THE ARDEN SHAKESPEARE

GENERAL EDITORS: HAROLD F. BROOKS AND HAROLD JENKINS

ANTONY AND CLEOPATRA

THE ARDEN EDITION OF THE
WORKS OF WILLIAM SHAKESPEARE

ANTONY AND
CLEOPATRA

Edited by
M. R. RIDLEY
BASED ON THE EDITION OF
R. H. CASE

LONDON
METHUEN & CO LTD
HARVARD UNIVERSITY PRESS
CAMBRIDGE, MASSACHUSETTS

The original editor of the Arden Shakespeare was W. J. Craig (1899-1906), succeeded by R. H. Case (1909-1944) and Una Ellis-Fermor (1946-1958).

Present general editors: Harold F. Brooks and Harold Jenkins.

R. H. Case's edition of Antony and Cleopatra first published in 1906. It was reprinted seven times Ninth Edition (M. R. Ridley) revised and reset, 1954 Reprinted four times reprinted 1964

9·5
CATALOGUE NO. 2/4729/10 (METHUEN)

PRINTED IN GREAT BRITAIN AT THE UNIVERSITY PRESS ABERDEEN
AND BOUND BY JAMES BURN & CO LTD., ESHER

CONTENTS

PREFACE TO REVISED EDITION

" Nothing recently written on Shakespeare, I venture to say, shows more thorough scholarship or better judgement than Mr. Case's edition in the Arden series." That is the comment of an exacting critic [1] on the first edition of *Antony and Cleopatra* in the Arden series. It was well justified, and the task of the reviser forty-five years later is correspondingly lightened, the sphere of his duties strictly circumscribed. When work is as sound and comprehensive as Case's introduction and the great bulk of his notes, tinkering with it is both needless and, I think, silly, as though one should set to work to renovate a period piece of furniture. Case's edition shows by its excellences how far English Shakespearean scholarship had at the time advanced, and by its limitations what fields of critical enquiry were still waiting for succeeding scholars to explore.

I can best explain what I have taken the reviser's job to be, and what I have done, with the reasons for it, under three heads, the text, the apparatus criticus, the introduction, notes and appendices.

1. The Text

Verbally the present text is much the same as that of the original (Arden) edition—which is to say much the same as that of all modern editions—except that in several places the Folio reading has been retained against a commonly accepted emendation. The punctuation, however, has been drastically revised.

The only authoritative text of the play is that of the First Folio. Dover Wilson [2] and Greg [3] agree that the copy for it was pretty certainly Shakespeare's own manuscript. The text is for the most part a good one, with two noticeable

---

[1] A. C. Bradley, *Oxford Lectures on Poetry* (1909), p. 307, note C.
[2] *Antony and Cleopatra*, in *New Shakespeare* edition (1951), p. 127.
[3] *The Editorial Problem* (1942), p. 148.

defects, (*a*) a considerable amount of mislineation (mainly in short speeches) and (*b*) some odd vagaries in the spelling of proper names.

As to (*a*) Greg says that this " seems mainly due to the author running on half-lines to economize space ", and Dover Wilson accepts this explanation, supporting it " by the fact that . . . speeches of 1½ to 2½ lines account for practically all the mislining." I do not think that the explanation is very convincing. In the first place, it is somewhat too much of a ' blanket' explanation, not reckoning with the different kinds of mislineation which the F text presents. But apart from that, so far as the half lines are concerned, it does not seem to me to square with the observable facts. If Greg means, as I think he must, that when a speech ended with a half-line Shakespeare was apt to run the half-line on at the end of the preceding complete line, then surely what we should expect to find in F is hypermetric lines in which the unwanted foot or two come at the end. For example, taking Cæsar's speech at II. ii. 37-40, we might expect it to end not with

> Did practise on my state, your being in Egypt
> Might be my question.

but with a single " line "

> Did practise on my state, your being in Egypt might be
> my question.

But in fact that kind of hypermetric line is rare, and much commoner is the kind in which the unwanted foot or two are at the beginning of the line, as for example, II. ii. 70-3, printed thus in modern editions

> for that you must
> But say, I could not help it.
> *Cæs.*   I wrote to you:
> When rioting in Alexandria you
> Did pocket up my letters. . . .

But which appears in F as

> for that you must,
> But say I could not help it.
> *Cæs.* I wrote to you, when rioting in Alexandria you
> Did pocket up my letters. . . .

thus producing an impossible first line for Cæsar. What I
think is clear is that the F compositor certainly, and
Shakespeare almost certainly, did not use the modern
typographical device whereby, when one speech ends and
the next begins in the middle of a line, the second speech
is indented, as at the opening of ii. i.

> *Pom.* If the great gods be just, they shall assist
> The deeds of justest men.
> *Mene.*   Know, worthy Pompey,
> That what . . .

I suspect that Shakespeare wrote the second line there as

The deeds of justest men.   *Mene.* Know worthy *Pompey*

but the F compositor, whenever he found himself con-
fronted by a fresh speech-heading, invariably started a new
line, and sometimes, with unhappy results, did the best he
could to divide the speech into some sort of lines. (The
point about how Shakespeare wrote the line above, and
others like it, has some importance, apart from the question
of mislineation. In F both speech-headings and proper
names are in italic, and it is natural to suppose that
Shakespeare indicated that this should be so. But if italic
speech-headings were apt to occur in the middle of lines
there is obvious danger of confusion between them and
italic proper names in the text.)
The question of mislineation is treated at greater
length in Appendix II ; I have there devoted a good
deal of space to exemplifying the kinds of mislineation which
F presents, and in notes on ii. v. 31-2 and 105-10 I have
discussed two typical passages in detail. I have done this
for two reasons. First, for reasons given in the relevant
section (p. xx below), I have omitted all references to mislineation from the apparatus criticus, and it is desirable
that the reader who is interested in such things should
be able to see examples of what happened more clearly
than he can reconstruct them from summary notes. Second,
it is important, I think, for the modern reader to realize
that " correction of frequent mislineation " does not imply a drastic revision of the original text, the sort of revision

of which he is suspicious (as with much cavalier emendation of words he is very rightly suspicious) that it may be taking him further from, rather than nearer to, what Shakespeare intended. It will be noticed from the examples, firstly, that a good deal of the so-called mislineation is not really *mis*lineation at all, but what one might call absence of lineation, consequent on the absence of an accepted modern typographical device, and secondly, that almost all the real mislineation can be easily, and for the most part with certainty, corrected.

To turn now to (*b*), the mis-spelling of proper names. F presents us with such oddities as " Scicion " [1] for Sicyon, " Towrus " for Taurus, and " Ventigius " for Ventidius, not to mention " Cleopater " three times in Act II for Cleopatra.[2] The mis-spellings are almost all corrected by whoever prepared the copy for F2, and they are intrinsically of small importance, but there is some interest in speculating how they arose. Dover Wilson says: " Working presumably with North under his eye, Shakespeare was nevertheless restrained by no habits of ' correctness ' or consistency so long as the names sounded all right on the stage." I find this very hard to swallow. Why should Shakespeare, working " with North under his eye," and often adhering to North very closely, go out of his way to alter words which were staring at him out of the page? It is no easier to write " Towrus " than " Taurus " or to give Ventidius a " g " instead of his proper " d." If we are to make Shakespeare responsible for the errors I can only suggest that he was *not* working with North under his eye, but knew him so well, almost by heart, that he could versify him without reference to the book, and when he came to a proper name relied on his memory of how he had heard it " in his head." But this will hardly work with " Cleopater." The other, and I think much more probable, explanation is that these are " auditory " errors. I know that the

[1] See note on I. ii. 110.

[2] It rather looks as though something had happened in Act II. Two of the three *Cleopater*'s come within a hundred lines of one another in scene ii, and all three *Ventigius*'s within ten lines in scene iii, though in III. i. he is three times spelt correctly.

hypothesis that copy was sometimes read to the compositor is at present somewhat blown upon, and that such external evidence as there is for it is readily (I think much too readily) dismissed. But it is quite clear that some errors in Shakespearean texts depend on an auditory link at *some* point in the chain of transmission, though not necessarily on the link between copy and compositor. For example, the famous " a dog so bade in office " for " a dog's obey'd in office " [1] is not accountable for by any misreading, but only by mishearing. And some at least of these proper names seem to me the results of mishearing, in particular " Ventigius," because he is not by any means always mis-spelt, and I do not see why Shakespeare should have been inconsistent. But some people naturally pronounce an " -idius " ending so that it sounds like " -igius." " Towrus," by the way, is interesting, on the " auditory " supposition, since it implies an " Italian " pronunciation, whereas Henslowe's " Fostus " for " Faustus " implies the English. [2]

Punctuation. Since Case's edition first appeared a great deal more attention has been paid to the punctuation of the early Quarto and First Folio texts than had been paid by earlier editors, who felt themselves free to play any old Harry they chose with the original punctuation. This increased attention was largely due to Percy Simpson's *Shakespearian Punctuation* (1911). To this book, some-thing of a landmark in Shakespearean scholarship, I will return later, but for the moment it is worth while to ask why earlier editors felt justified in allowing themselves such freedom. The assumption that punctuation could be properly treated much more high-handedly than words arose, I think, in part from a misconception which has nothing to do with Simpson's thesis, and which can be examined without reference to it. To editors accustomed to a style of punctuation mainly " syntactical," a guide to logical comprehension, the punctuation of early Shakespeare texts inevitably seemed very strange, and it was not un-natural that instead of looking for a principle behind it they dismissed it as haphazard and careless, and rectified

[1] *Lear*, iv. vi. 164.   [2] And see note on *Cicelie* at ii. vi. 45.

it according to their own principles.[1] But the idea that punctuation is anyway much more likely to have been carelessly handled than words depends on a misconception of how a compositor works. The compositor is a man who is trying to turn, as accurately as he can, the " copy " in front of him into something which, when duly dealt with by the printer, will reproduce that copy in a printed page. Before the invention of linotype or monotype machines the compositor did this by selecting, one by one, from the " cases " in front of him a series of pieces of type corresponding to the marks on the paper of the copy. Whether these " marks " are letters or marks of punctuation is a matter of indifference to him; each must be represented by its appropriate piece of type. He does not say " so long as I get the letters right it does not matter what happens to the punctuation." Give him the following four marks in the manuscript, *end:*, and he is no more likely to set a comma instead of the colon than to set an *e* for the *d* (in an Elizabethan printing-house he was in fact a good deal less likely, since in Elizabethan script *e* and *d* were very easily confused, so that we have *end* for an undoubted *due* in Sonnet LXIX). It is true that there may be with punctuation slightly more danger of " foul case," and also that punctuation seems to suffer somewhat readily from the malady known as " transposed pointing " where the compositor's eye registers the right symbol but puts it in the wrong place, or registers the right pair of symbols but transposes their positions.[2] But in general the " expectation of error "

---

[1] The attitude of almost all these editors, and most of their successors, is well expressed by Johnson, and his statement is significant, since it comes from an editor who, so far as the verbal text was concerned, was extremely conservative, and never emended himself or accepted the emendations of others except where he considered that there was overwhelming cause. " In restoring the authour's works to their integrity, I have considered the punctuation as wholly in my power; for what could be their care of colons and commas, who corrupted words and sentences. Whatever could be done by adjusting points is therefore silently performed. . . ." The right answer to Johnson's rhetorical question, " what care . . .," as I have tried to suggest, is " about the same " instead of the one which he implies, " none."

[2] Here is an example of " wrong place." *Coriolanus,* i. ix. 6 reads " And gladly quaked hear more; where the dull tribunes". A modern compositor, working under good conditions and from the printed page, none the less produced a line that made nonsense: " And gladly quaked hear more where;

should not be much higher with punctuation than with letters, unless the fault lies with the original copy.

If we put it at double we are putting it high. But editors till quite recently have put it far higher than that. For purposes of comparison I selected quite arbitrarily the last twenty lines of the first, third and fifth acts of *Antony and Cleopatra*, as they appear in the Folio and in three modern editions, the Arden (Case), the single volume Oxford (Craig), and the New Shakespeare (Dover Wilson). (The details of the three passages, together with some further examples, are given in Appendix III.) In these three passages F has comparatively few errors. There are four obvious misprints of words, and two, possibly four, in punctuation in sixty lines, so that the balance between errors in words and those in punctuation is about level— which is what with reasonable care on the compositor's part one would expect. But two of the modern editors allow themselves about ten times, and the third about eight times, greater freedom in altering the punctuation than in altering words. Further, the alterations are not all in one direction, since, though the majority make the

the dull tribunes". And here is, I think, an almost certain example of the transposition of symbols in an early text which has not, I judge, been previously observed. In *M.N.D.* III. ii. 382-7, all three early texts (except for a *dxile* in F) read as follows (spelling modernized but punctuation retained):

> damned spirits all,
> That in crossways and floods have burial,
> Already to their wormy beds are gone;
> For fear lest day should look their shames upon,
> They wilfully themselves exile from light,
> And must for aye consort with black-brow'd night.

That is not nonsensical or ungrammatical, but it is not wholly satisfactory. The semi-colon breaks the second couplet awkwardly, *exile* is an odd word for a hurried departure, and *wilfully* even odder when we are told in the next line that they *must* whether they will or no. Assume a transposed pointing and the commonest of all errors, the *e : d*, and we have a reading in which the rhythm is better and the point of the everlasting consort with night as punishment for the wilful exile from light is made.

> damned spirits all,
> That in crossways and floods have burial,
> Already to their wormy beds are gone,
> For fear lest day should look their shames upon;
> They wilfully themselves exil'd from light,
> And must for aye consort with black-brow'd night.

punctuation heavier, an appreciable number (about a third of the total) make it lighter. This has two effects; it slows up the general rate of delivery, but it also makes the tempo more monotonous and often destroys an effect of which Shakespeare—if for the moment we assume that the punctuation is his—was fond, that namely of giving three or four rapidly running phrases, separated only by commas, and following them by the heaviest pause at his command, a full stop. Shakespeare, that is, was writing for dramatic delivery, while his editors re-write him for logical comprehension from the page. Many readers must have noticed that the actor frequently does not deliver his lines in the least as his modern text has carefully prepared them for him, but reverts—often no doubt simply from his actor's just instinct, and not from consultation of the Folio—to the delivery that Shakespeare intended for him, and indicated as his intention.

But in the last few lines above I have of course been begging, or partly begging, a main question. Have we any justification for assuming that the punctuation which the early texts represent, or occasionally mis-represent, was Shakespeare's? Simpson's main thesis, in the book already mentioned, was this, that " Shakespearian " punctuation was not, like ours, an aid to understanding the syntactical construction of a sentence, but rather a guide to how the sentence should be delivered. It was " dramatic " or " rhetorical " rather than logical, and was, largely for that reason, usually considerably lighter than ours. Further, since it was not confined within the comparatively narrow limits of syntactical exposition, it was an instrument which could be used to indicate considerable and often subtle varieties of interpretation. It was a dramatic tool, not a a grammatical one.

Of the fundamental soundness of Simpson's general idea there is, I think, little doubt, and of its importance, if sound, no doubt at all. But it is true that in the natural enthusiasm created by the application of a new idea a good deal of nonsense was talked, and attempts were made, for example, to justify every apparently intrusive comma by over-subtle argument which would not stand up to examination. As a result there has been a strong reaction, and some critics, eager to pounce on absurdities of detailed example, have been led—I think misled—into dismissing the whole theory as moonshine.[1]

Two distinct questions arise. Is the punctuation of the early texts an approximation to Shakespeare's own? If not, has it any connection with theatrical performance, or is it the compositor's own, following " house-style " (if any), or his own temporary whim? Now those critics who hold that, except in a few special instances, it is idle to descry Shakespeare's, or any other playwright's, own intentions in the punctuation of the early texts, can justifiably point to the famous three pages of *Sir Thomas More*, which are most inadequately punctuated, and to some, though not all, of the other extant dramatic manuscripts of the period. But they seem tacitly to assume that if the punctuation is not the author's, then it is the compositor's. This is surely not so, and the view, I think, depends on a failure to imagine what must have happened to an author's manuscript after it was delivered to the players. Sir Edmund Chambers gives a clear account [2] of the operations of the man he calls the " stage-reviser "—the man, that is, who prepared the manuscript for direct use in the theatre, checking entries and exits, amplifying, if necessary, the stage-directions, and so on. But even Chambers does no more than glance by implication at another operation which this man must, so far as I can see, have conducted if it had not already been done. Before the play can go into production, each actor must be handed a transcript of his part. But no actor can efficiently study an unpunctuated, or very inadequately punctuated, part. Hence some one, whether the author himself or the " stage-reviser " (probably identical with the book-keeper), must complete the punctuation before these transcripts are made and handed out. And if the author is in close contact with the players (as, for example, Shakespeare and Heywood were) my guess is that the

---

[1] There is a balanced criticism of the theory in Chambers' *William Shakespeare*, I, pp. 190-6. I think he misses one point.
[2] *Op. cit.*, pp. 108-23.

" someone " is likely to have been the author himself. But
at least it seems moderately certain that the printed punctuation is the compositor's attempt to reproduce what was
before him, and that that was at least contemporary
theatrical punctuation.

But can we with any justification suppose that the
punctuation of the original manuscript was Shakespeare's
own? The probability, now generally accepted, that
the manuscript which went to the printer was either
Shakespeare's own original, or at worst at only one remove
from that, does not much help us, since it can always be
argued that though the words were his the punctuation was
not, but was inserted by someone else. We are reduced
therefore to an examination of a few bits of direct evidence
and to a consideration of likelihood. The question to
which we are trying to find what must be at best a largely
conjectural answer, is " Was Shakespeare a careless punctuator? "

In the first place it is demonstrable and generally
admitted that on occasion he was extremely careful. The
passage in *M.N.D.* v. i. 108-16 is punctuated (i.e. mis-
punctuated, beyond the range of the wildest compositor's
nightmare) to indicate the breathless mis-delivery of the
prologist; and the comments of Theseus and Lysander put
this beyond doubt. Chambers also admits as examples of
care on Shakespeare's part " Pistol's gabble when he eats the
leek or the pace of Margaret's tongue in *Much Ado About
Nothing* " (*Henry V*, v. i. 47, *Much Ado*, iii. iv. 78 onwards
—both passages are unhappily over-punctuated in most
modern editions). But I think that he misses the significance of the two passages, especially of Pistol's. The care-
fulness of the author, which is admitted, is shown not in
punctuation, but in *non*-punctuation. To secure a particular effect he deliberately omits normal punctuation.
But, if the whole manuscript had been very inadequately
punctuated, no one, whether compositor or transcriber,
would have noticed anything out of the way or suspected
any particular intention on Shakespeare's part; as a result,
surely, in would have gone some form of punctuation.
Either then Shakespeare inserted specific directions that

these passages were to be left almost unpunctuated, or these
passages were at variance with his normal practice. I
think the second alternative the more likely.

This is partly because I find it hard to accept the view
that Shakespeare was " normally a rapid writer, who did
not trouble about punctuation, but occasionally became
more careful." Rapid he may have been, and probably
was; but why therefore assume that he did not trouble
about punctuation? After all, punctuation (of whatever
type) is a tool of any writer's trade, and Shakespeare was
a skilled workman; more, he was a skilled *dramatic* workman,
who knew precisely the effects he wanted produced by the
spoken word. There seems to be a curious *non sequitur*
which lurks in a good deal of writing on the subject, and
every now and then emerges. " A few writers are always
careless in punctuation ; many writers are occasionally
careless ; therefore most writers are always careless."
Stated in those terms the absurdity is of course apparent,
but there does seem a tendency to assume that writers are
a careless race, and careless in particular about their stops.
It is of course impossible to prove a negative, but the
example of Keats is interesting. He was, so far as one can
judge, a rapid worker; though in the heat of composition
he would correct and correct till he got what he wanted,
he disliked cold-blooded revision; and in the ordinary run
of his letters he was if not a careless at least a very limited
punctuator—for long stretches there will be nothing but
full stops and dashes. But when, in these same letters, he
is being Keats the deliberate poet, when he wants to be sure
that a poem he cares about will be rightly read, he is very
far from either careless or limited. Some of the less important poems in the letters are inadequately punctuated,
but look at the verse epistle to his brother (letter 2 in
M. Buxton Forman's 3rd edition), at the *Ode to Psyche*
(letter 123), and *To Autumn* (letter 152). All are punctuated
with the greatest care, and so are many others, and not
infrequently the punctuation is more effective than that of
the printed text. I find it hard to believe that Shakespeare
was more careless than Keats, and even harder to believe
that by carelessness he robbed himself of a device by the

B

use of which he could go some way towards securing what he wanted.

I think therefore that in the punctuation of the early texts we have, pretty certainly, at least "playhouse" punctuation, and very possibly a great deal of Shakespeare's own. If this is so, it means that no modern editor can neglect the Q and F punctuation. I should go further, and be prepared to say that no editor can desert it without very careful consideration, and if he does so, does so at his peril. An alteration in the original punctuation should be regarded as no less an emendation than a change in a word, and should be felt to need the same kind of justification. The justification may often be much easier to find, but that is no excuse for not looking for it.

For these reasons I have in the text which follows retained an unusually high proportion of the F punctuation, and I think that any readers who are interested in the subject, and will compare the following passages in this edition with the same passages in others, will appreciate the difference in effect: i. iii. 71-3, and v. ii. 193-5. These passages, together with further examples, are given in full in Appendix III, and attention is drawn in the notes on a number of lines to the way in which the usual modern emendation of the F punctuation has wrecked the intended sense.

Stage directions, scene-divisions, etc. I have retained wherever possible the stage-directions of F, which are more complete and satisfactory than in many plays ; I have made the minimum of addition to them (from the copious store provided by the early editors) where, for example, a necessary exit has been omitted, or where the indication of "business" is helpful to the reader, and in a number of places I have, for reasons given in the notes, not accepted the usual modifications of them, since I think that Shakespeare's stage-directions, particularly in the matter of the order in which characters enter, not infrequently have a significance which facile modification has obscured.

I have retained the usual scene-divisions. They are convenient for reference, and so long as we remember that to the Elizabethans a new scene did not mean new scenery,

but simply the sequence of the exit of one group of characters, a momentarily bare stage, and the entry of a new
group, the retention does not do much harm.   In two places
(III. viii-x and IV. x-xii) I have tried to indicate something
of the Elizabethan continuity by omitting the vexatious
" another part of the plain " indication of locality.

Indications of locality at the beginning of scenes I have,
with some hesitation, retained in their simplest form.   I
dislike most of them, and I think we lose appreciably by
not becoming accustomed, in Shakespeare and other
Elizabethan drama, to " non-localised " scenes—some
characters meet " somewhere " to transact some necessary
business of the play, and where the " somewhere " is may
often be of small importance.   But the modern reader
expects them, and is perhaps needlessly distracted by their
absence, since, if he insists on knowing where he is, he
wastes time, better spent on listening to the characters, in
trying to deduce it from the text.   But I have bracketed
them, as well as the scene divisions, as a continued reminder
that they do not occur in F.   And I have omitted any notice
of them from the apparatus criticus.   It seems to me of
the least possible importance whether it was Rowe, or
Hanmer, or Capell who inserted this or that example of
them.   All that matters is that F has *none* of them.

The Text (verbally).   Here there is little to be said.
There is a comparatively small number of instances of
obvious corruption, of which the curative emendations
have been, since their promulgation, almost universally
accepted.   These are commented on in the apparatus
criticus and the notes.   There are a few other passages
where I am inclined to think that something has gone
wrong, and where I have made speculative suggestions.   I
am far from confident of any of the suggestions—certainly
not nearly confident enough to promote them to the text—
but there are two or three places where I am fairly confident that the possibility of corruption is at least worth
consideration, whatever the cure may be.[1]

---

[1] E.g. I. i. 40; I. iii. 80; II. i. 22; II. vi. 54; III. x. 32; IV. ii. 30, 31.
And at I. i. 50 I have substituted a new (so far as I know) emendation for
the hitherto accepted one.

2. THE APPARATUS CRITICUS

This I have considerably lightened. In an edition such as this, which does not pretend to present an exhaustive apparatus, like that of the Furness *Variorum*, it is, I think, important that what is given should be readily comprehensible, and should not obscure salient points by a cloud of minor ones.

I have therefore cut out all record of mislineations, and transferred the consideration of this problem to Appendix II. It is next to impossible for anyone, without long practice, to construct, from the abbreviated notes of an apparatus, a picture of what the F text in fact looks like, or to deduce from a series of such notes the types of mislineation which occur. The study of this problem—which in any case is of comparatively small importance—can be conducted only by an examination of a copy, or a facsimile, of the Folio. But something can be done by an examination of a number of examples, if they are given *in extenso*.

I have cut out almost all variants in proper names, and transferred this feature also of F to the introduction (p. x above). All that matters here is that some proper names are regularly, and some occasionally, mis-spelt, that F2 corrected most of them (indicating that some trouble was taken in preparing the copy for F2), and that mis-spellings of at least two names come in blocks. This last point, probably the least unimportant of the three, is hard to emphasize in an apparatus. I have, however, left in the apparatus an occasional example, as a reminder.

I have also cut out, for reasons given above, in the section on "Stage directions, etc.," all record of the various indications of locality inserted by editors.

I have made one change which I think is perhaps more important than it looks, namely, the excision throughout of the symbol Ff. Since Furness in the Variorum edition, printing the F1 text, meant by Ff an agreement of F2, F3 and F4, whereas Case in the original Arden edition meant an agreement of all the four Folios, the symbol is confusing anyway. But I think it is much worse than confusing, since it is apt to suggest to a reader not versed in textual problems that all four folios together have in some way or other a superior and overriding authority which F alone has not. And this is not so. The successive Folios, like successive Quartos, each printed from the last, occasionally emend, and occasionally introduce new errors, but none of them has any " authority," which only consultation of the original manuscript could have given. Johnson was wiser about this than many of his predecessors and successors: " In his enumeration of editions, he [Theobald] mentions the two first folios as of high, and the third folio as of middle authority; but the truth is, that the first is equivalent to all others, and that the rest only deviate from it by the printer's negligence." (A slight overstatement, since the latter Folios do occasionally emend.) For the same reason emendations in the later Folios derive no superior probability over those of later editions from greater proximity of date to the first Folio, and these emendations are to be judged by precisely the same standards as one would apply to an emendation of 1953, with one small qualification. The second Folio, printed nine years after the first, is less likely than eighteenth century editions to contain emendations which a more intimate knowledge of Elizabethan idiom would have shown to be needless, and such emendations as it may make are more likely to be consonant with that idiom.[1]

The present apparatus criticus therefore contains the following: (*a*) adequate material for the study of all the major and most of the minor textual cruces, giving the original reading and a selection from the often very numerous suggested emendations; (*b*) a record of additions to (other than those of locality), and departures from, the stage-directions of F; (*c*) a limited number of quite minor errors, and occasional oddities of spelling, in F, selected so far as possible for their relevance to the textual study of other plays as well as this—e.g. errors which depend on the common *e : d*, or the equally common minim, confusion, or, in spelling,

---

[1] Whoever prepared the copy for F2 took a good deal of trouble over his job. Apart from the proper names, he made a number of needless, and sometimes pedantic changes, but also a number of sensible, if pedestrian, emendations.

F's *bin* for *been*, which may have some bearing on, e.g. the odd *cliffe-cleefe* variant in *Hamlet*; (*d*) a few examples of the needless or wild conjecture, included simply as warning illustrations of the *cacoethes emendandi*.

It is apparent, therefore, that the apparatus is eclectic; eclectic to some extent it must be, for reasons already given, but is also sometimes so in a fashion, and on a principle, which are, I know, open to criticism. In constructing the apparatus, and deciding what to include and what to omit, I have tried to keep in mind two main types of reader, the student who is in the early or prentice days of his study of textual problems, and the ordinary reader who is mainly concerned with reading the plays as plays, who relies therefore on his edition primarily for discussion of points of meaning or dramatic presentation, but who is prepared every now and again to be interested in a technical problem. For both classes it is desirable to let the important things stand out, and not embed them in a mass of minor ones. Hence, for example, I have often, after giving the name of the editor who first made the emendation, said " and many other edd." instead of giving a string of names, which would be significant only to the mature scholar, already well-versed, or wanting to be better versed, in the habit of mind of this or that editor. But there is a type of what one may call " recurrent variant " which raises a problem. Many of these variants are matters of spelling, and some may be significant and some not. For example, the Folio's very frequent *loose* for *lose* is no more than a normal Elizabethan spelling, and is, I think rightly, silently modernized, in common with others of the same kind. On the other hand the Folio's frequent *bin* for *been* has some significance with regard to Elizabethan pronunciation, and therefore, possibly, with regard to problems elsewhere. But to record every occurrence of *bin* would be not only tiresome to the reader but, in an apparatus of this scope, disproportionate. I have therefore given only one instance of *bin*. I do not think that this is misleading so long as it is made clear (whether in the apparatus itself, as with *bin*, or in notes or introduction, as with mis-spelt proper names) that the instance recorded is not an isolated one, but is given as an example.

I have occasionally, following Case's example, admitted an explanatory word or two, when this seemed the way to direct the reader's attention to what matters and save him from wasting time on what does not.

There is one last point to which attention should be drawn. A mark of punctuation which in the text follows a word or phrase included in the apparatus is recorded only when it is the point, or one of the points, at issue (e.g. *chaps*, at III. v. 13). But to this rule there is, for typographical reasons, one general exception. Words which in the text are printed in roman type (i.e. all words except proper names which occur in speeches) are, in accordance with common practice, printed in italic in the apparatus, while those which are in italic in the text (i.e. stage-directions and (in F) proper names) appear in roman in the apparatus. But this, in the absence of some recognised symbol to separate the words cited from the name (also in roman) of the editor concerned has sometimes odd results. I have therefore retained in the apparatus the full stop which closes stage directions. This is admittedly inconsistent, but it avoids such entries as " They wake Rowe " or " Noise within Capell."

3. INTRODUCTION, NOTES AND APPENDICES

The introduction, for reasons already explained, I have left almost as it stood, venturing only on half a dozen minor verbal alterations where I thought that Case had not made his meaning as clear as he would have wished. Any matter of my own is by way of addition, not alteration, and is indicated by being included between a † and [R].

In the notes I have allowed myself a freer, but only slightly freer, hand. I have added, without comment, a certain number of glosses where Case had left unglossed a word or phrase which might puzzle a modern reader. I have occasionally (again without comment) cut out one of Case's more recondite illustrations—I think that Case's wealth and range of knowledge sometimes defeats its own ends and bewilders or wearies the reader instead of illuminating him—but on the other side I have on occasion given

in full a Shakespearean illustration to which Case gave
only a reference. Illustrations from a man's own work are
always, I think, more valuable than those from others, and
it is only, in my experience, the rarely assiduous student
who will look up a casual reference. Lastly, I have re-
written some notes, and made additions, whether by way
of amplification or doubt, to others, as well as making a
few suggestions of my own. It will not, I hope, be vexatious
to the reader to find all the modifications or additions in
this last category indicated by the same symbols († . . .
[R]). Where so much has been left untouched I see no
reason why I should foist onto Case, by the absence of any
such indication, the responsibility for comment with which
he might have seriously disagreed.

Appendices. I have incorporated most of Case's Appendix I in the notes on the passages concerned, but I have
left standing the long note on the arm-gaunt steed. This
unhappy animal has caused more trouble than he is worth,
but the note is worth retaining, partly as an example of
painstaking scholarship, and partly as an example (even an
awful example) of the vagaries of emenders. I have cut out
altogether his Appendix II. It was a presentation, almost
as exhaustive as the five pages of the Furness *Variorum*, of
the many explanations and emendations of ii. ii. 206-8.
Since most of the expositors expose little but themselves,
and demonstrate little but the fact that determined resolution can always find difficulties where no difficulties are,
the presentation of their labours throws little light on a
passage which we have, I think, as Shakespeare wrote it
and the Folio correctly presented it.

I have added three appendices of my own, one on the
mislineation of F, one containing examples of punctuation,
and one on the staging of certain scenes.

My thanks are due to Dr. H. F. Brooks for his scholarly
and generous help, particularly with the apparatus, but also
in making a number of illuminating suggestions about isolated points of text and interpretation.

M. R. R.

INTRODUCTION

(R. H. Case: 1906)

This edition of *Antony and Cleopatra* presents the first folio text with the majority of those emendations which in course of time have secured almost universal assent, no others, whether accepted in one or more editions or merely suggested, possessing, in the editor's judgement, that probability only short of certainty which alone justifies adoption. Certain changes countenanced by the best editions have, on the other hand, been rejected in favour of the original readings, and are here briefly indicated.

The plurals in *-th* and *-s*, so extremely common in the literature of the period, have been restored wherever they occur in the folio ; and similarly other slight variations from modern grammar: obsolete forms of words (mere difference of spelling excepted) are invariably given in place of following the usual eclectic plan: the folio forms of names, where they correspond with those of North and are consequently not press errors, are retained; and finally, also, besides the folio readings in certain places, its sense-affecting punctuation in the following passages, for reasons given in the notes in each case: I. i. 4, v. 74, 75; II. ii. 71, 72; III. xiii. 74; IV. xv. 73; V. ii. 291.

With regard to interpretation of identical readings, many instances of greater or less variation from the usually accepted senses will be found. The obstinate cruces of the play have been fully discussed, and, as a choice of evils, no ascertained difficulties have been avoided, though in cases of ambiguity where language is so freely wielded as in *Antony and Cleopatra*, it is a question whether a reader's cursory impressions are not less likely to mislead than laboured analyses. A particular aim has been to illustrate as far as possible from new sources, with acknowledgment of all illustrations—save sometimes those from Shakespeare —owed to their employment by others. In the critical apparatus, all material differences from the first folio text, including the re-arrangement of the lines, are recorded; and any corrections or variations worth noting in the later folios have been extracted from the collation in the Cambridge Shakespeare. This has also been used to determine the originators of emendations; but the editions and independent commentaries have been themselves examined.

The composition of *Antony and Cleopatra* is assigned to 1607, or the early part of 1608, for which dates the external evidence is the second of the following entries [1] in the Stationers' Registers (see Arber's *Transcript*, iii. 167*b*) under date 20 May 1608:

Edward Blount. Entred for his copie vnder thandes of Sir George Buck knight and Master Warden Seton A booke called. *The booke of* PERICLES *prynce of Tyre* . . . vj^d.

Edward Blunt Entred also for his copie by the lyke Aucthoritie. A booke Called. ANTHONY. *and* CLEOPATRA . . . vj^d.

Next year (1609) *Pericles* was published in quarto by another publisher, but the second entry either bore no fruit, or any resulting impression has disappeared. It is reasonably taken to refer to Shakespeare's play, which was registered by Master Blounte and Isaak Jaggard on 8 November 1623—in that case, for the second time—among " Master William Shakspeers *Comedyes Histories, and Tragedyes* soe manie of the said Copies as are not formerly entred to other men, *vizt.*" [Here follow sixteen plays under the several headings, the *Tragedies* being *Coriolanus, Timon of Athens, Julius Cæsar, Mackbeth, Anthonie and Cleopatra, Cymbeline* (see Arber's *Transcript*, iv. 69).] The play appeared in that year in the first folio, where it is placed between *Othello* and *Cymbeline*, and is consequently last but one in the book.

If, however, what I now put forward is not merely matter of coincidence, 1608 may be ruled out entirely and 1606 be granted a possibility beside 1607. Daniel's *Cleopatra* appeared in 1594, in that year's edition of his

---

[1] † Probably " blocking entries "; see Pollard, *Shakespeare Folios and Quartos* (1909), p. 78, and *Shakespeare's Fight with the Pirates* (1920), pp. 26-52. [R]

Delia: it was reprinted with some deletions and modifications in the *Poeticall Essayes* of 1599, in the folio editions of *Workes*, 1601 and 1602, and again in *Certaine Small Workes Heretofore Devulged by Samuel Daniel*, in 1605. In the next edition of *Certaine Small Workes*, however, namely that of 1607, an altered text appeared, which was repeated in the issues of 1609 and 1611, and also by itself in 1611. The *verso* of the general title-page of 1607 declared the play to be "newly altred," and the question is: what induced Daniel to reconstitute his play between 1605 and 1607? Was it merely due to re-reading Plutarch with a maturer eye, and a growing preference for dialogue as against relation; or had the author been stimulated by a new treatment of the story to improve his own version, and guided in some respects in so doing? There is at least a probability that a sudden remodelling of old work, once already textually revised, may be accounted for on the latter score.

Dr. Grosart, in his edition of Daniel (1885-86), drew attention to the additions of 1607 for the first time, as he thought, but Langbaine had long ago said—though apparently with muddling reference to the 1623 quarto: "this later Copy infinitly differs from the former, and far exceeds it; the Language being not only corrected, but it having another advantage in the Opinion of a Modern Poet, (°) since that which is only dully recited in the first Edition, is in the last represented" (*An Account of the Dramatick Poets*, 1691, p. 101). Dr. Grosart printed the additions before his reproduction of the earlier version as it reappeared in 1623, after Daniel's death, but without any hint of the comparison which I am suggesting. I have verified his statements by examining the various editions.

Cleopatra, especially as first written and first altered a few years later, is a stately rhymed tragedy after the Senecan model. It takes up the story of Cleopatra after Antony's death, and sadly dilutes its tragic force by pursuit of moral rather than romantic themes, in reflection on their conduct and its reward from Cæsar by the traitors Rodon and Seleucus, and on the faults and fortunes of Egypt by the philosophers Philostratus and Arius. It has, here and there

"(°) Mr. *Crown's* Epistle to *Andromache*."

in the earlier version, resemblances more or less slight to passages in *Antony and Cleopatra*, of which, omitting such as are traceable to the common source in Plutarch, the chief may be noticed here. The numbers I assign to the lines quoted are those of Dr. Grosart's edition, which run consecutively throughout the play.

In Act I, l. 54, compare " I have both hands, and will, and I can die " with IV. xv. 49 *post*, " My resolution and my hands I'll trust "; also in ll. 69, 70, " That I should passe whereas *Octavia* stands, To view my misery," etc., the same dislike to submit to the gaze of her rival in Rome that Cleopatra expresses in IV. xv. 27-9, and v. ii. 54, 55 *post*. In Act v, sc. ii, ll. 1475 *et seq.*, Cleopatra is described as sitting in all her pomp:

> as if sh' had wonne
> *Cæsar*, and all the world beside, this day:
> Euen as she was when on thy cristall streames,
> Clear *Cydnos*, she did shew what earth could shew; etc.

Compare v. ii. 227, 228 *post*, " I am again for Cydnus, To meet Mark Antony," and *ibid*. 345, 346 *post*, " As she would catch another Antony In her strong toil of grace."

Though, on the whole, I think Shakespeare had, as was natural, Daniel's and other predecessors' work before him, however small his use of it, such resemblances in thought, as, for instance, the effective retrospect to *Cydnus* here, might easily occur independently to writers of the same age exercising their genius on the same subject; and, if we take this view, their existence makes a little against the weight of any correspondences we may have to consider in the remodelled play. This, however, stands upon a different basis. It draws somewhat nearer to the contemporary drama by replacing relation and soliloquy to a great extent by dialogue, so that not only is the play more dramatic, but characters familiar to us in *Antony and Cleopatra* now play a greater part, viz. Charmian and Iras; others, Dercetas and Diomedes, are employed for the first time; Gallus becomes an interlocutor where he was but mentioned. It introduces the incident of " Dircetus " bringing Antony's sword to Cæsar (see v. i *post*); and, by means of his relation, the story of the events preceding Antony's death, on the lines followed by Shakespeare in IV. xii. (latter part), xiii, xiv, xv. *post*, though of course with the comparative brevity of a narration. This constitutes a new scene of Act I, and is a detail in which Daniel had not previously thought fit to follow the example of the Countess of Pembroke. Further: the new scene contains certain noticeable expressions. The second line is, " Will Antony yet struggle being undone? " and the second and third lines of Shakespeare's Act v *post*, on the same occasion:

> Being so frustrate, tell him he mocks
> The pauses that he makes.

Again, " Dircetus " says (l. 4): " His worke is ended. *Anthony* hath done." Compare *post*, IV. xiv. 35: " Unarm Eros, the long day's task is done." " Dircetus," describing Antony's last efforts with his forces, uses the phrase, " Had brought them to their worke," a possible reminiscence of Antony's " I'll bring you to't " in IV. iv. 34 *post*. Further —always remembering that I am not recording resemblances which may be due to Plutarch—there is a significant use of a similar conceit in both plays on the occasion of Antony's being drawn up into the momument: compare Daniel's (p. 8, Grosart):

> When shee afresh renewes
> Her hold, and with r'inforced power doth straine,
> And all the weight of her weake bodie laies,
> Whose surcharg'd heart more than her body wayes.

with IV. xv. 33, 34 *post:*

> Our strength is all gone into heaviness,
> That makes the weight.

The rest of the alterations of the play furnish nothing very material in the way of coincident thought, and remove some of the resemblances of the older version. The question rests on the parallels just given, the introduction of events from Plutarch treated also in certain scenes of *Antony and Cleopatra*, and the remodelling of the play in more dramatic form; and though this evidence is by no means overwhelming, so far as it goes it is consistent with a hypothesis that Daniel re-wrote his play because he had seen another treatment of the theme, namely, Shakespeare's, and just so much probability follows that we should finally exclude 1608 in considering the date of *Antony and Cleopatra*, and admit 1606 to competition with 1607. Unfortunately, the Stationers' Registers do not appear to contain any entry which would enable us to determine whether Daniel's altered text came early or late in the latter year.

The fact is slightly corroborative of Daniel's imitation that he is thought to have similarly profited by Shakespeare's *Richard II*, owing to changes made in the second edition of his *Civil Warres*, 1595.[1] His name is maliciously associated with Shakespeare's in *The Returne from Parnassus* (assigned to 1598 by Fleay, *Chronicle of the English Drama*, ii), III. i. 1015, *et seq.*, p. 57, in Macray's edition, and in the later play of the same name, acted 1601 or 1602, he is exhorted to use his own wit and " scorne base imitation." [2] I am, of course, not interpreting his revision of *Cleopatra* in any such way here.

Finally, in connection with the date of *Antony and Cleopatra*, some resemblances which occur in other plays are perhaps worth mentioning. In *Nobody and Somebody*, entered in the Stationers' Registers in 1606, and, though an older play, probably revised at that time (see Simpson, *School of Shakespeare*, i, p. 272, and Fleay, as before, under Heywood, No. 31), King Archigallo resembles Antony in a certain point:

> There's *Elydure*
> Your elder brother next unto the king;
> He plies his booke; when shall you see him trace
> Lascivious *Archigallo* through the streets,
> And fight with common hacksters hand to hand
> To wrest from them their goods and dignities? [3]

and in Barnabe Barnes's *The Divils Charter*, first played

---

[1] It should be observed that whether Daniel's second edition (dated, like the first, 1595) or Shakespeare's *Richard II* appeared first, is quite uncertain ; and that *1 Henry IV*, 1596-7, probably owes some detail to Daniel, as Dr. Moorman has shown : see his Introduction to that play in *The Warwick Shakespeare*. As regards *Cleopatra*, however, adoption in a late text of a more dramatic method and detail previously ignored, suggests, at least, a new model. [2] I. ii. 244-6, ed. Macray, 1886, p. 85.

[3] Ll. 34-9. *School of Shakespeare*, i. 278.

2 February 1607, entered 16 October, and printed same year after being " revised, corrected, and augmented," this passage occurs:

> *He draweth out of his boxes aspiks.*
> Come out here now you *Cleopatraes* birds.
> Fed fat and plump with proud *Egiptian* slime,
> Of seauen mouth'd *Nylus* but now turn'd leane:
> > *He putteth to either of their*
> > *brests an* Aspike.
> Take your repast vpon these Princely paps.
> Now *Ptolamies* wife is highly magnified,
> Ensigning these faire princely twins their death,
> And you my louely boys competitors,
> With *Cleopatra* share in death and fate.
>
> .   .   .   .
>
> I see their coulors chang and death sittes heauy.
> On their fayre foreheads with his leaden mace.
> My birds are glutted with this sacrefice.
> > *He taketh of the* Aspiks *and put*
> > *teth them vp in his box.*
> What now proud wormes ? how tasts yon princes blood.
> The slaves be plump and round ; into your nest,
> Is there no token of the serpents draught,
> All cleere and safe well now faire boyes good-night.[1]

A passage in Chapman's *Bussy D'Ambois*, which furnishes two important parallels with our text (see on IV. xii. 37, xiv. 2-7 *post*) exists substantially in the first edition, which appeared in 1607. This play, in Mr. Fleay's opinion, was written late in 1604,[2] and produced next year.

The internal evidence for the date of composition is not thrown out of correspondence by the slight recession of date suggested. It depends on the complete change in metrical style approached through the plays since Hamlet, which deprives Shakespeare's blank verse of much music in its effort to become a more spacious continent of his multiplying thought; the increased percentage of lines in which the

---

[1] See McKerrow's edition in *Materialen zur Kunde des älteren Englischen Dramas*, 1904, ll. 2546-69, p. [71].

[2] Chapman's latest editor, Mr. T. M. Parrott, maintains this date, approximately, against appeals to Henslowe's *Diary* in support of 1598 for a first version. See his article in *Modern Language Review*, January, 1908.

sense is carried on to the next without pause, and the consequent increase of stops within lines; the employment of the weak ending, prominent for the first time in *Macbeth* and now much more strikingly so; the increased use of the double or feminine ending. Dependence on elocution to make a pause within a line metrically equivalent to a syllable, or a long line musical, is frequent in this play, and there is a free disposition of accent which gives grip and strength at the cost of some ruggedness; but all this does but deceive the sense of space; ellipse and ambiguous phrase show that no relaxation of metrical restraints could accommodate the ideas and images demanding utterance. The theme of the play, ethically considered as the consequence of grave defect in a nature generously endowed with noble traits, has been compared with those of *Macbeth* and *Coriolanus*, between which it has taken its place on the different considerations already stated.

Shakespeare's debt to Plutarch, Amyot, and Sir Thomas North, through the medium of the last named and especially to him, has been displayed in its real extent and with fine enthusiasm by Mr. Wyndham, in his introduction to the reprint of North's *Plutarch* in the Tudor Translations. It has been necessary here only to make it as readily traceable as possible, by appending full extracts from the life of Antonius, and by giving complete references to them throughout the notes, sometimes for whole scenes, sometimes for particular passages, as the case demanded. The space they leave at my disposal will be divided between a few not very orthodox impressions of *Antony and Cleopatra*, whose excuse for non-suppression must be that they have survived long concern with the play, and some account of the other English plays on the same subject.

Since Coleridge's famous criticism of *Antony and Cleopatra* in his *Notes and Lectures*, there has been no danger of the play's being under-rated, and the impression received from many examens in which this criticism is cited is that there is a tendency for its doubt to be ignored and its limitations obscured. Coleridge expressed a " doubt . . . whether the *Antony and Cleopatra* is not, in all exhibitions of a giant power in its strength and vigour of maturity, a formidable rival of the *Macbeth, Lear, Hamlet,* and *Othello* "; but even if we replace the doubt by an absolute certainty, there remains the fact that a special point of comparison is indicated, viz. " all exhibitions of a giant power in its strength and vigour of maturity." It is in this respect only that comparison is possible with the other plays named by Coleridge,[1] for, in the first place, *Antony and Cleopatra* belongs to a type of play defective in construction and absorbing centre of interest. The Chronicle play has its compensations: we see in *Antony and Cleopatra* vivid presentation of the earlier processes which lead to tragedy, set before us in a series of significant pictures; but historical fact is lopped and telescoped only so far as is indispensable to a stage-plot, and it does not in this case provide any rousing incident till the play is far advanced. Secondly, there is in the theme at its intensest, and the characters at their deepest, a defect of tragedy in comparison with that of the greater plays. The world-tragedy—admitting for the sake of argument Dr. Brandes' contention that the play is really and intentionally " the picture of a world-catastrophe "—is here too little insistently obvious, and depends too much for its effect on the constitution of a reader's mind, to surround the sufferers with a deeper gloom than their destiny can bestow. The magnanimity of Antony sets him above fate at last, and the death of Cleopatra is her triumph. We see these lovers hasten to reunion " where souls do couch on flowers "; there is what meeting for Othello and Desdemona?

O ill-starr'd wench !
Pale as thy smock ! when we shall meet at compt,
This look of thine will hurl my soul from heaven
And fiends will snatch at it.

The appalling situations of Macbeth or Othello, set between retrospect and prospect of horror, have no parallel here, and the despairs of Antony and Cleopatra are never as theirs: the profundities of tragic feeling which awe us in

---

[1] Here, and perhaps again, I may seem to have conveyed and mismanaged a hint from an article on *Antony and Cleopatra*, of far wider scope than these impressions, in the *Quarterly Review* for April 1906, by Professor A. C. Bradley; but in these respects I set down " mine own rudeness rudely " months previously, and owe homage, not acknowledgment.

c

their words belong to an abyss of which the two who have
been erected to rivalry with them know nothing. The
utterance of the latter, for all its magnificence of poetry and
pathos, is more conscious, and has in it something of the
luxury of woe: it is of their own plane of enchantment,
where " all the haunt " is indeed theirs; it is not humanly
heart-rending, nor language of despair fit for a Hall of
Eblis.

An extraordinarily vivid presentment in Elizabethan
terms of events and characters of the ancient world, with
truth to life as its one restraining condition, *Antony and
Cleopatra* is almost as far removed from the tragedies as it is
from the decorous treatment of the same theme by the
Senecan school of poets. The ethical value of that theme
is considerable, and has its due weight. Events enforce it,
and draw from Enobarbus witty sarcasms, from Antony
many a bitter reflection on his own folly. But this is all:
the riotous life of pleasure betrays its charm beside its cost,
and the ultimate effects of all the moralist would condemn
are moral and not immoral. There is a temporary " diminution in our captain's brain " as a permanent one in his
fortunes, but all that is great in him, his heart-winning
magnanimity in its various manifestations, is conspicuous as
ever, and to this is now added the capacity for devotion and
self-forgetfulness which he pitifully lacked before. It is
absurd to shake our heads over Antony's love because, in
the sharp reversal of the situation of himself and Cleopatra
with respect to one another, he pays for the mortifications
and distresses he had once inflicted on her, in frenzied doubts
of a fidelity suspiciously unstable in our eyes as well as his.
It must be tested by the unselfish devotion at the supreme
hour which renders it incapable of differentiation from a
virtuous passion, and which (at first sight, at any rate) is in
such striking contrast with Cleopatra's care for her own
safety when love and pity should have exiled every other
thought.

It is said that Shakespeare softened or suppressed
Antony's worst traits as he found them in North; but his
instanced cruelties and oppressions precede as much of the
story as is retold in the play, and a dramatist must have

gone out of his way to reveal in him anything beyond what we gather from his treacherous and cold-blooded treatment of Octavia. It is even questionable whether his good qualities are not more conspicuous in Shakespeare than in Plutarch only because of the diminished size of the canvas; but the former certainly gives them full dramatic effect, and from the first we are attracted by glimpses of the " noble minde," " the rare and singular gifts," with which Plutarch loves to " soften to the heart " Antonius' story.

In this play, as in life, things extraneous to passion strengthen its hold for good or evil. In all probability, Antony must have returned to Cleopatra, but two factors besides infatuation are assigned, the " holy cold and still conversation " of Octavia, and, very definitely, the supposed subjection of his genius to Cæsar's. Similarly, something *apparently* stronger than her love for Antony, yet, perhaps, connected with it—her royal determination to endure no bonds nor ignominy—seem to transform Cleopatra after his death and to allow that passion to gain depth and dignity under its powerful shelter. She deceives Cæsar with exultant cunning, and throughout, in her unswerving purpose, in the tolerance with which she suffers the garrulous clown, in the wonderful language of her exultation, free now from all suspicious notes, she exerts, in this dilation to a tragic figure, a fascination which some may have so far heard more about than felt.

To create his Cleopatra, Shakespeare to some extent forsook Plutarch. His Queen of Egypt is a figure of coarser fibre than that which moves in the prose narrative, even allowing for the strong lights of dialogue; and the arts of irritating perverseness employed in I. iii, where Cleopatra's conduct is not indicated in Plutarch, are of harder cast than " the flickering enticements " with which, at a later time, the latter shows her seeking to keep Antony from Octavia; when she seemed to languish for love, contrived that Antony should often find her weeping, and then made show of hiding her tears, " as if she were unwilling that he should see her weepe." The original, with its subtlety preserved or augmented, is outgone in this draught of a type of the sex as well vehement and full-blooded as full of wiles and caprices, in whom qualities of brain and energetic life strike more than " the courteous nature that tempered her words and deeds," and the gift of " words . . . marvelous pleasant " less than its reverse; but the wondrous charm for which the character in its earlier manifestations is praised so unstintedly, seems, in the main, to be unconsciously transferred from the incomparable descriptions of Enobarbus.   Of course it does not matter how the illusion is produced, except as a question for the critic; but Cleopatra, as self-revealed merely, does not, I venture to think, altogether justify the somewhat Lepidian " kneel down, kneel down, and wonder " attitude of her admirers. Johnson spoke of " the feminine arts, some of which are too low, which distinguish Cleopatra," but an earlier and kinder critic has set the tune of comment, and the most fastidious almost outvie his " vilest things become themselves in her."

If we apply to Cleopatra, and extend, her own metaphor for Antony, one way we look on majesty ("Isis else defend!"), the other way is painted in hues that belong to Madam Cæsarean's; but full front she is " a very woman," and the question suggests itself: did Shakespeare intend to leave her a problem for this excellent reason? or was he unable to make up his own mind about her? We may probably dismiss from consideration any idea of the play's being incomplete as it stands, or even of vagueness due to haste.

We do not even know whether Cleopatra paltered with Cæsar after Actium, and there are ill-sounding notes in her protestations like the tuneless strings in a neglected instrument.   We undoubtedly receive an impression, which I hinted at just now, and which seems to go unquestioned, that Shakespeare intentionally represented Cleopatra less favourably than Plutarch in dealing with the motive of her death.   Such an impression goes for much, and the fewer the touches that produce it, the greater the writer's art; but even if the inquiry be narrowed to this last respect, it is worth making.

In Plutarch, there is no direct mention of what is so strongly enforced in Shakespeare, and previously in Daniel, Cleopatra's dread of being made part of Cæsar's triumph in Rome. He merely states the fact that Cleopatra would not open the gates of the monument, and later, that Dolabella, as she had requested him, informed her that Cæsar would within three days send her away before him with her children. In a moving speech at Antony's tomb, she lays stress on her preservation by Cæsar only that he may triumph over Antony: there is no word of her own fear of ignominy, and she implores Antony to help her to foil this attempt to triumph over him, and to save her from the misery she endures in living without him. Before this, Plutarch has already told us of her self-disfigurement for grief and her attempt to make the resulting fever fatal by the aid of starvation, from which she was only deterred by Cæsar's threat of slaying her children—a threat as little permanently effective as in Shakespeare, however, for Dolabella's news determines her action in Plutarch as in him.

Shakespeare's omissions throw into strong relief his development of the mere hint of a second motive for self-destruction, but it is not absolutely certain that he meant us to infer that this second motive was the only efficient one, and that Cleopatra would gladly have survived. He inserts in the final scene with Antony (l. 49) and after his death (l. 79 *et seq.*) expressions on the part of Cleopatra of determination to die, which rest as much or more on the desire not to outlive Antony as on the unwillingness to endure ignominy. He gives us no right to judge this determination weakened, for it is her first thought when we meet her next, and she reveals then, and in the ensuing scene with Proculeius, no incipient hope of life with grace at Cæsar's hands. She has her dagger ready when she is seized, her thought of starvation leaps to her lips, and the fact that, on such an occasion, what she naturally bursts out with is her dread and hatred of the triumph, does not exclude the continuance of her unwillingness to outlive Antony. Cæsar's lies cause her no hesitation, as they might be expected to do if she really cared to survive, or was only moved by fear of disgrace: her directions are at once given to Charmian (v. ii. 191), and this *precedes* Dolabella's final and positive information of Cæsar's purpose. Here, if anywhere, there

xxxviii ANTONY AND CLEOPATRA

is token of omission or confusion. Dolabella had previously assured her that Cæsar would lead her in triumph, and he had not, as he now says, been either commanded or sworn to obtain confirmation of that intention.

We have now once more a recurrence to the theme of Cæsar's triumph, this time partly to stimulate Iras (as Antony himself had used it to induce Eros to kill him), and it would be the height of absurdity to underrate the force of the desire to escape it as a motive in Cleopatra. I am only endeavouring to ascertain how far we are justified in regarding this, and this only, as what enabled her to " be noble " to herself; and perhaps the best plea I can put in for her love is an appeal to the first appearance of these " triumph " passages. It seems as if Shakespeare felt the necessity of accounting for Cleopatra's refusal to open the gates of the monument, and did so in a way which we interpret adversely to her; but let us recollect the lovers' last previous parting, and admit a doubt whether we should not, like Antony, " weep for " our " pardon." In language as forcible as he could make it, which has not the remotest suggestion in Plutarch, Antony had at once declared his belief in Cleopatra's willingness to grace Cæsar's triumph, and the miserable part she would play in it. Such words would surely haunt her; and by her action and the echo of them now, even of the reference to Octavia—a feminine touch, which, if it were not an echo, would go far to overthrow my plea—she took the readiest way to prove their untruth, and to assure Antony that she would help no triumph over him,[1] nor let what he had so jealously engrossed suffer ignominy. If it were so, all was indeed—

> well done, and fitting for a princess
> Descended of so many royal kings.

The familiar of these great figures, Enobarbus, a keen-sighted mocking observer, with lapses into tiresome forced wit, and exaltations into the finest poetry, proves to have understood every one but himself, and knows neither the

---

[1] There is some significance in the language of the various passages. To Antony, she will not *brooch* Cæsar's triumph; to Proculeius and Iras later, it is indignities she dwells upon.

strength of the ties that bind him to Antony, nor his risk of
remorse, nor his inability to bear it. With him, too, there
is something extraneous that helps to determine his fate:
we must add to remorse the small favour shown to master-
leavers by Cæsar, neither so honourable nor adequate a
help as the ague which carries him off in Plutarch. Cæsar
himself, though cold and hard in contrast with his generous
rival, is not heartless. The generous apostrophe to Antony
into which he suddenly breaks in I. iv, the warning appeal
in III. ii, beginning: "Most noble Antony, Let not the
piece of virtue," etc., forbid our taking this view; and
above all the pathos worthy of mighty rivals, lords of the
world, in his lament:

> O Antony !
> I have followed thee to this; but we do lance
> Diseases in our bodies: I must perforce
> Have shown to thee such a declining day,
> Or look on thine: we could not stall together
> In the whole world: . . .

Finally, I retain some impression that *Antony and Cleopatra*
was rather hastily written, with as much advantageous as
injurious result if this had anything to do with the daring
language and treatment, the "happy valiancy" that
Coleridge admired. Haste may have caused some peculi-
arities of construction, and caused the ready utilization of
similar thoughts and illustrations when they cropped up in
parallel cases: the number of reminiscences in *Antony and
Cleopatra* has been noted and is sometimes put down to
profound art. By supposing haste also, we may account
for the occasional occurrence of common-place exaggeration.

The English plays on the same subject would almost provide material for a study of the forms of English tragedy.
The Countess of Pembroke translated Garnier's *Marc-
Antoine*, as *The Trajedie of Antonie*, into monotonous blank
verse, with here and there a few eloquent lines (sometimes
affording illustrations for our text), and, in the choruses,
short measures, often intricately rhymed, which served as
models for Daniel in his *Cleopatra*, 1594. This latter play
—which occupied me in the beginning of this introduction
—is occasionally placed first owing to the date of impress

of *Antonie* (1595); but *Antonie* was finished "At Ramsbury
26. of November 1590," and was the cause, according to
Daniel's dedication, of his digression from Delia's unkindness
to a less absorbing subject. Till Shakespeare rescued it,
the theme remained in the possession of the classical school:
Fulke Greville, Lord Brooke, tells us in his life of Sidney,[1]
that his tragedies " were in their first creation three;
Whereof Antonie and Cleopatra, according to their irregular
passions, in forsaking empire to follow sensuality, were
sacrificed in the fire. The executioner the author him
selfe." It appears that it did not thus regrettably perish
as being inferior to his other plays, but owing to " Many
members in that creature—by the opinion of those few eyes
which saw it—having some childish wantonness in them,
apt enough to be construed or strained to a personating of
vices in the present governors and government."

Lord Brooke was followed by Samuel Brandon, whose
work has survived and is named for re-issue in the admirable series edited by Professor Bang, of Louvain, *Materialen
zur Kunde des älteren Englischen Dramas*. I have not seen this
Senecan play, *The Virtuous Octavia*, 1598, but Mr. Craig
has kindly examined for me the copy in the Dyce Library
at South Kensington, and has come to the conclusion, as
I have done with regard to the other early plays, that
Shakespeare had cast an eye over his predecessor's work.
There are two or three expressions recalling the like in
other plays of Shakespeare, and for *Antony and Cleopatra*,
putting aside as before coincidences traceable to Plutarch,
there is a possible hint for Cæsar's description of Octavia's
prevented welcome in an account of her reception at
Athens, where, says " Geminus (a Captaine) ":

> Long before we could approach the gates
> Of that faire citty, we encountered were
> With people of all ages and estates,
> Who in their handes did boughes of laurel bear,
> Some on their knees with joy and wonder filled,
> Salute the empress ; some rich gifts present,
> Some strew'd the way with flowers and some distill'd
> Their sweet perfumes along the fieldes we went. . . .

---

[1] Chap. xiv, *Works*, ed. Grosart, iv. 155.

Their loud applauses pierced the very skies,
Extoll'd Octavia past the reach of fame,
And silent Echo, waken'd with their cries,
Taught all the neighbour hills to blesse her name.

The play is thus—save, of course, in its choruses—written
in quatrains, like Daniel's *Cleopatra*. The scene is entirely in
Rome, but the action (licentiously for such a play) covers a
far longer period than that of the latter, and its dilutions
promise to be less dry, two virtuous ladies and a wanton, for
example, replacing Daniel's philosophers, and discussing
constancy and variety in love. One of the former, in a later
dialogue, excuses Antony's conduct on the ground of an
affinity between him and Cleopatra as inevitable as that of
the loadstone for iron.

After Shakespeare, Fletcher tried his hand on the delineation of Cleopatra, with some slight debt to him; but
Cleopatra in " the salad days " of her intrigue with Cæsar;
and in the prologue to his play, *The False One* (*circa*, 1620,
according to Fleay), he pleads this as an excuse for meddling
with the theme. The first to challenge comparison upon
the same ground was Thomas May, the translator of Lucan,
for whom, as a historical poet, much was said by Headley,
and might be repeated. His *Cleopatra* was acted in 1626,
printed in 1639, and its scheme is interesting, as coming
between Shakespeare and Dryden, and showing how a
learned and conscientious Caroline poet stood towards
Elizabethan drama. May does not quite dismiss the comic
element: he smooths out the actual representation of battle
and sea-fight, but his time is partly co-extensive with
Shakespeare's, as he takes up the theme before the Actium
disaster. Otherwise, his play disappoints, and its language
irritates by balking expectation of just the little better that
makes all the difference. But I except the *Thyreus* scene,[1]

---

[1] The scene is fine enough and inaccessible enough for rescue for comparison here:

  An. Hands on that Thyreus there, to prison with him.
  Thy. To prison!
  Ant.   Yes; away with him I say.
  Thy. *Cæsar* would not have us'd your messenger
      So ill.
  An.   Thou wert no messenger to me.
  Cle. For my sake dearest Lord.

in which his usually colourless Antony achieves a kind of despairing pathos. His Cleopatra is false a while, but repents when she finds Cæsar proof against her charms.

The rhymed heroic play now claimed the subject. Sir Charles Sedley's *Antony and Cleopatra* was acted at the Duke's

An.   O for your sake?
    I cry you mercy Lady, bear him hence.   [*Exit Thyreus.*
    I had forgot that *Thyreus* was your servant.
    But what strange act should he perform for you?
    Is it to help you to a happier friend?

Cle.   Can you suspect it? was my truest love
    So ill bestow'd? Can he, for whose dear sake
    A Queen so highly born as I preferr'd
    Love before fame, and fondly did neglect
    All names of honour when false *Fulvia,*
    And proud *Octavia* had the name of wives,
    Requite me thus? ungrateful *Anthony:*
    For now the fury of a wronged love
    Justly provokes my speech.

Ant.   Oh *Cleopatra,*
    It is not *Thyreus* but this heart of mine
    That suffers now, deep wounded with the thought
    Of thy inconstancie; did Fortune leave
    One only comfort to my wretched state
    And what a false one? for what conference
    Couldst thou so oft, and in such privacie
    With *Cæsar's* servant hold, if true to me?
    Which with the rack I could enforce from him.
    But that I scorn to do.

Cle.   You do not scorn
    To wrong with base unworthie jealousies
    A faithfull heart: but if you think me false
    Heer sheath your sword: make me the subject rather
    Of manly rage then childish jealousie.
    It is a nobler crime, and fitter farre
    For you to act, easier for me to suffer.
    For live suspected I nor can nor will.
    The lovely Aspe, which I with care have kept
    And was intended a preservative
    'Gainst *Cæsar's* crueltie, I now must use
    Against *Antonius* basenesse a worse fo
    Than Cæsar is: farewell, till death approve
    That I was true, and you unjust in love.

Ant.   Stay *Cleopatra,* dearest Love, forgive me
    Let not so small a winde have power to shake
    A love so grown as ours: I did not think
    That thou wert false: my heart gave no consent
    To what my tongue so rashly uttered
    Nor could I have outliv'd so sad a thought.
    Let *Thyreus* be releast, and sent to *Cæsar.*

Theatre, with Betterton as Antony, in 1676 or 1677, and
printed in the latter year, reappearing in 1702 as *Beauty the
Conqueror* or *The Death of Marc Antony.* Sir Walter Scott
(Dryden's *Works,* 1808, v. 293) and Dr. A. W. Ward, in his
History of English Dramatic Literature, treat it with severity,
but it cannot be accused of rant, and takes its place among
the heroic plays in which tragedy turns on manlike aims and
passions rather than on strained points of honour. The
story is taken up after Actium, the number of actors reduced,
Cleopatra refined, and comedy expelled, while the plot is
complicated by new loves; those of Mæcenas for Octavia,
of Photinus, the ambitious traitor of the piece, for Iras, of
Thyreus for Cleopatra. Antony and Cleopatra are, according to the kind, heroic and faithful lovers, and Canidius and
other Romans prefer death to faithlessness or surrender.
The play is full of life and bustle, combat and siege, and the
whole can appeal, if we forget Shakespeare, who influences
it in a general way.

In the meantime, or possibly owing to Sedley's example,
the subject attracted the former champion of the heroic
play: Dryden's *All for Love* was acted and printed in 1678.
In it he abandoned rhyme and restored to the drama the
art of writing good blank verse; this, too, without repro-
ducing that of any previous writer or coming under the
spell of Milton. The figures he drew deserve their own
observance, but, thanks to critics less generous than himself,
are seen only forlornly following Cæsar's triumph.

In *All for Love,* a close observance of the unities and
restriction to few characters does not prevent the contrivance of an interesting series of events, to the development of
which every scene contributes. The plot and characters
show Dryden still influenced to some extent by the love and
honour scheme of the heroic play. Cleopatra, save that
she would sooner see her hero ruined with her than secure
without her, is fidelity itself, and rejects Cæsar's ample
offers; Antony is torn either way by the truth of Cleopatra
and the generosity of Octavia. Love triumphs almost by
accident, when jealousy and a natural collapse of Octavia's
patience is vigorously marshalled to its aid. *All for Love*
certainly contains some imitation and reminiscence of

Antony and Cleopatra, but Dryden said truly that he had not copied his author servilely, and his play can be read and enjoyed as a study in a different manner, for its different conception of character, and its fine poetry, without the least compulsory reference to an all-belittling standard.

In preparing this edition I have been without the help of any on the same or a greater scale; but my obligations are many, as appears in the notes, and to the eighteenth-century editors of course incalculable.   I owe to Mr. Craig, the general editor of this Shakespeare, the most cordial thanks for help and encouragement throughout; and Mr. Henry Cuningham, the editor of *A Midsummer-Night's Dream* in the same series, obliged me by investigating some material points at the British Museum.   From my friend Mr. J. Roy Coventry I had a useful loan of some of the early critical editions, and from Mr. T. Harkness Graham, Assistant Librarian in the University of Liverpool, a most generous gift of time and scrupulous care in reading and correcting the whole of the proofs, and in verifying the numerous references, which will owe much of their exactness to him.

The following summarizes Mr. Daniel's Time-Analysis of the play: twelve days are represented on the stage with intervals after the first, third, fourth, fifth, sixth, seventh, and ninth, the historic time being about ten years, 40 to 30 B.C. :—

Day	1.	I. i-iv.
,,	2.	I. v, II. i-iii.
,,	3.	II. iv.
,,	4.	II. v-vii.
,,	5.	III. i, ii, iii.
,,	6.	III. iv, v.
,,	7.	III. vi.
,,	8.	III. vii.
,,	9.	III. viii-x.
,,	10.	III. xi-xiii, IV. i-iii.
,,	11.	IV. iv-ix.
,,	12.	IV. x-xv, V. i, ii. [R. H. C.]

† I have little to add to this introduction. Three judgements on the play and the characters deserve to have attention drawn to them. Bradley's article in the *Quarterly*, at which Case glances on p. xxxiii, was later republished in his *Oxford Lectures on Poetry* (1909). It is probably the finest piece of concentrated criticism which even this great critic achieved. (I say " great critic " because, though his reputation is at the moment suffering from a natural, and perhaps salutary, reaction, I cannot believe that his stature can long remain obscured.) In 1944 Lord David Cecil published a lecture on *Antony and Cleopatra* in which he presents the interest as " largely political." Shakespeare, he thinks, " conceived his play as a piece of history," and though there is a single presiding theme, " this theme is not love, it is success." He must find the play much duller than most of us do, but so odd a judgement, coming from a usually sane and sensitive critic, has at least the merit of making one think. Lastly, there is Dover Wilson's introduction to the play in the *New Shakespeare*. It exhibits, I think, a generous error to which he is liable: if he admires a character he cannot bear it to be less than almost wholly admirable; and this predisposition colours his judgement of both Antony and Cleopatra. But in the course of it he performs two signal services. The first is to draw attention to Dr. Tarn's presentation of Cleopatra in the *Cambridge Ancient History*, vol. X, ch. 2. The other is to discuss the Seleucus scene, and emphasize the interpretation of it which I am sure is the right one, but which, since Stahr is now little read, and in any case was not writing about Shakespeare's play but about Plutarch's Cleopatra, is apt to escape the modern reader and producer. Stahr [1] pointed out that Plutarch says, at the end of the account of Cæsar's interview with Cleopatra, " and so he took his leave of her, supposing he had deceived her, but indeed he was deceived himself " (North's translation); and North underlines this and makes the design explicit, by a marginal comment, " Cleopatra finely deceiveth Octavius Cæser *as though she desired to live* " (italics mine). That is to say, the whole scene with Seleucus

---

[1] A. Stahr, *Cleopatra* (1864), and see Furness, *Variorum* edition, pp. xiii, xiv.

is a put-up job, possibly even rehearsed beforehand. The easiest way of convincing Cæsar that she desires to live is to be exposed as having retained, and omitted from her declaration, half her fortune, to support not only life, but life in something like her former state.

This interpretation has two dramatic advantages. It prevents Cleopatra's assault on Seleucus being no more than an undignified repetition of the earlier scene with the messenger—a drop in tone which at this point of the play is hardly tolerable. And it gives us the pleasure of watching Cæsar out-played, not only walking headlong into the trap but (in ll. 183-8) thinking himself clever as he does so, so that Cleopatra's " My master, and my lord! " can carry its full charge of irony, since she knows that he is already the ass, unpolicied. The only trouble about the interpretation is whether it can be made plain to the audience, since if it cannot it is not what Shakespeare the practical playwright intended. But I think it can be done.[1] In the first place, the more quick-witted of the audience will wonder why Cleopatra brings in Seleucus at all—and it is her doing, not Cæsar's, that he is introduced. If Cæsar will not take her own word for her " brief " he is not likely to take that of a subordinate official, presumably under her thumb. " Hullo," says the suspicious spectator, " there is more here than meets the eye." But I think the vital point is the way in which the actress playing Cleopatra delivers the words " Speak the truth, Seleucus." They are his cue. After that both he and Cleopatra, by slight exaggeration, he of his fears and she of her tantrums and her humiliation, indicate that they are playing a game.

But if the interpretation is right in itself, I think that in the application of it Dover Wilson overplays his hand. He is so anxious to establish Cleopatra's unswerving nobility, to show that her resolution to follow Antony at once never wavered, that he takes this interpretation of the Seleucus scene as proof positive of the unwavering resolution, and he also neglects an awkward interval and the conversation with Proculeius. Now that conversation, though it is

---

[1] Dover Wilson says " the episode can readily be played so as to bring it out to the audience," but makes no attempt to show how.

possible to get round it, cannot safely be neglected; and the Seleucus scene turns out, on examination, to be irrelevant to the main issue. No one denies that Cleopatra contemplates suicide as at least a possibility. Even if she is only going to be driven to it as a last resort, still she will, when convinced of its necessity, need time for its achievement, and this time, she hopes, the scene with Seleucus will provide. If she finds that she can make satisfactory terms, little will have been lost; if she cannot, everything will have been gained. That is to say, the " put-up-job " interpretation of the Seleucus scene fits as neatly and as dramatically into either reading of Cleopatra's state of mind as into the other.

It is perhaps worth while examining for a moment the stages in Cleopatra's progress towards suicide. In the first place, at any time we like anterior to the climax of the play, she has pursued infinite conclusions of easy ways to die. In a crisis, therefore, her thoughts will not be exercised by the mechanics of suicide, but only by its necessity or desirability; and we guess that the compulsion will need to be strong that drives her to it. Under the immediate shock of Antony's death she rises to a mood of exaltation; the odds is gone, the world is a dull place, we have no friend but resolution and the briefest end, so let us act after the high Roman fashion, rush into the secret house of death and make death proud to take us. There is no mistake about that. But is it cynical to suggest that even here she does not exactly " rush " into the house of death, as Antony did or tried to do, but gains time even from her own resolution on the grounds of burying Antony? There is then an interval, during which we have no clue to her thoughts except that she sends the " poor Egyptian " to Cæsar to enquire his " intents." When next we see her (v. ii) she is again contemplating suicide, though in more philosophic fashion. She then has an interview with Proculeius, in which she expresses submission, states her terms, and suggests an interview with Cæsar. When captured by the guard she attempts suicide, and gives as reason for the attempt the hateful prospect of Cæsar's triumph—not a word of Antony. Her last message now to Cæsar is " I would die." Left alone with Dolabella she pays tribute to Antony, and having got Dolabella well-tempered she comes out with the direct question, " Know you what Cæsar means to do with me? " and forces an answer from him. She has no time to comment on it before Cæsar enters. She plays her scene with Cæsar and Seleucus, and after Cæsar has gone despatches Charmian, presumably to arrange for the introduction of the asps. While Charmian is away she receives from Dolabella further confirmation of Cæsar's intentions and paints for herself and Iras a picture of the degrading circumstances of Cæsar's intended triumph. From the moment of Charmian's return not only is her " resolution " indeed " placed " and she " marble-constant " but Antony at last is the expressed motive for the resolution. She is again for Cydnus to meet him, she claims him as her husband, and she will not, if she can help it, let Iras reach him first.

That, I think, is a fair statement of what the text shows us. Nothing can detract from Cleopatra's royal splendour at the end; but we should not allow our eyes to be so dazzled by it that we cannot examine what happens, or does not happen, earlier. There is, first, the short conversation with Proculeius before her capture. This reads to me like an honest attempt at negotiation. I admit that it may be construed as a dishonest playing for time; but if her resolution had been constant the time should not have needed to be played for. Far more crucial than the interview with Proculeius is the interval between the end of IV. xv and the opening of v. ii, an interval from which the supporters of the unwavering purpose resolutely avert their eyes, and do their best to avert the eyes of their readers. Dover Wilson, for example, says " She announces it [the resolution] at the end of 4.15 immediately after Antony's own death, reiterates it at the opening of 5.2, and is only forced to postpone it by her unexpected capture and the interview with Cæsar." " Only forced to postpone it " seems to me a piece of clever but somewhat disingenuous special pleading. It is true *of the moment*; but what has Cleopatra been doing with the interval before this moment? There is as yet, so far as we know, no guard through whom

the bearer of the asps has to be brought in, and so nothing
in the world to prevent her arranging for his arrival when
she chooses. I think that after her first moment of exaltation she would make terms with Cæsar if she could make her
own, and is brought back to her original resolution only by
her later conviction of Cæsar's intentions.

I have laboured the point only because I think that
Shakespeare's portrayal of Cleopatra at the end of the play
is far more subtly penetrating, and more unsparing, than
some of his critics would like it to be.

What little else I have to say, particularly about the
" echoes " of which the play is so full, and which Case
dismisses rather summarily on p. xxxviii, I have said some
fifteen years ago.[1] And since the re-writing, merely for the
sake of re-writing, of something which, whether well or ill
said, was at least as clear as the writer could make it, is an
unprofitable business, I am, by the courtesy of Messrs. J. M.
Dent & Sons, repeating it, with a few minor modifications.

To read this play is like watching a great tragic actor
playing, as it were for his amusement and relaxation, a
lighter part that is very far inside his compass. There is no
carelessness about it; every touch is as perfect as imagination
and long-trained technique can make it; but the perfection
is achieved with a felicity of ease which is enthralling.

In two ways the play is sharply differentiated from the
" four great " tragedies. In the first place it is a love
tragedy. Shakespeare opened his tragic career (if we may
not unreasonably leave *Titus* out of the reckoning) with
Romeo and Juliet, and he closed it (if again we may omit
Coriolanus as being of a somewhat different order of play)
with *Antony and Cleopatra*. These are both love tragedies,
the one of youth, the other of maturity, and the fact that
only twelve or thirteen years divide them shows the bitter
rapidity of the maturing. In the second place we are left at
the end of *Antony and Cleopatra* with less sense of waste than
at the end of any of the others, not excepting *Romeo and
Juliet*. When Antony says " the nobleness of life is to do
thus " we know that for himself, and perhaps also for
Cleopatra, he is stating the mere truth; but unless his

[1] *Shakespeare's Plays, a Commentary* (Dent, 1936).

D

values were wrong it would not be the truth. Their passion ennobles them as nothing else ever has or ever could, but also as, if they were themselves nobler, it would not. The world loses little by their passing; and indeed we know that for the world it is better that the course of the Roman State should on, cracking their link asunder. Finally the play has little dramatic tension, none of the complication followed by explication of plot which marks the others.

But all this is not to say that Shakespeare tried to write a tragedy like *Othello* or *Lear* and failed. He tried to write a drama of a different order, and royally succeeded. The different order may be also an inferior order, but there is no question about the success. The play is a brilliant *tour de force*, perhaps Shakespeare's high-water-mark of sheer technical brilliance. He is handling recalcitrant material. The story of Antony and Cleopatra, as narrated by Plutarch or elsewhere, is not in its essence dramatic at all. There is no proper forward progress, and so no plot; there is merely a series of oscillations on the part of Antony. Under various influences—a weak loyalty to Octavia, a rather stronger loyalty to Rome, and, by far the strongest, the love of being a great fighting general and leading to victory his adoring troops—Antony swings like a compass needle; but he always comes to rest again pointing to the inevitable north. And not only is this story not essentially dramatic, but it is in danger of being a trifle sordid. The spectacle of a man of at least considerable qualities wasting them in an infatuation is not an ennobling spectacle, certainly not a tragic one. If this subject is to be lifted to any sort of greatness, something must be added to it, and Shakespeare met the difficulty in the only way in which it could be met (and which Dryden missed realizing) by giving to Antony a greatness other than that of his character. We must be made to feel him as a man whose fate matters to the world, to the course of history from then till now; we must ourselves stand under the arch of the ranged empire; we must not only be *told* that he is the triple pillar of the world, we must *see* him so, or we care little whether or not he is transformed into a strumpet's fool; but show him to us as the great triumvir, in consultation with Octavius and the slight, unmeritable Lepidus, and we realize that his fall may cause the world to totter. And so Shakespeare neglects the unities, and hurries us about in space and time (bringing in, for example, stray captains from Syria) so that we feel the surge of great events, and Antony's greatness among them, as determined things hold their way to destiny. And the greater, even in this historical sense, that Antony can be made, the greater, by a natural, if illogical, process, do we feel to be the woman who so enslaves him; and, moving further round the same circle, the greater that Cleopatra becomes the less do we experience either wonder or distress at Antony's subjugation.

On the two main characters opinions have differed widely, as was indeed to be expected, human nature being what it is. A critic who sees mainly one side of Antony finds a man " of the most noble and high spirit, capable at times of a thoroughly soldier-like life, and full of kind and generous feelings." That is well said, and is true. Another, with his eyes rather on Antony's morals than his soldiership, sees that he is " dissolute and voluptuous, and Cleopatra's depravity is congenial to his nature"; that is also true, except that depravity is hardly the right word, and that it is only to one side of his nature that the " depravity " appeals. A third gives himself away by announcing that " the passion of Antony for Cleopatra is too obviously spurious to command our sympathy " (!). A fourth sees well round the subject from its various angles: " Antony appears as the soldier and the voluptuary, swayed alternately by love, by regret, by ambition, at one moment the great ruler of the divided world, at the next flinging his future away at the dictation of a passionate caprice." That I think is both justly and clearly said, and leaves little to add. Antony has a magnificent virility about him, to which both men and women react; but he is a creature of impulse, he has no eye for the stars, and cannot steer a course; he wants what he wants strongly, and he wants it immediately; he is generous, and even his faults are on the grand scale; he can descend to folly, but never to meanness.

Cleopatra gravels the critics of later ages as completely as she did those of her own.   She is " a brilliant antithesis " (whatever that may mean), " a compound of contradictions," or (perhaps the best example of the meaningless verbiage of befuddled bewilderment) " this glorious riddle, whose dazzling complexity continually mocks and eludes us."   She is often described as " the courtesan of genius," but to take that phrase in isolation is fair neither to Cleopatra nor to the penetrating criticism from which it is isolated. " Cleopatra is the greatest of the enchantresses.   She has wit, grace, humour;   the intoxication of sex breathes from her;   she unites the passion of a great temperament with the fathomless coquetry of a courtesan of genius. . . . It is this magnificence which invests Cleopatra's criminality with a kind of sublimity, so vast is the scale of her being, and so tremendous the force of her passions."   That also, I think, is just.   It is easy to miss the cutting and balanced precision of Shakespeare's delineation of Cleopatra.   If only we will hear, it is as though we were members of a jury, listening to the summing-up of the most dispassionate and brilliant of judges.   When once we have read the play it is hard not to reflect back upon the Cleopatra of the first four acts the light and colour of the Cleopatra of the last.   In the last act she is the great queen, and is indeed fire and air;   no doubt she would have made terms with Cæsar if she could have made her own, but, seeing that she cannot, she will follow Antony, and if she is to die, she will die indeed painlessly, but she will do it after the high Roman fashion;   and Death would be a poor creature if he was not proud to take her.   But if our eyes are not dazzled by this reflection we shall recognize that it would be hard to find anywhere in literature a more unsparing picture of the professional courtesan than Shakespeare's picture of Cleopatra in the first four acts.   Her aim indeed is not ignoble;   she is genuinely, and perhaps for the first time in her life, in love;   Antony at last realizes her ideal;   but the methods by which she achieves her aim and holds him are those of the pastmistress in her ancient art, learnt and perfected to the last finesse of technique in years in which she hung the scalps of Cæsar and Pompey, amongst others, at her belt.   The bafflement of the critics, or some of them, about her seems to depend on a confusion of complexity with variety. She is infinitely varied, but not in the least complex; she is as single-minded in pursuit of her aim as Lady Macbeth in pursuit of hers, and all the quick shifts of temper are little more than part of her brilliant technique. Perhaps in the end the best description of her is Enobarbus' simple " a wonderful piece of work." That at least avoids any idle questionings as to the morality or immorality of the love of Antony and Cleopatra.

Since, unless we suffer from a kind of moral myopia, we are little troubled as we read, and even less as we see, by questions of worthiness or unworthiness, still less of morality and immorality. We have been transported to a world in which such disputes seem to lose their meaning. Admittedly it is far from the noblest kind of world, as the two main figures are far from human nature at its noblest. But, being what they are, they are by their mutual passion lifted to the highest pitch to which they are capable of soaring. It is the merest fatuity of moralizing to deny the name of " love " to their passion, and write it off as " mere lust." No doubt it is not the highest kind of love; it is completely an *égoisme à deux*, and has no power to inspire to anything outside itself; but it has in it something that should be an element in the highest kind of love; and at least it is the passion of human beings and not of animals, of the spirit as well as of the body. It was not by her beauty (of which by all accounts the gods had not been lavish) but by her superb vitality that Cleopatra took Antony captive and held him.

And it is by that same vitality that she takes us captive also. We may attempt to analyse the play, to apply critical criteria to it, to examine the characters, and so on; and no doubt we are right to do so, and by so doing help our appreciation of the play. But in the end these intellectual exercises and their results drift down the wind like the idle thistledown that for this play they are; we know in our hearts that what in this play Shakespeare has to offer us is a thrill, a quickening of the pulses, a brief experience in a region where there is an unimagined vividness of life; and we surrender, with Antony, if anything so vitalizing can be called surrender, to the "strong toil of grace."

Octavius is an unattractive figure, but one worth study, not so much for himself as because he draws our wandering attention to a noticeable feature of the play. In the first three acts, by touch on subtle touch, the relentless power of Rome is forced on our subconscious notice. We are made to feel that it is something against whose ineluctable march no individuals, however great, can for one moment stand. Octavius, like the equally unattractive Aeneas, is the typical Roman; and at the end he, the "cold Cæsar," is more than himself: he is Rome, looking down, with a just and not unsympathetic estimation, on the "pair so famous" over whom her chariot wheels have rolled.

When all is said, the peculiar glory of this play is not in its dramatic quality at all. It is in its poetry. It is full, to begin with, of phrases in Shakespeare's best later manner, where the whole force depends on the use of a word, or a juxtaposition of words, which would startle us if we were not aware of their inevitable rightness before we have time be startled. For example:

> the odds is gone,
> And there is nothing left remarkable
> Beneath the visiting moon.

IV. xv. 66

Again, it is full of echoes, like:

Ant. Unarm, Eros, the long day's task is done,
And we must sleep.

IV. xiv. 35

Iras. Finish, good lady, the bright day is done,
And we are for the dark.

V. ii. 192

Or

Ant.   I will be
A bridegroom in my death, and run into 't
As to a lover's bed.

IV. xiv. 99

Cleo. The stroke of death is as a lover's pinch,
Which hurts, and is desir'd.

V. ii. 294

Or

Cleo. And when thou hast done this chare, I'll give thee leave
    To play till doomsday.

                                                        v. ii. 230

Char.   Your crown's awry,
    I'll mend it, and then play.

                                                        v. ii. 317

Or the triple chime on " royal " in the last scene, where
Shakespeare is stressing Cleopatra the queen:

Char.   Downy windows, close,
    And golden Phoebus, never be beheld
    Of eyes again so royal!

                                                        v. ii. 315

Char. It is well done, and fitting for a princess
    Descended of so many royal kings

                                                        v. ii. 325

Cæs.   Bravest at the last
    She levell'd at our purposes, and being royal
    Took her own way.

                                                        v. ii. 333

Finally, we have here beyond question Shakespeare's
topmost achievement in dramatic poetry, that kind of
poetry which apart from its context is little remarkable,
but in its dramatic setting is indefinably moving. The
earlier plays are full of pure lyric poetry which is quite
irrelevant to the action of the play, and not infrequently
even out of character for the person who speaks it; and even
down to the end of Shakespeare's dramatic career, down to
The Tempest, with its cloud-capped towers, there will occur
passages which can be lifted with little loss from their
contexts. But in this play, with the sole exception of the
description of Cleopatra's barge, most incongruously put
into the mouth of the prosaically, however penetratingly,
common-sensical Enobarbus, there is hardly a line which is
not in character, and perhaps no considerable memorable
passage which can stand by itself, none that can be ex-
cerpted, without losing half its force; while there is passage

after passage, line after line, of which the force in its setting
is electric. To take two examples only:

> I am dying, Egypt, dying:

IV. XV. 41

Four (or three) very ordinary words, and a proper name,
as they stand prosaic enough; but spoken by the dying
Antony, to his royal lover, his serpent of old Nile, they are
potent and poignant magic. Or again:

> Dost thou not see my baby at my breast,
> That sucks the nurse asleep?

V. ii. 308

Write that for its natural context, the description, let us
say, of a happy and carefree mother, and it is a piece of
quiet competence that no one will think of twice. Put
those same words in the mouth of the great queen, standing
in her full and final majesty, robed and crowned for the
stroke of her last fatal lover, with the asp at the breast that
had suckled her children, and the world catches its breath.

[R]

References to passages in other plays of Shakespeare's are to the single
volume Oxford edition (ed. W. J. Craig).
    For the other writers chiefly referred to the following list of editions may be
useful. In selecting the editions I have been guided not only by intrinsic
excellence but in part by considerations of accessibility and ease of reference.
Some otherwise admirable editions have no line-numbering, and it is a
vexatious business to try to locate a brief passage with nothing but act and
scene to help one.

Beaumont and Fletcher	Variorum edition (Bell & Bullen, 1904-12) so far as available; for other plays the Glover-Waller edn. (C.U.P. 1905-12).
Chapman	Plays, ed. Parrott (Routledge, 1910); Poems, ed. Shepherd (Chatto & Windus, 1875).
"Doubtful" plays	*Shakespeare Apocrypha*, ed. Tucker Brooke (Clarendon Press, 1908).
Gammer Gurton's Needle	*Representative English Comedies*, ed. C. M. Gayley (Macmillan Co., New York, 1903).
Jonson	ed. Herford and Simpson (Clarendon Press, 1925-52).
Kyd	ed. Boas (Clarendon Press, 1901).
Lyly	ed. Warwick Bond (Clarendon Press, 1902).
Marlowe	ed. Tucker Brooke (Clarendon Press, 1910).
Marston	ed. Bullen (Nimmo, 1887).
Middleton	ed. Bullen (Nimmo, 1885-6).
Nashe	ed. McKerrow (Clarendon Press, 1905-12).
Peele	ed. Bullen (Nimmo, 1888).
Ralph Roister Doister	as for *Gammer Gurton's Needle*.
Webster	ed. F. L. Lucas (Chatto & Windus, 1927).

ANTONY AND CLEOPATRA

ANTONY,
OCTAVIUS CÆSAR, } *triumvirs.*
LEPIDUS,

SEXTUS POMPEIUS.

DOMITIUS ENOBARBUS,
VENTIDIUS,
EROS,
SCARUS, } *friends of Antony.*
DECRETAS
DEMETRIUS,
PHILO,

MÆCENAS,
AGRIPPA,
DOLABELLA, } *friends of Cæsar.*
PROCULEIUS,
THIDIAS,
GALLUS,

MENAS,
MENECRATES, } *friends of Pompey.*
VARRIUS,

TAURUS, *lieutenant-general to Cæsar.*
CANIDIUS, *lieutenant-general to Antony.*
SILIUS, *an officer in Ventidius' army.*
A "*schoolmaster*" *acting as ambassador from Antony to Cæsar*
ALEXAS,
MARDIAN, *a eunuch,* } *attendants on Cleopatra.*
DIOMEDES,
SELEUCUS, *treasurer to Cleopatra.*
A *soothsayer.*
A *Clown.*

CLEOPATRA, *queen of Egypt.*
OCTAVIA, *Cæsar's sister.*
CHARMIAN, } *attendants on Cleopatra.*
IRAS,

Officers, Soldiers, Messengers, and other attendants.

SCENE: *In several parts of the Roman empire.*

---

[1] There is no list of *dramatis personæ* in F. It is first given (more or less) by Rowe, and expanded and emended by later editors. For Decretas and Thidias, instead of the more usual Dercetas and Thyreus, see notes on IV. xiv. 104 (S.D.) and III. xii. 31 respectively.

2

ANTONY AND CLEOPATRA

ACT I

SCENE I.—[*Alexandria. A room in Cleopatra's palace.*]

Enter DEMETRIUS *and* PHILO.

Phi. Nay, but this dotage of our general's
O'erflows the measure: those his goodly eyes,
That o'er the files and musters of the war
Have glow'd like plated Mars, now bend, now turn
The office and devotion of their view   5
Upon a tawny front: his captain's heart,
Which in the scuffles of great fights hath burst
The buckles on his breast, reneges all temper,

ACT I

Scene 1

Act 1. Scene 1.] Acts and Scenes not marked, save here, in F.

1. *general's*] Cf. *K.J.* ii. i. 65: "a
bastard of the king's," and i. ii. 71
post. The double genitive still occurs
in colloquial usage.

4. *plated*] See *R. II.* i. iii. 28:
"Thus *plated* in habiliments of war,"
and Heywood, *The Silver Age* (*Works*,
Pearson, iii. 132) :—
"Were his head brasse, or his
        breast doubly *plated*
With' best Vulcanian armour
        Lemnos yeelds; " etc.

bend, now turn] This is the pointing
of F. Editors place a comma after
turn, but *bend* may be independent,
expressing a contrast to the fiery out-
look inferred in *glow'd*, and without
influence on *the office*, etc. Cf.
Jonson, *The Poetaster*, v. ii. 92: "Nor
do her eyes once *bend* to taste sweet
sleep."

5. *office*] service, as in *R. II.* ii. ii.
136: "for little *office*, The hateful
commons will perform for us."

There seems no reason to deprive
devotion of its separate force, as some
do, by regarding *office and devotion* as
a hendiadys, equivalent to "devoted
service."

6. *front*] forehead, and so face.

8. *reneges all temper*] refuses *or* re-
nounces all self-restraint. Fletcher's
Maid's Tragedy concludes with :—
"May this a fair example be to me,
    To rule with *temper:* " etc.
A late instance of *renegue* is in Ferrand
Spence's *Lucian*, 1684, ii. 43: "*Lucian.
. . .* What say you, *Diogenes*, know
you this Dapper Blade? He's of your
Pond. *Diogenes.* I *renegue* him for
mine." Steevens quotes *Lear*, ii. ii. 82,
"*Renege*, affirm," and Stanyhurst's
Virgil, *Æneis*, 1582, book ii: "Too
liue now longer, Troy burnt, hee
flatlye *reneaged* " (see Arber's reprint,
p. 64, and also pp. 75, 143). For the
pronunciation, Halliwell quotes Sylvester's Du Bartas [*The Battail of Ivry,*

And is become the bellows and the fan
To cool a gipsy's lust.

Flourish.   Enter ANTONY, CLEOPATRA, *her Ladies, the Train,*
with Eunuchs fanning her.

Look, where they come: 10
Take but good note, and you shall see in him
The triple pillar of the world transform'd
Into a strumpet's fool: behold and see.
Cleo. If it be love indeed, tell me how much.
Ant. There's beggary in the love that can be reckon'd.   15
Cleo. I'll set a bourn how far to be belov'd.

---

lines 33, 34] and adopts the spelling suggested by Coleridge in *Notes and Lectures, reneagues* :—

> " All Europe nigh (all sorts of
>   Rights *reneg'd*)
>   Against the Truth and Thee un-
>   holy leagu'd."

9, 10. *bellows . . . To cool*] Johnson suggests *to kindle and to cool*, misled by the usual use of the bellows; for which, as a cooling implement, Steevens quotes Lyly's *Midas*, v. ii. 84: " methinks *Venus* and Nature stande with each of them a paire of *bellowes*, the one cooling my lowe birth, the other kindling my loftie affections." Malone cites also Spenser, *Faerie Queene*, II. ix. 30 :—

> " But to delay the heat, least by
>   mischaunce
>   It might breake out and set the
>   whole on fyre,
>   There added was by goodly ordi-
>   naunce
>   An huge great payre of *bellowes*,
>   which did styre
>   Continually, and cooling breath
>   inspyre."

10. *gipsy's*] Not colour only but conduct is aimed at in the word. For its contemptuous or insulting application to any woman, see Shirley, *The Traitor*, II. i :—

> " *Gipsy*, use better language,
>   Or I'll forget your sex."

See also on IV. xii. 28 *post*, on the word and its further supposed application to Cleopatra.

12. *triple pillar*] Applied to Antony as one of the three, the Triumvirs, who governed the world between them. Cf. Sir Thomas Browne, *Religio Medici*, section xix: " I have therefore always endeavoured to compose those feuds and angry dissensions between Affection, Faith and Reason; for there is in our soul a kind of Triumvirate, a Triple Government of Three Competitors, which distracts the Peace of this our Commonwealth not less than did that other the state of *Rome*." For *triple*＝third, cf. *All's Well*, II. i. 111 : " Which . . . He bade me store up, as a *triple* eye," etc.

13. *strumpet's fool*] There were professional fools whose places entitled them to this description. Such is the fool in *Timon of Athens*. See Douce, *Illustrations of Shakespeare*, 1807, i. 151; ii. 73, 304 *et seq.*

15. *There's beggary . . . reckon'd*] Steevens furnishes references to *R. and J.* II. vi. 32 : " they are but *beggars* that can count their worth "; Martial, lib. vi, ep. 34: " [Basia] pauca cupit, qui numerare potest "; *beggary* is niggardliness, meanness, cf. *Cymbeline*, I. vi. 115.

16. *bourn*] boundary, as in *Hamlet*, III. i. 79.

Ant. Then must thou needs find out new heaven, new earth.

Enter an Attendant.

Att. News, my good lord, from Rome.

Ant.   Grates me, the sum.

Cleo. Nay, hear them, Antony:
    Fulvia perchance is angry; or who knows   20
    If the scarce-bearded Cæsar have not sent
    His powerful mandate to you, " Do this, or this;
    Take in that kingdom, and enfranchise that;
    Perform't, or else we damn thee."

Ant.   How, my love?

Cleo. Perchance? nay, and most like: 25
    You must not stay here longer, your dismission
    Is come from Cæsar, therefore hear it, Antony.
    Where's Fulvia's process? Cæsar's I would say. Both?
    Call in the messengers. As I am Egypt's queen,
    Thou blushest, Antony, and that blood of thine   30
    Is Cæsar's homager: else so thy cheek pays shame

17. Enter an Attendant] Capell; Enter a Messenger. F.   18. Att.] Capell ; Mes. F.

17. (S.D.). Enter an Attendant] The " messengers " are waiting outside.

18. *Grates me, the sum*] offends me : be brief. See Middleton, *No Wit [Help] Like a Woman's*, I. i. 9 :—

    " but I'm *grated* [=vexed]
    In a dear, absolute friend," etc.

F's comma (as against many editors' colon) gives Antony's impatience.

19. *them*] i.e. the news. *News* is sometimes singular, as in III. vii. 54 *post*; *Lear*, IV. ii. 87; sometimes plural, as in *R. & J.* II. v. 22.

23. *Take in*] subdue, occupy. See III. vii. 23 *post*, on which Steevens quotes Chapman's Homer, *Iliad*, ii. 10. The expression occurs again and again in that book, e.g. line 22 :—

    " Thy strong hand the broad-way'd
    town of Troy
    Shall now *take in*."

enfranchise] set free.

26. *dismission*] Similarly for *dismissal* in *Cymbeline*, II. iii. 57.

28. *Fulvia*] Antony's wife.

process] summons ; the name of the whole course of proceedings in a cause, being so applied, according to Minshew, because the calling into court " *is the* beginning *or the* principall part thereof, *by which the rest of the* business is directed," etc. See Forman's *Diary* (ed. Halliwell, 1849), under 1590: " The 26. of Julii I was served with *proces* to apeare at the Star chamber, before the counsell " ; Overbury, *Characters*, 1616, *An Apparatour* : " Thus lives he in a golden age, till Death by a *processe*, summons him to appeare."

31. *homager*] vassal. So Browne, *Britannia's Pastorals*, I. iii. 742 : " A many *homagers* to Tamar's crown."

else so . . .] or else (even more humiliating) it is your usual reaction to Fulvia's reproaches.

When shrill-tongued Fulvia scolds.   The messengers!
Ant. Let Rome in Tiber melt, and the wide arch
  Of the rang'd empire fall!   Here is my space,
  Kingdoms are clay: our dungy earth alike   35
  Feeds beast as man; the nobleness of life
  Is to do thus: when such a mutual pair, [*Embracing.*
  And such a twain can do't, in which I bind,
  On pain of punishment, the world to weet
  We stand up peerless.

Cleo.   Excellent falsehood! 40

34. *rang'd*] *raing'd* F. 37. Embracing] Pope; not in F.

32. *shrill-tongued Fulvia*] See North, *post*, pp. 258-9.

33. *Let Rome . . . melt*] Cf. II. v. 78 *post*.

33, 34. *arch . . . rang'd empire fall!*] *rang'd* is probably ordered, having its parts in due succession. The main conception is elusive. Should the mind momentarily image a structure supported by a vast arch, or " a fabric standing on pillars " (Johnson), or the mighty vault of a great hall or nave? The alternative would be to suppose the words imply an arch only, itself the empire, with Rome as keystone, and the extent on either side implied in *rang'd*. The well-known passage in *Coriolanus*, III. i. 203:—

 " That is the way to lay the city flat;
  To bring the roof to the foundation,
  And bury all, which yet distinctly *ranges*,
  In heaps and piles of ruin; "

is cited in *O.E.D.* under : " Of things, especially buildings and their parts, . . . to stretch out or run in a line, to extend." I find in Laneham's *Letter*, etc., 1575 (Ballad Society, 1871, p. 50), in the account of a large building used as an aviary, the architrave described as " *raunging* aboout the Cage." Malone having remarked that *range* was apparently " applied, in a peculiar way, to mason-work in our author's time," and having quoted Spenser, *Faerie Queene*, II. ix. 29, " With many raunges reard along the wall," without a hint that these *raunges*, however constructed, were merely kitchen ranges, Steevens subjoined : " What in ancient mason's or bricklayer's work was denominated a *range*, is now called a *course*." Rowe read *the rais'd empire*. Bearing on the possibility of a misprint, Mr. Craig notes that the spelling *raing'd* is exceptional.

35. *dungy*] Cf. *The Winter's Tale*, II. i. 155-6 :
 " There's not a grain of it [honesty] the face to sweeten
  Of the whole *dungy* earth."

37. *a mutual pair*] i.e. a pair who interchange equal love.

39. *to weet*] to wit, i.e. to know. So Spenser, *Faerie Queene*, III. i. 19, and often. See also *Gammer Gurton's Needle*, II. iii. 10 : " Tush, man, is Gammers neele found? that chould gladly *weete*."

40-42. *Excellent . . . not*] Johnson marked this as an aside, a plausible though not convincing conjecture.

Excellent] † surpassing; here, as often, in uncomplimentary sense ; cf. *R. III.* IV. iv. 52, " *excellent* grand tyrant," and *Lear*, I. ii. 132, " *excellent* foppery."

Why did he marry Fulvia, and not love her?
I'll seem the fool I am not; Antony
Will be himself.
Ant.   But stirr'd by Cleopatra.
Now for the love of Love, and her soft hours,
Let's not confound the time with conference harsh: 45
There's not a minute of our lives should stretch
Without some pleasure now.   What sport to-night?
Cleo. Hear the ambassadors.
Ant.   Fie, wrangling queen!
Whom every thing becomes, to chide, to laugh,
To weep: how every passion fully strives   50
To make itself, in thee, fair and admired!
No messenger but thine, and all alone,
To-night we'll wander through the streets, and note

---

47. *now*] F; *new* Warburton.   50. *how*] *who* F; *whose* F 2; see note.

I suspect that we should read a comma after *Why*. Cleopatra is not asking why Antony married Fulvia, but saying: "The fact that he married her proves that he loved her." [R]

42, 43. *Antony . . . Cleopatra*] It is slightly in favour of a previous aside (see last note) that "Antony will be himself" (i.e. noble, peerless as he is), may revert to *peerless*, the whole being equivalent to, Antony will show himself noble, as he is. *Ant.* Only if inspired by Cleopatra. This is, in any case, substantially the usual interpretation. Johnson, taking *but* in its exceptive sense (cf. III. xi. 47 *post*), understood: " Antony will recollect his thoughts," "Unless kept in commotion by Cleopatra "; and I have sometimes thought that Cleopatra's reference might be to Antony's conduct at the moment; and the sense: Antony will be Antony, play the lover, embrace. *Ant.* Yes, unless angered by Cleopatra. What follows is a plea against such angering. Cf. Beaumont and Fletcher, *Philaster*, I. i. 268 :—

"Be more yourself, as you respect
    our favour;
You'll stir us else: " etc.

45. *confound*] waste. See I. iv. 28 *post*, and *Coriolanus*, I. vi. 17.

50. *how*] † F's *who* is clearly impossible, and F 2's emendation, *whose*, has been universally accepted. But it is not wholly satisfactory, and I suggest *how*. It is graphically a trifle easier, assuming the transposition of one letter by the compositor rather than the omission of two, and it regularises somewhat confused syntax, since *in thee* is redundant after *whose*. This second argument goes for little, since the redundancy is not un-Shakespearean, but I think that the picture with *how* is the better of the two. The passions are not Cleopatra's possessions, but independent things, looking for someone in whom to display themselves to the best advantage, and finding their show-ground in Cleopatra. [R]

52. *No . . . thine:* etc.] For Antony's treatment of ambassadors, see North, *post*, p. 260; for the rest, *ibid.*, p. 264.

The qualities of people.   Come, my queen,
Last night you did desire it.   Speak not to us.   55
     [*Exeunt Ant. and Cleo. with their Train.*
Dem. Is Cæsar with Antonius priz'd so slight?
Phi. Sir, sometimes, when he is not Antony,
 He comes too short of that great property
 Which still should go with Antony.
Dem.   I am full sorry
 That he approves the common liar, who   60
 Thus speaks of him at Rome; but I will hope
 Of better deeds to-morrow. Rest you happy!   [*Exeunt.*

[SCENE II.—*The same.   Another room.*]

Enter ENOBARBUS, LAMPRIUS, *a* Soothsayer, RANNIUS,
 LUCILLIUS, CHARMIAN, IRAS, MARDIAN *the Eunuch,* and
 ALEXAS.

Char. Lord Alexas, sweet Alexas, most any thing Alexas,
 almost most absolute Alexas, where's the soothsayer

---

55. Exeunt . . .] Capell; Exeunt with the Traine. F.

Scene II

1. *Lord*] Johnson; *L.* F.

54. *qualities*] characters or characteristics. The word is also frequent in the sense function, profession, as in *Hamlet,* II. ii. 461. Cf. Whetstone, *Promos and Cassandra,* v. i (*Six Old Plays,* Nichols, i. 49) :—

 " but now tell me
What *quality* hast, that I may use
 thee?
Rosk. I am a Barbour."

55. *speak . . . us*] To the messenger who waited with the news.

58. *property*] distinctive quality.

60. *approves*] corroborates. So in *Lear,* II. ii. 167: " Good king, that must *approve* the common saw "; *Hamlet,* I. i. 29: " He may *approve* our eyes," i.e. confirm their witness. Malone rather unnecessarily takes " the common liar " to be Fame.

61. 62. *hope Of*] So in *M. for M.* III. i. 1: " So then you *hope of* pardon from Lord Angelo?"

62. *Rest you happy*] Cf. " Rest you merry," *R. and J.* I. ii. 65; " Sit you merry, sir," Johnson, *Bartholomew Fair,* IV. vi. 55, said ironically to Waspe when he is put in the stocks. The full phrase appears in *A.Y.L.* v. i. 66: " God rest you merry, sir."

Scene II

Enter . . .] † Of the nine characters in F's entry (or eight if we take " Lamprius " to be the name of the soothsayer) four (or three) have nothing to say throughout the scene, and three of the names occur nowhere else in the play. The usual way, since Steevens, of treating this

that you prais'd so to the queen?   O that I knew
this husband, which, you say, must charge his horns
with garlands!   5

4. *charge*] Theobald (Warburton and Southern MS.); *change* F.

entry has been to excise Lamprius, Rannius, Lucilius and Mardian, to bring in Charmian, Iras, Alexas and the soothsayer together, and defer Enobarbus' entry till after line 10. I do not think that this at all represents Shakespeare's intention. And it is a good example of what happens when one starts playing fast and loose with Shakespeare's stage-directions, and neglects to keep an eye on the stage. In the first place it makes something near nonsense of Charmian's opening question; if a group of four people enter together it is merely silly for one to ask a second where the fourth member of the quartet is; and Alexas' " Soothsayer!" is clearly in the nature of a summons. (This no doubt could be met by giving the soothsayer his entry after line 6.) In the second place there is no reason why Enobarbus should not be among the first entrants. No doubt, again, he could enter after line 10, throwing his order over his shoulder as he comes in, but he is then left up in the air, since the others neglect him, and he has no more to say till line 44, which would not matter with a character on already but is dramatically clumsy with a fresh entrant. With this in mind it is worth examining F's entry again, and in particular the *order* of it, since I think that the order of a Shakespearean entry is sometimes significant (see note on II. vi below, and compare Hamlet's first entry (in Q 2), universally and disastrously emended by all editors from F inclusive downwards till Dover Wilson saw the dramatic point and restored the Quarto reading). The characters fall into two groups, one of Enobarbus, a soothsayer, and two (or three) non-

speaking figures who, from their names, are presumably Romans ; and an Egyptian group, of Cleopatra's waiting women, Mardian and Alexas. (There is just this much to be said for thinking Lamprius to be the soothsayer that this would give the two speaking characters first, followed by the two supers.) Dover Wilson saw this, and brings in " Enobarbus and three other Romans talking with a Soothsayer," and then " a little after," the Egyptian group. I do not think that this is a possible interpretation of F's entry. A scene-opening in which the entrants are engaged in an inaudible conversation is surely unparalleled in Shakespeare (on the modern stage even a silent entry can be covered by business, arranging cushions or a coffee tray or what not, but this sort of cover is not possible on the Elizabethan stage; Shakespeare often covers an entry with *irrelevant* conversation till the characters are well down stage, but he invariably gives the entrants *something* to say). I do not understand why Wilson, having gone seven-eighths of the way, failed to make the final step to what seems the obvious solution. The two groups come in simultaneously, but by different doors. The entry of both is covered by the brisk conversation of one, Enobarbus is there to give his order, and the soothsayer is where we want him, in the non-Egyptian group, so that Alexas can call him over. [R] (Plutarch gives his " grandfather Lampryas " as the authority for one of his stories. See *post*, p. 263. He does not mention Rannius or Lucillius.)

1-5. *Lord . . . garlands*] This speech has a suspicion of mutilated verse

E

Alex. Soothsayer!

Sooth. Your will?

Char. Is this the man?   Is't you, sir, that know things?

Sooth. In nature's infinite book of secrecy
　　　A little I can read.

Alex.　　　　　　　　　Show him your hand.　　　　10

Eno. Bring in the banquet quickly; wine enough,
　　　Cleopatra's health to drink.

Char. Good sir, give me good fortune.

Sooth. I make not, but foresee.

Char. Pray then, foresee me one.　　　　　　　　15

Sooth. You shall be yet far fairer than you are.

---

about it.   Capell (omitting *Lord*) printed as six lines of verse.   S. Walker conjectures verse, lines 3-5 : " O . . . garlands! "

4-5. *charge . . . garlands*] This reading is taken to imply cuckoldom for Charmian's wished husband—which is Alexas' prediction—but cuckoldom garlanded, i.e. rich and honourable (Warburton) or contented (Malone) or triumphant (Steevens), an idea which Charmian herself would more probably contribute. Steevens might have quoted *Jack Drum's Entertainment* (1616), v. 334 (Simpson's *School of Shakspere*, ii. 207) : " I'le weare this Crowne [a compulsory ' Coronet of Cuckolds,' line 316 *ante*] and triumph in this horne."   I doubt these inferences, " rich," etc.   Quite possibly the horns are credited in advance, and *must charge*, etc., merely means : must marry me, wear the bridegroom's chaplet.   Cf. Sylvester's Du Bartas, *The Magnificence* (1621 ed. p. 462) : " A *Garland*, . . . The Royall Bridge-groom's radiant brow bedights."   Or may the jest be, after all, only the equivalent (with cuckoldom thrown in) of modern banter, in an allusion to the *victim*, and the phrase=must come as a sacrifice to the altar?   Cf. D'Avenant, *Gondibert* (1651), III. iii. 61 :—

　　" Who lets this guilded Sacrifice
　　　　proceed

To *Hymen's* Altar, by the king adorn'd,
　As Priests give Victims *Garlands* ere they bleed."

Some would retain *change*. Steevens quotes *Cymbeline*, I. v. 55 ; *Paradise Lost*, iv. 892 (" to *change* Torment with ease ") for *change with*=*change for*, and interprets much as the advocates of *charge*.   Thiselton has : " take his horns in exchange for [wedding] garlands," aptly comparing Jonson, " To Celia " (*The Forest*, ix) :—

　" But might I of Jove's nectar sup,
　　I would not *change* for thine."

Upton's " new dress and adorn " or Johnson's suggestion " dress, or dress with changes of garlands," reappears in Staunton, who reads *change* as = " vary or garnish."   Schmidt gives *change*=make of another appearance, and cf. *Coriolanus*, v. iii. 152 (F reading), on which Malone relied as an unmistakable instance of *change* in error for *charge*.

16. *fairer . . . are*] Mr. Craig points out that the soothsayer whose later deliverances (II. iii. *post*) are so pregnant, probably does not speak idly in this scene, and that the present prediction is perhaps fulfilled in Charmian's *character*, by the fairer, nobler qualities displayed in Act v (or the fame resulting from them) which made her mistress call

Char. He means in flesh.

Iras. No, you shall paint when you are old.

Char. Wrinkles forbid!

Alex. Vex not his prescience, be attentive.   20

Char. Hush!

Sooth. You shall be more beloving than belov'd.

Char. I had rather heat my liver with drinking.

Alex. Nay, hear him.

Char. Good now, some excellent fortune! Let me be   25
married to three kings in a forenoon, and widow
them all: let me have a child at fifty, to whom
Herod of Jewry may do homage. Find me to

---

20. *prescience*] F; *patience* F 3.

---

her " noble " (v. ii. 229 *post*), and
Cæsar exclaim of her last movements :
" O noble weakness " (v. ii. 342 *post*).

17. *in flesh*] Charmian takes *fair* in
the sense " plump, in good condition." Cf. *A.Y.L.* i. i. 11 : " His
horses are bred better ; for, besides
that they are *fair* with their feeding,"
etc. (Craig).

20. *his prescience*] Delius thinks this
a title like *his worship*, used jocosely.

22. *You . . . belov'd*] " i.e. [as the
soothsayer means it, not as Charmian
takes it] You shall expend all your
love on your queen and mistress, and
so will not gain the affection of male
admirers " (Craig). Or possibly it
refers to the love between Charmian
and her mistress. The further *direct*
predictions may be conveniently
noted here as literally true, viz., those
in lines 31, 33-4, and that to Iras in
line 52 : " Your fortunes are alike."

23. *heat . . . drinking*] So in *M. of V.*
i. i. 81 : " And let my liver rather
heat with wine." The same effect
was formerly attributed to love,
whence Charmian's expression of
preference. Cf. *The Tempest*, iv. i.
55-6, and Webster, *Appius and
Virginia*, iv. i. 255, where the lust
of Appius is aimed at : " We have
not such hot livers : mark you that."
That love has its seat in the liver was

an opinion of the ancients, and is
amusingly discussed in Prior's *Alma*,
i. 351 *et seq.* Unlike the generality,
Phineas Fletcher (*The Purple Island*,
iii. x, and his note thereon) gives
the liver a Platonic tenant :—
        " Not Cupid's self but Cupid's
            better brother : . . .
        By whose command we either
            love our kinde,
        Or with most perfect love affect
            the minde " ; etc.

27. *let me . . . fifty*] On this jesting
wish of Charmian to be one of very
few mothers, Steevens observes :
" This is one of Shakespeare's
natural touches. Few circumstances are more flattering to the
fair sex than breeding at an advanced period of life." Cf. the jest
in *Histriomastix*, Act vi. 192 (Simpson,
School of Shakspere, ii. 82), where,
when his unpaid hostess says : " Go
to, I'll bear no longer," Posthast
replies : " What, and be under
fifty? "

28. *Herod of Jewry*] As Steevens
pointed out, Charmian bespeaks a
son powerful enough to subdue even
the fiercest of blustering tyrants.
Herod is the type of these in the
Miracle plays. The York play of *The
Coming of the Three Kings to Herod* opens
with a rant in which Herod claims

marry me with Octavius Cæsar, and companion
me with my mistress.   30
Sooth. You shall outlive the lady whom you serve.
Char. O excellent, I love long life better than figs.
Sooth. You have seen and prov'd a fairer former fortune
    Than that which is to approach.
Char. Then belike my children shall have no names: pri-   35
    thee, how many boys and wenches must I have?

---

the clouds, Saturn, Sun and Moon, etc., as his subjects; and in that of the Nativity, in the Coventry series, occurs the direction: " Here Erode ragis in thys pagond and in the strete also." See III. iii. 3 *post*: *M.W.W.* II. i. 20: " What a *Herod of Jewry* is this! " and *Hamlet*, III. ii. 16, of rant: " It out-herods Herod." Furness cites, and unwillingly inclines to accept, the suggestion of Th. Zielinski (*Philologus*, p. 19) that in Charmian's speech, the child is Christ, and the three Kings are the three wise men, or three Kings [of Cologne] as they were usually called.

Find] i.e. in the lines of the hand, as Delius notes. See line 10 *ante*.

32. *I . . . figs*] a proverbial expression, say Steevens and Schmidt, regrettably without references to distinguish the assertion from an easy surmise. I can only doubtfully suggest possible clues for the choice of figs (if, indeed, there was any occult reason for it) in (1) " The Fig-tree is more fruitful than other trees, for it beareth fruit three or four times in one year," etc. (Charmian's mind was running on fruitfulness); " Figs do away rivels [i.e. wrinkles] of old men, if they ate thereof among their meat " (see " Wrinkles forbid! " line 19 above), *Bartholomew* (*Berthelet*, 1535), *De Proprietatibus Rerum*, bk. xvii. § 61 ; (2) the poisoned fig of Spain so often alluded to as a secret means of removing an enemy, e.g. by Shirley, *The Maid's Revenge*, III. ii. (*Works*, 1833, i. 141): " A rat! give him his bane: . . . our own

country figs shall do it rarely "; (3) the following passages, particularly the second, from Sir T. Browne, *A Letter to a Friend*, etc., 1690 (*Religio Medici*, etc., Canterbury, 1894, p. 138): " Upon my first visit I was bold to tell them who had not let fall all hopes of his recovery, that in my sad opinion he was not like to behold a grasshopper, much less to pluck another fig; " . . . " for he lived not unto the middle of May, and confirmed the observation of *Hippocrates* of that mortal time of the year when the leaves of the fig-tree resemble a Daw's claw." Perhaps, as there is more in the soothsayer's words than meets the eye, so we ought not to forget here the basket of figs which brings death to Charmian, v. ii. *post*, though Warburton has been ridiculed for detecting an omen.

35. *Then . . . names*] Then, I suppose, my children will be bastards. Steevens quotes *T.G.V.* III. i. 324.

" *Speed.* She hath many nameless
    virtues.
    Launce. That's as much as to say,
      bastard virtues, that indeed
      know not their fathers and
      therefore have no names."

See also Beaumont and Fletcher, *A King and No King*, III. i. 175 :—

    " else I shall live
Like sinfull issues that are left in
    streets
By their regardless Mothers, and
    no name
Will be found for me."

Sooth. If every of your wishes had a womb,
  And fertile every wish, a million.
Char. Out, fool! I forgive thee for a witch.
Alex. You think none but your sheets are privy to your   40
  wishes.
Char. Nay, come, tell Iras hers.
Alex. We'll know all our fortunes.
Eno. Mine, and most of our fortunes to-night, shall be—
  drunk to bed.   45
Iras. There's a palm presages chastity, if nothing else.
Char. E'en as the o'erflowing Nilus presageth famine.
Iras. Go, you wild bedfellow, you cannot soothsay.
Char. Nay, if an oily palm be not a fruitful prognostica-
  tion, I cannot scratch mine ear. Prithee tell her   50
  but a worky-day fortune.

38. *fertile*] Theobald (Warburton); *foretell* F.

37. *every*] similarly a pronoun in *A.Y.L* v. iv. 179: "*Every* of this happy number."

38. *fertile*] The frequent spelling *fertill* supports the emendation. Pope reads *foretold*, Collier MS. *fruitful.* Johnson thought *foretell* might stand, explaining, on the supposition of an unlikely ellipse: "And [if] I should foretel all those wishes, I should foretel a million of children." Malone objects that the supposition of wombs without a second of fertility, would not be a sufficient hypothesis.

39. *I . . . witch*] Professor Herford says: "*for a witch*, i.e. as being a wizard, and hence privileged to utter home-truths"; and a frank admission would not be unlike the Charmian who has just said: "Then belike my children," etc. On the other hand, there is much to be said for repudi-ation, and the usual explanation, which = I'll answer for your being no witch, if this is a sample of your skill. The phrase is not unlike, "I'll warrant him for drowning" (*The Tempest*, I. i. 51); "*R. Royster.* Except I have hir to my Wife, I shall runne madde. *M. Mery.* Nay un-wise perhaps, but I warrant you for

madde" (*Roister Doister*, I. ii. 79). Steevens quotes "a common pro-verbial reproach to silly ignorant females: 'You'll never be burnt for a witch.'" The gender of witch was formerly common; it is masculine again in *Cymbeline*, I. vi. 166.

49. *oily palm*] A moist palm was supposed to indicate a wanton dis-position. See Middleton, *Blurt Master Constable*, I. ii. 20: "*Lazarillo.* A woman, Pilcher, the moist-handed Madonna Imperia, a most rare and divine creature. *Pilch.* A most rascally damned courtesan." Malone quotes *Othello*, III. iv. 37: "This hand is moist, my lady," and 39: "This argues fruitfulness and liberal heart"; but see the whole passage, 37-44, and *Venus and Adonis*, 25, 26. See also Overbury's *Characters*, under "A very whore."

fruitful prognostication] presage of fertility.

51. *worky-day*] ordinary. Cf. *A.Y.L.* I. iii. 12: "working-day world." The noun occurs in *Two Wise Men and All the Rest Fools*, 1619, II. i: "I ha' more weeds grown in one Holy-day than in three worky-days."

Sooth. Your fortunes are alike.

Iras. But how, but how? give me particulars.

Sooth. I have said.

Iras. Am I not an inch of fortune better than she?   55

Char. Well, if you were but an inch of fortune better than
     I, where would you choose it?

Iras. Not in my husband's nose.

Char. Our worser thoughts heavens mend! Alexas,—
     come, his fortune, his fortune! O, let him marry a   60
     woman that cannot go, sweet Isis, I beseech thee,

59, 60. *Alexas,—come*] Theobald; Alexas. *Come,* F, apparently assigning
the speech from *Come* onward to Alexas.

58. *Not . . . nose*] The author of
Tristram Shandy may be consulted
here.   See Book III, chap. xxxi;
Book v. chap. i. *ad fin.* Cf. also *The
Unnatural Combat,* IV. ii. (Gifford's
Massinger, ed. Cuningham, p. 58*a*):—
     "It hath just your eyes; and such
          a promising *nose,*
     That, if the sign deceive me not,
          in time
     'Twill prove a notable striker,
          like his father."

59, 60. *Alexas,—come*] † The F
reading is an interesting example of the
confusion that may be caused by the
italicization of proper names in text as
well as in speech-headings. The compositor presumably found the proper
name indicated for italicization in
his copy and took it for a speech-
heading. It is even possible, I think,
that he did not at first regard it as a
speech-heading, but, having barely
room for it in the line after *mend,*
started a new line with it and in-
advertently inset it level with the
speech-headings, since it is noticeable (and Rolfe noted it) that this is
the only place where the name is
given in full as a speech-heading, and
not in the abbreviated form *Alex.* [R]

61. *that cannot go*] *Go* is constantly
employed for walk, etc., and go
upright, as opposed to creep, especially in a varying proverb: "blood
(kind, love, bairns, etc.) will creep

where it (they) *cannot go,*" in print
as early as 1481 (Caxton, *Reynard
the Fox,* ed. Arber, p. 70): "one
shal alway seke on his frendis, though
he haue angred them, for blood must
krepe, where it *can not goo.*" Does
Charmian, then, mean here an old,
crippled, or bed-rid woman, whom,
on second thoughts, she wills to die
and give place to a series of worse
in another kind, who will cuckold
Alexas as she could not? Another
common sense of *go* is "be pregnant," and *go*=go with child,
actually occurs, without the time-
expression which usually makes the
sense unmistakable, in *A Cure for a
Cuckold,* II. iii. 102: "And, Urse,
how goes all at home? or cannot all
go yet? lank still! will 't never be
full sea at our wharf? *Wife.* Alas,
husband! *Comp[ass].* A lass, or a
lad, wench, I should be glad of
both." In *L.L.L.* v. ii. 676, 677,
Costard says: "The party is *gone*;
fellow Hector, she is *gone*: she is
two months on her way." Charmian,
who wished to bear at fifty (see line
27 *ante*), would account sterility a
severe wish, not to mention that it
would imprecate on Alexas one of
the things that are said to be never
satisfied. Thiselton—the only commentator, I believe, to offer an
explanation—makes "that cannot
go" = "that is never satisfied,"

and let her die too, and give him a worse, and let
worse follow worse, till the worst of all follow him
laughing to his grave, fifty-fold a cuckold! Good
Isis, hear me this prayer, though thou deny me a 65
matter of more weight: good Isis, I beseech thee!
Iras. Amen, dear goddess, hear that prayer of the
people! for, as it is a heart-breaking to see a handsome man loose-wiv'd, so it is a deadly sorrow to
behold a foul knave uncuckolded: therefore, dear 70
Isis, keep decorum, and fortune him accordingly!
Char. Amen.
Alex. Lo now, if it lay in their hands to make me a
cuckold, they would make themselves whores, but
they'ld do't. 75
Eno. Hush, here comes Antony.

Enter CLEOPATRA.

Char. Not he, the queen.
Cleo. Saw you my lord?
Eno. No, lady.
Cleo. Was he not here?
Char. No, madam.
Cleo. He was dispos'd to mirth; but on the sudden
A Roman thought hath struck him. Enobarbus! 80
Eno. Madam.
Cleo. Seek him, and bring him hither. Where's Alexas?
Alex. Here at your service. My lord approaches.

---

76. Enter Cleopatra] after *do 't*, line 75, F. 77. *Saw you my lord?*]
F 2; *Saue you, my lord.* F.

---

without remark or evidence to support
his view.

Isis] Originally the Egyptian goddess of the earth and fertility, later
of the moon. See Spenser, *Faerie
Queene*, v. vii. 4 :—

"They wore rich Mitres shaped
like the Moone,
To shew that *Isis* doth the
Moone portend; " etc.

67, 68. *that prayer . . . people*]

" seems to mean ' that universal
prayer ' " (Thiselton).

76. (S.D.)] F puts the entry before
Enobarbus' remark at the beginning
of the line, but this is hardly possible,
since the actual presence of Cleopatra
on the stage would make the remark
nonsensical.

80. *A Roman thought*] Perhaps a
thought such as Roman virtue would
inspire, and not merely, as Schmidt
explains it, " A thought of Rome."

Cleo. We will not look upon him: go with us.   [*Exeunt.*

Enter ANTONY, *with a Messenger.*

Mess. Fulvia thy wife first came into the field.   85
Ant. Against my brother Lucius?
Mess. Ay:
    But soon that war had end, and the time's state
    Made friends of them, jointing their force 'gainst Cæsar,
    Whose better issue in the war, from Italy,   90
    Upon the first encounter, drave them.
Ant.   Well, what worst?
Mess. The nature of bad news infects the teller.
Ant. When it concerns the fool or coward. On:
    Things that are past are done, with me. 'Tis thus,
    Who tells me true, though in his tale lie death,   95
    I hear him as he flatter'd.
Mess.   Labienus—
    This is stiff news—hath with his Parthian force

84-85. (S.D.)] Again F puts the entry a line earlier. It is impossible to place it rightly, since Cleopatra's exit and Antony's entry are simultaneous.

85-91. *Fulvia,* etc] See North, *post,* p. 264.

89. *jointing*] The past part. of the same verb occurs in *Cymbeline,* v. iv. 143; v. v. 441.

92. *The nature . . . teller*] So in *2 H. IV.* i. i. 100:—

    " Yet the first bringer of unwel-
       come news
    Hath but a losing office, and his
       tongue," etc.

Cf. also ii. v. 85, 86 *post.*

94. *done, with me. 'Tis thus*] Dover Wilson, adopting a suggestion of Capt. E. G. Spencer-Churchill, re-punctuates *done. With me, 'tis thus.*

96. *as he flatter'd*] as (readily as) if he. . . .

96-101. *Labienus . . . whilst*] † F prints thus :—

    Labienus (this is stiffe-newes)
    Hath with his Parthian Force

Extended Asia : from Euphrates
    his conquering
Banner shooke, from Syria to Lydia,
    And to Ionia, whil'st ——,

a typical example of F mislineation, corrected by most editors as in text here, though Pope, followed by Theobald, tried a different, and rhythmically much duller, arrange-ment. But there has been a con-spiracy of most editors, including Case and Dover Wilson, to tinker also with F's punctuation and read

    Extended Asia from Euphrates,
    His conquering banner shook from
      Syria
To Lydia and to Ionia, whilst . . .

which (apart from producing two rhythmically repetitive lines) misses the point that Shakespeare was merely versifying North's " Labienus con-quered all Asia with the armie of the Parthians, from the river of Euphrates, and from Syria, unto the contries of Lydia and Ionia " (p. 264, *post*). [R]

98. *Extended*] seized upon. *Extent* is a legal phrase from the words of

　　　　Extended Asia: from Euphrates
　　　　His conquering banner shook, from Syria
　　　　To Lydia, and to Ionia;　　　　　　　　　100
　　　　Whilst—
Ant.　　　　　Antony, thou wouldst say,—
Mess.　　　　　　　　　　　　　　O, my lord!
Ant. Speak to me home, mince not the general tongue:
　　　　Name Cleopatra as she is call'd in Rome;
　　　　Rail thou in Fulvia's phrase, and taunt my faults
　　　　With such full license, as both truth and malice　105
　　　　Have power to utter.　O then we bring forth weeds,
　　　　When our quick minds lie still, and our ills told us

107. *minds*] Hanmer (Warburton) ; *windes* F.

a writ—*extendi facias*—authorizing
full valuation of land before seizure.
See *A.Y.L.* III. i. 17: "let my
officers . . . Make an *extent* upon
his house and lands"; Nashe, *The
Unfortunate Traveller*, II. p. 311, line
11: "Ere the officers come to
extend, Ile bestow a hundred pound
on a doale of bread," etc.

　　Asia . . . Euphrates] *Asia* a trisyllable and *Euphrates*, as usually at
this period, "Euphrǎtes". So Drayton, in a passage (of which Steevens
quotes line 2) recalling the famous
lines of Denham in *Cooper's Hill*:—
　　"Give me those lines, (whose
　　　　touch the skilful eare to please)
　　That gliding flow in state, like
　　　　swelling *Euphrates*, etc.
Polyolbion, pt. ii. 1622, Song xxi.

　　102. *home*] directly (cf. "strike
home") as in *Cymbeline*, III. v. 92.

　　mince] diminish, fine down. Now
used only in "*mince* the matter *or*
matters," as in *Othello*, II. iii. 249;
but compare Charles Cotton, *Poems*
(1689), p. 182:—
　　"The man, upon this, comes me
　　　　running again,
　　But yet *minced* his Message, and
　　　　was not so plain," [i.e. so
　　peremptory].

　　104. *Fulvia's phrase*] See on I. i. 32
ante.

　　107. *minds*] So most editors, the
sense of this passage being thus
either: (1) we accumulate faults
when our reason forgets its natural
activity and exerts no corrective
force; and to be told of these is as
salutary as earing (ploughing) to
weed-grown fields; or (2) when
our *minds*, with their gift of fertility,
lie idle and uncultivated, they produce evil growths; and, etc. Ascham,
Toxophilus, 1545 (Arber, 1868, p. 93),
similarly appeals to the value of
ploughing for eradicating weeds, in
support of his receipt about the
weeds of the mind; ". . . euen as
plowing of a good grounde for
wheate, doth not onely make it
mete for the seede, but also riueth
and plucketh vp by the rootes, all
thistles, brambles and weedes . . . :
Euen so shulde the teaching of youth
to shote, not only make them shote
well, but also plucke awaye by the
rootes all other desyre to noughtye
pastymes, as disynge," etc. See also
next note; and for *quick*, compare
Ascham, as before, p. 40: "Muche
musike . . . recreateth and maketh
quycke a mannes *mynde*"; also *H. V.*
IV. i. 20: "And when the *mind* is
quickened." On *winds*, which several
editors retain, Johnson says: "The
sense is, that man, not agitated by

Is as our earing.   Fare thee well awhile.

Mess. At your noble pleasure.   [*Exit.*

Enter another Messenger.

Ant. From Sicyon how the news ?   Speak there!   110

110. *how the news?*] F; *ho, the news !* Dyce.

censure, like soil not ventilated by *quick winds*, produces more evil than good." See *3 H. VI.* II. vi. 21 : " For what doth cherish weeds but gentle air? " quoted by Steevens. Capell thought *quick winds* = friends. Another explanation, beginning with a suggestion of Blackstone, is technical : Steevens thinks *quick winds* = teeming fallows, because " the ridges left in lands turned up by the plough, that they may sweeten during their fallow state, are still called *windrows*." In Collier *winds* = (perhaps) *wints*, " in Kent and Surrey two furrows ploughed by the horses going to one end of the field and back again." He refers to Cooper's *Glossary of Provincialisms*, etc. (Sussex, 1836), and Holloway, *Gen. Prov. Dict.* (1838).

108. *earing*] ploughing. See I. iv. 49 *post*: Herbert, *A Priest to the Temple* (1652), chap. xxxiv : " the usuall seasons of summer and winter, *earing* and harvest "; *Arden of Feversham*, III. v. 24 : " For Greene doth *ear* the land and weed thee up, To make my harvest nothing but pure corn."

109-14. †I have retained F's S.D.s, since I am not clear that the seeming difficulties justify the drastic changes which have been followed by almost all editors. Rowe cut out the S.D. at lines 109-10 altogether, and Capell turned the messengers of lines 111 and 112 into attendants. This runs smoothly enough, but the " Enter another Messenger " at lines 109-10 is obstinately there and I do not think that F is at all impossible as it stands. The entering messenger finds that he has

come from the wrong place, and calls to a group at the door to see whether there is another messenger who will give Antony what he wants; a second messenger in the group, eager to please, reports that there is such a messenger, waiting.   I think that this perhaps gives better the general bustle of the scene, with messengers from various places coming with news, than he somewhat formal business with attendants summoning messengers in their proper turn.

And I retain F's " how the news." Antony's speech is usually given as " From Sicyon, ho, the news !", and admittedly " how " often in Shakespearean text stands for " ho." But " how the news?" is a quite possible phrase (cf. Shallow's " How a score of ewes now ?" in *2 H. IV.* III. ii. 55) and fits rather better than " ho " if we retain F's entries. [R]

110. *Sicyon*] † F's *Scicion* may easily be no more than a blunder— the sort of repeating of a letter to which we are all liable with an unfamiliar name.   But it may also be quite reasonably adduced as evidence supporting the view that the copy for this play was Shakespeare's autograph, in view of the fact that " scilens " (for " silence ") occurs in the " addition " to *Sir Thomas More*, and " Scilens " occurs eighteen times in Q I of *2 H. IV* as the name of the character whom we know as Silence.

Perhaps I may without impertinence interject a word about the famous three pages in *Sir Thomas More* which are so often alluded to in

First Mess. The man from Sicyon,—is there such an one?
Sec. Mess. He stays upon your will.
Ant.   Let him appear.
These strong Egyptian fetters I must break,
Or lose myself in dotage.

Enter another Messenger, with a letter.

                                    What are you?
Third Mess. Fulvia thy wife is dead.
Ant.   Where died she?   115
Third Mess. In Sicyon:
Her length of sickness, with what else more serious
Importeth thee to know, this bears.   [*Gives a letter.*
Ant.   Forbear me.
                                    [*Exeunt Messengers.*
There's a great spirit gone!   Thus did I desire it:
What our contempts doth often hurl from us,   120

---

118. Gives a letter] Johnson; not in F.   120. *doth*] F; *do* F 2; *contempt*
doth Staunton and some other edd.

discussion of textual problems. It
has not, I think, been *proved* (indeed
it is a thing hardly susceptible of
proof) that they are in Shakespeare's
autograph, though I think that the
cumulative evidence makes it much
more likely that they are than that
they are not. Arguments, therefore,
which use the three pages as con-
clusive evidence of Shakespeare's
practice in such things as spelling,
punctuation, or italicization of proper
names, are based on an assumption
and not on a fact. On the other hand,
I think the evidence makes it almost
certain that even if the pages are
not Shakespeare's autograph they
are in a hand so nearly identical with
his that in considering such things as
" probability of error "—that whole
section of the field of emendation
which depends on the probable
formation of letters in the original—
we can safely operate as though the
three pages had Shakespeare's sig-
nature on them. [R]

112. *stays upon*] So in *All's Well*,
III. v. 45 : " I thank you and will
stay upon your leisure."
115. *Fulvia . . . dead*] See North,
post, p. 265.
118. (S.D.). Exeunt . . .] I think
Dover Wilson is clearly right that
Antony should here be left alone.
F has no S.D.
120. *contempts doth*] As the old
Southern plural in -*th* occurs elsewhere in F, and very frequently in
contemporary writings, in the verbs
do and *have*, I have retained it. Cf.
in F, p. 174, *M. of V.* III. ii. 33 :—
" I, but I feare, you speake vpon
        the racke,
    Where men enforced *doth* speake
        anything."
So Queen Elizabeth (Harington's
Nugæ Antiquæ (1769), i. 59) : " But
clouds of joys untry'd *Doth* cloke
aspyring mynds." It is scarce in the
case of other verbs, but see Sidney's
Apologie for Poetrie (ed. Arber, p. 31) :
" the generalities that contayneth it."

We wish it ours again. The present pleasure,
By revolution lowering, does become
The opposite of itself: she's good, being gone,
The hand could pluck her back that shov'd her on.
I must from this enchanting queen break off,   125
Ten thousand harms, more than the ills I know,
My idleness doth hatch. Ho now, Enobarbus!

Re-enter ENOBARBUS.

Eno. What's your pleasure, sir?
Ant. I must with haste from hence.

122. *By revolution lowering*] Carried
to a lower and lower pitch in our
estimation by the changes in ourselves and circumstances which ac-
company the revolution of time, or of
" the Wheel of things," as Sir T.
Browne calls it (*Christian Morals*, § 16).
Warburton saw an allusion to the
sun's diurnal course and its termina-
tion opposite to the point of rising;
but the figure is no doubt merely that
of the turning of a wheel, so often and
variously applied. See *Lear*, v. iii.
176, of the correspondence between
a vicious act and its final consequences : " The wheel is come full
circle " ; *Twelfth Night*, v. i. 388 :
" and thus the whirligig of time
brings in his revenges." In the present
case the wheel has not come full
circle : " Opinions do find, after
certain revolutions [of time], men
and minds like those that first
begat them " (Sir Thomas Browne,
Religio Medici, § 6), and by-and-by
the advantages of losing Fulvia would
again find a mind *in Antony* to appreciate them ; at the moment,
appreciation of these advantages is
at its greatest distance in the revolution.

123. *she's good, being gone*] Cf. *All's
Well*, v. iii. 60 : " Crying ' That's
good that's gone.' "

124. *could*] would be ready to.
The line resembles one in Lyly's
The Woman in the Moone, II. i. 139 :

" Whether thou drawe me on, or
put me back."

125. *I must . . . off*] Cf. Countess
of Pembroke's *Antonie* (1595), i. 83,
84 :—
  " Thou breakest at length from
      thence as one encharmed
  Breaks from the enchanter that
      him firmly held,
  For thy first reason, (spoiling of
      their force
  The poisoned cups of thy fair
      sorceress)
  Recured thy spirit;" etc.

128-9. †F reads as follows :—
  My idlenesse doth hatch.
                  Enter Enobarbus.
  How now *Enobarbus.*
This is precisely parallel to II. i. 27,
where Varrius' entry interrupts a
speech (as indicated by a long dash
in F), and he is greeted with
" How now *Varrius?*" At first sight
there seems to be little that needs
doing with either passage ; insert
a comma after " now " in both,
and give F's question mark after
Varrius after Enobarbus also, and
all is well.   But in fact all is not
at all well, since, though the text
is the same in the two passages,
the situation is not. Varrius enters
hurriedly with news, whereas Enobarbus, as seems clearly implied by
his first words, enters in answer to a
summons. This has led most editors
to shift the entry of Enobarbus to

Eno. Why, then we kill all our women. We see how 130
mortal an unkindness is to them; if they suffer our
departure, death's the word.

Ant. I must be gone.

Eno. Under a compelling occasion let women die: it
were pity to cast them away for nothing, though 135
between them and a great cause, they should be
esteemed nothing. Cleopatra catching but the
least noise of this, dies instantly. I have seen her
die twenty times upon far poorer moment: I do
think there is mettle in death, which commits some 140
loving act upon her, she hath such a celerity in
dying.

Ant. She is cunning past man's thought.

Eno. Alack, sir, no, her passions are made of nothing
but the finest part of pure love. We cannot call 145
her winds and waters sighs and tears; they are
greater storms and tempests than almanacs can

---

134. *a compelling occasion*] Rowe; *a compelling an occasion* F; *so . . . an
. . .* Nicholson conj.; *as . . . an . . .* Anon, conj.

half a line later, but retaining " How
now," and led Capell, and (independently) Dyce to read " Ho,
Enobarbus!" " How " is not infrequently printed for " Ho " (cf.
IV. xiv. 104 *post*) and Dyce makes
the just comment, " It would be
impossible, I presume, to point out,
in any old writer, an instance of
" How now!" used as *the exclamation
of a person summoning another into his
presence.*"
The crucial point is Enobarbus'
" What's your pleasure?" which is
almost nonsensical as a reply to a
question (" How now?"), but natural
as the reply to a summons, and,
though reluctant to tamper with F,
I think that Capell and Dyce were
probably right, and that those who
go half-way, retaining the words but
shifting the S.D., are certainly
wrong, making poor sense either
way, as is the usual fate of such
compromises. (I have retained F's

" now," since, though it makes the
line hypermetrical, it is not impossible,
but Capell and Dyce may well have
been right in omitting it, on the
grounds that, as Furness suggests, a
compositor, taking " How " to mean
" How " and not " Ho " might
easily insert the natural " now.") [R]
    132. *death's the word*] So in *Cym-
beline*, v. iv. 155: " Hanging is the
word, sir."
    138. *noise*] rumour. Cf. *T. and C.*
I. ii. 12: " The *noise* goes, this:
there is," etc.
    139. *upon . . . moment*] for causes
much less weighty.
    139-42. *I do . . . dying*] Enobarbus
pictures death as a vigorous lover to
whom Cleopatra yields willingly.
    145-6. *We . . . tears*] Malone sus-
pected an inversion on all fours with
" To make your house our Tower "
(*H. VIII.* v. i. 107) and equivalent
to " we cannot call her sighs and
tears, winds," etc.; but this is failing

report. This cannot be cunning in her; if it be,
she makes a shower of rain as well as Jove.

Ant. Would I had never seen her!   150

Eno. O, sir, you had then left unseen a wonderful piece
of work, which not to have been blest withal, would
have discredited your travel.

Ant. Fulvia is dead.

Eno. Sir?   155

Ant. Fulvia is dead.

Eno. Fulvia?

Ant. Dead.

Eno. Why, sir, give the gods a thankful sacrifice. When
it pleaseth their deities to take the wife of a man 160
from him, it shows to man the tailors of the earth;
comforting therein, that when old robes are worn
out, there are members to make new. If there were
no more women but Fulvia, then had you indeed a
cut, and the case to be lamented: this grief is 165
crown'd with consolation, your old smock brings
forth a new petticoat, and indeed the tears live in
an onion, that should water this sorrow.

to think in Enobarbus' fashion. For
an elaboration of a similar metaphor,
see *R. and J.* III. v. 131-8; and for
what follows, the storms and tempests
of almanacs, cf. Ben Jonson, *E.M.O.*
I. iii. 51, where the grain-hoarding
chuff Sordido rejoices in the almanac
prediction: " great tempest of rain,
thunder and lightning ".

153. *discredited your travel*] proved
you a bad sight-seer.

159-63. *When . . . new*] Malone
explains: " When the deities are
pleased to take a man's wife from
him, this act of theirs makes them
appear to man like the tailors of the
earth; affording this comfortable
reflection, that the deities have made
other women to supply the place of
his former wife; as the tailor, when
one robe is worn out, supplies him
with another." It is possible that the
bereaving deities are neither called
nor resembled to " the tailors of the

earth ": these may be merely re-
productive man. In the following
passage, the bereaved lover, Pan, is
apparently the *workman* (see Good-
win's Browne, *Britannia's Pastorals*,
II. iv. 672) :—

  " If thou the best of women didst
        forego,
    Weigh if thou found'st her, or
        didst make her so;
    If she were found so, know there's
        more than one;
    If made, the workman lives,
        though she be gone."

165. *cut*] blow. So Lady Kix, of
her childlessness after seven years'
marriage: " Can any woman have
a greater *cut*? " (Middleton, *A
Chaste Maid in Cheapside*, II. i. 135).

167, 168. *the tears . . . sorrow*] i.e.
an onion would bring to your eyes
all the tears that this sorrow deserves.
Cf. *The Noble Soldier*, 1634 (Bullen's
Old Plays, i. 268), quoted in part by

Ant. The business she hath broached in the state
  Cannot endure my absence.   170
Eno. And the business you have broach'd here cannot
  be without you, especially that of Cleopatra's,
  which wholly depends on your abode.
Ant. No more light answers. Let our officers
  Have notice what we purpose. I shall break 175
  The cause of our expedience to the queen,
  And get her leave to part. For not alone
  The death of Fulvia, with more urgent touches,
  Do strongly speak to us; but the letters too
  Of many our contriving friends in Rome 180
  Petition us at home. Sextus Pompeius

---

174. *light*] F; *like* F 2.   177. *leave*] Pope; *loue* F.

Steevens: " If you had buried nine husbands, so much water as you might squeeze out of an Onyon had been teares enow to cast away upon fellowes that cannot thanke you "; see also *T. of S.* Induction, i. 124-8. *Onion-ey'd* occurs IV. ii. 35 *post.*

172. *that of Cleopatra's*] Hanmer read *Cleopatra:* but see on I. i. I *ante.*

173. *abode*] stay. See *Cymbeline*, I. vi. 53 ; Fairfax, *Godfrey of Bulloigne,* 1600, p. 98 :—

 " Thus spake the king, and soone
  without *aboad*
 The troope went forth in shining
  armour clad," etc.

176. *expedience*] The word usually means *haste* in Shakespeare (cf. *R. II.* II. i. 287) and may very well = *haste* here, as Dyce explains it, for the departure was to be sudden. It is, however, generally explained as *expedition* with Warburton, and compared with *I H. IV.* I. i. 33, where " this dear *expedience* " *seems* to stand for the expedition to the Holy Land. But even there, it probably rather means " matter demanding haste," else why the next line : " My liege, this *haste* was hot in question "?

177. *leave to part*] Several editors retain *love*, understanding with Steevens : " And prevail on her love to consent to our separation "; but strong probability favours *leave*, and Malone remarked a similar misprint (*loves* for *leaves*) in *Titus Andronicus*, III. i. 291 : *part* = depart, as often.

178. *more urgent touches*] " things that touch us more sensibly, more pressing motives " (Johnson).

180. *many . . . contriving friends*] many who occupy themselves in my interests. The usual sense of *contrive* is plot, conspire, as in *J.C.* II. iii. 6 : " If not, the Fates with traitors do *contrive* "; and S. Walker scents a Latinism here for " spending the time," " sojourning." Cf. *T. of S.* I. ii. 279 : " Please ye we may *contrive* this afternoon." The difference of the cases, however, makes the point very doubtful, and even in the instance just quoted this sense is questioned by Schmidt. For the position of *many*, cf. *T. of A.* III. vi. 11 : " *many* my near occasions."

181. *Petition . . . home*] beg for my presence in Rome.

181-90. *Sextus Pompeius*, etc.] See North, *post*, p. 265; I. iii. 45, etc. ; I. iv. 36, etc., *post.*   The clause

Hath given the dare to Cæsar, and commands
The empire of the sea.   Our slippery people,
Whose love is never link'd to the deserver
Till his deserts are past, begin to throw   185
Pompey the Great, and all his dignities
Upon his son, who high in name and power,
Higher than both in blood and life, stands up
For the main soldier: whose quality, going on,
The sides o' the world may danger.   Much is breeding,
Which like the courser's hair, hath yet but life,   191
And not a serpent's poison.   Say our pleasure,

182. *Hath*] F 2; *Haue* F.

"Whose . . . past," lines 184, 185, has been taken of Pompey the Great, but would be less true of him, and seems to be definitely confirmed to Sextus by I. iv. 43 *post*; "the ebb'd man, ne'er lov'd till ne'er worth love."

188. *blood and life*] high mettle and vital energy.

189. *quality*] nature and condition, including their potentialities. Some, however, connect it more especially with "the main soldier," as, e.g., Delius: "If Pompey progresses preeminently in this *rôle* of soldier," etc. See also on I. i. 54 *ante*. It is worth noting that *quality* in *1 H. IV.* IV. iii. 36, "Because you are not of our *quality*, But stand against us like an enemy," is explained "party." It is given in *O.E.D.* as the sole known instance, but this sense, if admissible, would suit the passage before us. So Kinnear takes it.

190. *The sides . . . danger*] So in *Cymbeline*, III. i. 49-51 :—

"Cæsar's ambition
Which swelled so much that it did almost stretch
The sides of the world."

See also on I. iii. 16, and IV. xiv. 39 *post*.

191. *the courser's hair*] In a passage in Holinshed's Chronicles, 1587, *The*

Description of England, p. 224, to which Steevens refers, is a sceptical account of this old popular belief: "it [i.e. the getting a brood of eels from a turf cut beside a fenny river and placed in contact with the water] would seeme a wonder; and yet it is beleeued, with no lesse assurance of some, than that an horse haire laid in a pale full of the like water will in short time stirre and become a liuing creature." Coleridge, *Shakespeare Notes and Lectures*, says on the passage in the text: "This is so far true to appearance, that a horse hair, 'laid,' as Hollinshead says, 'in a pail of water,' will become the supporter of seemingly one worm, though probably of an immense number of small slimy water-lice. . . . It is a common experiment with schoolboys in Cumberland and Westmoreland." Mr. Craig tells me that he recollects being shown, as a child, by his Irish nurse, some horsehairs wriggling about in a tributary of the Bann in Derry, and being informed that they were turning into eels. The thought of a serpent as yet only potentially venomous occurs also in *Macbeth*, III. iv. 29-31.

192-4. *Say . . . from hence*] †The reading of the text is that of F, with the transposition of the comma from after *us* to after *require*. Most editors

To such whose places under us require,
Our quick remove from hence.
Eno. I shall do't.   [*Exeunt.*

[SCENE III.—*The Same.*]

Enter CLEOPATRA, CHARMIAN, ALEXAS, *and* IRAS.

Cleo. Where is he?
Char.   I did not see him since.
Cleo. See where he is, who's with him, what he does:
I did not send you.   If you find him sad,
Say I am dancing; if in mirth, report
That I am sudden sick.   Quick, and return.   [*Exit Alexas.*
Char. Madam, methinks if you did love him dearly,   6
You do not hold the method, to enforce
The like from him.
Cleo.   What should I do, I do not?
Char. In each thing give him way, cross him in nothing.
Cleo. Thou teachest like a fool: the way to lose him.   10
Char. Tempt him not so too far.   I wish, forbear;
In time we hate that which we often fear.
                 Enter ANTONY.
But here comes Antony

193. *whose places . . . require*]; *whose places under us, require* F; *whose place
is under us, requires* F 2; *who've places . . . requires* Mason conj.
195. Exeunt] not in F.

                              Scene III

5. Exit Alexas] Capell; not in F.

follow F 2, an interesting example,
I think, of the dangers of too readily
deserting F. No doubt F's reading
would have been an easy " auditory
error," but it gives the right sense,
which I suggest F 2 does not.
Antony does not want *all* his subordinates informed. He is saying,
more practically, " Convey my intention (our immediate departure)
to *those of* my subordinates whose
positions make it essential for them
to be informed." [R]

                         Scene III

3. *I did . . . you*] Malone compares
similarly elliptical phrasing in *T.
and C.* IV. ii. 73 :—

" I will go meet them : and, my
    lord Æneas,
  We met by chance : you did not
    find me here."

sad] probably " serious " merely,
as so commonly.

11. *I wish, forbear*] Prithee, forbear. Dover Wilson adopts an

F

Cleo.   I am sick, and sullen.

Ant. I am sorry to give breathing to my purpose,—

Cleo. Help me away, dear Charmian, I shall fall.   15
   It cannot be thus long, the sides of nature
   Will not sustain it.

Ant.   Now, my dearest queen,—

Cleo. Pray you stand farther from me.

Ant.   What's the matter?

Cleo. I know by that same eye there's some good news.
   What, says the married woman you may go?   20
   Would she had never given you leave to come!
   Let her not say 'tis I that keep you here.
   I have no power upon you; hers you are.

Ant. The gods best know—

Cleo.   O, never was there queen
   So mightily betray'd! yet at the first   25
   I saw the treasons planted.

Ant.   Cleopatra,—

Cleo. Why should I think you can be mine and true
   (Though you in swearing shake the throned gods)
   Who have been false to Fulvia? Riotous madness,
   To be entangled with those mouth-made vows,   30
   Which break themselves in swearing!

Ant.   Most sweet queen,—

---

20. *What, says . . . go?*] *What sayes . . . goe?* F; *What says the married woman?*
you may go; Rowe and others.

anonymous conjecture " iwis " =
" certainly " (*not* " I wis ").

16. *the sides of nature*] Steevens
compares *Twelfth Night*, II. iv. 95 :—
   " There is no woman's *sides*
   Can bide the beating of so strong
   a passion," etc.
See also on I. ii. 190 *ante:* IV. xiv. 39
post.

20. *What says . . . go?*] † F's
question mark is probably right,
whether we supply a comma (" What,
says the married woman you may
go?") or another question mark
(" What says the married woman?
You may go?"). But since exclamation and question marks were fre-

quently confused, and, from Fulvia,
must would be more natural than
may, perhaps Cleopatra is *assuming*
that Fulvia has issued a summons,
and we should read " What says the
married woman? You may go!"
[R]

26. *planted*] either in the gardener's
sense, or = placed (like mines, etc.) :
so Braithwaite, *Strappado for the
Diuell*, 1615 (1878 reprint, p. 92),
The Wooer; " He *plants* his engines
deeper," etc.

32. *colour*] A very common metaphor for pretext, specious excuse.
See *H. VIII.* I. i. 178. Lyly plays on
the word in *Campaspe*, v. iv. 94:

Cleo. Nay, pray you, seek no colour for your going,
But bid farewell, and go: when you sued staying,
Then was the time for words: no going then;
Eternity was in our lips, and eyes,   35
Bliss in our brows' bent; none our parts so poor,
But was a race of heaven. They are so still,
Or thou, the greatest soldier of the world,
Art turn'd the greatest liar.
Ant.   How now, lady?
Cleo. I would I had thy inches, thou shouldst know   40
There were a heart in Egypt.
Ant.   Hear me, queen:
The strong necessity of time commands
Our services awhile; but my full heart
Remains in use with you. Our Italy

" You lay your *colours* grosely;
though I could not paint in your
shop, I can spy into your excuse ";
ibid. III. i. 14: " You have bin so
long used to colours, you can doe
nothing but *colour* "; and John
Harington in a letter to Sir Antony
Standen, dated from Athlone, 1559:
" On Sunday last the Governor
marched with one and twenty companies, or colours (for indeed some
of them were but mere *colours* of
companies, having sixty for a hundred
and fifty) from Tulske," etc. See
Harington's *Nugæ Antiquæ*, 1769, i. 51 ;
also the extracts from North, *post*,
pp. 269, 275.

36. *bent*] arch. In Ben Jonson, the
arches of the brow are Love's
" double bow ": see *Underwoods*,
Elegy xix :—
" By that fair Stand, your forehead,
    whence he bends
His double Bow, and round his
    Arrowes sends ";
also *ibid.*, *A Celebration of Charis*, v :
" Both her *Brows*, *bent* like my
bow."

37. *race of heaven*] As eternity was
in her lips and eyes (cf. Marlowe,
Dr. Faustus, 1330 (sc. 14): " Sweet

Helen, make me immortal with a
kiss "), bliss in her brows, so he had
found the same or other marks of
heaven in her other beauties. *A race
of heaven* probably = as Malone
thought, " of heavenly origin " (cf.
the use of *race* in *The Tempest*, I. ii.
358); but Warburton says *race* is
" smack or flavour of heaven," and
Johnson approves, observing that
" *the race* of wine is the taste of the
soil "; see Massinger, *New Way to
Pay Old Debts*, I. iii. 8 :—
" There came, not six days since,
    from Hull, a pipe
Of rich Canary. . . .
Greedy. Is it of the right *race?*"

41. *Egypt*] i.e. Cleopatra, as *post*
line 78, and elsewhere.

44. *in use with you*] yours to enjoy,
to have the usufruct of; *perhaps* in
trust with you, as in *M. of V.* IV. i.
384, where, however, the context
puts the phrase in strict accord with
its counterpart in legal terminology,
when a third party is possessed with
land for the express purpose of con-
veying it to one person after the
death of another (*seisitus in usum
alicujus*). See in Dyce's *Glossary*, a
note by Anon., apud Halliwell, and

Shines o'er with civil swords; Sextus Pompeius   45
Makes his approaches to the port of Rome,
Equality of two domestic powers
Breed scrupulous faction: the hated, grown to strength,
Are newly grown to love: the condemn'd Pompey,
Rich in his father's honour, creeps apace   50
Into the hearts of such as have not thriv'd
Upon the present state, whose numbers threaten,
And quietness, grown sick of rest, would purge
By any desperate change. My more particular,
And that which most with you should safe my going, 55
Is Fulvia's death.
Cleo. Though age from folly could not give me freedom,
It does from childishness. Can Fulvia die?
Ant. She's dead, my queen.

Look here, and at thy sovereign leisure read   60
The garboils she awak'd: at the last, best,
See when and where she died.

---

the aforesaid passage in *M. of V.* :—

" I am content; so he will let me
  have
The other half *in use*, to render it,
Upon his death, unto the gentle-
  man
That lately stole his daughter."

45-52. *Sextus Pompeius*, etc.] Cf.
I. ii. 182-90 *ante:* I. iv. 36-47 *post.*

46. *port of Rome*] More probably
Ostia, the natural objective of a
fleet, than = gate of Rome, though
port = gate in IV. iv. 23 *post.*

48. *Breed . . . faction*] Favour the
rise of parties which profess a
hesitancy in determining where their
allegiance is due. Some editors read
breeds with Pope, to correspond with
Equality: but the plural is no doubt
due to the proximity of *powers.* See
Abbott, *Shakespearian Grammar,* § 412.

48, 49. *the hated . . . to love*] those
who were hated are beginning to be
ved.

53. *sick of . . . purge*] *ill* through
rest, as well as tired of it, would, etc.
The diseases of peace and tranquillity

similarly suggest purgation (by letting
blood) in *2 H. IV.* IV. i. 54-66, e.g.
lines 63-6 :—

" But rather show awhile like
  fearful war,
To diet rank minds *sick of* happiness
And *purge* the obstructions which
  begin to stop
Our very veins of life."

54. *My more particular*] What is
more especially my own affair. Cf.
IV. ix. 20 *post,* and *T. and C.* II. ii. 9 :
" As far as toucheth *my particular.*"

55. *safe my going*] make you feel
secure in letting me go. See IV. vi.
26, and note.

58. *It does . . . die*] A mere expression of incredulity, to which it would
be needless to draw attention if
Steevens and Malone had not shown
that it could be mistaken.

61. *garboils*] tumults, commotions,
from the old French *garbouil.* Cf.
II. ii. 67 *post.* The word occurs
fairly often. See Steevens's instances
in 1821 Variorum, and Collier's in a

Cleo.   O most false love!
Where be the sacred vials thou should'st fill
With sorrowful water?   Now I see, I see,
In Fulvia's death, how mine receiv'd shall be.   65
Ant. Quarrel no more, but be prepar'd to know
The purposes I bear; which are, or cease,
As you shall give the advice.   By the fire
That quickens Nilus' slime, I go from hence
Thy soldier, servant, making peace or war,   70
As thou affects.

71. *affects*] F; *affectst* F 2 and many edd.

note to Barry's *Ram Alley* (Hazlitt's *Dodsley*, x. 287) ; also *The Weakest Goeth to the Wall*, v. i. 52 (Hazlitt's *Webster*, IV. p. 287) : " these sweating *garbolds* " ; *Manningham's Diary*, p. 147 (Camden Society, 1868) : " There was a diligent watch and ward kept . . . to prevent *garboiles* " ; Drayton, *The Harmonie of the Church* (Percy Society, 1843), p. 35 : " They chose them gods ; then *garboils* did within their gates abound." It occurs several times in Drayton's *Barons' Wars*.

at the last, best] Surely this means that the cream of the correspondence is in the part to which her attention is last directed—possibly also the last part of a letter—and consists of convincing intelligence of Fulvia's death. Steevens, however, perceives a " conjugal tribute to the memory of Fulvia," comparing *Macbeth*, I. iv. 7, 8 : " nothing in his life Became him like the leaving it " ; while Boswell interprets : " her death was the *best* thing I have known of her, as it checked her garboils."

† The F punctuation, with comma (not semicolon) after " best," supports Case's interpretation and makes Boswell's almost impossible. [R]

63. *vials*] " Alluding," says Johnson, " to the lachrymatory vials, or bottles of tears, which the Romans sometimes put into the urn of a friend." That the vials found in

tombs were so employed is now considered very doubtful. It has been maintained that they really held unguents. Theobald (and later Steevens) refers to *The Two Noble Kinsmen*, I. v. 4 :—

" Balms, and gums, and heavy cheers,
Sacred *vials* fill'd with tears."

In Browne's *Britannia's Pastorals*, I. v. 736, the walls of the house of Repentance are hung with " crystal *vials* of repentant tears " ; and, similarly, Death's cave, " In bottles tears of friends and Louers vaine," in Peacham's *Period of Mourning* (1613), Vision iii. See also Angel Day, *The English Secretarie* (1599), pt. i, 125 : " I have prepared a golden boxe wherein I mean to consecrate all the teares you shed for that accident, to *Berecynthia* the beldame of the Gods, as a relique of your great kindship and curtesie."

68. *By the fire*] i.e. the sun. Steevens prefixed *Now* to satisfy his ear, quoting *K.J.* II. i. 397 : " Now by the sky," etc. The metrical value of the marked pause (see Abbott, *Shakespearian Grammar*, § 508) was not yet appreciated.

71. *affects*] choosest.

Cut my lace] However inappropriate to Cleopatra's unfettered beauty, the first thought, under emotion, real or pretended, of the coarser female

Cleo.   Cut my lace, Charmian, come,
But let it be, I am quickly ill, and well,
So Antony loves.
Ant.   My precious queen, forbear,
And give true evidence to his love, which stands
An honourable trial.
Cleo.   So Fulvia told me.   75
I prithee turn aside and weep for her,
Then bid adieu to me, and say the tears
Belong to Egypt.   Good now, play one scene
Of excellent dissembling, and let it look
Like perfect honour.
Ant.   You'll heat my blood: no more.
Cleo. You can do better yet; but this is meetly.   81

80. *blood: no more.*] Rowe (semicolon); *blood no more?* F.

character in old plays. See Dekker, *The Honest Whore*, pt. i (*Works*, Pearson, ii. 30): " Fie, fie, *cut my lace*, good servant; I shall ha' the mother presently, I'm so vext," etc.; Webster, *Northward Hoe!* ii. i (*Works*, Hazlitt, i. 200): " *Doll.* O, I shall burst, if I *cut not my lace*, I'm so vext!"

72, 73. *I . . . So Antony loves*] I am no sooner ill than well again, provided Antony loves. In thus withdrawing the threat of hysterics implied in " Cut my lace," etc., Cleopatra seems to angle for some convincing evidence of love, which Antony's reply does not afford to her satisfaction. The words are less likely to refer to what precedes, viz. the sworn devotion of lines 68-71; it did not prevent the threat, and probably no admission of its force as a proof of love is involved in the words of withdrawal. Steevens, Capell, and several editors interpret differently, making *so* = thus, and punctuating accordingly, with sense: " Antony's love is as fluctuating and uncertain as my health." I have not seen it proposed to make *so* refer wholly to Antony's purpose, disconnecting it altogether from line 72.

In that case it would mean: " This, then, is your love for me."

74. *give . . . evidence*] bear true witness. The Collier MS. corrector substitutes *credence* for *evidence*, and *audience* has been proposed by L. Campbell; but the phrase as it stands has the right ring, and the " witness " is probably the testimony of being composed and *well*.

78. *to Egypt*] " To me, the Queen of Egypt " (Johnson). See line 41 *ante*, and note.

good now] " please you," as in *Hamlet*, i. i. 70.

80. *You'll heat . . .*] † Rowe's repunctuation will no doubt serve well enough. It leaves Antony saying " You'll make me lose my temper. Enough of this." But the F question mark is obstinately there, and I think it is tempting to transfer the " no more?", retaining the question mark, to Cleopatra, who thus says, in reply to Antony's " You'll make me lose my temper," " Is that the best you can do by way of retort? You can do better than that, though you've made quite a good start." [R]

81. *meetly*] reasonably well. Not elsewhere in Shakespeare.

Ant. Now, by my sword,—
Cleo.   And target.   Still he mends.
But this is not the best.   Look, prithee, Charmian,
How this Herculean Roman does become
The carriage of his chafe.   85
Ant. I'll leave you, lady.
Cleo.   Courteous lord, one word:
Sir, you and I must part, but that's not it:
Sir, you and I have lov'd, but there's not it;
That you know well, something it is I would,—
O, my oblivion is a very Antony,   90
And I am all forgotten.
Ant.   But that your royalty

82. *my*] F 2; not in F.

84. *And target*] "making it a swashbuckler's oath, cf. *1 H. IV.* i. iii. 230 " (Dover Wilson).

84. *Herculean*] as descended from Anton, son of Hercules. See extracts from North's *Plutarch, post,* p. 258; and cf. iv. xii. 44 *post.*

84, 85. *How . . . chafe*] How he becomes, or lends grace to, his furious bearing. There is still some allusion to playing a part. Staunton is unwarrantably positive that *chafe* is " a silly blunder of the transcriber or compositor for *chief* [the reading in his text], meaning Hercules, the *head* or *principal* of the house of Antonii."

90, 91. *O, my oblivion . . . forgotten*] my " oblivious memory " is as faithless as Antony, and, like him, has forgotten my power over it. " Oblivious memory " is Steevens's phrase, but it is unnecessary to follow him in further taking here " I am all forgotten " as = " I forget everything," much like the sense in " How comes it, Michael, you are thus forgot? " (*Othello,* ii. iii. 190). It seems to mean, not " I am all forgetful," but " I am every way forgotten," viz. by Antony and my own faculties († surely it means both. [R]) Marston, however, who imi-

tates Shakespeare here and there in *The Insatiate Countess,* has in that play, iv. ii. 67, 68 :—

" Thy intellectual powers oblivion
    smothers,
    That thou art nothing but for-
    getfulness."

91-3. *But that . . . itself*] Under the surface meaning—which contains its own rebuke—that Cleopatra can't be both queen and subject, or might be taken for a personification of idleness or trifling, possibly lies the insinuation: Were you not liege lady of trifling, *and able to make her serve* (or : *command her arts for*) your purposes, I should take you, etc. Malone suggests something like this last, and it is substantially the explanation preferred by Clarke and Rolfe. With *idleness,* Steevens compares Webster, *Vittoria Corombona,* iv. i. 114, where Francesco, taking Isabella's ghost to be the product of his imagination, and having asked, " How cam'st thou by thy death? " continues :—

" how idle am I
To question mine own *idleness!*"

His own best interpretation is: " holds *idleness* in subjection to you, exalting you far above its influence."

Holds idleness your subject, I should take you
For idleness itself.
Cleo.   'Tis sweating labour,
To bear such idleness so near the heart
As Cleopatra this.   But sir, forgive me,   95
Since my becomings kill me, when they do not
Eye well to you.   Your honour calls you hence,
Therefore be deaf to my unpitied folly,
And all the gods go with you!   Upon your sword
Sit laurel victory, and smooth success.   100
Be strew'd before your feet!
Ant.   Let us go.   Come;
Our separation so abides and flies,
That thou, residing here, goes yet with me;
And I, hence fleeting, here remain with thee.
Away!   *[Exeunt.*   105

100. *laurel*] F (*Lawrell*); *Lawrell'd* F 2, and some edd.   103. *goes*] F;
goest F 2, Rowe; *go'st* Capell and others.

96. *Since my becomings,* etc.] I see
here the expression of feelings hurt by
Antony's cold answer to the sudden
and emotional conversion from mockery to pathos in lines 86-91. Cleopatra says, in effect: " I have done;
even the regrets, the emotion, the
fears that become me at such a time,
I repress, since it is anguish to me to
displease you." The usual explanation of *becomings* is, however, "graces."
Steevens suspected in the word an allusion to Antony's phrase in I. i. 49
ante.
    99, 100. *Upon . . . victory*] Cf.
Edward III. III. iii. 190: " Be still
adorn'd with laurel *victory*," which
confirms the reading, *laurel,* of F,
as do similar cases of noun as adjective, e.g. " the honey of his *music*
vows " (*Hamlet,* III. i. 165). For the
figure cf. *Tryall of Chevalry,* 1605,
" Successful action sit *upon* thy
sword " (Bullen's *Old Plays,* iii. 333,

where other examples are given);
also *Selimus,* 1594 (ed. Grosart, line
2447): " And white-wing'd *victory*
sits on our swords."
    102-4. *Our separation . . . thee*]
Their separation is said to *abide* as
resulting from Cleopatra's *abode* in
Egypt, and to *fly,* as resulting from
Antony's fleeting thence. With the
conceit in the whole sentence, cf.
Mucedorus, I. i. 12 :—
    " 'tis from the realm, not thee :
    Though lands part bodies, hearts
        keep company " ;
and Donne's famous poem, *A Valedic-
tion: Forbidding Mourning.* Steevens
quotes Sidney's *Arcadia,* book i. (see
lines 169, 170 of the poem at its
close), as possibly having suggested
the thought to Shakespeare:—
    " She went, they staid ; or rightly,
        for to say,
    She staid in them, they went in
        thought with her."

[SCENE IV.—*Rome.   Cæsar's house.*]

Enter OCTAVIUS *reading a letter,* LEPIDUS,
and their Train.

Cæs. You may see, Lepidus, and henceforth know,
It is not Cæsar's natural vice to hate
Our great competitor. From Alexandria
This is the news: he fishes, drinks, and wastes
The lamps of night in revel; is not more manlike   5
Than Cleopatra; nor the queen of Ptolemy
More womanly than he: hardly gave audience, or
Vouchsaf'd to think he had partners. You shall
   find there
A man who is the abstract of all faults
That all men follow.
Lep.   I must not think there are   10
Evils enow to darken all his goodness:
His faults, in him, seem as the spots of heaven,

Scene IV

3. *Our*] Singer (Heath and Johnson conj.); *One* F.   8. *Vouchsaf'd*]
Johnson; *vouchsafe* F; *did vouchsafe* F 2.   9. *abstract*] F 2; *abstracts* F.

Scene IV

3. *competitor*] Here, as often, partner, associate. Cf. II. vii. 70 *post*, and
R. III. IV. iv. 505 :—
   " And every hour more *competitors*
      Flock to the rebels," etc.
See also the quotation on I. i. 12,
" *triple pillar.*"
   4-33. *he fishes, drinks,* etc.] With the
charges in these speeches, cf. North,
post, pp. 263-4, 258, 261.
   6. *queen of Ptolemy*] Cleopatra was
nominally married by Cæsar to the
younger of her two brothers of that
name, a mere child, whom she is
said to have made away by poison.
Cf. *Egypt's widow*, II. i. 37 *post*.
   9, 10. *is the abstract . . . follow*]
exhibits in himself, and in their
highest degree, all the faults of mankind. In respect of faults, he is, like

Dryden's Zimri (*Absalom and Achito-
phel*, i. 546): " Not one, but all
mankind's epitome." Cf. Jonson,
The Devil is an Ass, IV. iv. 245:
" The top of woman! all her sex
in *abstract* ": Massinger, *The City
Madam*, III. iii : " Heaven's *abstract*
or epitome."
   12, 13. *His faults . . . blackness*]
His faults are made more conspicuous
by his goodness, as the stars by night's
blackness. The simile aims only at
force of contrast, disregarding correspondence of quality in the things
compared, *faults* and *stars*, *goodness*
and *blackness*. It is otherwise in
Hamlet, v. ii. 266-8, as Malone
indicates :—
            " in mine ignorance
   Your skill shall, like a star i' the
         darkest night,
   Stick fiery off indeed."

More fiery by night's blackness; hereditary,
Rather than purchas'd; what he cannot change,
Than what he chooses.   15
Cæs. You are too indulgent.   Let's grant it is not
Amiss to tumble on the bed of Ptolemy,
To give a kingdom for a mirth, to sit
And keep the turn of tippling with a slave,
To reel the streets at noon, and stand the buffet   20
With knaves that smells of sweat: say this becomes
     him,—
As his composure must be rare indeed
Whom these things cannot blemish,—yet must Antony

---

16. *Let's*] F; *Let us* Pope and edd.   21. *smells*] F (*smels*); *smell* F 2.

Quarles, in *The Author's Dream*, compares his sins to the stars in brightness :—

" My Sins are like the Stars within the Skies,
     In view, in number, ev'n as bright, as great," etc.

With *spots of heaven*, cf. Peele, *Edward I*, sc. iii, line 74 : " The welkin, spangled through with golden spots," etc.

14. *purchas'd*] acquired, as commonly. Cf. Nashe, *The Unfortunate Traveller*, II. p. 253, line 2 : " With him we travelled along, having *purchast* his acquaintance a little before." The legal origin of the use is played upon in the following passage from Shirley's *Love Tricks*, III. v (*Works*, 1833, i. pp. 54, 55) : " . . . got a great estate of wealth by gaming and wenching, and so *purchas'd* unhappily this state of damnation you see me in. *Infor.* Came you in it by *purchase?* then you do not claim it by your father's interest as an heir :" etc. See Cowel's *Interpreter* (ed. Manley, 1684, *s.v.*) : " it signifieth the buying of Lands or Tenements with Money, or by any other Agreement, and not the obtaining of it by descent," etc.

18. *a mirth*] So Beaumont and

Fletcher, *Philaster*, III. ii. 95 : " made it [danger] but *a mirth*."

20. *stand the buffet*] So in *1 H. IV.* III. ii. 66 : " To laugh at gibing boys and *stand the push* Of every beardless vain comparative." Cf. also the whole passage, and see Introduction, *ante*, p. xxxiv.

21. *smells*] The old Northern plural (?) in *s* is extremely common, occurring in all kinds of writers, and often, as here, in F. Cf. line 49 *post*: *The Tempest*, III. iii. 2, " bones akes "; *M. of V.* III. ii. 18, " times Puts," and quotation in note on IV. xiv. 76, 77 *post*.

22. *As his composure*] Composure = composition, as in *T. of C.* II. iii. 254 ; Brome, *A Mad Couple*, etc., IV. i. (*Works*, Pearson, p. 63) : " hee is of so sweete a *Composure*," etc. For *As* Johnson proposed to read *And*: but the inconsequence he detected is more apparent than real, as the inference in *As* is from the idea of an untarnishable Antony involved in " say this becomes him." The whole equals : Grant he is a prodigy, as prodigy he must be to carry off such faults. Dr. Ingleby's account of the use of *as* in this and other passages will be found in II. ii. 53 *post*, but can, I think, be dispensed with in the present case at least.

No way excuse his foils, when we do bear
So great weight in his lightness. If he fill'd   25
His vacancy with his voluptuousness,
Full surfeits, and the dryness of his bones
Call on him for't. But to confound such time,
That drums him from his sport, and speaks as loud
As his own state, and ours,—'tis to be chid: 30
As we rate boys, who being mature in knowledge,

24. *foils*] F (*foyles*); *soils* Malone.
most edd.; *chid*, Hanmer, Johnson.

30. *chid:*] F; *chid* Capell and

24. *foils*] The retention of *foils* in
the text seems inevitably to follow
the evidence of *O.E.D.* as to the
sense disgrace, stigma, with mixture
of the sense of the verb *foil* = to foul,
etc. The quotation there given from
Porter, *Angry Women of Abingdon*
(Percy Soc.), 26, "It hath set a
foyle upon thy fame," is precisely
apt and unmistakeable:—

"And it [a fault] hath set a foil
    upon thy fame,
Not as the foil doth grace the
    diamond"

(Hazlitt's *Dodsley*, VII. 288). Equally
with Malone's otherwise probable
soils, *foils* agrees with the defiling
pursuits just detailed, and no longer
merely depends on Collier's explanation as the vices "which foil or defeat" Antony's virtues, or on
Schmidt's citation of *Tempest*, III. i.
46, for the sense "blemish": or
again on the possibility that Cæsar
—who has just granted, for argument's sake, that Antony's faults
may become him—might refer to
them as the foils of his virtues, as
Lepidus makes the virtues set off his
faults, and as Prince Hal (*1 H. IV.*
I. ii. 234-7) makes his "fault" the
"foil" to set off his reformation.

24, 25. *when . . . lightness*] when
"his trifling levity throws so much
burden upon us" (Johnson).

26. *vacancy*] Similarly used for
leisure by Heywood, *ΓΥΝΑΙΚΕΙΟΝ*
(1624), p. 318: "Neither remember

I, O king, . . . that Agamemnon, in
all the time of the tenne yeeres siege
of Troy had such *vacancie* as thou
hast now to prie into the Boothes of
his soulders;" etc.

28. *Call on him for 't*] Insist on a
reckoning for it. Cf. Braithwaite,
Nature's Embassie (1621), Satire ii, st.
2, of the deferred wrath of Nature:—

"Though she delay assure thee she
    will *call*,
And thou must pay both vse and
    principall."

O.E.D. quotes the passage under
"To impeach, challenge," adding
"1740 Chesterfield Lett. J, clx. 295:
You *call* upon me for the partiality
of an author to his own works," and
another late passage.

confound] See on I. i. 45 *ante*.

31-3. *As we rate*, etc.] such conduct merits the scolding we give
boys, who being old enough to know
better, gratify their present desires
against their judgment. Non-existent
difficulties have been found here.
Hanmer read (and Warburton accepted) *immature*, offended at the
idea of maturity in connection with
boys. Daniel conjectures *he's to be
chid . . . who . . . Pawns his . . . to
his . . . rebels. . . .* If we are to press
the meaning in *Pawn*, it is possible
to say that experience (which gives
foreknowledge of consequences) is
pledged to pleasure in the sense that
it must be redeemed, or reinforced,
by the undergoing of the foreseen

Pawn their experience to their present pleasure,
And so rebel to judgment.

Enter a Messenger.

Lep.   Here's more news.

Mess. Thy biddings have been done, and every hour,
Most noble Cæsar, shalt thou have report   35
How 'tis abroad.   Pompey is strong at sea,
And it appears he is belov'd of those
That only have fear'd Cæsar: to the ports
The discontents repair, and men's reports
Give him much wrong'd.

Cæs.   I should have known no less ;
It hath been taught us from the primal state   41
That he which is was wish'd, until he were;
And the ebb'd man, ne'er lov'd till ne'er worth love,
Comes dear'd, by being lack'd.   This common body,

---

44. *dear'd*] Theobald (Warburton);   *fear'd* F.

---

consequences of pleasure; but I
doubt if the thought goes beyond
the necessity of parting with the
valuable, the guidance of experience,
for the occasion: cf. Braithwaite,
Strappado for the Diuell, 1615 (1878
reprint, p. 291):—
          " oh why should we,
   To get a little sport, *paune*
      modesty? "
   † But as to *rate* Mr. J. C. Maxwell
makes the interesting suggestion that
it here means " estimate "—i.e. " In
the same way that we count as mere
boys those men who, being. . . ."
The F colon after *chid* helps it. [R]
   36-47. *Pompey,* etc.] Cf. I. ii. 181-
90 ; I. iii. 45-52 *ante.*
   39. *the discontents*] the discontented,
or malcontents, as in *1 H. IV.* v. i. 76.
Similar instances of the abstract for
the concrete occur in II. ii. 47 *post*:
Lear, III. i. 24, etc. Cf. *Edward III.*
III. iii. 156 :—
   " For what's this Edward but a
      belly-god,
   A tender and lascivious wanton-
      ness," etc.

40. *Give him*] represent him as ; as
in *Coriolanus,* I. ix. 55 ; Shirley, *The
Wedding,* v. ii (*Works,* 1833, I. 441):
" my nephew *gives* you valiant," etc.
   41. *from the primal state*] since
government began.
   42. *That he . . . were*] that the man
in power was always the popular
candidate for it till, and only till,
he obtained it. Cæsar glances at
his own loss of popular favour.
   43. *ebb'd man*] Copley uses a similar
figure in *A Fig for a Fortune,* 1596,
p. 6 : " What booteth it to liue . . . A
muddie ebbe after a Chrystall flood?"
   44. *Comes dear'd*] becomes en-
deared.   Collier (1843) retained
fear'd, but reads *lov'd* in his second
edition, with the Collier MS. Cf.
Coriolanus, IV. i. 15 : " I shall be *loved*
when I am lack'd." Knight retains
fear'd on the ground that the notions
of fear and love are almost synony-
mous in the mind of one who aims
at supreme power. But the messenger's distinction between these notions
in lines 37, 38, confirms the emendation. Cf. I. ii. 183-5 *ante.*

Like to a vagabond flag upon the stream,   45
Goes to, and back, lackeying the varying tide,
To rot itself with motion.

Enter a second Messenger.

Mess.   Cæsar, I bring thee word,
Menecrates and Menas, famous pirates,
Makes the sea serve them, which they ear and wound
With keels of every kind.   Many hot inroads   50
They make in Italy, the borders maritime
Lack blood to think on't, and flush youth revolt:
No vessel can peep forth, but 'tis as soon
Taken as seen; for Pompey's name strikes more
Than could his war resisted.

46. *lackeying*] *lacquying* Theobald (Anon. MS.); *lacking* F.   47. Enter
. . .] Capell; not in F.

45. *common body*] the common
people.
flag] a common species of iris.
46. *lackeying*] The servility of popular favour is united with its instabil-
ity by Theobald's reading. Pope's
was *lashing*. For the use of the verb,
Steevens quotes, among other passages, Chapman's Homer, *Iliad*,
xxiv [ed. Shepherd, 1875, p. 285] :—
    " I could wish thy grave
    affairs did need
    My   guide   to   Argos,   either
    shipp'd, or *lackeying* by thy
    side," etc.
47. *Enter . . .*] †F has no S.D.
and so attributes *Cæsar, I bring . . .*
to the messenger who has already
come. But I have little doubt that
Capell (supported by Steevens) was
right in thinking that we must have a
second messenger. Quite apart
from the expectation of a series of
messengers created by " every hour
shalt thou have report " (lines 34, 35),
the opening " Caesar, I bring thee
word," natural in the mouth of a
second messenger, is awkward as no
more than the introduction to a second
item of news from the same messenger
who has already addressed Cæsar;

and Cæsar's seven lines of philosophic
comment are equally awkward if
they interrupt the delivery of a piece
of news, though natural enough if
they follow a report which has clearly
terminated. [R]
48. *Menecrates . . . pirates*] See
North, *post*, p. 265.
49. *Makes*] See on line 21 *ante*;
ear, plough. Cf. I. ii. 108 *ante*.
52. *flush*] lusty, full of vigour. Cf.
Hamlet, III. iii. 81 : " As *flush* as
May." *O.E.D.* gives further examples of a derived sense, " self-
confident," " self-conceited," and it
is interesting to note also here another
flush, of uncertain etymology and
dialectal, = fledged.
54, 55. *Pompey's name . . . resisted*]
† The commentators are mostly silent,
but I do not find this so obvious as
the silence suggests it should be. If
" war resisted " = " resistance to his
armed forces " (as " Cæsar inter-
fectus " can mean " the death of
Cæsar "), then the whole means
" His mere name causes you more
loss than armed resistance would."
But if we take " resisted " as conditional, it means " His mere name
is more effective than his armed

Cæs.   Antony,   55
Leave thy lascivious wassails.   When thou once
Was beaten from Modena, where thou slew'st
Hirtius and Pansa, consuls, at thy heel
Did famine follow, whom thou fought'st against,
Though daintily brought up, with patience more   60
Than savages could suffer.   Thou didst drink
The stale of horses, and the gilded puddle
Which beasts would cough at: thy palate then did deign
The roughest berry, on the rudest hedge;
Yea, like the stag, when snow the pasture sheets,   65
The barks of trees thou browsed.   On the Alps

56. *wassails*] Pope; *Vassailes* F, F 2; *Vassails* F 3; *Vassals* F 4.   57.
Was] F; *Wast* Steevens (1778) and edd.; *Wert* F 2.   66. *browsed*]
brows'd F; *browsed'st* F 2.

forces would be, if only you opposed
them." I do not think the two
meanings are identical, but perhaps I
am merely nosing out difficulty
where there is none. [R]

56. *wassails*] Carousals attended
with lust are naturally contrasted
with the scant and repulsive diet, and
severe hardships stoically endured,
which the next lines describe. Some,
however, prefer the old reading
vassals, to which alone, and not to
" drunken revelry " (*wassails*), Knight
unaccountably considers the epithet
lascivious appropriate.

57. *Modena*] accented on second
syllable (as also by the Countess of
Pembroke in *Antonie*, Act III),
whereas Italian, " Módena," Latin,
" Mútina." For the whole passage,
to line 71, see North, *post*, p. 259-60.

59 *whom*] Abbott (*Shakespearian
Grammar*, § 264) shows that *who*
stands for irrational antecedents
where there is any approach to personification; but adds that *whom* is
rare, comparing *The Tempest*, III. iii.
62: " The elements Of *whom*," etc.

61. *Than . . . suffer*] explicable, I
think, as a case of cognate accusative,
and = " Than that which savages
could suffer." For the thought, cf.
D'Avenant, *Gondibert*, II. ii. 25 :—

" Still I have fought, as if in
Beauty's sight,
Outsuffer'd patience, bred in
Captives Breasts ; " etc.

It is usually taken as an instance of
omission to repeat the preposition in
relative sentences (see Abbott, *Shakespearian Grammar*, § 394) and =
" Than savages could suffer *with*," or
" Than that with which," etc.

62. *gilded*] overspread with irides-
cent scum ; " filthy-mantled," as in
The Tempest, IV. i. 182.

63. *deign*] not disdain.

66. *The barks . . . brows'd*] So Nashe,
in *Christ's Tears*, II. p. 70, line 2 :
" All the bushes and boughes, within or rounde about Ierusalem, were
hewd down and feld, for men (like
brute beasts) to *brouse* on " ; Browne,
Britannia's Pastorals, book ii (1616),
Song i. 663-7 :—

" As in a forest well complete with
deer
We see the hollies, ashes, everywhere
Robb'd of their clothing by the
browsing game :
So near the rock all trees where'er
you [i.e. Limos or Famine]
came,
To cold December's wrath stood
void of bark."

It is reported thou didst eat strange flesh,
Which some did die to look on: and all this—
It wounds thine honour that I speak it now—
Was borne so like a soldier, that thy cheek   70
So much as lank'd not.

Lep.   'Tis pity of him.

Cæs. Let his shames quickly
Drive him to Rome, 'tis time we twain
Did show ourselves i' the field, and to that end
Assemble we immediate council; Pompey   75
Thrives in our idleness.

Lep.   To-morrow, Cæsar,
I shall be furnish'd to inform you rightly
Both what by sea and land I can be able
To front this present time.

Cæs.   Till which encounter,
It is my business too. Farewell.   80

Lep. Farewell, my lord; what you shall know meantime
Of stirs abroad, I shall beseech you, sir,
To let me be partaker.

Cæs.   Doubt not, sir,
I know it for my bond.   [*Exeunt.*

---

75. *we*] F 2; *me* F.   84. *know*] Walker; *knew* F.

71. *lank'd*] grew thin.

75. *Assemble we*] *we*, the reading of
F 2, sorts with *we twain*, line 73, and
our, line 76, as well as with the fact
that, as Malone says, Cæsar is ad-
dressing an equal. *Me* is retained by
one or two editors, among whom
Knight thinks "the commentators
forget Cæsar's contempt for Lepidus
and the crouching humility of Lepidus
himself." Neither of these ascribed
qualities appears in this scene.

78. *what . . . I can be able*] what
my powers can be.

79. *front*] face, confront. Cf. 2 *H.
IV.* IV. i. 25: "What well-appointed
leader *fronts* us here?" See also
II. ii. 61 *post*.

84. *I know . . . bond*] †I recognize
it as part of my engagements. F's
knew is no doubt possible, in the sense
"I knew what my commitments
were when we came to our original
agreement (and have not forgotten
them since)" but the emendation is
graphically easy, and attractive.
[R]

[SCENE V.—*Alexandria.   Cleopatra's palace.*]

Enter CLEOPATRA, CHARMIAN, IRAS, *and* MARDIAN.

Cleo. Charmian!
Char. Madam?
Cleo. Ha, ha!
    Give me to drink mandragora.
Char.   Why, madam?
Cleo. That I might sleep out this great gap of time   5
    My Antony is away.
Char.   You think of him too much.
Cleo. O, 'tis treason!
Char.   Madam, I trust not so.
Cleo. Thou, eunuch Mardian!
Mar.   What's your highness' pleasure?
Cleo. Not now to hear thee sing.   I take no pleasure
    In aught an eunuch has: 'tis well for thee   10

Scene v

5. *time*] Rowe (*time,*); *time:* F.   8. *Thou, eunuch*] F; *Thou eunuch,* Pope.

Scene v

3. *Ha, ha!*] "A yawn of ennui" (Kittredge).

4. *mandragora*] the juice of mandragora or mandrake, a plant with strong narcotic qualities. "The juice thereof with woman's milk laid to the temples maketh to sleep, yea though it were in the most hot ague" (*Bartholomew* [*Berthelet*], Book XVII, § 104). Cf. *Othello*, III. iii. 330:—

"Not poppy, nor mandragora,
  Nor all the drowsy syrups of the world,
Shall ever medicine thee to that sweet sleep
Which thou ow'dst yesterday."

How a Man may Choose a Good Wife, etc. III. ii (Hazlitt's *Dodsley*, ix. 48) :—

      "in this paper is
The juice of mandrake, by a doctor made
To cast a man, whose leg should be cut off,

Into a deep, a cold, and senseless sleep;
Of such approved operation
That whoso takes it, is for twice twelve hours,
Breathless, and to all men's judgments past all sense;" etc.

9-12. *Not now . . . affections?*] † Mardian is the official singer; cf. II. v. 2 (S.D.). '*Tis well for thee* that means, I think, not " it's just as well for you that . . ." (i.e. " you escape blame because . . .," Cleopatra-like remark though that would be), but " you are happy in that. . . ." Cleopatra is, or pretends to be, congratulating him on his sexless immunity from desire, when her own " freer," and far from unsexed, thoughts are flying with passionate longing to Rome (cf. line 21, *to bear the weight,* a characteristic, purely physical, touch). *Affections* is nearer to " passions " or " desires " than our modern sense. [R]

That, being unseminar'd, thy freer thoughts
May not fly forth of Egypt.   Hast thou affections?
Mar. Yes, gracious madam.
Cleo. Indeed?
Mar. Not in deed, madam, for I can do nothing   15
But what indeed is honest to be done:
Yet have I fierce affections, and think
What Venus did with Mars.
Cleo.   O Charmian!
Where think'st thou he is now?   Stands he, or sits he?
Or does he walk?   or is he on his horse?   20
O happy horse to bear the weight of Antony!
Do bravely, horse, for wot'st thou whom thou mov'st,
The demi-Atlas of this earth, the arm
And burgonet of men.   He's speaking now,
Or murmuring, " Where's my serpent of old Nile?" 25
For so he calls me.   Now I feed myself
With most delicious poison.   Think on me,
That am with Phœbus' amorous pinches black,
And wrinkled deep in time.   Broad-fronted Cæsar,

29. *time.*] F; *time?* Capell.

16. *honest*] in the restricted sense
of " chaste "; cf. *M.W.W.* IV. ii.
110, " Wives may be merry, and
yet *honest* too."
18. *What Venus . . .*] Venus, wife
of Vulcan, was Mars's paramour,
and Vulcan trapped them in the
act.
23-4. *arm And Burgonet*] † I suppose we must be content, as most
commentators seem to be, to take
this as meaning simply " the complete soldier," equipped both for
offence with his own strong arm, and
for defence with the most efficient
helmet yet devised.   But it seems
something of an anti-climax after
" the demi-Atlas," and it is difficult
to feel happy about it. [R]
24. *burgonet*] a helmet of Bur-
gundian invention, whence its name.
" It was so fitted to the gorget that
the head moved freely, without producing a chink through which an

enemy might pierce the neck."   So
Morley, on stanza 82, canto vi of
Drayton's *Barons' War* (1887 edn.).
27-9. *Think . . . time*] † Capell's
question mark (adopted by both
Case and Dover Wilson) is not
wholly convincing.   It makes Antony,
rather awkwardly, the subject of
think.   F makes Cleopatra address
Charmian, " it's me that he loves,
in spite of my wrinkles," and then
she goes on, characteristically, to
say that it is not so surprising after
all, considering her other conquests.
But it is true that *think on* often
means " to think kindly of," as in
Coriolanus, II. iii. 61 and 196. [R]
28. *amorous pinches*] † cf. v. ii. 294,
" The stroke of death is as a lover's
pinch."   She includes both the sun
and death among her lovers. [R]
29. *Broad-fronted*] obviously, " with
a broad forehead."   Henley and
Singer fancy there is an allusion to

G

When thou wast here above the ground, I was   30
A morsel for a monarch: and great Pompey
Would stand and make his eyes grow in my brow,
There would he anchor his aspect, and die
With looking on his life.

Enter ALEXAS *from Antony.*

Alex.   Sovereign of Egypt, hail!
Cleo. How much unlike art thou Mark Antony!   35
Yet coming from him, that great med'cine hath
With his tinct gilded thee.
How goes it with my brave Mark Antony?
Alex. Last thing he did, dear queen,
He kiss'd—the last of many doubled kisses—   40
This orient pearl. His speech sticks in my heart.

34. (S.D.).   from Antony] Collier MS.; from Cæsar. F.   40. *kiss'd—the*
. . . *kisses*—] Theobald (substantially); *kist the . . . kisses* F.

Cæsar's baldness, and Seward proposed *bald-fronted Cæsar.* See on II.
vi. 68-70 *post*, and North, *post*, p. 261,
for his intrigue with Cleopatra.

31. *great Pompey*] Cneius, son of
Pompey the Great, as in III. xiii. 118
post, *q.v.*, and North, *post*, p. 261.
The epithet is misleading.

33. *anchor his aspect*] Cf. Sonnet
cxxxvii. 6 :—
    " If eyes corrupt by over partial
        looks
    Be *anchored* in the bay where all
        men ride," etc. ;
and *M. for M.* II. iv. 4.

36, 37. *great med'cine . . . thee*] The
terms the medicine or great medicine,
tinct or tincture, were applied by the
alchemists to the supreme result of
their labours, regarded rather as the
agent for transmuting metals than the
elixir to renew youth. See *All's Well*,
v. iii. 102 : " That knows the tinct
and multiplying *medicine* ": Donne,
Resurrection (Nonesuch   Donne, ed.
Hayward, p. 290) :—
    " He was all gold when he lay
        down, but rose
    All tincture, and doth not alone
        dispose

Leaden and iron wills to good,"
    etc. ;
Jonson, *The Alchemist*, *passim*, but
especially II. i. 37 *et seq.*, " But when
you see th' effects of the *great med'cine*,"
etc. In the text, as in *The Tempest*,
v. i. 280, where a similar allusion
underlies the expressed cause and
effect of drunkenness :—
        " where should they
    Find this grand liquor that hath
        gilded them ?"
the effect is but external. *Tincture* is
often used for a mere surface deposit ;
so Lord Brooke, " An Inqvisition vpon
Fame and Honovr," 10 (*Works*, ed.
Grosart, ii. 70) : " Goodnesse puts
only *tincture* on our gall " ; on which
the editor observes : " Tincture was
supposed to turn the basest metal
into gold. *Supra*, it means a golden
covering as of a pill in medicine."
Walker (*Critical Examination of the
Text of Shakespeare*, 1860) suggests
medicine possibly = physician, as it
may possibly in *All's Well*, II. i. 75.

41. *orient*] bright, lustrous. *Pearl*
and this epithet were almost insepar-
able. Cf. " What a sight would it be
to embrace one whose haire were as

Cleo. Mine ear must pluck it thence.

Alex.   " Good friend," quoth he,
    " Say the firm Roman to great Egypt sends
    This treasure of an oyster; at whose foot
    To mend the petty present, I will piece   45
    Her opulent throne with kingdoms. All the east,
    (Say thou) shall call her mistress." So he nodded
    And soberly did mount an arm-gaunt steed,
    Who neigh'd so high, that what I would have spoke
    Was beastly dumb'd by him.

Cleo.   What, was he sad, or merry?

48. *an arm-gaunt*] *an Arme-gaunt* F.
. . . *merry*] *What was he sad, or merry* F;

50. *dumb'd*] Theobald; *dumbe* F. *What
was he, sad or merry* Furness conj-

orient as the pearle!" (Lyly, *Endimion*,
v. ii. 95:—
        " to make a pearl more pure
    We give it to a dove, in whose
        womb pent
    Some time, we have it forth most
        orient."
(Wm. Browne, *An Elegy on Sir
Thomas Overbury*, etc., lines 26-8).
O.E.D. says the epithet is applied
to pearls " as coming anciently from
the East," and cites 1555 Eden
Decades 39 : " Many of these perles
were as bygge as hasell nuttes, and
oriente (as we caule it), that is, lyke
unto them of the Easte partes."
Pearl of Orient = orient pearl, oriental
pearl (*O.E.D.*) also supports this,
but a quotation supplied by Mr.
Craig shows that another derivation
was current : Harrison, *Description
of England*, Book III. chap. i (New
Shakes. Soc., ed. Furnivall, part i,
p. 80) : " They [pearles] are called
orient because of the cleerenesse
which resembleth the colour of the
cleere air before the rising of the sun."

43. *firm*] constant.

45. *piece*] To *piece* can mean to
make additions to as well as simply
to mend. See Earle's *Microcosmo-
graphie*, 1628, *A young rawe Preacher;*
" He has more tricks with a sermon,
then a Tailer with an old cloak, to

turne it, and *piece* it," etc.; Lyly's
Campaspe, IV. i. 12 : " He hath found
Dedalus old waxen wings, and hath
beene *peecing* them this moneth, he
is so broade in the shoulders " ;
Kyd, *1 Ieronimo*, III. iv. 10 :—
                        " My armes
    Are of the shortest ; let your loues
        peece them out."
Antony will lay his conquests at
Cleopatra's feet to extend her
dominion.

48. *arm-gaunt*] See App. I.

50. *beastly dumb'd*] " Deep clerks
she *dumbs* " (*Pericles*, v, prol. 5),
quoted by Steevens, supports this
reading. See also Sylvester's *Du
Bartas*, 1621 ed., p. 910 (*Job Triumphant*) : " He dulls the Learned,
dumbs the Eloquent," etc. Shake,
speare uses *beastly* as an adverb in
Cymbeline, v. iii. 27, and elsewhere.

What . . . merry?] †Furness' punctuation is undeniably attractive, and
Dover Wilson promotes it to the text.
But I do not feel very happy about it.
I fancy that the most natural Elizabethan for what it makes Cleopatra
say would have been " *Whether* was
he sad or merry?", and the *What*
followed by comma of most editors
(precisely the oratorical Latin
" Quid ? " = " now for the next
point ") is common Elizabethan. [R]

Alex. Like to the time o' the year between the extremes   51
    Of hot and cold, he was nor sad nor merry.
Cleo. O well-divided disposition!   Note him,
    Note him, good Charmian, 'tis the man; but note him.
    He was not sad, for he would shine on those   55
    That make their looks by his; he was not merry,
    Which seem'd to tell them, his remembrance lay
    In Egypt with his joy; but between both.
    O heavenly mingle!   Be'st thou sad, or merry,
    The violence of either thee becomes,   60
    So does it no man else.   Met'st thou my posts?
Alex. Ay, madam, twenty several messengers:
    Why do you send so thick?
Cleo.   Who's born that day
    When I forget to send to Antony,
    Shall die a beggar.   Ink and paper, Charmian.   65
    Welcome, my good Alexas.   Did I, Charmian,
    Ever love Cæsar so?
Char.   O that brave Cæsar!
Cleo. Be chok'd with such another emphasis,
    Say the brave Antony.
Char.   The valiant Cæsar!
Cleo. By Isis, I will give thee bloody teeth,   70

61. *man*] F 2; *mans* F.

54. *but*] just, only (not adversa-
tive).
56. *That make . . . his*] Cf. *K.J.*
v. i. 50 :—
        " inferior eyes
  That borrow their behaviours
    from the great," etc.
59. *mingle*] As a noun, not elsewhere in Shakespeare save IV. viii.
37 *post*. Cf. *Poems on Several Occasions*, Sir R. Howard, 1696, *To the
Reader*, sig. A 4: " the *Mingle* it
has with my private Papers, was the
greatest cause, that it received its
share in the publick Impression."
60. *The violence . . . becomes*] the
compliment of I. i. 49 *ante*, returned.
   † But *violence* is an odd word to
use of either sadness (even if here

probably nearer to the modern use
than the frequent Elizabethan meaning of " soberness ") or merriment,
and even odder when both Alexas
and Cleopatra have been stressing
that Antony's behaviour has been
the happy mean *between* two extremes.   I suppose that Cleopatra
must be taken to mean " *Even if*
he had to run to either extreme it
would still have become him." [R]
65. *Shall die a beggar*] According to
Deighton, she implies that the day
will be so ill-fated as to carry with it
such consequences.   Perhaps, however, there is nothing more than a
quaint way of expressing the certainty of a daily despatch.

If thou with Cæsar paragon again
　My man of men.

Char.　　　　　　　　　By your most gracious pardon,
　I sing but after you.

Cleo.　　　　　　　　　My salad days,
When I was green in judgment, cold in blood,
To say as I said then.　But come, away,　　　75
Get me ink and paper,
He shall have every day a several greeting,
Or I'll unpeople Egypt.　　　　　　　[*Exeunt.*

71. *paragon*] match *or* compare. See note on the word in *Othello*, II. i. 62 (*Arden Shakespeare*).

74, 75. *green . . . then*] I have restored the pointing of F. The reading generally adopted, *green in judgment; cold in blood, To . . . then!* is Warburton's, who says: "*Cold in blood* is an upbraiding expostulation to her maid. ' Those (says she) were my sallad days, when I was green in judgment; but your blood is as cold as my judgment, if you have the same opinion of things now as I had then.' " Boswell justly objected that *cold* as well as *green* seems " to be suggested by the metaphor *sallad* days "; but besides this, it is more probable that Cleopatra should strengthen her contention with regard to *herself*, and further, do so by adding the physical sensation to the mental attitude, than that she should break off to reproach her maid, whose judgment might be in question, but whose blood was not supposed to take its temperature from Antony. Judgment and beauty only are touched in North, see *post*, p. 262.

ACT II

[SCENE I.—*Messina.   Pompey's house.*]

Enter POMPEY, MENECRATES, *and* MENAS, *in warlike manner.*

Pom. If the great gods be just, they shall assist
    The deeds of justest men.
Mene.   Know, worthy Pompey,
    That what they do delay, they not deny.
Pom. Whiles we are suitors to their throne, decays
    The thing we sue for.
Mene.   We, ignorant of ourselves,   5
    Beg often our own harms, which the wise powers
    Deny us for our good; so find we profit
    By losing of our prayers.
Pom.   I shall do well:
    The people love me, and the sea is mine;
    My powers are crescent, and my auguring hope   10
    Says it will come to the full.   Mark Antony
    In Egypt sits at dinner, and will make
    No wars without doors.   Cæsar gets money where

ACT II

Scene 1

3. *what*] F; *which* F 2.

Scene 1

4, 5. *Whiles . . . sue for*] cf. Cassio in *Othello*, III. ii. 13-18.

5-8. *We . . . prayers*] Mr. Churton Collins (*Studies in Shakespeare*, 1904, p. 29) quotes these lines as a " terse translation " of Juvenal, *Satire* x. 346-52, not attributable to mere coincidence. But it would be surprising if the reflection could be proved to have been any less common in Shakespeare's time than it is to-day.

10. *My powers are crescent*] Cf. *Hamlet*, I. iii. 11 : " For nature,

crescent, does not grow alone," etc. Theobald obtained concord with the following *it* by reading *My pow'r 's a crescent*. Cf. *M.N.D.* v. i. 248 : " He is no *crescent* "; but the metaphor from the waxing moon, which accounts for *it*, was probably a second thought, and usage did not forbid *it* to relate to a plural noun. So in *T. of A.* III. vi. 102 :—

    " Who, stuck and spangled with
        your flatteries,
    Washes *it* off," etc.

13. *No wars . . . doors*] An allusion to a commonplace of love poetry :—

He loses hearts: Lepidus flatters both,
Of both is flatter'd: but he neither loves,   15
Nor either cares for him.
Men.   Cæsar and Lepidus
Are in the field, a mighty strength they carry.
Pom. Where have you this? 'tis false.
Men.   From Silvius, sir.
Pom. He dreams: I know they are in Rome together
Looking for Antony: but all the charms of love,   20
Salt Cleopatra, soften thy wan'd lip!
Let witchcraft join with beauty, lust with both,
Tie up the libertine in a field of feasts,

16, 18, 38. Men.] Malone; Mene. F.   21. *wan'd*] Steevens, 1793
(Percy conj.); *wand* F; *wan* Pope.

" Love calls to war ;
    Sighs his alarms,
  Lips his swords are,
    The field his arms."
So Chapman, *Epithal. Teratos* in *Hero
and Leander*, 5th Sestiad.
    15. *neither*] object of *loves* (not
correlative to the following *nor*).
    16. Men.] Malone altered *Mene.*
(Menecrates) to *Men.* for Menas both
here and in line 18 conjecturally, as
well as in line 38, where the context
demands the change. As he says :
" It is a matter of little consequence."
Johnson gave all to Menas, observing:
" I know not why Menecrates appears;
Menas can do all without him."
    20. *Looking for*] waiting for.
    21. *Salt*] lustful ; as in *M. for M.*
v. i. 402. So D'Avenant, *Albovine*, iv
(*Dramatists of Restoration*, i. 81) :—
              " Let 'em revel
    With their *salt* lips. Th' other
              sport is fulsome."
wan'd] In reading *wan'd* Steevens
does not decide between the sense
" *waned*, declined, gone off from its
perfection ; comparing Cleopatra's
beauty to the moon past the full "
(Percy), and that of *wanned* or *made
wan*, for which he quotes *Hamlet*, II.
ii. 588, where F has *warm'd* but Q
wand : " That from her [i.e. his
soul's] working all his visage *wann'd.*"

With *waned*, the more natural and
usually accepted epithet, compare
wither'd in Webster, *The White Devil*,
II. i. 168 :—
    " You have oft, for these two lips,
      Neglected cassia or the natural
            sweets
      Of the spring-violet ; they are
            not yet much *wither'd.*"
Waned frequently occurs in conjunction with cheek, but not with
lip. Steevens quotes (anent *wan*
or *wanned*) Beaumont and Fletcher,
Queen of Corinth [IV. i ; (Camb.
vi. 51)] : " Now you look *wan* and
pale, lips, ghosts ye are." Collier
(1843) reading *wand*, suggests *wand-
lip* = lip potent as a wand, i.e.
similarly commanding enchantment,
and saw confirmation of his view in
witchcraft, next line ; but Z. Jackson
had urged all this in 1819. Collier
(1858) reads *wan'd.*
    22. *join*] † F· reads *ioyne*; is this
perhaps the common *e; d* error for
ioynd? [R].
    23. *Tie . . . field of feasts*] Mr. Craig
supplies me with the following from
*A Glossary of Words in the County of
Chester* by Robert Holland (Eng.
Dial. Soc. 1886, pt. ii) : " *Tied by
the tooth*, idiom., a curious expression,
explaining why sheep and cattle do
not break through fences, though

Keep his brain fuming; Epicurean cooks
Sharpen with cloyless sauce his appetite,   25
That sleep and feeding may prorogue his honour,
Even till a Lethe'd dulness—

Enter VARRIUS.

                         How now, Varrius?

Var. This is most certain, that I shall deliver:
Mark Antony is every hour in Rome
Expected: since he went from Egypt, 'tis   30
A space for farther travel.

Pom.   I could have given less matter
A better ear. Menas, I did not think
This amorous surfeiter would have donn'd his helm
For such a petty war: his soldiership
Is twice the other twain: but let us rear   35
The higher our opinion, that our stirring
Can from the lap of Egypt's widow pluck
The ne'er-lust-wearied Antony.

they are bad, because the pasture is good, which prevents rambling. L." The source (L) is Col. Egerton Leigh's *Glossary*, etc., 1877. Perhaps, as Mr. Craig further suggests, though Antony would be like an animal in such a fat pasture, the reference (if any) is merely to the large pasture fields of Shakespeare's day, in which the severally owned portions were not enclosed. The following passages from Elton's *Wm. Shakespeare, his Family and Friends* (1904), are relevant: " The rights incidental to Shakespeare's ' yard-lands ' comprised privileges on other people's fallows, called ' hades, leys, and tyings ' " (p. 142): " The word ' tyings ' meant the right of tethering a horse, hobbled with a ' tye ' or chain, so as to graze on the neighbour's herbage " (p. 144). Deighton sees, apparently, an implied contrast in " field of feasts," as he explains: " where he may . . . forget all thoughts of the field of battle."

25. *cloyless*] Apparently only used here and in Hogg's *Queen's Wake* (1813), p. 251 : " *Cloyless* song, the gift of heaven," quoted by *O.E.D.*

26, 27. *prorogue . . . Lethe'd dulness*] suspend the operation of his honour till it becomes too insensible to prompt. For *prorogue* = put off, see *R. and J.* II. ii. 78, IV. i. 48. Nashe also uses the word in this sense in *The Unfortunate Traveller*, II, p. 220, line 16, and p. 325, line 1113 in the sense " prolonged" " No paines I will refuse how euer *prorogued*, to have a little respite to purifie my spirit."

30, 31. *since he went . . . travel*] There has been time enough, since he left Egypt, for him to have got further than Rome. For *space* meaning " space of time " cf. *Lear*, v. iii. 54, " To-morrow, or at further *space*."

35, 36. *rear . . . opinion*] think more highly of ourselves.

37. *Egypt's widow*] See on I. iv. 6 *ante*.

Men.   I cannot hope
Cæsar and Antony shall well gree together:
His wife that's dead did trespasses to Cæsar,   40
His brother warr'd upon him, although I think
Not mov'd by Antony.
Pom.   I know not, Menas,
How lesser enmities may give way to greater.
Were't not that we stand up against them all,
'Twere pregnant they should square between them-
        selves,   45
For they have entertained cause enough
To draw their swords: but how the fear of us
May cement their divisions, and bind up
The petty difference, we yet not know.

---

39. *gree*] Furness conj., *greet* F.   41. *warr'd*] F 2; *wan'd* F.
43, 44. *greater. Were't . . . all,*] Rowe's pointing; *greater, Were't . . .
all;* F.

38. *hope*] expect; as, e.g. in *Henry V.*
III. vii. 82, and Rowley, *A Woman
Never Vexed*, II. (Hazlitt's *Dodsley*, xii.
132): " I *hope* thou'lt vex me."
Boswell cites Puttenham (*The Arte
of English Poesie*, 1589, lib. iii, p. 263
in Arber's ed.) for ridicule of the
word's use in this sense: " Such
manner of vncouth speech did the
Tanner of Tamworth vse to king
Edward the fourth, which Tanner
hauing a great while mistaken him,
and vsed very broad talke with him,
at length perceiuing by his traine
that it was the king, was afraide he
should be punished for it, said thus
with a certain rude repentance: *I
hope I shall be hanged to-morrow.* For
[*I feare me*] *I shall be hanged*, whereat
the king laughed a good, not only
to see the Tanners vaine feare, but
also to heare his ill shapen terme,"
etc.

39. *gree*] † Furness's suggestion
seems to me almost certain. " Greet
together " is an awkward phrase
(apparently unknown except in this
passage); and a doubling of a letter
is an easy error. For *gree* = *agree*
(a common form) see, e.g., II. vi 37. [R]

45. *pregnant*] extremely probable,
big with the consequence; one of
many figurative uses of the word.
Cf. *Othello*, II. i. 240: " Now, sir,
this granted, as it is a most *pregnant*
and unforced position," etc.

square] quarrel; as in *M.N.D.*
II. i. 30, where Mr. Cuningham
cites Cotgrave, " *Se quarrer*; to
strout, or square it, looke big on't,
carrie his armes a-kemboll bragga-
dochio-like," which shows how this
sense became attached to the word.
Cf. H. Gifford, *A Posie of Gilloflowers*,
1580 (p. 103, Grosart's reprint):—

" When men doe *square* for every
        fly,
    To make them friends the women
        runne," etc.

48. *cement*] accented as commonly
(*cément*). Cf. Massinger, *The Unnatural Combat*, I. i:—

" Being made up again and
        cemented
With a son's blood "

and Donne, *The Extasie*, lines 5, 6:—

" Our hands were firmly cimented
    With a fast balme, which thence
        did spring."

Be't as our gods will have't! It only stands   50
Our lives upon to use our strongest hands.
Come, Menas.   [*Exeunt.*

[SCENE II.—*Rome.   The house of Lepidus.*]

Enter ENOBARBUS *and* LEPIDUS.

Lep. Good Enobarbus, 'tis a worthy deed,
 And shall become you well, to entreat your captain
 To soft and gentle speech.
Eno.   I shall entreat him
 To answer like himself: if Cæsar move him,
 Let Antony look over Cæsar's head,   5
 And speak as loud as Mars. By Jupiter,
 Were I the wearer of Antonius' beard,
 I would not shave't to-day.
Lep.   'Tis not a time
 For private stomaching.
Eno.   Every time
 Serves for the matter that is then born in't.   10
Lep. But small to greater matters must give way.
Eno. Not if the small come first.
Lep.   Your speech is passion:

Scene II

7. *Antonius'*] Steevens (1773); Anthonio's F.

50, 51. *stands Our lives upon*] is a
matter of life and death; cf. *Errors*,
IV. i. 68, " Consider how it stands
upon my credit." The more usual
sense is *be incumbent on*, as in *Hamlet*,
v. ii. 63.

Scene II

8. *I . . . shave't*] i.e. I would not
remove the temptation to pluck or
shake it, if he dare. Cf. *Lear*, III.
vii. 76, 77:—
 " If you did wear a beard upon
  your chin,
 I'd *shake* it in this quarrel ";
Hamlet, IV. vii. 32, etc. My interpretation conflicts with the accepted one
(Johnson's), which imports that the
speaker would not even show Cæsar
the respect of a shorn chin. This is
too tame for what precedes.

9. *private stomaching*] indulgence of
personal resentments or dislikes. See
on III. iv. 12 *post*, and cf. the verb
in *Ralph Roister Doister*, IV. iii. 34:—
 " And where ye halfe *stomaked* this
  gentleman afore,
 For this same letter, ye wyll love
  hym now therefore," etc.

12. *Your speech is passion*] You are
letting your feelings run away with
you.

But, pray you, stir no embers up.　Here comes
The noble Antony.

Enter ANTONY *and* VENTIDIUS.

Eno.　　　　　　　And yonder, Cæsar.

Enter CÆSAR, MÆCENAS, *and* AGRIPPA.

Ant.　If we compose well here, to Parthia:　　　15
　　Hark, Ventidius.
Cæs.　　　　　　　I do not know,
　　Mæcenas; ask Agrippa.
Lep.　　　　　　　Noble friends,
　　That which combin'd us was most great, and let not
　　A leaner action rend us.　What's amiss,
　　May it be gently heard.　When we debate　　20
　　Our trivial difference loud, we do commit
　　Murther in healing wounds.　Then, noble partners,
　　The rather for I earnestly beseech,
　　Touch you the sourest points with sweetest terms,
　　Nor curstness grow to the matter.
Ant.　　　　　　　'Tis spoken well. 25
　　Were we before our armies, and to fight,
　　I should do thus.　　　　　　　　[*Flourish.*

---

15. *compose*] come to an agreement.
Cf. *composition*, II. vi. 58 *post*, and
Jonson, *The New Inn*, IV. iv. 86:—
"*Compose* with them, and be not
　　angry valiant."
14-17. As Antony and Cæsar come
in, by different doors, each is in
brisk conversation with his own
friends till interrupted by Lepidus.
17-25. *Noble friends*, etc.] "the
frendes of both parties would not
suffer them to unrippe any old
matters," etc. See North, *post*, p. 265.
21, 22. *commit . . . wounds*] A
surgeon may handle trifling wounds
—which would heal themselves if
left alone—so clumsily as to cause
death.

25. *Nor curstness . . . matter*] "Let
not *ill-humour* be added to the real
subject of our difference" (Johnson).
Cf. Puttenham, *Arte of English Poesie*,
1589, III. xix (Arber's reprint, p. 209
[cited in *O.E.D.*]): "With spitefull
speach, *curstnesse* and crueltie";
Mabbe's *Celestina*, 1631, ix (Tudor
Trans., p. 168) : "There is . . . not
any that can indure their tartnesse
and *curstnesse*," etc.　Ladies who
have maid-servants are here the
offenders.
27. *I . . . thus*] Some welcoming
action or embrace must be understood here, unless Antony is merely
asserting that his words would be
temperate in any event.

Cæs. Welcome to Rome.
Ant.   Thank you.
Cæs.   Sit.
Ant.   Sit, sir.
Cæs.   Nay, then.
Ant. I learn, you take things ill which are not so:
Or being, concern you not.
Cæs.   I must be laugh'd at,   30
If or for nothing, or a little, I
Should say myself offended, and with you
Chiefly i' the world: more laugh'd at, that I should
Once name you derogately, when to sound
Your name it not concern'd me.
Ant.   My being in Egypt,
Cæsar, what was't to you?   36
Cæs. No more than my residing here at Rome
Might be to you in Egypt: yet if you there
Did practise on my state, your being in Egypt
Might be my question.
Ant.   How intend you, practis'd?   40
Cæs. You may be pleas'd to catch at mine intent
By what did here befall me.   Your wife and brother
Made wars upon me, and their contestation
Was theme for you, you were the word of war.

44. *theme*] F 3;   *theame* F;   *theam'd* Warburton;   *then* (*thenne*) Deighton (*Old Dramatists*, 1898).

28. *Sit . . . Nay, then*] † Steevens and Johnson both detected in this interchange a resentment on Antony's part at Cæsar's arrogating to himself the right to give Antony his gracious permission to be seated. But surely Malone was right in seeing in it no more than an exchange of " After you " courtesies, which Cæsar, anxious to get on with business, terminates by yielding. [R]

34. *derogately*] in a detracting manner, with disparagement. The sole instance of the word in *O.E.D.*

39. *practise on*] plot or intrigue against, as in *Lear*, III. ii. 57. Common in this and the sense " craftily play upon," as in *Much Ado*, II. i. 401.

40. *my question*] " my business," " a matter that I should particularly enquire into " (Beckett).

42, 43. *Your wife . . . me*] See North, *post*, p. 264.

44. *Was theme for you*] The sense accepted as *intended* by Shakespeare is that conveyed in Staunton's conjecture, *Had you for theme*, i.e. was about *you:* and is also implied in Johnson's *Had theme for you* or *You were theme for*, Malone's *Was them'd from you*, and in other conjectures. Malone argues the necessity of this meaning, and consequent existence

Ant. You do mistake your business, my brother never　45
　　Did urge mè in his act: I did inquire it,
　　And have my learning from some true reports
　　That drew their swords with you. Did he not rather
　　Discredit my authority with yours,
　　And make the wars alike against my stomach,　50
　　Having alike your cause? Of this, my letters
　　Before did satisfy you. If you'll patch a quarrel,
　　As matter whole you have to make it with,
　　It must not be with this.

53. *you have to make*] F; *you have to take* F 2; *you have not to make* Rowe (*you've*) and most edd.

of corruption, from what immediately follows. If, however, we are to stand by the text, it is possible to connect *Was theme for you* with *practise* instead, making the words *You were the word of war* confirmatory or evidential rather than explanatory, and punctuating accordingly. (F has a comma after *for you.*) In this event, Cæsar says : " By ' practised ' I mean that their quarrel with me supplied you with a theme to work upon, a ground for your intrigues, *witness as proof* the use of your name in the war." Antony deals at once and solely with the *proof* of practice (which my supposition would confine to these last words) without troubling himself to deny the *charge* of practice which depends on it. Steevens quotes *Coriolanus*, I. i. 226 : " throw forth greater *themes* For insurrections' arguing," and perhaps was not far wrong in explaining our text : " Was proposed as an example for you to follow on a yet more extensive plan, as *themes* are given for a writer to dilate upon."
　† After all which, is there not much to be said for Deighton's straightforward emendation? [R]
　word of war] Cf. III. i. 31 *post*, and *R. III.* v. iii. 350 : " Our ancient word of courage, fair Saint George," etc.
　46. *Did urge . . . act*] Represented his wars as waged in my cause, made

capital of my name in the war. Cf. *The Weakest Goeth to the Wall*, II. ii. 55 (Hazlitt's *Webster*, IV. 245) : " I trust you will not *urge me* in the matter," where the speaker deprecates being cited as the source of certain information.
　47. *reports*] reporters. See on *discontents*, I. iv. 39 *ante*.
　49. *Discredit*] i.e. Bring into discredit, as in *M. for M.* IV. ii. 30.
　with] along with.
　50. *stomach*] inclination. Cf. *The Tempest*, II. i. 113 :—
　　" You cram these words into mine
　　　ears against
　　The *stomach* of my sense."
　51. *Having . . . cause*] Since I had as much cause to resent them as you. So I understand the words, but the usual explanation (Steevens's and Malone's) is = Since I was engaged in the same cause with you.
　53. *as matter whole you have*] † Rowe emended *you have* to *you've not* and Capell to *you have not*, and almost all editors since have accepted this insertion of the negative, including Case (though in a balanced note he gave a selection of argument on the other side), and Dover Wilson (surprisingly, since in his glossary he gives a sense for *as* which seems to make needless, if not to preclude, the insertion).

Cæs.   You praise yourself,
By laying defects of judgment to me; but   55
You patch'd up your excuses.

Ant.   Not so, not so;
I know you could not lack, I am certain on't,
Very necessity of this thought, that I,
Your partner in the cause 'gainst which he fought,
Could not with graceful eyes attend those wars   60
Which fronted mine own peace. As for my wife,
I would you had her spirit in such another;
The third o' the world is yours, which with a snaffle

60. *graceful*] F; *grateful* Pope.

The case for the retention of F's reading is, I think, much simpler than one would suppose from the tortuous ingenuity of many of the arguments used to support it. There are two crucial points, the first purely linguistic, namely, what does *as* mean in this context, the second more general, namely, what sense is demanded by the general drift of the whole passage, lines 29-98. As to *as*, there is a section in *O.E.D. sub voc.* B. II. 8d, which is exactly apposite (more exactly, I think, than that cited by Dover Wilson, which is B. I. 3b) " In antithetical or parallel clauses, introducing a known circumstance with which a hypothesis is contrasted; . . . whereas. *Hamlet*, v. ii. 347, Had I but time (as this fell sergeant death is strick'd in his Arrest)." The *Hamlet* parallel seems to me wholly convincing. As to the more general point, Antony, if we accept this meaning of *as*, is saying in effect " If you will insist on patching a quarrel, even when you have whole cloth to cut it from, this particular patch will not serve your turn." And that seems to me exactly in line with Antony's general tactics in the scene, which are worth watching, and have not always been watched. He knows from the start that on one point, and one only, — the " arms and aid " of line 88—

Cæsar has an irrefutable case, and on that point he is prepared to " play the penitent." But he would prefer to come to this main point at once, and not waste time over accusations which he can either flatly deny, or deal with by a plea of ignorance, or dismiss as trivial. It is just worth notice that when Cæsar does come to the main point, the " article of the oath," Antony is impatient of interruption. [R]

55. *laying . . . but*] † As the line stands it is impossible to throw the apparently required emphasis on to *me*. Capell therefore printed the line as *By laying to me defects of judgement; but*. It is to be noticed that F, giving what precedes and follows as verse, prints this speech alone as prose, which perhaps suggests some confusion in the manuscript. [R]

60. *with graceful . . . attend*] favourably regard. The only instance of *graceful* in this sense in *O.E.D.*
† And *c: t* with Elizabethan script is an easy error, so that Pope was very probably right. [R]

61. *fronted*] opposed. Cf. I. iv. 79 *ante*.

62. *her spirit*] See North, *post*, pp. 258-9, 265.

63. *snaffle*] Flecknoe, *Heroick Portraits* (1660), sig. H *verso*, uses this figure from horsemanship in speaking of the subjects of Charles I *as*

> You may pace easy, but not such a wife.
>
> *Eno.* Would we had all such wives, that the men might   65
> go to wars with the women!
>
> *Ant.* So much uncurbable, her garboils, Cæsar,
> Made out of her impatience, which not wanted
> Shrewdness of policy too, I grieving grant
> Did you too much disquiet: for that you must   70
> But say, I could not help it.
>
> *Cæs.*   I wrote to you,
> When rioting in Alexandria you
> Did pocket up my letters; and with taunts
> Did gibe my missive out of audience.
>
> *Ant.*   Sir,
> He fell upon me, ere admitted, then: 75
> Three kings I had newly feasted, and did want
> Of what I was i' the morning; but next day
> I told him of myself, which was as much
> As to have ask'd him pardon. Let this fellow
> Be nothing of our strife; if we contend,   80
> Out of our question wipe him.
>
> *Cæs.*   You have broken
> The article of your oath, which you shall never
> Have tongue to charge me with.
>
> *Lep.*   Soft, Cæsar!
>
> *Ant.* No, Lepidus, let him speak;

---

75. *admitted, then:*] F; *admitted: then*] Rowe.

" onely rid with a *snaffle*, and gentle hand."

64. *pace*] train; cf. *Pericles*, IV. vi. 68-70, " My lord, she's not paced yet; you must take some pains to work her to your manage."

65, 66. *that the men . . . women*] Probably purposely ambiguous. The lines have always been printed as prose.

67. *garboils*] See on I. iii. 61 *ante*.

71, 72. *I . . . you*] The punctuation (Lloyd conj.) is substantially that of the folio. I agree with Mr. Thiselton in thinking it no improvement to read with modern editors :—

" I wrote to you

When rioting in Alexandria; you ".

74. *missive*] messenger. So in *Macbeth*, I. v. 7, Macbeth's letter speaks of Ross and Angus as " missives from the king." For Antony's action, see note on I. i. 52.

75. *admitted, then:*] † Rowe's emendation is an example of needless tinkering with F's punctuation. " Transposed pointing " is always possible, but why assume it here? Antony's *then* is contrasted with *next day*, when the messenger was admitted in proper form. [R]

80. *Be nothing of*] Have no place in.

82. *article*] precise terms.

The honour is sacred which he talks on now,   85
Supposing that I lack'd it.   But on, Cæsar,
The article of my oath.

Cæs.   To lend me arms and aid when I requir'd them,
The which you both denied.

Ant.   Neglected, rather;
And then when poisoned hours had bound me up
From mine own knowledge; as nearly as I may,
I'll play the penitent to you.   But mine honesty
Shall not make poor my greatness, nor my power
Work without it.   Truth is, that Fulvia,
To have me out of Egypt, made wars here,   95
For which myself, the ignorant motive, do
So far ask pardon, as befits mine honour
To stoop in such a case.

Lep.   'Tis noble spoken.

Mæc.   If it might please you, to enforce no further
The griefs between ye: to forget them quite   100
Were to remember that the present need
Speaks to atone you.

Lep.   Worthily spoken, Mæcenas.

85, 86. *The honour . . . it*] Malone is probably right in his view of " Supposing," etc., which governs his (the usual) interpretation of the passage : " The theme of honour which he now speaks of, namely, the religion of an oath, for which he supposes me not to have a due regard, is sacred ; it is a tender point, and touches my character nearly. Let him therefore urge his charge, that I may vindicate myself." Yet in what follows, Antony practically admits that his honour slept in poisoned hours, and the following sense seems not impossible : " He is speaking of an undeniable point of honour, even supposing mine failed me."

90, 91. *bound . . . knowledge*] drugged me so that I was not myself.

94. *without it*] " without mine honesty." So Malone, on whose side is,

perhaps, the accentuation of *it*. It may be a question, however, whether he and others do not too readily identify *power* with *greatness*. Perhaps *it* refers to greatness, and Antony declines to exert his *power*, except his *greatness* in no respect suffer diminution, either by his stooping too far or by the way in which his admissions are taken.

95. *To have . . . here*] See North, *post*, p. 265.

98. *noble*] Adjective as adverb. Very common. Cf. *J.C.* v. i. 60.

100. *griefs*] grievances ; a frequent sense. Cf. *J.C.* I. iii. 118.

102. *atone*] make at one, reconcile, as in *Cymbeline*, I. iv. 44. So Jonson, *The Silent Woman*, IV. v. 165 : " Nay, if he had been cool enough to tell us that, there had been some hope to *atone* you."

Eno. Or if you borrow one another's love for the instant,
     you may, when you hear no more words of Pompey,
     return it again: you shall have time to wrangle in,   105
     when you have nothing else to do.
Ant. Thou art a soldier only, speak no more.
Eno. That truth should be silent, I had almost forgot.
Ant. You wrong this presence, therefore speak no more.
Eno. Go to, then: your considerate stone.   110
Cæs. I do not much dislike the matter, but
     The manner of his speech; for't cannot be
     We shall remain in friendship, our conditions
     So differing in their acts. Yet, if I knew
     What hoop should hold us staunch from edge to
       edge   115
     O' the world, I would pursue it.
Agr.   Give me leave, Cæsar.
Cæs. Speak, Agrippa.

107. *soldier only,*] *soldier only;* Theobald; *Souldier, onely* F.   115, 116. *staunch from . . . world,*] F; *staunch, from . . . world* Pope.

108. *That truth,* etc.] Cf. *Lear,* I. iv. 124: " *Truth's* a dog must to kennel." Grey quotes Ray's *Proverbs*: "All *truth* must not be told at all times."

109. *presence*] august company; as often in Shakespeare. Cf. *Ancient Popular and Romance Poetry of Scotland* (ed. Laing and Small, 1885), xvii. 18:—

  " The God of most magnificence,
  Conserf this high *presens,*" etc.

110. *your considerate stone*] Much needless tinkering here began with Johnson's *You considerate ones*. With the metaphor, compare Steevens's excellent examples (1821 Variorum), e.g. *Titus Andronicus,* III. i. 46: "A *stone* is silent, and offendeth not"; *Jacob and Esau* [1568, IV. vi. 18-23, Hazlitt's *Dodsley,* ii. 237]: "Bring thou in thine, Mido, and see thou be a *stone. Mido.* A *stone?* how should that be, mistress? . . . *Rebecca.* I meant thou shouldest nothing say"; or a new one from Beaumont and

Fletcher, *The Captain,* IV. iv (Camb. v. 297):—

  " Think she is a *stone.*
  She is a kind of bawdy confessor,
  And will not utter secrets."

Considerate is here = considering, reflective, as in *R. III.* IV. ii. 30:—

  " none are for me
  That look into me with *considerate* eyes";

D'Avenant, *Gondibert* (1651), II. ii. 10: " on whose *considerate* brow, Sixtie experienc'd summers he discern'd." Enobarbus obviously means: Very well; have me dumb, but reflective, i.e. none the less aware that your friendship will be hollow. *Consideration* occurs in IV. ii. 45 *post.*

113. *conditions*] dispositions, as often. Cf. *Lear,* IV. iii. 35.

115. *What hoop . . . staunch*] Steevens quotes *2 H. IV.* IV. iv. 43: "A *hoop* of gold to bind thy brothers in." See also *Hamlet,* I. iii. 63.

H

Agr. Thou hast a sister by the mother's side,
Admir'd Octavia ? Great Mark Antony
Is now a widower.

Cæs.   Say not so, Agrippa: 120
If Cleopatra heard you, your reproof
Were well deserv'd of rashness.

Ant. I am not married, Cæsar: let me hear
Agrippa further speak.

Agr. To hold you in perpetual amity,   125
To make you brothers, and to knit your hearts
With an unslipping knot, take Antony
Octavia to his wife; whose beauty claims
No worse a husband than the best of men;
Whose virtue, and whose general graces, speak   130
That which none else can utter. By this marriage,
All little jealousies which now seem great,

120. *not so,*] Rowe; *not, say* F.   121. *reproof*] Hanmer (Warburton
conj.); *proofe* F; *approof* Theobald.

118. *Thou hast,* etc.] For hence to
line 170, see North, *post,* p. 265.

118. *sister by . . . side*] Octavia was
the emperor's own sister, daughter of
C. Octavius and his second wife,
Atia. An elder sister, daughter of
Ancharia, and also named Octavia,
is given to Antony by Plutarch (see
post, p. 265), but this does not
account for Shakespeare's "sister
by the mother's side" as some
appear to fancy.

119. *Octavia?*] † I think that F's
question mark may well be retained,
though it has been almost universally
changed to exclamation mark or
semicolon. Agrippa's is a half-
rhetorical question—" you can't have
forgotten that. . . ." [R]

121, 122. *your reproof . . . rashness*]
Abbott (*Shakespearian Grammar,* § 423)
thinks we have here a case of the pro-
nominal adjective being placed before
the first of two nouns connected by *of,*
and that, therefore, *your reproof* connected with *of rashness* is used " where
we should say, ' the reproof of your
rashness ' (unless ' of ' here means

' about,' ' for ')." The latter alternative, or that *of* = *by* or as a consequence of, seems far more likely in
view of the position of the nouns.
Cf. II. iii. 26 *post.*

your reproof] † It is tempting to
guess that what the compositor
found in front of him was *yourreproofe,*
which he read as *youre proofe,* and
regularized the *youre* to *your,* which is
the normal F spelling. But the temptation must, I think, be resisted,
however easy it makes the emendation.
There is no evidence, so far as I know,
that Shakespeare normally wrote
youre, and some that he did not.
Writers of an earlier generation,
like More, naturally wrote the word
with the final *e,* but by Shakespeare's
time this spelling was fading out
(and for what it is worth the spelling
in the " three pages " of *Sir Thomas
More* is not even *your* but *yor*). The
compositor, therefore, accustomed
to *your* or *yor* would naturally break
the hypothetically run-together words
after *your* and not after *yourre.*
Possibly it was an auditory error. [R]

And all great fears, which now import their dangers,
Would then be nothing: truths would be tales,
Where now half tales be truths: her love to both   135
Would each to other and all loves to both
Draw after her.   Pardon what I have spoke,
For 'tis a studied, not a present thought,
By duty ruminated.

Ant.   Will Cæsar speak?

Cæs. Not till he hears how Antony is touch'd,   140
With what is spoke already.

Ant.   What power is in Agrippa,
If I would say, " Agrippa, be it so,"
To make this good?

Cæs.   The power of Cæsar, and
His power unto Octavia.

Ant.   May I never
To this good purpose, that so fairly shows,   145
Dream of impediment!   Let me have thy hand
Further this act of grace: and from this hour,
The heart of brothers govern in our loves,
And sway our great designs!

Cæs.   There's my hand.
A sister I bequeath you, whom no brother   150

134, 135. *truths*] F 3; *truth's* F.   146, 147. *hand Further*] F; *hand; Further*
Theobald and most edd.   See note.   149. *There's*] F; *There is* Theobald.

133. *import*] carry with them, in-   believed, *or* deprive even true ones
volve. Cf. *Lear,* IV. iii. 5 : " which   of significance.
imports to the kingdom so much   135. *both*] †? *each.* [R]
fear and danger."   138. *present*] on the spur of the
134. *truths . . . tales*] Cf. Yarington, moment.
Two Lamentable Tragedies, 1601 (Bul-   144-6. *May . . . impediment*] Cf.
len's *Old Plays,* iv. p. 9) : " Would   Sonnet cxvi :—
Truth were false, so this were but a   " Let me not to the marriage of
tale!"   Pope read *but tales,* and   true minds
various other insertions before *tales*   Admit *impediments.*"
have been proposed, for want of   146, 147. *hand Further*] † A good
appreciating the metrical force   example of a tinkering with F's
of the pause.   The sense is that   punctuation which destroys the in-
whereas, under present circumstances,   tended sense.   Antony means " I hope
reports only partially true are   your hand-clasp will ratify this act of
credited [and cause distrust], this   grace."   For this use of " have " cf.
marriage would make even true   *Othello,* v. ii. 87 : " I would not
ones [of a disturbing nature] dis-   have thee linger in thy pain."   [R]

Did ever love so dearly.   Let her live
To join our kingdoms, and our hearts, and never
Fly off our loves again!

Lep.   Happily, amen!

Ant. I did not think to draw my sword 'gainst Pompey,
For he hath laid strange courtesies and great   155
Of late upon me: I must thank him only,
Lest my remembrance suffer ill report;
At heel of that, defy him.

Lep.   Time calls upon's,
Of us must Pompey presently be sought,
Or else he seeks out us.

Ant.   Where lies he?   160

Cæs. About the Mount Misena.

Ant.   What is his strength?

Cæs. By land, great, and increasing: but by sea
He is an absolute master.

Ant.   So is the fame.
Would we had spoke together!   Haste we for it,
Yet ere we put ourselves in arms, despatch we   165
The business we have talk'd of.

---

162. Cæs. *By land*] Hanmer; see note.

153. *Fly off*] Cf. *Lear*, II. iv. 91:
"The images of revolt and *flying off*":
R. Flecknoe, *Heroick Portraits* (1660),
sig. F 2: "and if you deceive them
when it comes to the push indeed,
and *fly off*, shrink, frown," etc.

157. *remembrance*] memory for favours.

159. *presently*] immediately, as
commonly. Cf. Pepys's *Diary*, 7 May
1660: "This morning Captain Cut-
tance sent me 12 bottles of Margate
ale. Three of them I drank *presently*
with some friends," etc.; also North,
post, p. 264.

161. *Mount Misena*] As North (see
post, p. 266) has "the Mount of
Misena," Shakespeare certainly did
not write "Misenum," as corrected
by Rowe and successive editors.

161. † The Hanmer emendation
seems to me almost as certain as
such things can be, though it has
had few followers. F reads "*Anth.*
What is his strength by land?
Cæsar. Great, and increasing. . . ."
But Antony was not likely to narrow
the scope of his question to the
enemy's land forces, whereas the two
abrupt questions from him, with
Cæsar's itemized reply to the second,
seem to me much more effective and
more in character. [R]

164. *spoke together*] joined battle.
Cf. II. vi. 25 *post*, and *Coriolanus*,
I. iv. 4. † But I think Dover Wilson
undoubtedly right that Antony's *we*
means not himself and Pompey, but
himself and Cæsar. "If only we
had had a chance of consultation,
this danger from Pompey would
never have arisen." [R]

Cæs.   With most gladness,
    And do invite you to my sister's view,
    Whither straight I'll lead you.
Ant.   Let us, Lepidus,
    Not lack your company.
Lep.   Noble Antony,
    Not sickness should detain me.   170

[*Flourish. Exeunt all but Enobarbus, Agrippa, and Mæcenas.*

Mæc. Welcome from Egypt, sir.
Eno. Half the heart of Cæsar, worthy Mæcenas! My
    honourable friend Agrippa!
Agr. Good Enobarbus!
Mæc. We have cause to be glad, that matters are so 175
    well disgested.   You stay'd well by 't in Egypt.
Eno. Ay, sir, we did sleep day out of countenance; and
    made the night light with drinking.
Mæc. Eight wild-boars roasted whole at a breakfast, and
    but twelve persons there; is this true?   180
Eno. This was but as a fly by an eagle: we had much
    more monstrous matter of feast, which worthily
    deserved noting.
Mæc. She's a most triumphant lady, if report be
    square to her.   185

170. Exeunt . . .] Capell ; Exit omnes.   Manet Enobarbus, Agrippa,
Mecenas. F.

166. *most*] the greatest, as in *1 H.
VI.* iv. i. 38 : "But always resolute
in *most* extremes"; Googe, *Eglogs*,
1563 (Arber's repr., p. 126) : "Syth
that the *most* misfortune nowe," etc.
167. *do*] I do. So in *Lear*, v. i. 68,
shall = they shall.
172. *Half . . . Cæsar*] Beloved of
Cæsar. Deighton: "the translation
of a Latin poetical phrase used by
Horace of Vergil, *Odes*, i. iii. 8:
animæ dimidium meæ."
176. *stay'd well by't*] † Not, I think,
so obvious as the silence of most
commentators suggests that it is.
Dover Wilson's reference to *Coriolanus*,
II. ii. 176 is not very helpful, since

"stay'd by him" there need mean
no more than "continued to fight
him." Onions gives "kept things
going." I think it means "you stuck
well to your guns" or, almost with the
racing sense of *stay*, "your stamina
must have been pretty good." [R]
177, 178. Day was disconcerted by
being treated as night, and night
made light in a two-fold sense, i.e.
bright, and either of light behaviour
or light-headed.
179. *Eight wild-boars*] See North,
post, p. 263.
181. *by*] compared with.
184. *square*] just; cf. *T. of A.* v. iv.
36.

Eno. When she first met Mark Antony, she purs'd up
　his heart upon the river of Cydnus.
Agr. There she appear'd indeed; or my reporter
　devis'd well for her.
Eno. I will tell you.   190
　　　The barge she sat in, like a burnish'd throne
　　　Burn'd on the water: the poop was beaten gold;
　　　Purple the sails, and so perfumed that
　　　The winds were love-sick with them; the oars were
　　　　　silver,
　　　Which to the tune of flutes kept stroke, and made 195
　　　The water which they beat to follow faster,
　　　As amorous of their strokes.　For her own person,
　　　It beggar'd all description: she did lie
　　　In her pavilion—cloth of gold, of tissue—

---

187. *Cydnus*] F 2; *Sidnis* F.
pointing; *love-sicke.　With them the* F.

194. *love-sick with them: the*] Pope's

---

187. *Cydnus*] The river of Cilicia on
which Tarsus is situated.　For the
rest of the scene, see North, *post*,
p. 262.　Mason thinks it due to
negligence that Antony is represented as captivated by Cleopatra
on *Cydnus*, he being all the time in
the market-place (line 215), nay,
we may add, being made to yield
up his heart later at supper (line 225).
But in the mind of Enobarbus, " the
quick forge " already glowing with
the task before it, I think Antony
was already won on *Cydnus*: and,
undoubtedly, knowing Antony as he
did, he must have reckoned him as
good as won when he saw what he
reports.　Indeed, the emotions of
Antony—left in the magically dis-
peopled city—would carry him far
on the road to love.

188. *There . . . indeed*] Dover Wilson,
very reasonably, " suspects an omission, perhaps of ' triumphantly ' or
' in triumph '."

devis'd] invented; " *devis'd* well
for her " may contain the sense,
invented a fine description of her.

191, 192. *The barge . . . Burn'd*]

Cf. Fairfax's Tasso, *Godfrey of Bulloigne* (1600), XVI. iv, of a representation of the battle of Actium :—
　" The waters *burnt* about their
　　　vessels good,
　　Such flames the gold therein en-
　　　chased threw," etc.

199. *cloth of gold, of tissue*] One of
the two current explanations, viz.,
" cloth of gold in tissue or texture,"
may, I think, be dismissed; for, like
" of Damaske " in " his grace was
apparelled in a garment of Clothe of
Silver, of Damaske, ribbed with Cloth
of Golde, so thicke as might bee "
(Hall's *Chronicle*, 1548, Henry VIII.
xii. yere, f. lxxvi), " *of tissue* " added
to the otherwise sufficient " *cloth of
gold* " must denote something, in view
of the independent existence of *tissue*
and *cloth of tissue*: whether the inter-
mixture of coloured silks, or else quality, depending on the number of
threads in the warp.　Cf. " Which sat
behynde a traues of sylke fyne *Of
golde of tessew*, the fynest that might
be " (Skelton, *Bouge of Court*, prologue, st. 9), and the following
definitions: " *Tissu* of the French

O'er-picturing that Venus where we see   200
The fancy outwork nature. On each side her,
Stood pretty dimpled boys, like smiling Cupids,
With divers-colour'd fans, whose wind did seem
To glow the delicate cheeks which they did cool,
And what they undid did.

Agr.   O, rare for Antony!   205

204. *glow*] Rowe; *gloue* F; *glove* F 2.   205. *undid did*] F; *did, undid*
Johnson conj.; *undy'd, dy'd* Staunton.

Tissu, i.e. woven cloth of Tissu, with us cloth of silke and silver, or of silver and gold woven together" (Minshew, *Guide to the Tongues,* 1617) ; " *Tissue,* made of three threads of divers colours of Tissue " (*ibid.*): " to weave cloth *of tissue* with twisted threads both in woofe and warp, and the same in sundry colours was the invention of Alexandria," etc. (Mr. Craig from Holland's *Pliny,* Bk. VIII, chap. xlviii, pt. i, p. 228, ed. 1634).

The other explanation current is Staunton's, " *cloth of gold* on a ground *of tissue,*" which suggests no objection save that the reversal of the positions of *gold* and *tissue* is possible, indeed probable, judging by the frequency of examples. Cf. " in a coate of rich *tyssue* cut on cloth of silver " (Hall's *Chronicle,* 1548, Henry VIII, year ix. f. lxv) ; " This gold-ground *Tissue* " (Sylvester's *Du Bartas,* ed. 1621, p. 442, week 2, day 4, bk. ii. line 22) ; " With gold-ground Velvets, and with silver *Tissue* " (*ibid.* p. 71, week 1, day 3, line 1181). Shakespeare had the phrase from North (see *post,* p. 262), now first supported by other instances : " The Kyng of Englande mounted on a freshe courser, the trapper of *clothe of golde, of Tissue* " (Hall, as before, xii yere, f. lxxviii; I owe this reference to Mr. Craig); " The aultars of the Chapell were hanged with riche revesture of *clothe of golde, of Tissue,* Embroidered with pearles " (*ibid.* f. lxxiii). The Collier MS. correction, " *cloth of gold, and tissue,*"

was therefore needless, though the phrase apparently occurs. See Nichols, *Progresses of James I* (1828), ii. 550.

200, 201. *O'er-picturing . . . nature*] Surpassing the picture of Venus in which artistic imagination has out-done nature. Warburton (whose suggestion is still frequently quoted) has : " Meaning the Venus of Protogenes, mentioned by Pliny, l. xxxv, c. x " ; but as Pliny records no Venus by Protogenes we must surely substitute that of Apelles (Pliny, *Nat. Hist.* lib. xxxv. 36 [x]), whose famous Venus Anadyomene was inferentially said to outdo nature in the poetical assertion that Juno and Pallas would contend no further for the prize of beauty if they saw her. Sylvester says that certain works of art, including Apelles' Venus, " Are proofs enow that learned Painting can, [*sic*] Can (Goddess-like) another Nature frame " (*Du Bartas,* week 1, day 6, 1621, ed. p. 133). North has merely : " apparelled and attired like the goddesse Venus, commonly drawen in picture." Theobald had correctly referred to Apelles' Venus.

203-5. *fans . . . undid did*] According to the syntax the *fans* cooled or " undid " heat, their *wind* seemed to produce it, or " did " the reverse of the action; but the imagination readily identifies the fans with the wind and makes it equally un-necessary to read *winds* or refer *they* to *boys* (line 202). Helen, in Venus'

Eno. Her gentlewomen, like the Nereides,
　　So many mermaids, tended her i' the eyes,
　　And made their bends adornings.　At the helm
　　A seeming mermaid steers: the silken tackle
　　Swell with the touches of those flower-soft hands,　210
　　That yarely frame the office.　From the barge
　　A strange invisible perfume hits the sense
　　Of the adjacent wharfs.　The city cast
　　Her people out upon her; and Antony,
　　Enthron'd i' the market-place, did sit alone,　215
　　Whistling to the air; which, but for vacancy,

209. *tackle*] F; *tackles* F 2.

Show (Peele, *The Arraignment of Paris*, II. i. 79), has " four Cupids attending on her, each having his *fan* in his hand to fan fresh air in her face."

206, 207. *Nereides . . . mermaids*] As Steevens observed, the fifty daughters of Nereus and Doris, divinities of the Ægean Sea, were unlike mermaids in having complete human shapes.

207. *tended her i' the eyes*] waited in her sight, i.e. were not just a group of attendants in the background. The following new example seems especially to favour this common interpretation : Chapman translates " Flos Asiae ante ipsum " (Juvenal, *Sat.* v. line 56) by " *In his eye* waits the flower of Asia," where the intention is to contrast a rich host's personal attendant with the rude slaves who minister to his guests. Steevens quotes *Hamlet*, IV. iv. 6 : " We shall express our duty *in his eye*." See also *M.N.D.* III. i. 172 : " Hop in his walks and gambol *in his eyes*."

208. *made . . . bends adornings*] † There are five close-packed pages of selected comments on this and the preceding line in the Furness Variorum, from which we learn, amongst many other things, that the *bends* are Cleopatra's eyebrows, which the attendants are " adjusting," or, alternatively, the thickest outer planks of

the ship's side ; while the *eyes* are either the hawse-holes or " dead-eyes." I am not clear what all the pother is about, and one quotation from Drayton, given by Case, seems to me almost decisive in favour of the obvious meaning : *Mortimeriados* (slightly varied in *The Barons' Wars*, vi) :—

　" The naked nymphs, some up,
　　　some downe descending,
　　Small scattering flowres one at
　　　another flung,
　　With pretty turns their lymber
　　　bodies bending."

Cleopatra's attendants, as they wait on her, fall into such graceful postures that they compose a lovely frame for the central figure. [R]

209. *tackle*] collective ; sails, ropes, etc.

211. *yarely*] readily, nimbly. So in *The Tempest*, I. i. 3 : " fall to't, *yarely*, or we run ourselves aground." *frame*] perform, manage. See *Lear*, I. ii. 109 ; Basse, *Works* (ed. Bond), p. 232 : " wish'd to *frame* these rites to you," etc.

213. *wharfs*] banks. So in *Hamlet*, I. v. 33 : " on Lethe *wharf*."

216. *but for vacancy*] except that it would have created a vacuum. " Alluding to an axiom in the peripatetic philosophy then in vogue, that *Nature abhors a vacuum* " (Warburton). Cf. Sylvester's *Du Bartas*,

Had gone to gaze on Cleopatra too,
And made a gap in nature.

Agr.   Rare Egyptian!

Eno. Upon her landing, Antony sent to her,
Invited her to supper: she replied,   220
It should be better he became her guest,
Which she entreated: our courteous Antony,
Whom ne'er the word of " No " woman heard speak,
Being barber'd ten times o'er, goes to the feast;
And for his ordinary, pays his heart,   225
For what his eyes eat only.

Agr.   Royal wench!
She made great Cæsar lay his sword to bed;
He plough'd her, and she cropp'd.

Eno.   I saw her once
Hop forty paces through the public street,
And having lost her breath, she spoke, and panted,   230
That she did make defect perfection,
And, breathless, power breathe forth.

232. *breathless, power breathe*] Pope; *breathless power breathe* F 3, 4; *breath-lesse powre breath* F; *breathlesse power breath* F 2.

p. 9, in ed. 1621 : " To all, so odious is *Vacuitie*."

225. *ordinary*] supper. The ordinary, or regular public dinner, was a very flourishing institution in Shakespeare's time, and a convenient centre for news-gathering, discussion, dicing, etc. For its humours, see Dekker, *The Gull's Hornbook*, 1609, chap. v, *How a yong Gallant should behaue himselfe in an Ordinary*. His instructions begin thus : " First, hauing diligently enquired out an Ordinary of the largest reckoning, whither most of your Courtly Gallants do resort, let it be your vse to repaire thither some halfe houre after eleuen; for then you shall find most of your fashionmongers planted in the roome waiting for meate."

227. *Cæsar*] See on II. vi. 68-70 *post*.

228. *cropp'd*] bore fruit. See North, *post*, p. 271, and North's *Julius*

Cæsar (Tud. Trans. v. 52): " Thereuppon Cæsar made Cleopatra his [the king's] sister Queene of Ægypt, who being great with childe by him, was shortly brought to bedde of a sonne, whom the Alexandrians named Cæsarion "; and *ibid.* in margin : " Cæsarion, Cæsars sonne, begotten of Cleopatra." Marston uses the word in a similar connection, but transitively, see 2 *Antonio and Mellida*, I. i. 26 :—

" He wan the ladie to my honours death,
And from her sweetes *cropt* this Antonio."

232. *power . . . forth*] did breathe forth charm, i.e. made her want of breath a source of fascination. F text yields rather Daniel's *pour breath forth*, and might forbid change, were the clause co-ordinate with *spoke, and panted*. But as a consequence of speaking and panting it is

Mæc. Now Antony must leave her utterly.

Eno. Never; he will not:

 Age cannot wither her, nor custom stale   235
 Her infinite variety: other women cloy
 The appetites they feed, but she makes hungry,
 Where most she satisfies. For vilest things
 Become themselves in her, that the holy priests
 Bless her, when she is riggish.   240

Mæc. If beauty, wisdom, modesty, can settle
 The heart of Antony, Octavia is
 A blessed lottery to him.

Agr.   Let us go.
 Good Enobarbus, make yourself my guest,
 Whilst you abide here.

Eno.   Humbly, sir, I thank you. 245

             [Exeunt.

[SCENE III.—*The same. Cæsar's house.*]

Enter ANTONY, CÆSAR, OCTAVIA *between them.*

Ant. The world, and my great office, will sometimes
 Divide me from your bosom.

Octa.   All which time
 Before the gods my knee shall bow my prayers
 To them for you.

---

238. *vilest*] F 4 and edd.; *vildest* F.

lame, and if = *sing* (Staunton, *Athenæum*, 1873, Apl. 12) becomes lamer.

234. *Never ; he will not*] †I have retained the accepted punctuation. But " he will not " is something of an anticlimax after the emphatic " never," and I suspect that F's unpunctuated reading, " Never he will not," with double negative, is right; or perhaps even more probably that " Never " and " he will not " were alternatives, neither of which was clearly marked for omission. [R]

238, 239. *for vilest . . . her*] Cf. I. iv. 21 *ante.*

240. *riggish*] wanton. So in Lane's *Tom Tel-Troth's Message*, etc., 1600 (New Shakespeare Soc. 1876), stanza 52 : " Their *riggish* heads must be adorned with tires," etc. The substantive *rig* = strumpet is common ; the verb (= to gad) occurs in Lyly's *Midas*, I. ii. 90.

243. *lottery*] allotment, prize. Similarly *lotteth* = allotteth : " Thee towns neglecting, that to hym set destenye lotteth " (Stanyhurst's *Virgil*, iv. [ed. Arber], p. 102) ; *lotted* = allotted : " thou didst spend thy lotted days " (*A Collection of Seventy-nine Black-letter Ballads*, etc., p. 264, Lilly, 1867).

Ant.   Good night, sir.   My Octavia,
Read not my blemishes in the world's report :   5
I have not kept my square, but that to come
Shall all be done by the rule.   Good night, dear lady.
Octa. Good night, sir.
Cæs. Good night.   [*Exeunt Cæsar and Octavia.*

Enter Soothsayer.

Ant.   Now, sirrah; you do wish yourself in Egypt?   10
Sooth. Would I had never come from thence, nor you
    Thither!
Ant.   If you can, your reason?
                                        I see it in
My motion, have it not in my tongue: but yet
Hie you to Egypt again.

Scene III

8. *Good night, sir*] see note.   9. Exeunt Cæsar and Octavia] Rowe;
Exit. F.

Scene III

6. *kept my square*] † Not, I think,
"kept within due bounds," as it is
sometimes explained, but "kept to
the straight line." The metaphor is
from a carpenter's set square, by
which a line can be ruled not only
straight but in the right relation to
another. Cf. *squier* (a common
Elizabethan form of *square*) meaning
a footrule, as in *1 H. IV.* II. ii. 14,
"four foot by the squire." [R]

7, 8. *Good night, dear lady. Good
night, sir*] † F gives both sentences to
Antony, so that Octavia has no farewell speech. F 2, almost certainly
rightly, gives *Good night, sir* to Octavia.
Antony has already said good night
to Cæsar in line 4. He now says
good night to Octavia, and both
Octavia and Cæsar reply. [R]

10. For remainder of scene, see
North, *post*, pp. 266-7.

12. *Thither*] † Mason boldly proposed to read "Hither," and F's
reading is undeniably awkward.
It makes the soothsayer regret

(*a*) that he ever left his own country,
and (*b*) that Antony had ever gone
to it. But the second regret, implying
that it is Antony's visit to Egypt
which has caused all the later trouble,
is not only quite irrelevant to his
line of argument, but contrary to it.
Antony's "demon" would have
been just as much subdued by Cæsar's
if he had stayed in Rome, and the
only hope for him is to get back to
Egypt as soon as may be. It would
be just possible to retain F's words,
but repunctuate

Would I had never come from
    thence, nor you.
Thither!

making "Thither" a command.
But though "Thither again" would
serve well enough, and be picked up
by "Hie you to Egypt again,"
"Thither" by itself is a weak word
to take the necessary stress. [R]

12, 13. *in My motion*] in the in-
voluntary movement of my brain,
i.e. intuitively, "by self-unable
motion" (*All's Well*, III. i. 13).

Ant.   Say to me,
Whose fortunes shall rise higher, Cæsar's or mine?   15
Sooth. Cæsar's.
　　　Therefore, O Antony, stay not by his side:
Thy demon, that thy spirit which keeps thee, is
Noble, courageous, high, unmatchable,
Where Cæsar's is not.　But near him, thy angel   20
Becomes afeard; as being o'erpower'd, therefore
Make space enough between you.
Ant.   Speak this no more.
Sooth. To none but thee; no more but when to thee.
　　　If thou dost play with him at any game,
Thou art sure to lose; and of that natural luck,   25
He beats thee 'gainst the odds.　Thy lustre thickens,
When he shines by: I say again, thy spirit
Is all afraid to govern thee near him;
But he away, 'tis noble.

18 *that thy*] F; *that's thy* F 2.　　19. *high, unmatchable*] F 3; *high unmatchable*
F, F 2; *high-unmatchable* anon. conj.　　21. *afeard,*] Thirlby; *a feare;* F.
23. *To . . . thee*] Theobald's pointing; *To none but thee no more but: when
to thee,* F.　　29. *he away, 'tis*] Pope; *he alway 'tis* F.

Cf. Lord Herbert, *Occasional Verses*
(1665), in preface: " belief . . .
that their Poets, as Orpheus, Linus,
and Musæus, were descended of the
Gods, and divinely inspired, from
the extraordinary *Motions* of their
Minds," etc.; F. Spence's *Lucian*
(1684), *The Epistle Dedicatory*, sig.
B 7: " In his Works he has couch't
. . . a perfect *Anatomy* of the Passions
and *inward Motions* of Man," etc.
Shakespeare seems to use the singular
variously for the operation of the
mind and the natural impulses. Cf.
Othello, I. ii. 75; I. iii. 95. On the
Soothsayer, see notes on Act. I. sc. ii.
ante.

18. *that thy*] Some editors read
that 's with F 2-4, comparing North,
q.v., p. 266 *post.* In support of the
text Rolfe refers to III. v. 18; IV. xiv.
79 *post* ; *Macbeth*, I. vii. 53, etc.

18-21. See North, *post*, p. 266, for
this allusion to the ancient belief
that a guardian spirit attends each

of us from birth to guide and ad-
monish; and cf. *Macbeth*, III. i. 54-7:—
　　" There is none but he
　Whose being I do fear: and
　　under him,
　My Genius is rebuk'd, as it is
　　said
　Mark Antony's was by Cæsar."
21. *afeard*] † The *e* : *d* confusion is
so usual, and the consequent emendations such common form, that there
is little to guide us in choosing between F and Thirlby except " suita-
bility." *Afeard* has been scorned, and
a fear praised as " characteristically
Shakespearean "; which no doubt
it is, but is it characteristic of the
soothsayer? In lines 28, 29 he makes
precisely the same distinction between *afraid* and *noble*; and see
North, p. 266 *post.* [R]
25. *of*] in consequence of.
26. *thickens*] grows dim, is no longer
clear and bright. So in *Macbeth*, III.
ii. 50, " Light *thickens*."

Ant.   Get thee gone:
Say to Ventidius I would speak with him.   30
                                    [*Exit Soothsayer.*
He shall to Parthia. Be it art or hap,
He hath spoken true. The very dice obey him,
And in our sports my better cunning faints
Under his chance: if we draw lots, he speeds,
His cocks do win the battle still of mine   35
When it is all to nought; and his quails ever
Beat mine, inhoop'd, at odds. I will to Egypt:
And though I make this marriage for my peace,
I' the east my pleasure lies. O, come, Ventidius.

Enter VENTIDIUS.

You must to Parthia, your commission's ready;   40
Follow me, and receive 't.   [*Exeunt.*

30. Exit Soothsayer] Exit. F.   30, 39. *Ventidius*] F 2; Ventigius F.

36. *all to nought*] even when the odds are infinite in my favour.

37. *inhoop'd, at odds*] If confined within a hoop the birds could not avoid fighting. Farmer quotes the first two lines of one of John Davies of Hereford's Epigrams [*Vpon English Proverbes*, No. 287; *Scourge of Folly*, p. 47 (*Works*, ed. Grosart, vol. ii)] :—
   " ' Hee sets cocke on the hoope ' in you wou'd say:
   For cocking in hoopes is now all the play.
   And therefore no maruell mens stockes often droope,
   That still vse the cocke-pit to set cocke *in hoope.*"
The first line is in the original incorrectly, " ' Hee sets cocke on the hoope in,' " etc.; the sense of the phrase in the last is illustrated by a reference of Mr. Craig's to Horman's *Vulgaria*; " He setteth all things at cock in the *hope*; omnia in fortunae casibus ponit." This epigram makes it clear

that Shakespeare embellished what he took here from North, by an allusion to the practice of his own time in cock-fighting; and disposes of Capell's reading (Seward's conjecture), *in whoop'd-at odds*, i.c. odds so much in Antony's favour as to excite the cries of the onlookers), notwithstanding frequent spellings like *Hoop'd* for *Whoop'd* in *Coriolanus*, IV. v. 84. Douce (*Illustrations of Shakespeare*, 1807, ii, pp. 867) says: " Quail combats were well known among the ancients, and especially at Athens. Julius Pollux relates that a circle was made in which the birds were placed, and he whose quail was driven out of this circle lost the stake," etc. He also gives an illustration of the sport among the Chinese, copied from a Chinese miniature painting, in which the quails are actually placed within a hoop, a small, low circular enclosure, set on a table.

[SCENE IV.—*The same.   A street.*]

Enter LEPIDUS, MÆCENAS, *and* AGRIPPA.

Lep. Trouble yourselves no further: pray you hasten
    Your generals after.
Agr.   Sir, Mark Antony
    Will e'en but kiss Octavia, and we'll follow.
Lep. Till I shall see you in your soldiers' dress,
    Which will become you both, farewell.
Mæc.   We shall,   5
    As I conceive the journey, be at the Mount
    Before you, Lepidus.
Lep.   Your way is shorter,
    My purposes do draw me much about,
    You'll win two days upon me.
Both.   Sir, good success!
Lep. Farewell.   [*Exeunt.*   10

[SCENE V.—*Alexandria.   Cleopatra's palace.*]

Enter CLEOPATRA, CHARMIAN, IRAS, *and* ALEXAS.

Cleo. Give me some music; music, moody food
    Of us that trade in love.
All.   The music, ho!

Scene IV

6. *at the*] F 2; *at* F.

Scene IV

6. *Mount*] Mount Misenum. See
II. ii. 161 *ante*, and North, *post*, p. 266.
   9. *win . . . upon me*] Cf. Jonson,
The New Inn, II. ii. 25 : " You will
win upon me in compliment."
   good success] so in *Lear*, v. iii. 196 :
" this *good success*." The word was
used for result, good or bad. Cf.
Daniel, *Hymen's Triumph*, III. ii (line
1133) (*Works*, ed. Grosart, iii. 372) :—
   " That learns his errours but by
      their *successe*,
   And when there is no remedie."
see also III. v. 5 *post*.

Scene v

1. *moody food*] Cf. *Twelfth Night*,
I. i. 1. : " If music be the *food* of
love, play on." Moody = melancholy : Quarles uses it nobly of the
passing bell : " This *moody* musick of
impartial *death*." See his " Pente-
logia," *Mors Tua*, i. 9.
   2. *trade in*] Probably much as now,
" have dealings in," etc.; but the
word (verb and noun) retained
senses nearer that of its source, *tread*.
Cf. Sylvester's *Du Bartas*, week 11,
day 11, part iii, p. 282, ed. 1621 :
" Ships . . . To *trade* the seas ";

Enter MARDIAN *the Eunuch.*

Cleo. Let it alone, let's to billiards: come, Charmian.
Char. My arm is sore, best play with Mardian.
Cleo. As well a woman with an eunuch play'd,   5
  As with a woman.   Come, you'll play with me, sir ?
Mar. As well as I can, madam.
Cleo. And when good will is show'd, though 't come
  too short,
  The actor may plead pardon.   I'll none now,
  Give me mine angle, we'll to the river there,   10
  My music playing far off.   I will betray
  Tawny-finn'd fishes, my bended hook shall pierce
  Their slimy jaws; and as I draw them up,
  I'll think them every one an Antony,
  And say " Ah, ha! y'are caught."
Char.   'Twas merry when 15
  You wager'd on your angling, when your diver
  Did hang a salt-fish on his hook which he
  With fervency drew up.

Scene v

3. *billiards*] F 2;   *billards* F. 12. *Tawny-finn'd*] Theobald;   *Tawny fine* F.

Cartwright, *Poems*, 1651, p. 312 :—
 " Thine equall skill thus wresting
  nothing, made
  Thy Pen seem not so much to
  write, as *Trade*."
Turbervile, *The Speech of Reason against
Love* (repr. in *The Muses Library*, 1741,
p. 192), uses the noun of lustful
intercourse :—
 " They spent their youthfull Yeares
  In foule, and filthie *Trade*," etc.

3. *billiards*] In a citation by Dr.
Furness from A. A. Adee in *Lit.
World*, 21 April 1883, Boston, it is
urged that " Shakespeare got the
idea that billiards was an Egyptian
game, and a favourite pastime of
women " from Chapman, *The Blind
Beggar of Alexandria*, iv. 11 : " go,
Aspasia, Send for some ladies to go

play with you, At chess, at billiards,
and at other game."
 10. *angle*] fishing tackle.
 15-18. '*Twas merry*, etc.] See North,
post, p. 264. Nashe, *Lenten Stuffe*,
III. p. 212, lines 11-28, has a story
of a scholar in Cambridge who
amused the " gaping rural fools " by
drawing up a red herring, with which
he had secretly baited his hook, at
the town-bridge there.   There is also
a story quoted by Dr. Grey (*Critical*,
etc., *Notes on Shakespeare*, 1754, ii. 198)
from *Memoirs of the English Court*,
1707, pp. 489, 490, that Nell Gwynn
similarly caused Charles II to draw
up a dozen fried smelts, and the
Prince of Newburg a purse containing " the picture of my Lady ——"
set in gold and jewelled.   " Cleopatra," said the king, " caused a

Cleo.   That time? O times!
I laugh'd him out of patience; and that night
I laugh'd him into patience, and next morn,   20
Ere the ninth hour, I drunk him to his bed;
Then put my tires and mantles on him, whilst
I wore his sword Philippan.   O, from Italy!

Enter a Messenger.

Ram thou thy fruitful tidings in mine ears,
That long time have been barren.
Mess.   Madam, madam,—
Cleo. Antonius dead!—If thou say so, villain,   26
Thou kill'st thy mistress: but well and free,

---

18. *time? O times!*] *time? oh times:* F.
25. *been*] *bin* F (and often elsewhere).
F; *Anthony's* F 2.

24. *Ram*] F; *Rain* Hanmer.
26. *Antonius*] Delius; *Anthonyo's*

---

sardian to be tied to *Mark Anthony's*
hook, but you exceed her in your
contrivance; for you bestow pictures, which are much more accept-
able."

21. *ninth hour*] probably 9 a.m.
rather than 3 p.m. Cf. *J.C.* II. iv. 23.

22. *tires*] usually understood here
as = head-dresses. Cf. *M.W.W.* III.
iii. 60; Chapman, *A Justification of
a Strange Action of Nero*, 1629: " it
shall no more be tortured with
curling bodkins, tied up each night
in knots, wearied with *tires,*" etc. In
sense *attire*, the word is also common.
Cf. Heywood, *The Brazen Age* (*Works*,
Pearson, iii. 245): " Hence with
these womanish *tyres,*" said by
Hercules, Antony's supposed ancestor, with whose treatment by
Omphale in this point there is a
resemblance here, intentional or
otherwise, as has been observed. Cf.
also Rowlands, *The Knave of Hearts*,
1613 (Percy Society, No. xxxiv, p.
74): " Reach me my stockings, and
my other *tire.*"

23. *Philippan*] The contrast is
heightened by selecting the sword
which triumphed in the overthrow
of Brutus and Cassius at Philippi.

Philippan is doubtless noun, not
adjective, though, as Theobald points
out, we have no warrant for supposing
swords to have received names till
very much later times.

24. *Ram*] Some read *Rain* with
Hanmer, but *Ram* is thoroughly
characteristic, and is supported by
Malone's references to *J.C.* v. iii. 74:
" thrusting this report Into his ears,"
and *The Tempest*, II. i. 113: " You
cram these words into my ears," etc.
Cf. also Jonson's use of *rammed*;
" And for his poesy, 'tis so *ramm'd*
with life " (*The Poetaster*, v. i. 136).

26. *Antonius*] † Dover Wilson takes
F's spelling to " suggest intimacy,
natural to the context "; over-subtle,
I think. And what about II. ii. 7?
[R]

27. *mistress*] The word may be tri-
syllabic here, like *frustrate*, v. i. 2
post, and according to a very common
practice of syllabifying *r*. Cf. *R.J.*
II. iv. 207, and Sylvester's *Du
Bartas*, week 1, day 3, p. 67, in 1621
ed. :—

    " Wherewith he wooes his *Iron
        Misteriss*,
    And never leaues her till he get
        a kiss," etc.

If thou so yield him, there is gold, and here
My bluest veins to kiss; a hand that kings
Have lipp'd, and trembled kissing.   30
Mess. First, madam, he is well.
Cleo.   Why, there's more gold.
But, sirrah, mark, we use
To say, the dead are well: bring it to that,

---

28. *him, there*] Pope (ed. 2); *him.   There*] F.

But the pause after *mistress* is sufficient for metre, and the quicker enunciation more in agreement with the speaker's mood.

31, 32. *First, madam . . . we use*]
† F lineates thus:—

Mes. First Madam, he is well.
Cleo. Why there's more Gold.
But sirrah marke, we use
To say, . . .

That is, we have three incomplete lines, of which either the first and second, or the second and third, taken together make a regular complete line. The narrowness of the Folio column is probably here, as in some other places, the cause of F's lineation, since the first and second half-lines will not go into the column at all, and the second and third, though in fact they just will, would have been so tight a squeeze that a compositor might very naturally, looking at them in manuscript, conclude that he could not get them in, and so start a new line without wasting time on an experiment. We are therefore entitled to re-lineate. But there are two ways of doing it, and they are worth a moment's examination, since something like the same problem with two or more solutions, is presented in other places where re-lineation is called for. Which of the two ways one prefers depends on where one prefers to retain the incomplete line which we cannot avoid somewhere. Dr. Brooks prefers the following:—

Mes. First, madam, he is well.

I

Cleo. Why, there's more gold.   But, sirrah, mark, we use
To say, . . .

That is, clearly, perfectly possible, and there is a certain effectiveness in leaving the messenger's brief announcement standing by itself. I prefer the arrangement of the text, for these reasons: Cleopatra's impulsive offer of more gold comes, I think, the moment his words are out of the messenger's mouth; but she then has a second, and alarming, thought, and makes a new start with it. And it will be observed that Cleopatra's second incomplete line may be regarded rhythmically not as unfinished but as "un-begun," the gap at the beginning being occupied by the giving of the gold. This would be made plainer in a modern text, more lavish of stage-directions for business even when the business is clearly implied, thus:—

Why, there's more gold.
(*gives him gold*) But sirrah, mark, we
use
To say, . . . [R]

33. *the dead are well*] Cf. *2 Kings*, iv. 26. The same thought occurs in *Macbeth*, IV. iii. 176, 177: " *Macd.* How does my wife? *Ross.* Why, well. *Macd.* And all my children? *Ross.* Well too "; *2 H. IV*, v. ii. 3; *R. and J.*, IV. v. 76, etc. Mr. Churton Collins (*Studies in Shakespeare*, 1904, p. 54) notes the parallel with Euripides, *Troades*, 268: εὐδαιμόνιζε παῖδα σήν· ἔχει καλῶς.

The gold I give thee will I melt and pour
Down thy ill-uttering throat.   35
Mess. Good madam, hear me.
Cleo.   Well, go to, I will;
But there's no goodness in thy face, if Antony
Be free and healthful,—so tart a favour
To trumpet such good tidings!   If not well,
Thou shouldst come like a Fury crown'd with
    snakes,   40
Not like a formal man.
Mess.   Will't please you hear me?
Cleo. I have a mind to strike thee ere thou speak'st:
Yet if thou say Antony lives, is well,
Or friends with Cæsar, or not captive to him,
I'll set thee in a shower of gold, and hail   45
Rich pearls upon thee.
Mess.   Madam, he's well.
Cleo.   Well said.
Mess. And friends with Cæsar.

---

37. *face, if*] *face if* F; *face: if* F 2.
Capell (Tyrwhitt conj.); *'tis* F.

38. *so*] F; *why so* Rowe.   43. *is*]

34, 35. *The gold . . . throat*] Perhaps
suggested by the treatment of
Crassus' body by Orodes. See on
III. i. 2 *post*.

38, 39. *so tart . . . tidings*] so sour
an aspect, etc. Cf. *R. and J.* II. v. 23,
24 :—

> " If good, thou sham'st the music
>   of sweet news
>   By playing it to me with *so sour
>   a face*."

Also *Cymbeline*, III. iv. 11-14. *Favour*
is very common for " face,"
" appearance," etc. ; so in *Othello*,
I. iii. 346.

41. *a formal man*] Here merely, I
think, with Malone, a man in shape
or form, though in *C. of E.*
v. i. 105, the phrase means a man in
his normal condition of mind ; as
also elsewhere. Chester, *Love's Martyr*
(ed. Grosart, New Shakespeare Soc.
p. 108), speaks of the bear bringing
forth :—

" A lump of flesh without all fashion,
  Which she by often licking
    brings to rest,
  Making a *formal* body good and
    sound," etc.

" A mere *formall man* " in Earle's
Micro-cosmographie (1628) is one that
is mere outside, all he does or says
being pure imitation : " When you
have seen him *outside*, you have lookt
through him, and need imploy your
discouery no further."

45, 46. *I'll . . . thee*] Warburton is,
doubtless, too specific in making this
= " I will give thee a kingdom,"
because of an Eastern coronation
ceremony alluded to by Milton,
Paradise Lost, II. 4 :—

" Or where the gorgeous East with
    richest hand
  Showrs on her Kings *Barbaric*
    Pearl & Gold."

Cleopatra, however, proffers a province in line 68 *post*.

Cleo.   Th'art an honest man.

Mess. Cæsar, and he, are greater friends than ever.

Cleo. Make thee a fortune from me.

Mess.   But yet, madam,—

Cleo. I do not like " But yet," it does allay   50
    The good precedence, fie upon " But yet,"
    " But yet " is as a gaoler to bring forth
    Some monstrous malefactor.   Prithee, friend,
    Pour out the pack of matter to mine ear,
    The good and bad together: he's friends with
      Cæsar,   55
    In state of health, thou say'st, and thou say'st, free.

Mess. Free, madam, no; I made no such report,
    He's bound unto Octavia.

Cleo.   For what good turn?

Mess. For the best turn i' the bed.

Cleo.   I am pale, Charmian.

Mess. Madam, he's married to Octavia.   60

Cleo. The most infectious pestilence upon thee!
                           [*Strikes him down.*

Mess. Good madam, patience.

Cleo.   What say you?   Hence,
                              [*Strikes him.*
Horrible villain, or I'll spurn thine eyes
Like balls before me; I'll unhair thy head,
                    [*She hales him up and down.*
Thou shalt be whipp'd with wire, and stew'd in brine,
Smarting in lingering pickle.

50, 51. *does allay . . . precedence*]
qualifies the good [news] that pre-
ceded it. Cf. for *precedence*, *L.L.L.*
III. i. 83.   Daniel, in *Hymen's
Triumph* (1615), II. iv (line 901
in Grosart's *Daniel*) imitates with:—
  " But—*Clo.* Ah now comes that
    bitter vvord of But
  Which makes all nothing, that
    vvas said before."
There are several verbs *allay* (whence
confusion, see *O.E.D.*), and the
word here is not *allay* = alleviate,
but belongs to *allay* = put down,
abate, confused with *allay* = alloy;

whence comes: temper or qualify
by admixture of something undesirable, as here: cf. *Coriolanus* II. i. 53,
" a cup of hot wine with not a drop
of allaying Tiber in't."

54. *pack*] Cleopatra thinks of the
messenger with his news as like a
pedler with his pack, and elaborates
the image later, in lines 104-6.

58. *turn*] purpose (but the messenger takes the straightforward sense).

65. *whipp'd with wire*] So in Nashe,
The Unfortunate Traveller, II. p. 315,
line 34: " Then did they scourge
hys backe parts so blistered and

Mess.   Gracious madam,   66
    I that do bring the news made not the match.
Cleo. Say 'tis not so, a province I will give thee,
    And make thy fortunes proud: the blow thou hadst
    Shall make thy peace for moving me to rage,   70
    And I will boot thee with what gift beside
    Thy modesty can beg.
Mess.   He's married, madam.
Cleo. Rogue, thou hast liv'd too long.   [*Draw a knife.*
Mess.   Nay, then I'll run.
    What mean you, madam?   I have made no fault.
                               [*Exit.*

Char. Good madam, keep yourself within yourself,   75
    The man is innocent.
Cleo. Some innocents 'scape not the thunderbolt:
    Melt Egypt into Nile! and kindly creatures
    Turn all to serpents!   Call the slave again,
    Though I am mad, I will not bite him: call!   80
Char. He is afeard to come.
Cleo.   I will not hurt him.
    These hands do lack nobility, that they strike

---

basted, with burning whips of red hot *wire* "; Sylvester's *Du Bartas, The Decay*, p. 503, in ed. 1621: " With *wyery* Rods, thou shalt to death bee *whipt.*"

66. *lingering pickle*] *either* long-continuing pickle, *or* pickle whose effects will be so.

71. *boot thee with*] give thee into the bargain, *or merely* benefit thee with; *O.E.D.* " benefit, increase, enrich," giving this passage only for this sense. The noun (= something over and above, advantage) occurs in IV. i. 9 *post.*

73. *Draw a knife*] The not infrequent " imperatival " S.D.

75. *keep . . . yourself*] control yourself.

77. *innocents*] This is perhaps a play on the sense fools, naturals, occurring, e.g. in *Lear*, III. vi. 9.

78. *Melt . . . Nile*] Cf. I. i. 33 *ante.*

81-5 (S.D.s)† I have kept the single S.D. of F. Dyce, followed by others, inserted an *Exit Charmian* after *I will not hurt him,* and read *Re-enter Charmian and Messenger* just before *Come hither, sir.* But this misses the stage business. Charmian does not leave the stage, but goes to the door to call the messenger, whom she finds trembling outside, and reports accordingly. Then Cleopatra sees him in the doorway and encourages him with *Come hither, sir,* and he enters. [R]

82, 83. *These hands . . . myself*] Steevens saw an allusion here to the laws of chivalry, which " forbade a knight to engage with his inferior "; but chastisement has nothing to do with combat on equal terms. There is another difficulty: are there two reasons for lack of nobility? (1) the blow to an inferior, (2) the wrong assignment of blame; or, as I am half inclined to think, only one, the

A meaner than myself; since I myself
Have given myself the cause.

Come hither, sir.

Enter the Messenger again.

Though it be honest, it is never good   85
To bring bad news: give to a gracious message
An host of tongues, but let ill tidings tell
Themselves, when they be felt.

Mess.   I have done my duty.

Cleo. Is he married?
I cannot hate thee worser than I do,   90
If thou again say " Yes."

Mess.   He's married, madam.

Cleo. The gods confound thee, dost thou hold there still?

Mess. Should I lie, madam?

Cleo.   O, I would thou didst,
So half my Egypt were submerg'd and made
A cistern for scal'd snakes! Go get thee hence,   95
Hadst thou Narcissus in thy face, to me
Thou wouldst appear most ugly. He is married?

Mess. I crave your highness' pardon.

Cleo.   He is married?

Mess. Take no offence that I would not offend you:
To punish me for what you make me do   100
Seems much unequal: he's married to Octavia.

---

latter, thus: My hands act ignobly in bestowing blows on any less person than myself, for I myself am the real offender (by my infatuation for Antony) who has deserved them. Malone (see also III. iii. 14) sees a probable hit at Queen Elizabeth's temper, after her death, when it "*might be safely hazarded!*" The italics are mine.

95-7. *Go . . . ugly*] Steevens quotes *K.J.* III. i. 36, 37:—

"Fellow, be gone! I cannot brook thy sight:
This news hath made thee a most *ugly* man."

96. *Narcissus*] See Golding's Ovid's *Metam.*, Bk. III, line 428 *et seq.*:—

". . . freckled Lyriop, whome sometime surprised in his streame,
The floud Cephisus did inforce. This lady bare a sonne,
Whose beauty at his very birth might justly love have wonne.
Narcissus did she call his name," etc.

99. *Take . . . you*] Don't be angry at my reluctance to give a reply which I know will anger you.

101. *unequal*] unjust. So *2 H. IV.* IV. i. 102; Jonson, *Volpone*, III. ii. 14:

Cleo. O that his fault should make a knave of thee,
That art not what th'art sure of.   Get thee hence,
The merchandise which thou hast brought from Rome
Are all too dear for me: 105
Lie they upon thy hand, and be undone by 'em!

                                           [Exit Messenger.

Char. Good your highness, patience.
Cleo. In praising Antony, I have disprais'd Cæsar.
Char. Many times, madam.
Cleo. I am paid for't now.   Lead me from hence; I faint,
O Iras, Charmian! 'tis no matter.   110

---

103. *That . . . th' art sure of.*] F; *That say'st but what thou'rt sure of!* Hanmer; *That art not!—what? thou'rt sure of't!*—Mason conj., adopted by Steevens and others; *That art but . . .* Grant White; *That art in . . .* Hudson.   106. Exit Messenger] Rowe; not in F.

" You are *unequal* to me," etc.; Lord Brooke, *Life of Sidney* (*Works*, Grosart, iv. 8) : " Witnes his sound establishments both in Wales and Ireland, where his memory is worthily grateful unto this day : how *unequall* and bitter soever the censure of provincialls is usually against sincere monarchall governours," etc.

102, 103. *O, . . . sure of*] The first of these two lines seems to me to require some stress on *his,* and to be suggested by the messenger's complaint in line 100. He says, in effect : " You are unjust : *you make* me commit the fault you punish me for "; she replies : " O that it should be *his* fault that makes you a subject for punishment." What follows : " That art not what thou'rt *sure of,*" seems to imply Cleopatra's recognition that the messenger's offence to her lies in the obstinate persistence that his news is authentic, out of which he can neither be beaten nor cajoled. (This is precisely the offence in Marston's imitation in *The Insatiate Countess,* IV. ii.) In this view the sense of the whole will be : " O that it should be *his* fault that makes thee a subject for punishment, that art not thyself the thing of which thou art so hatefully positive."

† Case is, I think, right about the first line, but doubtfully so about the second. It is one of those Shakespearean phrases, common in his later work, of which the sense has to be " felt " and not arrived at by syntactical analysis. Cleopatra " means " " It is the *fact* of which you are so positive that deserves my anger, and not *you,* the bringer of the news." [R]

105-10. † *Are all . . . no matter.*] An admirable example of the lineation problem, " admitting a wide solution." F has this :—

  Are all too deere for me:
  Lye they vpon thy hand, and be
    undone by em.
    Char. Good your Highnesse
    patience.
    Cleo. In praysing *Anthony,* I
    haue disprais'd *Cæsar.*
    Char. Many times, Madam.
    Cleo. I am paid for't now: lead
    me from hence,
  I faint, oh *Iras, Charmian* : 'tis no
    matter.
I first adopted, without much conviction, the usual relineation (which derives from Capell), thus :—

  Are all too dear for me: lie they
    upon thy hand,
  And be undone by 'em!

Go to the fellow, good Alexas, bid him
Report the feature of Octavia; her years,
Her inclination, let him not leave out
The colour of her hair: bring me word quickly.

[Exit Alexas.

Let him for ever go, let him not—Charmian,   115
Though he be painted one way like a Gorgon,

---

114. Exit Alexas] Capell; not in F.

Char.   Good
   your Highness, patience.
Cleo. In praising Antony, I have
   disprais'd Cæsar.
Char. Many times, madam.
Cleo.   I am paid for't now.
   Lead me from hence;
   I faint, O Iras, Charmian! 'tis
   no matter.

Well, that bed of Procrustes no doubt
produces something more regular
than F, but at the cost of an awkwardly
hypermetrical line to start with,
which can only be regularized by a
slurring which destroys the emphasis,
and of a suspicious half line for
Cleopatra. The following was then
suggested to me, with the comment
" Is this too fanciful?":—

   Are all too dear for me: lie
      they upon
   Thy hand, and be undone by
      'em.
Char.   Good your highness
   Patience.
Cleo.   In praising Antony,
   I have
   Disprais'd Cæsar.
Char.   Many times,
   Madam.
Cleo.   I
   Am paid for't now.—Lead me
      from hence,
   I faint, O Iras, Charmian! 'tis
   no matter.

That seems to me not too fanciful,
but too jerky. And if one looks again
at F, is there really much the matter
with it? In the first two lines it

retains the contrasted emphasis on
me and *thy*. At *for me* Cleopatra has
said all she has to say, and pauses, and
then spits out her vituperative
dismissal; and though the second
line is, by count of syllables, hypermetric, the last three syllables (*-done
by 'em*) amount in naturally rapid
delivery to no more than a feminine
ending. Half-lines like Charmian's
are not uncommon (cf., e.g. Mardian's
line 7 in this scene). But what is
suspicious is Cleopatra's awkwardly
incomplete line starting eleven lines
of continuous verse. But a glance at
the Folio shows that after *hence*,
there is room for only at most six
letters (less, that is, than *I faint*, by a
space and a comma) and suggests as a
reasonable conjecture that Shakespeare wrote the complete line as in
the text above, and intended a pause
in the next line between *Charmian* and
'tis no matter, while Cleopatra re-
covers herself. [R]

   112. *feature*] applies most commonly to the shape of the whole body,
as in *R. III.* i. i. 19; sometimes to
facial characteristics more especially,
as in *K.J.* IV. ii. 264.

   113. *inclination*] temperament; to
which Henley (1821 Variorum)
thought Cleopatra expected to find
an index in the colour of Octavia's
hair.

   115. *him*] i.e. Antony.

   116, 117. *Though . . . Mars*] Alluding, as Staunton pointed out, to the
pictures formerly called perspectives
(cf. *Twelfth Night*, v. i. 227; *Henry V.*

The other way's a Mars.   Bid you Alexas
                                    [_To Mardian._
Bring me word how tall she is.   Pity me, Charmian,
But do not speak to me.   Lead me to my chamber.
                                    [_Exeunt._

[SCENE VI.—_Near Misenum._]

Flourish.   _Enter_ POMPEY _at one door, with drum and trumpet;
    at another_ CÆSAR, LEPIDUS, ANTONY, ENOBARBUS,
    MÆCENAS, AGRIPPA, MENAS _with Soldiers marching._

Pom. Your hostages I have, so have you mine;
    And we shall talk before we fight.
Cæs.   Most meet
    That first we come to words, and therefore have we
    Our written purposes before us sent,

117. To Mardian] Capell; not in F.

v. ii. 347) and still to be seen.
Different objects are painted on the
opposite surfaces of any suitable
material (care being taken to paint
one in the reverse direction), which
is then cut into regular strips and
attached to a third painted surface
at small equal intervals, and at right
angles to it.   An example sometimes
seen in village inns shows Lord
Beaconsfield from one side, Mr.
Gladstone from the other, and a
basket of flowers if the observer
faces it. In [Sir George Mackenzie's]
Religio Stoici (1665), sig. A 7, occurs :
" Thus we see, that one may account
that a miracle which another looks
upon as a folly; and yet, none but
Gods Spirit can decide the contro-
versie.   Matters of Religion and
Faith, resembling some curious Pictures, and Optick Prismes, which
seems to change shape and colours,
according to the several stances from
which the aspicient views them."

Gorgon] presumably the particular
Gorgon, Medusa, the sight of whose
face turned men to stone.

117. _way's_] Surely "The other
way " = the other way of the
picture.   But Hanmer and others
print _way he's_, and _way's_ is so explained by recent editors.

Scene VI (see North, _post_, p. 266).

S.D.]   † I have, with hesitation,
retained F's S.D., since, though
odd, it is not impossible.   The usual
practice has been to bring in Menas
with Pompey, and then excise Agrippa
altogether, both somewhat drastic
changes.   But the S.D. is inter-
pretable as it stands.   There enter
first, by their respective doors,
Pompey, the triumvirs, Enobarbus
and Maecenas; they are followed by
Agrippa (who does not talk at all)
and Menas (who does not talk till all
but he and Enobarbus have left),
each as leader of a group of soldiers,
and they stand in the background.
(" Door " is the usual terminology of
the Elizabethan playhouse, in which
all entries to the main stage, whether
the scene represented was indoors or
not, were by " doors "). [R]

Which if thou hast considered, let us know   5
If 'twill tie up thy discontented sword,
And carry back to Sicily much tall youth,
That else must perish here.

Pom.   To you all three,
The senators alone of this great world,
Chief factors for the gods: I do not know   10
Wherefore my father should revengers want,
Having a son and friends, since Julius Cæsar,
Who at Philippi the good Brutus ghosted,
There saw you labouring for him.   What was't
That mov'd pale Cassius to conspire?   And
      what   15
Made the all-honour'd, honest Roman, Brutus,
With the arm'd rest, courtiers of beauteous freedom,
To drench the Capitol, but that they would
Have one man but a man?   And that is it
Hath made me rig my navy: at whose burthen   20
The anger'd ocean foams, with which I meant
To scourge the ingratitude that despiteful Rome
Cast on my noble father.

Cæs.   Take your time.
Ant. Thou canst not fear us, Pompey, with thy sails.

Scene VI

10. *gods: I*] gods. *I* F; *gods, I* most edd.   16. *the*] F 2; not in F.
honest Roman, Brutus,] most modern edd.; *honest, Roman Brutus,* F and Delius.

7. *tall*] stout, bold; as often in
Shakespeare. Also used sportively, in
other connections than plain valour,
as e.g. by Massinger, *The Unnatural
Combat*, III. i. 23 :—
    " As *tall* a trencherman, that is
      most certain,
    As e'er demolish'd pye-fortifica-
      tion," etc.
See also *M.W.W.* I. iv. 26, for " *tall
. . .* of his hands," i.e. formidable
in combat.
    10. *gods: I*] † The heavy punctu-
ation of F is surely right. Pompey
starts with a formal address, and
then states his case; and *To you I do
not know* is almost impossibly awkward. [R]

10-14. *I do . . . for him*] This appears to mean, in brief: Julius
Cæsar found active avengers in you;
I do not see why my father, who has
a son alive, and friends likewise,
should go without revenge.
    13. *ghosted*] haunted.   See *J.C.*
IV. iii. 275-87; v. iii. 94-6; v. v.
17-19. Steevens quotes Burton, *Anatomy of Melancholy*, 1632 ed., preface,
p. 22: " What madnesse *ghosts* this
old man? but what madnesse
ghosts us all?"
    24. *fear*] frighten; as often. Cf.
Jonson, *Bartholomew Fair*, III. ii. 129:
" Well said, brave Whit! in, and
fear the ale out o' the bottles into
the bellies of the brethren," etc.

We'll speak with thee at sea. At land thou know'st   25
How much we do o'er-count thee.

Pom.   At land, indeed,
Thou dost o'er-count me of my father's house:
But since the cuckoo builds not for himself,
Remain in't as thou may'st.

Lep.   Be pleas'd to tell us—
For this is from the present—how you take   30
The offers we have sent you.

Cæs.   There's the point.

Ant. Which do not be entreated to, but weigh
What it is worth embrac'd.

Cæs.   And what may follow,
To try a larger fortune.

Pom.   You have made me offer
Of Sicily, Sardinia; and I must   35
Rid all the sea of pirates.   Then, to send

25. *speak with thee*] encounter thee. Cf. II. ii. 164 *ante*.

27. *o'er-count . . . house*] Plutarch relates that Antony, having bought the elder Pompey's house at auction, afterwards refused to pay for it. See North, *post*, pp. 258, 266. Hence, as Malone observes, the phrase is equivocal; *out-number* me by your possessing my father's house, and *cheat* me out of it by your sharp practice.

28. *But, since the cuckoo,* etc.] " Since, like the cuckoo, that seizes the nests of other birds, you have invaded a house which you could not build, keep it while you can " (Johnson). A sharp taunt, emphasizing the insinuation of cheating. Cf. R. Chester, *Love's Martyr*, 1601 (New Shakespeare Soc., 1878, p. 118) :—

" She scornes to labour or make vp
    a nest,
But creeps by stealth into some
    others roome,
And with the *Larkes* deare yong,
    her yong ones rest,
Beeing by subtle dealing ouer-
come," etc.

The cuckoo's usual victim is the hedge-sparrow. See *1 H. IV.* v. i. 60; *Lucrece,* 849.

30. *this . . . present*] this (the matter of the house) is beside the present point.

32, 33. *Which do not . . . embrac'd*] Do not regard this as a plea; simply consider your own interests.

33, 34. *And . . . fortune*] understood as a veiled menace in case his ambition rejects all offers and resorts to arms. It may, however, be meant for encouragement (as implied in Schlegel and Tieck's translation), and signify : " And what it may lead to, if you take the chance of develop-ments in this alliance." *To try,* the infinitive used indefinitely, as often. Cf. *The Winter's Tale,* II. ii. 57: " I know not what I shall incur to pass it, Having no warrant."

36. *to send*] The insertion of *to* before a second infinitive depending on an auxiliary verb is frequent in Shakespeare and elsewhere. Cf. *The Parliament of Criticks,* 1702, p. 79: " Let the *Keeper of Bedlam* take such distracted *gentlemen* as those into his

Measures of wheat to Rome; this 'greed upon,
To part with unhack'd edges, and bear back
Our targes undinted.
Cæs. Ant. Lep.   That's our offer.
Pom.   Know, then,
I came before you here a man prepar'd   40
To take this offer.   But Mark Antony
Put me to some impatience: though I lose
The praise of it by telling, you must know,
When Cæsar and your brother were at blows,
Your mother came to Sicily, and did find   45
Her welcome friendly.
Ant.   I have heard it, Pompey,
And am well studied for a liberal thanks
Which I do owe you.
Pom.   Let me have your hand:
I did not think, sir, to have met you here.
Ant. The beds i' the east are soft, and thanks to you,   50
That call'd me timelier than my purpose hither;
For I have gain'd by 't.
Cæs.   Since I saw you last,
There is a change upon you.

---

39. Cæs. Ant. Lep.] Capell; Omnes. F.   45. *Sicily*] *Cicelie* F.   53.
There is] Rowe; *Ther's* F.

Care, and consider whether their *Madness* be in the *Brain* or the *Blood,* and to report to the above-mentioned censors," etc.

39. *targes*] said to be monosyllabic here (*targs*), and in *Cymbeline,* v. v. 5.

45. *Sicily*] † F's *Cicelie* is a real oddity. One can see Shakespeare misspelling some of the less familiar proper names, but hardly so common a geographical name as this (with which elsewhere, by the way, as in *Winter's Tale,* he had apparently no difficulty). But it is an easy " auditory " error, and I wonder whether in the light of it one should not examine with a more suspicious eye the easy writing-off of other similar errors as " Shakespeare's mis-spellings." Apart from *Ventigius-Ventidius,* elsewhere commented on, what about *Sidnis* for *Cydnus?* As a " misspelling " it is surely extravagantly " far wide." But as a mis-hearing it is easy enough. [R]

47. *am well studied,* etc.] See II. ii. 154-6 *ante.* I am well equipped for amply thanking you, by much thought of my debt. Cf. II. ii. 138 *ante; M. of V.* II. ii. 211 : " Like one *well studied* in a sad ostent, To please his grandam," etc.; Dekker, *The Bel-man of London,* 1608 (*Temple Classics,* p. 133) : " so *well studied* that he hath the principles of the *Black-Art,* and can 'pick a lock if it be not too much cross warded," etc.

Pom.   Well, I know not
What counts harsh fortune casts upon my face,
But in my bosom shall she never come,   55
To make my heart her vassal.
Lep.   Well met here.
Pom. I hope so, Lepidus, thus we are agreed:
I crave our composition may be written
And seal'd between us.
Cæs.   That's the next to do.
Pom. We'll feast each other, ere we part, and let's   60
Draw lots who shall begin.
Ant.   That will I, Pompey.
Pom. No, Antony, take the lot: but, first or last,
Your fine Egyptian cookery shall have
The fame. I have heard that Julius Cæsar
Grew fat with feasting there.
Ant.   You have heard much. 65
Pom. I have fair meanings, sir.
Ant.   And fair words to them.
Pom. Then so much have I heard,
And I have heard Apollodorus carried—

---

54. *casts*] *cast's* F.   57. *Lepidus, thus*] F; *Lepidus. Thus* most edd.
66. *meanings*] Malone (Heath conj.); *meaning* F.

---

54. *counts*] reckonings. So George
Herbert, *The Discharge*, line 6 : " Hast
thou not made thy *counts*, and summ'd
up all? " In his careless answer,
Pompey makes Fortune *score* on his
face the record of her cruelties to
him. Cf. *Edward III* (1596), ed.
Moore Smith, IV. iv. 128, 129 :—
    " And stratagems forepast with
        iron pens
    Are texted in thine honourable
        face."
casts] used, of course, in the technical sense : " Dost thou not know
numbers ? Canst thou not *cast?* "
(*The Puritan*, 1607, III. i. 42.)
    † Should we perhaps read *fortune's
cast* (i.e. *has cast*)] which might account
for F's odd apostrophe? [R]
57. † I think F's punctuation
makes Pompey more deliberately

courteous to the unimportant member of the triumvirate. *Thus* then =
" if you also are content." [R]
58. *composition*] agreement. Cf.
the use of *compose*, II. ii. 15 *ante.*
64, 65. *Cæsar . . . feasting there*]
Cæsar beganne thenceforth to spend
all the night long in *feasting* and
bancketing " (North's Plutarch, 1579,
Julius Cæsar, Tudor Trans. v. 50).
68-70. *Apollodorus . . . mattress*]
[Cæsar] " secretly sent for Cleopatra
which was in the contry to come
unto him. She onely taking Apollodorus Sicilian of all her friendes,
tooke a litle bote and went away
with him in it in the night, and came
and landed hard by the foote of the
castell. Then having no other meane
to come in to the court, without
being knowen, she laid her selfe

Eno. No more of that: he did so.

Pom. What, I pray you? 70

Eno. A certain queen to Cæsar in a mattress.

Pom. I know thee now: how far'st thou, soldier?

Eno. Well,
　　And well am like to do, for I perceive
　　Four feasts are toward.

Pom. Let me shake thy hand,
　　I never hated thee: I have seen thee fight,
　　When I have envied thy behaviour.

Eno. Sir, 75
　　I never lov'd you much, but I ha' prais'd ye,
　　When you have well deserv'd ten times as much
　　As I have said you did.

Pom. Enjoy thy plainness,
　　It nothing ill becomes thee.
　　Aboard my galley, I invite you all: 80
　　Will you lead, lords?

Cæs. Ant. Lep. Show 's the way, sir.

Pom. Come.

　　　　　[*Exeunt all but Menas and Enobarbus.*

Men. [*aside*] Thy father, Pompey, would ne'er have
　　made this treaty.—You and I have known, sir.

---

69. *more of that*] F 3; *more that* F. 　　 81. *Show 's*] F (*Shew's*); *Shew us*
Hanmer. Exeunt . . .] Exeunt. Manet Enob. and Menas. F. 　　82. aside]
Johnson.

downe upon a mattresse or flockbed,
which Apollodorus her frend tied
and bound up together like a bundle
with a great leather thong, and so
tooke her up on his backe, and
brought her thus hamperd in this
fardell unto Cæsar, in at the castell
gate. This was the first occasion, (as
it is reported) that made Cæsar to
love her: but afterwards, when he
sawe her sweete conversation and
pleasaunt entertainment, he fell then
in further liking with her, and did
reconcile her againe unto her brother
the king, with condition, that they
two joyntly should raigne together "
(*ibid.* Tudor Trans., pp. 50, 51).

73. *toward*] impending; as in
Hamlet, v. ii. 378 :—
　　　" O proud Death!
　What feast is *toward* in thine
　　　eternal cell," etc.;
Jonson, *E.M.I.* i. i. i (F): " A
goodly day toward! and a fresh
morning!"

78. *Enjoy thy plainness*] Cf. Brome,
The Damoiselle, i. ii (Pearson's
Brome, i. 391) : " Youle give me leave
to use my *plainnesse*[?]," i.e. to speak
plainly.

Enjoy] give rein to, " indulge."

83. *known*] been acquainted. So
in *Cymbeline*, i. iv. 38 : " Sir, we have
known together in Orleans," on which

Eno. At sea, I think.

Men. We have, sir.   85

Eno. You have done well by water.

Men. And you by land.

Eno. I will praise any man that will praise me, though it
     cannot be denied what I have done by land.

Men. Nor what I have done by water.   90

Eno. Yes, something you can deny for your own safety:
     you have been a great thief by sea.

Men. And you by land.

Eno. There I deny my land service.   But give me your
     hand, Menas: if our eyes had authority, here   95
     they might take two thieves kissing.

Men. All men's faces are true, whatsome'er their hands are.

Eno. But there is never a fair woman has a true face.

Men. No slander, they steal hearts.

Eno. We came hither to fight with you.   100

Men. For my part, I am sorry it is turned to a drinking.
     Pompey doth this day laugh away his fortune.

Eno. If he do, sure he cannot weep't back again.

Men. Y'have said, sir.   We looked not for Mark
     Antony here: pray you, is he married to   105
     Cleopatra?

Eno. Cæsar's sister is called Octavia.

Men. True, sir, she was the wife of Caius Marcellus.

Eno. But she is now the wife of Marcus Antonius.

Professor Dowden quotes Jonson
Cynthia's Revels, IV. iii. 76: "he
salutes me as familiarly as if we had
known together since the Deluge," etc.

95. *authority*] i.e. as constables.

96. *two thieves kissing*] i.e. fraternis-
ing, in a general sense, if the speakers
are the " two thieves," as lines 92, 93
indicate; but line 97 points rather to
their hands, which the word *kissing*
would suit very well. Cf. *R. and J.*
I. v. 103, 104 :—
  " For saints have hands that pil-
    grims' hands do touch."
  "And palm to palm is holy Palmer's
    kiss: "
and *Hamlet*, III. ii. 355, " by these
pickers and stealers."

97. *true*] honest, as in *1 H. IV.*
II. ii. 25. S. Rowlands, *The Four
Knaves* (Percy Society, 1843, p. 89),
versifies on the proverb: " When
theeves fall out *true* men come by
their goods." In the next line there
appears to be a play on the word as
meaning unsophisticated as well as
honest. Mr. Craig suggests that in
" All men's faces are true," *true*
means (as well as " honest ") " true
indices of character, of their
thoughts," and that Enobarbus infers
the contrary of women, as he thinks
of the inscrutable eyes of Cleopatra.

102, 103. *laugh away . . . weep't
back*] Proverbial, perhaps, but I fail
to trace it.

Men. Pray ye, sir?   110
Eno. 'Tis true.
Men. Then is Cæsar and he for ever knit together.
Eno. If I were bound to divine of this unity, I would
    not prophesy so.
Men. I think the policy of that purpose made more in 115
    the marriage than the love of the parties.
Eno. I think so too. But you shall find the band that
    seems to tie their friendship together will be the
    very strangler of their amity: Octavia is of a
    holy, cold, and still conversation.   120
Men. Who would not have his wife so?
Eno. Not he that himself is not so; which is Mark
    Antony. He will to his Egyptian dish again:
    then shall the sighs of Octavia blow the fire up in
    Cæsar; and (as I said before) that which is the 125
    strength of their amity shall prove the immediate
    author of their variance. Antony will use his
    affection where it is. He married but his occasion
    here.
Men. And thus it may be. Come sir, will you aboard? 130
    I have a health for you.
Eno. I shall take it, sir: we have us'd our throats in
    Egypt.
Men. Come, let's away.   [*Exeunt.*

---

119. *strangler*] F; *stranger* F 2-4; *estranger* Rowe.

115. *made*] counted.
119. *strangler*] † Rowe's reading is
an excellent example of the dangers
of paying attention to the later Folios,
since what he was doing was emending them (not the first, which
needed no emendation) and so
moving steadily further from the
first. [R]
120. *conversation*] behaviour, system of life. So in *Pericles*, II, Gower,
9: "The good in *conversation*":
Rosse, *Mel Heliconium* (1640), p. 8:

"Before Christ came, the *Gentiles*
were but Ants, men of Earthly *conversation*," etc.; *Life and Death of
Sir Henry Vane* (1662), p. 23: "men
of debauched consciences and bruit-
ish *conversations*."
128. *affection*] passion.
but his occasion] i.e. merely with
an eye to expedience.
132. *us'd*] Whether we take this
as = made use of *or* accustomed,
the inference of practised pledging
is the same.

[SCENE VII.—*Aboard Pompey's galley, off Misenum.*]

Music plays.   Enter two or three Servants with a banquet.

First Serv. Here they'll be, man. Some o' their plants
are ill-rooted already, the least wind i' the world
will blow them down.
Sec. Serv. Lepidus is high-coloured.
First Serv. They have made him drink alms-drink.   5
Sec. Serv. As they pinch one another by the disposition,

Scene VII

1, 4, etc. First (Sec.) Serv.] 1. (2.) Ser. Rowe; 1. 2. F.   4. *high-coloured*]
F 2; *high Conlord* F.

Scene VII

a banquet] i.e. as often, a dessert
with wine. Malone quotes *The Life
and Death of Thomas, Lord Cromwell,*
1602 [III. iii, *Supplement to Shakespeare,* ii. 411] :—
    " 'Tis strange, how that we and
    the Spaniard differ ;
    Their dinner is our *banquet* after
    dinner," etc.
See also Osborne, *Historical Memoires,*
etc., 1658 (James I, pt. i, § 39) :
" And after such suppers huge
banquets no lesse profuse, a waiter
returning his servant home with a
cloak-bag full of dried sweetmeats
and confects, valued to his lordship
at more than ten shillings the
pound."
    1. *plants*] A play, as Johnson noted,
on the two senses of *plants*. For
plants, a common Latinism for the
soles of the feet and the feet themselves, cf. Jonson, *Oberon*, line 403 :
" Knotty legs, and *plants* of clay " ;
Nashe, *Christ's Tears,* II. 63, line 7 :
" . . . you Pilgrims, that . . . weare
the *plants* of your feete to the like-
nesse of withered rootes, by bare-
legd processioning (from a farre) to
the Sepulcher," etc.
    5. *alms-drink*] Ordinarily " the re-
mains of liquor reserved for alms-
people" (*O.E.D.*) ; hence, perhaps,

" leavings " here, possibly mixed
leavings, not likely to agree with the
recipient. Beaumont (Letter to Ben
Jonson) speaks of water and claret
lees as drink :—
    " So mixt that given to the
        thirstiest one
    'Twill not prove *alms* unless he
        have the stone."
Warburton is apparently the sole
authority for " almsdrink " 's being
" a phrase among good fellows to
signify that liquor of another's share
which his companion drinks to ease
him." Can it here = *drink taken as
a work of charity,* i.e. to further the
reconciliation? See next speech.
Almsdrink supplies a bitter reflection
in Churchyard's *Tragicall Discourse
of the Vnhappy Man's Life,* stanza 70
(reprinted in *Bibliographical Miscellanies,* Oxford, 1813, p. 31) :—
    " I see some bring from doells an
        empty cup
    Yet craues an *almes,* and shoes a
        needye hand ;" etc.
    6. *pinch . . . disposition*] Some later
editors decline to accept the natural
explanation that the differing dispositions of the newly reconciled
three occasionally clashed.   Mr.
Deighton says : " we have no reason
for thinking they were quarrelsome
in their cups " : but the probability

he cries out " No more ";   reconciles them to his
entreaty, and himself to the drink.

First Serv. But it raises the greater war between him and
his discretion.   10

Sec. Serv. Why, this it is to have a name in great men's
fellowship: I had as lief have a reed that will do
me no service, as a partisan I could not heave.

First Serv. To be called into a huge sphere, and not to
be seen to move in't, are the holes where eyes   15
should be, which pitifully disaster the cheeks.

---

12. *lief*] Capell; *liue* F; *lieve* F 3.

---

of some friction was great, and the
next speech has far more point if it
signifies that the means (more drink)
whereby Lepidus *healed strife between
the others*, increased that between
himself and his discretion. That
pinch . . . disposition should mean :
" as they ply each other hard with
the mischievous desire of seeing one
another under the table " (Deighton),
or = stint themselves by the disposal of alms, (i.e. an extra share) to
Lepidus, which is according to Mr.
A. E. Thiselton, or that it refers to
" the sign they give each other regarding ' the disposition ' of Lepidus
to drink " (Collier), is surely unlikely ;
as also the consequence that *No more*
= no more drink, instead of being
an exclamation like " Soft, Cæsar!"
(II. ii. 83 *ante*), and that " reconciles
them to his entreaty," etc. = ob-
tains their assent to his taking no
more and yet persuades himself to
take it.

12, 13. *a reed that will do me no
service*] † Not, I think, " a reed which
will not serve me well *qua* reed," but
" a reed, which (in the nature of the
case) is no use as a weapon." [R]

13. *partisan*] " a sharp two-edged
sword placed on the summit of a
staff for the defence of foot soldiers
against cavalry " (Fairholt).

14-16. *To . . . cheeks*] According to
the construction, two circumstances,

the call to occupy a high position and
the failure to make a figure in it, are
compared to eyeless sockets. An allusion in *spheres* has been pointed out
to the Ptolemaic system of astronomy,
and the hollow concentric spheres,
each of the first seven with its planet,
with which that system surrounds
the earth. The servant's elliptical
speech seems to compare (1) such
spheres, supposing their planets were
unseen, to disfiguring eyeless sockets ;
(2) great positions in life, meanly
tenanted, to spheres in such a case ;
and, finally, Lepidus, the man of
no account, to the hypothetically
non-luminous planets. Malone quotes
for Shakespeare's use of *sphere* in
connection with *eyes*, Sonnet cxix.
7, and *Hamlet*, I. v. 17. The spheres
aforesaid are those of the Moon,
Mercury, Venus, the Sun, Mars,
Jupiter, Saturn ; after them is that
of the fixed stars, and, finally, en-
folding all, the *Primum Mobile*, which
was the first moved and communi-
cated its motion to the inner spheres.
See also on IV. xv. 10, 11 *post*.

16. *disaster*] A word of astrological
origin, and so probably suggested
here, as Rolfe notes, by the preceding figure. An adjective *disastered* (cf. " ill-starred ") occurs
thrice in the Countess of Pembroke's
Antonie (1595), e.g. in Act II : " us
disastered men," " this *disastered* woe."

K

A sennet sounded.   Enter CÆSAR, ANTONY, POMPEY, LEPIDUS,
    AGRIPPA, MÆCENAS, ENOBARBUS, MENAS, *with other
    captains.*

Ant. [*To Cæsar*] Thus do they, sir: they take the flow o'
        the Nile
    By certain scales i' the pyramid; they know,
    By the height, the lowness, or the mean, if dearth
    Or foison follow.   The higher Nilus swells,   20
    The more it promises: as it ebbs, the seedsman
    Upon the slime and ooze scatters his grain,
    And shortly comes to harvest.
Lep. Y'have strange serpents there ?
Ant. Ay, Lepidus.   25
Lep. Your serpent of Egypt is bred now of your mud by
    the operation of your sun: so is your crocodile.

17 To Cæsar] Capell.

A sennet] A particular set of notes (not now known) on the trumpet, differing from a flourish. Cf. *Satiromastix* (Pearson's *Dekker*, i. 222): " Trumpets sound a florish, and then *a sennate.*" See the derivation discussed in Naylor's *Shakespeare and Music* (1896), p. 178. The forms *sonet*, *sonnet*, have suggested *sonare*,—*synnet*, *signet*, etc., *signum*, as the source.

18. *By certain scales*, etc.] Cf. Lyly, *Campaspe*, The prologue at the Blacke Friers: " It was a signe of famine to Ægypt, when Nylus flowed lesse than twelve cubites, or more than eighteene." Malone thinks Shakespeare got his information from Pory's translation of Leo's *History of Africa* (1600): " Upon another side of the island standeth an house alone by itselfe, in the midst whereof there is a foure-square cesterne or channel of eighteen cubits deep, whereinto the water of Nilus is conveyed by a certaine sluice under ground. And in the midst of the cisterne there is erected a certaine *piller*, which is *marked and divided into so many cubits*

as the cisterne containeth in depth. . . . If the water reacheth only to the fifteenth cubit of the said *piller*, they hope for a fruitful yeere following; but if [it] stayeth between the twelfth cubit and the fifteenth, then the increase of the yeere will prove but mean: if it resteth between the tenth and twelfth cubits, then it is a sign that corne will be solde ten ducates the bushel." Reed quotes Holland's *Pliny* (1601), Bk. v, chap. ix, but the resemblance there is more distant.

20. *foison*] profusion, plenty. Cf. *The Tempest*, II. i. 170; IV. i. 110, etc.

26. *Your*] A common colloquialism. So in *Hamlet*, IV. iii. 22 : " *Your* worm is *your* only emperor for diet," etc. On its occurrence in the text, Abbott (*Shakespearian Grammar*, § 221) observes: " Though in this instance the *your* may seem literally justified, the repetition of it indicates a colloquial vulgarity which suits the character of Lepidus." It certainly sets off his temporary condition.

bred . . . mud] The doctrine (abiogenesis or equivocal generation) was

Ant. They are so.

Pom. Sit,—and some wine!   A health to Lepidus!

Lep. I am not so well as I should be: but I'll ne'er out.   30

Eno. Not till you have slept; I fear me you'll be in till
then.

Lep. Nay, certainly, I have heard the Ptolemies'
pyramises are very goodly things; without contra-
diction I have heard that.   35

Men. [*Aside to Pom.*] Pompey, a word.

Pom.   [*Aside to Men.*] Say in mine ear, what is't?

Men. [*Aside to Pom.*] Forsake thy seat, I do beseech thee,
captain,
And hear me speak a word.

Pom.   [*Aside to Men.*] Forbear me till anon.—
This wine for Lepidus!

Lep. What manner o' thing is your crocodile?   40

36-38. As Asides first by Rowe.
Eare. F.

38. *anon.*—] *anon.*   Whispers in 's

current in Shakespeare's day, that
living matter can be produced from
matter without life. So Jonson, *The
Alchemist*, II. i. 171 :—

"Beside, who doth not see, in
daily practice,
Art can beget bees, hornets,
beetles, wasps,
Out of the carcasses, and dung
of creatures ;
Yea, scorpions of an herb, being
rightly placed?"

Cf. also Shirley, *The Traitor*, IV. ii·
(Mermaid ed., p. 157) :—

" oh that my voice
Could call a serpent from corrupted Nile," etc. ;

and Sylvester's *Du Bartas*, week 1,
day 2, p. 31 in 1621 ed. : " As on the
edges of som standing Lake . . . The
foamy slime itselfe transformeth oft
To green half-Tadpoles, . . . Half
dead, half-living ; half a frog,
half-mud." At the present time
the question has been re-opened
owing to the results of certain
experiments.

30. *I'll ne'er out*] I'll never refuse a
pledge, never stand out. See *2 H.
IV.* v. iii. 68 (of drinking) : " A' will
not out ; he is true bred " ; Massinger, *The Parliament of Love*, II. i,
at end : " *I'll not out* for a second,"
where it is said by the second person
to take up a bet ; F. Spence's *Lucian*
(1684), *The Epistle Dedicatory*, sig.
C 2 : " Yet *Custom* so requiring, I
have very slavishly imitated *Others*,
and fancy myself like those *Sparks*,
who will ever be in the *Fashion*, Let
it never be so damn'd Foppish, silly
and Troublesome : Nay, rather than
be *out*, we'll go upon *Trust for
Ridiculousness* and *Mortification*," etc.

31. *in*] A play on the opposite
phrase to " be out " (so Felltham,
Lusoria, 1661, xxxv, p. 33 : " being
in, I must go on ") and the sense
" *in* drink."

34. *pyramises*] A plural peculiar to
the bibulous Lepidus, but corresponding with the Latin singular
pyramis, the common form in Shakespeare's time. For the usual plural
pyramides, cf. v. ii. 61 *post*.

Ant. It is shap'd, sir, like itself, and it is as broad as it
    hath breadth: it is just so high as it is, and moves
    with it own organs. It lives by that which
    nourisheth it, and the elements once out of it, it
    transmigrates.   45

Lep. What colour is it of?

Ant. Of it own colour too.

Lep. 'Tis a strange serpent.

Ant. 'Tis so, and the tears of it are wet.

Cæs. Will this description satisfy him?   50

Ant. With the health that Pompey gives him, else he is
    a very epicure.

Pom. [*Aside to Men.*] Go hang, sir, hang! Tell me of
    that? away!
    Do as I bid you.—Where's this cup I call'd for?

Men. [*Aside to Pom.*] If for the sake of merit thou wilt
    hear me,   55
    Rise from thy stool.

Pom. [*Aside to Men.*] I think th'art mad. The
    matter?   [*Rises and walks aside.*

Men. I have ever held my cap off to thy fortunes.

53-57. As asides first by Johnson.   57. Rises . . .] Johnson; not in F.

43, 47. *it*] its. A common flexion-
less form, transitional between the
usual neuter possessive *his* and the
later *its*. Cf. *Lear*, I. iv. 238, 9 : " The
hedge-sparrow fed the cuckoo so long,
That it had it head bit off by it young."

44, 45. *elements . . . transmigrates*]
Here " elements " apparently = the
vital elements, life, not the complete
group of four which compose everything (see on v. ii. 288 *post*). In
" transmigrates " is probably, as
Delius says, a facetious allusion to
the Pythagorean doctrine of the
transmigration of souls, as in *A.Y.L.*
III. ii. 188, and *Twelfth Night*, IV. ii.
55-66; unless the word be merely
" rots," " passes into other forms of
matter," in a quaint disguise.

49. *tears*] A by-allusion to the
popular belief which furnishes a
figure in *Othello*, IV. i. 257; *2 H. VI.*
III. i. 226. " If the Crocodile findeth

a man by the brim of the water, or
by the cliff, he slayeth him if he may,
and then he weepeth upon him, and
swalloweth him at the last. . . ."
(*Bartholomew* [*Berthelet*], Bk. XVIII §33.)

58. *held my cap off to*] been a servant
to, followed. The phrase here seems
rather to derive from the etiquette of
service at a time when head-coverings
were more constantly worn than now,
than from occasional acts of deference
or courtesy, such as " *Off-capp'd* to
him " in *Othello*, I. i. 10 (F). Cf.
Beaumont and Fletcher. *The Honest
Man's Fortune*, I. i (Camb. x. 213):—

  " *Long.* Counsel's the office of a
    servant," . . .
  " *Mont.* Stay, sir, what one example
    since the time
  That first you put your *hat off* to
    me, have
  You noted in me to encourage you
    To this presumption?"

Pom. Thou hast serv'd me with much faith: what's
    else to say?
    Be jolly, lords.

Ant.   These quick-sands, Lepidus,
    Keep off them, for you sink.   60

Men. Wilt thou be lord of all the world?

Pom.   What say'st thou?

Men. Wilt thou be lord of the whole world?   That's
    twice.

Pom. How should that be?

Men.   But entertain it,
    And though thou think me poor, I am the man
    Will give thee all the world.

Pom.   Hast thou drunk well? 65

Men. No, Pompey, I have kept me from the cup.
    Thou art, if thou dar'st be, the earthly Jove:
    Whate'er the ocean pales, or sky inclips,
    Is thine, if thou wilt ha't.

Pom.   Show me which way.

Men. These three world-sharers, these competitors,   70
    Are in thy vessel.   Let me cut the cable,
    And when we are put off, fall to their throats:
    All there is thine.

---

60. *for*] F; *'fore* Theobald; *or* Dyce, ed. 2 (S. Walker conj.).   73. *there*]
F; *then* Pope, and Southern MS. notes in F 4; *theirs* Steevens conj.

In some notes on England quoted
by Sir W. Besant (*London in the
Time of the Tudors*, 1904, p. 191)
as written in 1558, and translated
for and published in *The Antiquarian
Repertory*, vol. iv, occurs: "The
servants wait on the master bare-
headed, and leave their *caps* on the
buffet."

59, 60. *These quick-sands . . . sink*]
Perhaps Lepidus collapses here. Pompey's health (see line 84 *post*) is too
late.   There is a drinking scene in
Heywood's *Iron Age*, I. (Pearson's
Heywood, iii. 281) in which Paris is
similarly overcome, but feignedly, as
afterwards appears, while Thersites
has something of the mocking spirit

of Enobarbus and the temperance of
Cæsar.

61, etc.] See North, *post*, p. 266.

68. *pales . . . inclips*] fences in, as
with pales . . . embraces. Cf. *clip*.
IV. viii. 8 *post*.

70. *competitors*] confederates. See
on I. iv. 3 *ante*.

73. *All there is thine*] † Pope's *then*
is attractive, and makes easy sense.
But we can retain F, I think, so long
as we do not take *there* as a demon-
strative, and do, in thought if not in
type, insert a comma: *All there is,
thine*, i.e. "then all the world is
yours." This is almost Furness's
conjecture (*All there is, is thine*) but
his second *is* is needless. [R]

Pom.   Ah, this thou shouldst have done,
    And not have spoke on't!   In me 'tis villainy,
    In thee, 't had been good service.   Thou must know, 75
    'Tis not my profit that does lead mine honour;
    Mine honour, it.   Repent that e'er thy tongue
    Hath so betray'd thine act.   Being done unknown,
    I should have found it afterwards well done,
    But must condemn it now.   Desist, and drink.   80
Men. [*Aside*] For this,
    I'll never follow thy pall'd fortunes more.
    Who seeks and will not take, when once 'tis offer'd,
    Shall never find it more.
Pom.   This health to Lepidus!
Ant. Bear him ashore, I'll pledge it for him, Pompey.   85
Eno. Here's to thee, Menas!
Men.   Enobarbus, welcome!
Pom. Fill till the cup be hid.
Eno. There's a strong fellow, Menas.
                [*Pointing to the Attendant who carries off Lepidus.*
Men. Why?
Eno. 'A bears the third part of the world, man; see'st
    not?   90
Men. The third part, then, is drunk: would it were all,
    That it might go on wheels!

---

81. Aside] Capell.   88. Pointing . . .] Steevens; Pointing to Lepidus.
Rowe; not in F.   91. *part, then, is*] *part, then he is* F; *part, then is* Rowe.

82. *pall'd*] decayed, dwindled. Compare *Hamlet*, v. ii. 9: " When our deep plots do *pall* "; Kyd, *1 Ieronimo*, ii. iv. 54 : " Which strooke amazement to their *pauled* speeche," etc. *Pall* is said to be an abbreviated form of *appal*, both originally meaning to become or be made pale. So of wine when it loses colour and becomes vapid by standing. Compare Spence's *Lucian*, 1684, ii. 78 : " swallow delitious Wine, whilst you must only drink such as is *pall'd* and Taplash."

92. *go on wheels*] Proverbial for " go fast," and especially of the world. Cf. *T.G.V.* iii. i. 320; B. Rich, *The Honestie of this Age*, 1614 (Percy Society, 1844, p. 30) : " They were wont to say, the world did runne on *wheeles*: and it may well bee it hath done so in times past, but I say now it goes on crouches, for it is waxen old," etc. ; A. Wilson, *The Inconstant Ladie*, i. i. 11 :—

        " I am angrie
    To see the guiddie world run thus
        o' *wheeles*
    In such untoward tracks," etc. ;

Mabbe's *Celestina*, 1631, ix (Tudor Trans. p. 169) : " But such is this world, it comes and goes upon *wheeles*."

Eno. Drink thou; increase the reels.

Men. Come.

Pom. This is not yet an Alexandrian feast. 95

Ant. It ripens towards it; strike the vessels, ho!
Here's to Cæsar!

---

93. *increase the reels*] Cf. line 116 *post*, and example in note on line 124; *Coriolanus*, ii. i. 123; also *Histriomastrix*, iv. i. 28 (Simpson's *School of Shakspere*, ii. 57): "Why should this *reeling* world (drunke with the juice Of *Plenties'* bounty)," etc.; Heywood, *Rape of Lucrece* (Pearson's reprint, v. 168): "heres a giddy and drunken world, it *Reeles*, it hath got the staggers," etc. Douce conjectured *revels* for *reels*, and there is another word *rule*, signifying revel, bustle, rowdy behaviour: cf. *Twelfth Night*, ii. iii. 133; Middleton, *A Chaste Maid*, etc. i. i. 208: "Come now, we'll see how the *rules* go within": but there seems no need of change. Steevens cleverly conjectured "and grease the wheels."

96. *Strike the vessels*] ?Tap the casks. So Weber, the editor of Beaumont and Fletcher's works, which supply: "Home, Launce, and *strike* a fresh piece of wine," etc. (*Monsieur Thomas*, v. x. 42); "*Strike* me the oldest Sack," etc. (*Love's Pilgrimage*, ii. iv (Camb. vi, p. 272). Dyce adds from Prior's *Alma*, chap. iii. 425:—

"*Strikes* not the present tun for, fear
The vintage should be bad next year," etc.

The demand comes rather late in the feast, but its giver had had to call thrice for wine, lines 29, 39, 53 *ante*. On the other hand, I suspect that a sense "fill the vessels (i.e. the cups) full" may some day find at least excuse. A "strike" was "an instrument with a straight edge for levelling (striking off) a measure of grain" (Skeat, *Etymol. Dict.* § v), whence came "strike," a measure of varying amount, and a verb meaning to level corn to the top of the measure with a "strike"; and further (see Wright, *Eng. Dial. Dict.*), the adverb *strike* = full to the top. Again, the sense "fill" might conceivably be reached from that of "to lade a fluid from one vessel into another," as cane juice into a cooler in sugar making. This is clearly the sense in Harrison's directions for brewing (Holinshed's Chronicle, 1587, *Description of England*, book ii, chap. vi. p. 170): "and when it hath sodden, . . . she *striketh* it also, and reserveth it vnto mixture with the rest when time dooth serue therefore." Just before (p. 169) we have "where it is *stricken* ouer, or from whence it is taken againe," etc. The suggestion of Holt White again, that the vessels were kettledrums, though entirely neglected, is backed up by the likelihood of a call for a *noisy* toast in response to Pompey's request for Alexandrian riot. He quotes *Hamlet*, v. ii. 284, and Enobarbus, line 108 *post*. The idea of healths to music was familiar apart from Danish customs. Cf. Beaumont and Fletcher, *The Scornful Lady*, i. i. 6: "at a gulp, without trumpets"; D'Avenant, *Albovine*, 1629, ii. (*Dram. Works*, 1872, i, p. 36), where, if he had this scene in view, he is a valuable witness for Holt White:—

"*Cuny.* Sound high!
Alb. More wine and noise! Now boy, I celebrate
Valdaura's health—
Cuny. Bid their instruments speak louder."

Cf. also Shadwell, *The Miser*, iii. ii (*Works*, 1720, iii. 52): "Come on, Musicianers, strike up, hey: Here Forsooth, here's your Health; . . ·

Cæs.   I could well forbear't.
It's monstrous labour when I wash my brain
And it grow fouler.
Ant.   Be a child o' the time.
Cæs. Possess it, I'll make answer: 100
But I had rather fast from all, four days,
Than drink so much in one.
Eno.   [*To Antony*]   Ha, my brave emperor,
Shall we dance now the Egyptian Bacchanals,
And celebrate our drink?
Pom.   Let's ha 't, good soldier.
Ant. Come, let's all take hands,   105
Till that the conquering wine hath steep'd our sense
In soft and delicate Lethe.

---

99. *And it grow*] F; . . . *grows* F 2.

102. To Antony] added by Capell.

[*He drinks, they flourish.*] Ha, Ha; this is the prettiest way of drinking, I vow; it encourages us, as Drums and Trumpets do, when we let off our Guns at a Muster"; *Ibid.* (IV. i), p. 71: " Oh, if I had but Fiddles to play a Health now!" Steevens's view that " strike the vessels " may be compared with " chink glasses," found a supporter in Cowden Clarke among modern editors.

98. *wash my brain*] Mr. Craig compares Nashe, *Anatomie of Absurditie*, 1589 (ed. McKerrow, p. 41, line 3): " Euery one knowes that he that *washeth his braines* with diuers kinds of wines, is the next doore to a drunken man," etc.

99. *And it grow*] Editors (save Singer, ed. 2, " *An it grow* ") read with F 2. But *and* = if (whence the usual *an*) is used by Shakespeare. Cf. *The Tempest*, II. i. 187 :—
 " *Ant.* What a blow vvas there giuen?
  Seb. And it had not falne flat-long."
† I think that *and* is more probably the ordinary copula, and *grow* a subjunctive, caused by the feeling that *when* is in effect a conditional, not temporal, conjunction. [R]

100. *Possess it*] Have your way, enjoy your wish to pledge me; a somewhat freer, but quite intelligible, use of *possess* than e.g. in Jonson's *Volpone*, v. iv. 15 :—
 " He says, sir, he has weighty affairs of state,
  That now require him whole, some other time
  You may *possess* him."
Indeed we might boldly explain "take it." Cf. *The Tempest*, III. ii. 102: " Remember First to *possess* his books; " etc. Among unnecessary conjectures are *Profess it* (Collier MS. and ed. 2), *Propose it* (Staunton).
† An anonymous explanation, quoted by Furness, is " Rather be its master, say I," which would be wholly convincing if it were not for the " But " at the opening of the next line, where we should rather expect " Nay," or " Indeed." Even so, I prefer it to any of the others. [R]

106, 107. *steep'd* . . . *Lethe*] Cf. *Twelfth Night*, IV. i. 66: " Let fancy still my sense in *Lethe steep* "; and Armin, *Two Maids of Moreclacke* (1609), Grosart's *Occas. Issues*, vol. xiii, p. 99: " What is thy haste in *leathe steep't?* speak," etc.

Eno.   All take hands.
Make battery to our ears with the loud music:
The while, I'll place you, then the boy shall sing.
The holding every man shall bear as loud   110
As his strong sides can volley.

[*Music plays.   Enobarbus places them hand in hand.*

THE SONG.

Come, thou monarch of the vine,
Plumpy Bacchus with pink eyne!
In thy fats our cares be drown'd,

110. *bear*] Theobald; *beate* F.

110. *holding*] Malone quotes a pamphlet, *The Servingman's Comfort* (1598): "A song is to be song, the undersong or holding whereof is, It is merrie in Haul, when Beardes wagges all." This suggests the same meaning as the Somonour's "stif burdoun" in Chaucer (*Prol.*, line 673), a bass part or "ground melody." But the meaning here must be rather "refrain," since if Enobarbus' directions were followed the boy's song would be drowned by an "undersong."

113. *pink eyne*] "small, winking, half-shut eyes." Steevens quotes Holland's *Pliny*, bk. xi, [cxxxvii, p. 335 E in vol. i, 1601 ed.] : "also them that were *pinke-eyed* and had verie small eies they termed *ocellae*." Dyce cites Cotgrave, *Fr. and Eng. Dict.*: "*Oeil de rat*, a small eye, *pinke-eye*, little sight." Cf. also Minshew, *Guide to the Tongues* (1617): "to Pinke, or *winke in slumbering*, *pinck-eyd*, *somniculosus*"; Lyly's *Euphues* (W. Bond, I. p. 254, line 25): "if she be gagge toothed, tell hir some merry ieste, to make hir laughe, if *pinke eyed*, some dolefull Historye, to cause hir weepe, in the one hir grinning will shewe hir deformed, in the other hir whining, lyke a Pigge halfe rosted"; Kyd, *Soliman and Perseda* (v. iii. 7 in *Works*, ed. Boas, who prints *pinky-ey'd*) : "The mightie *pinckanyed* brand-

bearing God"; *Laneham's Letter* (*Captain Cox*, etc., Ballad Society, 1871, p. 17): "the bear with his *pink nyez* leering after his enmiez approch"; Harrison's *Description of England* (Holinshed's *Chronicle*, 1587, bk. ii. chap. vi, p. 170): "and either fall quite vnder the boord, or else not daring to stirre from their stooles, sit still *pinking* with their narrow *eies* as halfe sleeping, till the fume of their aduersarie be digested that he may go to it afresh"; D'Avenant, *The Platonic Lovers*, II. i (*Dramatic Works*, 1872 ed. ii. 26) :—

"O Sir, she hath the prettiest *pinking eyes;*
    The holes are no bigger than a pistol bore."

Even the indefinite among these examples and others, point rather to smallness than redness, a sense some think may be also referred to. In two or three allusions to the colour of Bacchus' eyes which I have come upon the word *red* is used. Compare S. Rowlands, *More Knaves Yet?* etc. (Percy Society, xxxiv, 1843, p. 100): "What rhume's in Bacchus's eyes? how *red* they looke:" etc.

114. *fats*] vats, which is the Southern form of the word. Cf. Browne, *Britannia's Pastorals*, II. i, 373: "Within a tanner's *fat* I oft have eyed . . . a large ox-hide In liquor mix'd" etc.

With thy grapes our hairs be crown'd: 115
          Cup us till the world go round,
          Cup us till the world go round!

Cæs. What would you more? Pompey, good-night.
          Good brother,
Let me request you off: our graver business
Frowns at this levity. Gentle lords, let's part,   120
You see we have burnt our cheeks. Strong Enobarb
Is weaker than the wine, and mine own tongue
Splits what it speaks: the wild disguise hath almost
Antick'd us all. What needs more words? Good
          night.
Good Antony, your hand.

Pom.   I'll try you on the shore.
Ant. And shall, sir; give's your hand.
Pom.   O Antony,   126
You have my father's house. But what, we are friends?
Come down into the boat.
Eno.   Take heed you fall not.

          [*Exeunt all but Enobarbus and Menas.*
          Menas, I'll not on shore.

119. *you off: our*] Rowe (semicolon); *you of our* F.   123. *Splits*] F 4;
Spleet's F.   128, 129. *fall not. Menas,*] *fall not* Menas; F. Exeunt . . .]
Camb. edd.; not in F;   129. Men.] Capell; not in F. See note.

123. *Splits what it speaks*] a peril-
ously fissile combination of sounds.
    disguise] O.E.D. cites Jonson,
Masque of Augurs, line 46: "*Disguise!* what mean you by that? do
you think that his majesty sits here
to expect drunkards?" See also
Shirley, *The Wedding*, v. ii (*Works*,
1833, i. 448): "*Raw.* I am not
drunk. *Lod.* No, but thou art *dis-
guis'd* shrewdly."
    124. *Antick'd us*] Made antics or
grotesques of us. Cf. Dekker, *The
Bel-man of London*, pt. i, 1608 (*Temple
Classics* ed., p. 86): "At the length,
drunken healths reeled up and downe
the table. . . . The whole *Roome*
showed a farre off (but that there was
heard such a noyse) like a Dutch
peece of *Drollery*: for they sat at table

as if they had beene so many *Anticks*;"
etc.
    125. *I'll try . . . shore*] This may
mean "I'll test your hospitality
ashore," with time of so doing un-
defined; but more probably Pompey,
fired by the "Alexandrian feast,"
wants to continue the debauch, offers
to vie drinking powers on shore then,
and actually accompanies the other
"great fellows." This suits Antony's
reply and his own: "Come down
into the boat" (line 128), which is
otherwise rather abrupt to a depart-
ing guest.
    127. *my father's house*] See on II. vi.
27 *ante*.
    128, 129. † I have given the
usually accepted reading, but it is
not, I think, satisfactory. Enobarbus'

Men.   No, to my cabin.

These drums, these trumpets, flutes! what!   130
Let Neptune hear we bid a loud farewell
To these great fellows: sound and be hang'd,
    sound out!   [*Sound a flourish, with drums.*
Eno. Hoo! says 'a. There's my cap.
Men. Hoo! Noble captain, come.   [*Exeunt.*

131. *a loud*] Rowe, ed. 3; *aloud* F.

warning would be more naturally
addressed (in spite of his " plainness")
to his equal, Menas, than to the
triumvirs and Pompey; "Menas" is
a rather awkwardly formal opening
to " I'll not on shore "; and would
even Enobarbus thus force his continued company on Menas? F
reads as follows :—

  Eno. Take heed you fall not
    Menas: Ile not on shore,
    No to my cabin: . . .

thus giving the whole speech to
Enobarbus, which is clearly wrong,
since the cabin is Menas's. I
suggest that the MS. had *Menas*
twice, once as vocative, and once as

speech heading, and that we should
read :—

  Eno. Take heed you fall not, Menas.
  Men. I'll not on shore. No, to
    my cabin.

Menas is then saying, in effect,
" No need for your kindly warning;
I'm not going ashore; no, we're both
going to my cabin, but let's give the
great fellows a good send-off." [R]

  133. *says a'*] † Again I retain the
usual reading (F *Hoo saies a*), but
with even more doubt, and suggest
Hoo! Sessa! (an easy " auditory
error "); cf. *Taming of the Shrew*,
Induc. i. 5, 6, " Let the world slide.
Sessa!" [R]

ACT III

[SCENE I.—*A plain in Syria.*]

Enter VENTIDIUS *as it were in triumph, with* SILIUS, *and other Romans, Officers, and Soldiers; the dead body of* PACORUS *borne before him.*

Ven. Now, darting Parthia, art thou struck, and now
Pleas'd fortune does of Marcus Crassus' death
Make me revenger. Bear the king's son's body
Before our army. Thy Pacorus, Orodes,
Pays this for Marcus Crassus.

Sil.   Noble Ventidius,   5
Whilst yet with Parthian blood thy sword is warm,
The fugitive Parthians follow. Spur through Media,
Mesopotamia, and the shelters whither
The routed fly. So thy grand captain Antony
Shall set thee on triumphant chariots, and   10
Put garlands on thy head.

ACT III

Scene 1

Enter . . .] F, but omitting "with Silius . . . soldiers."   5. Sil.]
Theobald; Romaine F.   8. *whither*] F 2; *whether* F.

<table>
<tr><td>

Scene 1

[See North, *post*, p. 267.]

1. *darting Parthia*] Alluding to the well-known tactics of Parthian horsemen, who, having flung their darts, avoided close quarters by swift retreat, shooting flights of arrows backward as they fled.

2. *Crassus' death*] Crassus (who formed the first triumvirate with Pompey and Cæsar) was defeated 53 B.C. in the plains of Mesopotamia, by Surenas, the general of Orodes, King of Parthia and father of Pacorus; and was treacherously killed during a conference proposed by the victor.

</td><td>

Orodes poured melted gold into the dead man's mouth, bidding him take his fill of what he had so coveted in life. This act possibly suggested II. v. 34, 35 *ante*.

9. *grand captain*] as often. So e.g. John Heywood, *The Spider and the Flie*, 1556 (Spenser Soc., 1894, pp. 218, 223, etc.) :—

"The *ground Captaine* standing
    amid mong this rought,
Was the flie, that " etc. ;

Roister Doister, IV. viii. 26: "I my selfe will mounsire *graunde captaine* undertake."

</td></tr>
</table>

100

Ven.   O Silius, Silius,
I have done enough.   A lower place, note well,
May make too great an act.   For learn this, Silius;
Better to leave undone, than by our deed
Acquire too high a fame, when him we serve's away.
Cæsar and Antony have ever won   16
More in their officer than person: Sossius,
One of my place in Syria, his lieutenant,
For quick accumulation of renown,
Which he achiev'd by the minute, lost his favour.   20
Who does i' the wars more than his captain can,
Becomes his captain's captain: and ambition,
The soldier's virtue, rather makes choice of loss,
Than gain which darkens him.
I could do more to do Antonius good,   25
But 'twould offend him.   And in his offence
Should my performance perish.
Sil.   Thou hast, Ventidius, that
Without the which a soldier and his sword
Grants scarce distinction.   Thou wilt write to Antony?
Ven. I'll humbly signify what in his name,   30
That magical word of war, we have effected;
How with his banners, and his well-paid ranks,
The ne'er-yet-beaten horse of Parthia
We have jaded out o' the field.
Sil.   Where is he now?

12, 13. *A lower ... act*] Subordinate
position may make an achievement
too great for safety.

20. *by the minute*] continually.

lost his favour] There is possibly no
authority for this statement.   It is
not in North (see *post*, p. 267) or
Plutarch, as was kindly pointed out
to me by Professor A. C. Bradley.

22. *captain's captain*] So is Desdemona called (*Othello*, II. i. 74).

22, 23. *ambition ... virtue*] Compare
Othello, III. iii. 350: " the big wars
That make *ambition virtue!* "

24. *darkens him*] him, i.e. the soldier,
as ambition and the rest shows;
otherwise it is equally true that he
who becomes his captain's captain

darkens *him*.   With *darkens*, compare
Coriolanus, IV. vii. 5: " And you are
darken'd in this action, sir, Even by
your own."

29. *Grants scarce*] Equivalent to
" scarcely admit of."   Warburton
first explained lines 28, 29 to mean
that, without discretion, there would
be very little difference between a
soldier and his sword.   Steevens
quotes *Coriolanus*, I. iv. 52-54 :—

        " O noble fellow!
    Who sensibly out-dares his sense-
        less sword,
    And, when it bows, stands up."

31. *word of war*] cf. II. ii. 44 *ante*.

34. *jaded*] " driven like worn-out
nags " (Kittredge).   Cf. Beaumont

Ven. He purposeth to Athens, whither, with what haste 35
　　The weight we must convey with 's will permit,
　　We shall appear before him.　On there, pass along!
　　　　　　　　　　　　　　　　　　　　　[*Exeunt.*

[SCENE II.—*Rome.　An ante-chamber in Cæsar's house.*]

Enter AGRIPPA *at one door,* ENOBARBUS *at another.*

Agr. What, are the brothers parted?
Eno. They have despatch'd with Pompey, he is gone,
　　The other three are sealing.　Octavia weeps
　　To part from Rome; Cæsar is sad, and Lepidus,
　　Since Pompey's feast, as Menas says, is troubled 5
　　With the green-sickness.
Agr.　　　　　　　　　　'Tis a noble Lepidus.
Eno. A very fine one: O, how he loves Cæsar!
Agr. Nay, but how dearly he adores Mark Antony!
Eno. Cæsar?　Why he's the Jupiter of men.
Agr. What's Antony?　The god of Jupiter. 10
Eno. Spake you of Cæsar?　How, the nonpareil?
Agr. O Antony, O thou Arabian bird!
Eno. Would you praise Cæsar, say "Cæsar," go no
　　further.
Agr. Indeed he plied them both with excellent praises.

Scene II

11. *Spake*] F; *Speak* F 3.

and Fletcher, *Philaster*, I. i. 179:
"Oh! this same whorson Con-
science, how it *jades* us!"

Scene II

6. *green-sickness*] The form of
anæmia supposed peculiar to love-
sick damsels. "Lepidus, it is in-
sinuated, is languishing for love of
Cæsar and Antony" (L. in *The
Eversley Shakespeare*).　And they are
parodying his ecstasies.

7. *A very fine one*] This comment
was possibly evoked by the sound of
the word *Lepidus*, which, to me, at

least, is rather suggestive of some kind
of sea creature of the inerter type.
But perhaps this is seeing too much:
(† and why not evoked by the Latin
meaning of *lepidus* = elegant. [R])
Lepidus is presently a "shard-borne
beetle" (line 20 *post*).

12. *Arabian bird*] A frequent phrase
for the fabulous phœnix, of which but
one was supposed to exist at a time.
Cf. *Cymbeline*, I. vi. 17.

13. "*Cæsar*"; *go no further*] So
"Cæsar" implies the perfection of
generous clemency in III. xiii. 55 *post*;
"Further than he is Cæsar."

Eno. But he loves Cæsar best, yet he loves Antony: 15
  Hoo! hearts, tongues, figures, scribes, bards, poets, cannot
  Think, speak, cast, write, sing, number, hoo,
  His love to Antony.   But as for Cæsar,
  Kneel down, kneel down, and wonder.
Agr.   Both he loves.
Eno. They are his shards, and he their beetle, so: 20
         [*Trumpet within*]
  This is to horse.   Adieu, noble Agrippa.
Agr. Good fortune, worthy soldier, and farewell.

  Enter CÆSAR, ANTONY, LEPIDUS, *and* OCTAVIA.

Ant. No further, sir.
Cæs. You take from me a great part of myself;
  Use me well in 't.   Sister, prove such a wife   25
  As my thoughts make thee, and as my farthest band
  Shall pass on thy approof.   Most noble Antony,

16, 17. *Hoo*] F 1-3; *Ho* F 4. 16. *figures*] Hanmer; *Figure* F. 20. *beetle, so:*] F; *beetle;* [Trumpet within] *so,* Capell, and, with minor modifications, most edd.   No trumpet in F.

16, 17. *Hoo! hearts . . . Think . . .*] I retain *Hoo!* of F as characteristic of the speaker and also appropriate to the semi-hysterical adulation of Lepidus which he mimics. A common practice of sonneteers is aimed at in the ensuing correspondence of a succession of nouns with another of verbs, in separate lines. Cf. B. Griffin, *Fidessa*, 1596, Sonnet xlvii :—
 "I see, I hear, I feele, I know, I rue,
  My fate, my fame, my praise, my losse, my fall ; " etc.
figures] metaphors and similes.
17. *cast*; compute. Cf. II. vi. 54 *ante.*
number] versify, put into "numbers."
20. *They . . . beetle*] Steevens : "They are the *wings* that raise this *heavy lumpish insect* from the ground. So, in *Macbeth* [III. ii. 42] : ' the shard-borne beetle.' " See also *Cymbeline*, III. iii. 20, "The *sharded beetle*." The shards are properly the horny cases or sheaths of the insect's wings.
beetle, so.] † I can see no good reason for deserting the pointing of F, though from Capell various editors have inclined to insert the S.D. (which is not in F) between *beetle* and *so*, making the latter a part of Enobarbus' comment on the trumpet-call. [R]
21-2. It looks as though there must have been some second thoughts here. Two more unmistakable exit lines it would be hard to find, but the passage of asides later in the scene is effective.
26, 27. *as my farthest band . . . approof*] such as I would stake anything that you will prove to be. *Band* is frequent for *bond*, as in *Two Wise Men*, etc., 1619, I. i (see Chapman, ed.

Let not the piece of virtue which is set
Betwixt us, as the cement of our love
To keep it builded, be the ram to batter   30
The fortress of it; for better might we
Have lov'd without this mean, if on both parts
This be not cherish'd.

Ant.   Make me not offended
In your distrust.

Cæs.   I have said.

Ant.   You shall not find,
Though you be therein curious, the least cause   35
For what you seem to fear: so, the gods keep you,
And make the hearts of Romans serve your ends!
We will here part.

Cæs. Farewell, my dearest sister, fare thee well,

---

31. *for better*] F; *for far better* Capell.

1875, *Poems*, etc., p. 388, col. 1, line 46: " a friend of mine must use a thousand pound and intreats my *band*"; etc. For *approof* indicating the proved possession of a quality, compare *All's Well*, II. v. 3: " Of very valiant *approof*." † And for *pass on* cf. *M. for M.* II. i. 22, 23 :—

" what knows the laws
That thieves do *pass on* thieves?"
about which there has been needless difficulty, since it does not mean that thieves pass laws, but that the law takes no cognisance of the fact that thieves (in the jury) may be *passing verdicts on* thieves (in the dock). [R]

28. *piece of virtue*] So in *The Tempest* I. ii. 56: " Thy mother was a *piece of virtue* "; Sir T. Browne, *Hydriotaphia*, Epistle Ded.: " A complete *piece of Virtue* must be made from the Centos of all Ages, as all the beauties of *Greece* could make but one handsome *Venus*." *Piece* often = masterpiece, as here (most probably) and in v. ii. 99 *post*, but is also used merely for " creature " and the like words. So in *The Taming of a Shrew* (*Six Old Plays*, Nichols, 1779,

p. 212) : " *Ferando.* 'Tis wel done *Kate. Emelia*, I sure, and like a loving *peece*," etc.

29. *cement*] accented on first syllable, like the verb in II. i. 48 *ante*. So commonly.

31. *for*] † Capell's emendation is graphically easy, and tempting. [R]

32. *mean*] *mean* and *means* were used indifferently. Cf. Adlington's *Apuleius*, 1566, chap. xxii (Tudor Trans. p. 124) : " shewing a *mean* to Psyches to save her life," etc. † But I suspect that *mean* here has the sense of " intermediary." [R]

33, 34. *Make . . . In your distrust*] This does not seem to = " In your distrust of me, don't offend me," but rather " Make me not offended *with*, or *at* your mistrust," the use of *in* being comparable to one or other of those remarked by Abbot (*Shakes. Grammar*, § 162). Cf. *T. and C.* II. iii. 150 " *In* second voice we'll not be satisfied."

35. *curious*] particular, minute in inquiry. The word is used of careful or over-exactness of any kind. See *R. and J.*, I. iv. 31, " What *curious* eye doth quote deformities."

handwritten: brother // sister relationship.

The elements be kind to thee, and make   40
Thy spirits all of comfort! fare thee well.
Oct. My noble brother!
Ant. The April's in her eyes, it is love's spring,
And these the showers to bring it on.   Be cheerful.
Oct. Sir, look well to my husband's house; and—
Cæs.   *[handwritten: look after 'cause]* What,   45
Octavia?
Oct.   I'll tell you in your ear.——   *[handwritten: Ant + Oct going away]*
[handwritten: shows intimacy + affection]
Ant. Her tongue will not obey her heart, nor can
Her heart inform her tongue—the swan's down
   feather, — *[handwritten: Octavia]*
That stands upon the swell at the full of tide, *[handwritten: which way??]*
And neither way inclines.   *[handwritten: Slack water — surely not??]*   50
Eno. [*Aside to Agr.*] Will Cæsar weep? *[handwritten: surely not??]*
Agr.   [*Aside to Eno.*] He has a cloud in's face.
Eno. [*Aside to Agr.*] He were the worse for that were he a horse,   *[handwritten: joke. He might cry / rain cloud]*
So is he being a man.

49. *at the full*] F; *at full* F 2, and many edd.   51-59. Aside . . .] Capell.

40, 41. *The elements . . . comfort*]
Most likely a parting wish for favourable weather; Mason quotes *Othello*,
II. i. 45. Johnson, however, thought
that the elements composing the
human body are invoked to act har-
moniously and induce cheerfulness.
See on v. ii. 288 *post*.

43, 44. *The April's . . . on*] Cf.
Bodenham's *Belvedere*, 1600, (Spenser
Soc., 1875, p. 28) :—

" *MAY is not loues month, MAY is
   full of flowers,
   But dropping APRIL: Loue is full
   of showers.*"

47, 48. *nor can . . . her tongue*]
Cleopatra, at parting, is similarly at
a stand in I. iii. 89: " something it is
I would,——"

48-50. *the swan's . . . inclines*] It is
not clear whether Octavia's heart is
the swan's down feather, swayed
neither way on the full tide of emotion
at parting with her brother to accom-
pany her husband, or whether it is
merely the *inaction* of heart and

tongue, which is compared to that of
the feather. († Surely *the full of tide*
= slack water, just before the ebb
starts. [R])

52. *were he a horse*] According to
Madden (*Diary of Master William
Silence*) " a cloud " was simply the
absence of a white star. His auth-
orities are Gervase Markham (*Caval-
arice*) for the star as " an excellent
good marke " and the viciousness
of " the horse that hath no white at
all "; and Sadler, *De Procreandis*, etc.,
equis, 1587: *Equus nebula (ut vulgo
dicitur) in facie, cujus vultus tristis est et
melancholicus, jure vituperatur.* Such a
horse he says later (p. 339 in 1907
ed.) is Arcite's unlucky steed in *The
Two Noble Kinsmen*, v. iv. 63, " a
blacke one, owing Not a hayre worth
of white," etc. The Duke of New-
castle, who wrote both on horsemanship and the management of horses,
uses the phrase something like Shakespeare in *The Triumphant Widow, or
The Medley of Humours. A comedy*,

L

Agr.   [*Aside to Eno.*] Why, Enobarbus ?
When Antony found Julius Cæsar dead,
He cried almost to roaring; and he wept   55
When at Philippi he found Brutus slain.

Eno. [*Aside to Agr.*] That year, indeed, he was troubled
        with a rheum;
What willingly he did confound, he wail'd,
Believe 't, till I wept too.

Cæs.   No, sweet Octavia,
You shall hear from me still; the time shall not   60
Out-go my thinking on you.

Ant.   Come, sir, come;
I'll wrestle with you in my strength of love: *—embrace/hand shake*
Look here I have you, thus I let you go,
And give you to the gods.

Cæs.   Adieu; be happy!

---

59. *wept*] Theobald; *weepe* F.

1677 (see extracts in Lamb's *Speci-mens*, Bohn's ed., p. 511), of a footpad going to execution :—

  2nd Woman. Look, what a down
            look he has!
  1st Woman. Ay, and what a cloud
            in his forehead,
            goody Twattle,
            mark that.
  2nd Woman. Ay, and such frown-
            ing wrinkles, I
            warrant you; not
            so much as a smile
            from him.

57. *a rheum*] a running at the eyes. Cf. D'Avenant, *The Just Italian*, IV. (*Works*, i. 258 in *Dramatists of Restoration*) :—

    " This is a sickly *rheum*, and not
        Compunction in my eyes."

and *Othello*, III. iv. 52, " salt and sullen *rheum*."

58. *What willingly . . . wail'd*] Cf. v. i. 28-30 *post*.

59. *wept*] Steevens and Capell retain *weep* of F. The latter unaccountably thinks it out of character for Enobarbus to weep, and says on *Believe't till I weep too*, " Which he thought would

be never." The former defends it as implying something like this: Believe it till you see me weeping on the like occasion, and then I'll thank you for the same undeserved credit for compassion.

61. *Out-go . . . you*] Outstrip, etc., i.e. my loving thought of you shall keep pace with the passage of time.

62. *I'll wrestle . . . love*] After what precedes, this gives the impression of meaning that Antony would contend with Cæsar—with whom Octavia was finding it so hard to part —by putting forth the strength of his love to separate them; till we read the next line (63) which seems to confine Antony's expression of love to Cæsar, whom he embraces. *Wrestle* thus refers at once to their embrace and rivalry in mutual good-will.

63-66. † The speech distribution does not seem wholly satisfactory. Lepidus' " thy " must surely be addressed to Octavia, as Cæsar's " Adieu; be happy " presumably also is. But I feel that " thus I let you go, and give you to the gods "

Lep. Let all the number of the stars give light   65
    To thy fair way!
Cæs.   Farewell, farewell! [*Kisses Octavia.*
Ant.   Farewell!
              [*Trumpets sound. Exeunt.*

     [SCENE III.—*Alexandria.   Cleopatra's palace.*]

    Enter CLEOPATRA, CHARMIAN, IRAS, *and* ALEXAS.

Cleo. Where is the fellow?
Alex.   Half afeard to come.
Cleo. Go to, go to.   Come hither, sir.

      Enter the Messenger as before.

Alex.   Good majesty,
    Herod of Jewry dare not look upon you,
    But when you are well pleas'd.
Cleo.   That Herod's head
    I'll have: but how, when Antony is gone,   5
    Through whom I might command it? Come thou near.
Mess. Most gracious majesty!
Cleo.   Didst thou behold
    Octavia?
Mess.   Ay, dread queen.
Cleo.   Where?
Mess.   Madam, in Rome;
    I look'd her in the face, and saw her led
    Between her brother and Mark Antony.   10
Cleo. Is she as tall as me?
Mess.   She is not, madam.
Cleo. Didst hear her speak? is she shrill-tongu'd or low?
Mess. Madam, I heard her speak; she is low-voic'd.
Cleo. That's not so good: he cannot like her long.

---

is much more appropriate from
Cæsar to Octavia than from Antony
to Cæsar. However, any attempts
at readjustment, even if one could
find any warranty for them, only
create new difficulties. [R]

   3. *Herod of Jewry*] See on I. ii. 28
ante.
   14. *That's . . . good*] That is less
favourable news. Those who suppose the words to mean " That is no

Char. Like her? O Isis! 'tis impossible.   15

Cleo. I think so, Charmian: dull of tongue, and dwarfish!
  What majesty is in her gait?   Remember,
  If e'er thou look'st on majesty.

Mess.   She creeps:
  Her motion and her station are as one;
  She shows a body, rather than a life,   20
  A statue, than a breather.

Cleo.   Is this certain?

Mess. Or I have no observance.

Char.   Three in Egypt
  Cannot make better note. *not 3 people in Egypt more*

Cleo.   He's very knowing, *observant.*
  I do perceive 't, there's nothing in her yet.
  The fellow has good judgment.

Char.   Excellent.   25

Cleo. Guess at her years, I prithee.

Mess.   Madam,
  She was a widow—

Cleo.   Widow?   Charmian, hark.

Mess. And I do think she's thirty.

Cleo. Bear'st thou her face in mind? is 't long or round?

Mess. Round, even to faultiness.   30

---

18. *look'st*] F; *lookd'st* Pope.

great commendation," on the strength
of what immediately follows, and of
" dull of tongue " (line 16), perhaps
do not sufficiently consider Cleopatra's hopeful mood after her recent
despair.   " He cannot like her long "
is probably merely a rebound from a
momentary doubt, and = Nevertheless, he cannot, etc. As to " dull of
tongue "—in her now mood of interpreting everything to her own advantage, she so presently construes
low-voic'd, just as she degrades any
lower stature than her own to
dwarfish, though she would doubtless
have preferred the messenger to say
" shrill-tongued." Cf. i. i. 32 *ante.*
On the contrary supposition, Malone
(a: in ii. v. 82, 83) again applauds a

suggestion of Queen Elizabeth in
Cleopatra, because, forsooth, the
Continuator of Stowe's *Chronicle* says :
" She was *tall of stature,* . . . her *voyce
loud and shrill.*"   († I think Case got
entangled in his own argument, and
that the second explanation is the
right one. [R])

19. *station*] manner of standing, as
in *Hamlet,* iii. iv. 58.

28. *she's thirty*] †Cleopatra passes on
without comment. She was herself
thirty-eight (see North, *post,* p. 262).
[R]

30, 31. *Round . . . so*] Steveens derives Cleopatra's comment from the
old writers on physiognomy, quoting
inexactly Hill's *Pleasant History,* etc.
(1613), p. 218.   The information is

Cleo. For the most part, too, they are foolish that are so.
Her hair what colour?

Mess.   Brown, madam: and her forehead
As low as she would wish it.

Cleo.   There's gold for thee,
Thou must not take my former sharpness ill,
I will employ thee back again; I find thee   35
Most fit for business. Go, make thee ready,
Our letters are prepar'd.   [*Exit Messenger.*

Char.   A proper man.

Cleo. Indeed he is so: I repent me much
That so I harried him. Why, methinks by him,
This creature's no such thing.

Char.   Nothing, madam.   40

Cleo. The man hath seen some majesty, and should know.

Char. Hath he seen majesty? Isis else defend!
And serving you so long.

Cleo. I have one thing more to ask him yet, good Charmian:
But 'tis no matter, thou shalt bring him to me   45
Where I will write; all may be well enough.

Char. I warrant you, madam.   [*Exeunt.*

37. Exit . . .] Hanmer; not in F.

given repeatedly of both head and
face: "The face very *rounde*, argueth
such an one to be foolish," etc. (p.
86*b*); "The head spericall or
thoroughly *round*, doth denote a
quicke mouing, vnstablenesse, forget-
fulnesse, small discretion, and little
wit in that person" (p. 26 *b*); "The
head short and very *round*, to be for-
getfull and foolish. The head long
in fashion to the Hammer, to be
prudent and wary" (p. 218, wrongly
paged 118); "The face very little
and *round*, to be foolish" (p. 220,
wrongly 120). In Mabbe's *Celestina*,
1613, i (Tudor Trans. p. 32), Calisto,
enumerating Melibea's beauties, says:
"The forme of her face rather long
then *round*."

32. *hair, what colour*] See II. v. 114
ante.

33. *As low . . . it*] "The phrase
employed by the Messenger is still

a cant one. I once overheard a
chambermaid say of her rival,—'that
her legs were as thick *as she could wish
them*'" (Steevens). A low forehead
discredits beauty in *I Antonio and
Mellida*, IV. i. 179.

"Her beautie is not half so ravishing
    As you discourse of; she hath a
        freckled face,
    A *lowe* forehead, and a lumpish
        eye."

Similarly in *The City Wit*, IV. i (Pearson's *Brome*, i. 339): "*Rufflit* here, he
writes that you [i.e. Josina] have a
grosse body, a dull eye, a *lowe* forehead, a black tooth, a fat hand, and
a most lean purse."

39. *harried*] harassed, maltreated;
from the original sense ravaged, laid
waste. Minshew, *The Guide to the
Tongues*, 1617 (cited by Malone) has
"to *Harrie*, turmoile or vex."

by him] from his account.

[SCENE IV.—*Athens.   A room in Antony's house.*]

Enter ANTONY *and* OCTAVIA.

Ant. Nay, nay, Octavia, not only that,—
That were excusable, that and thousands more
Of semblable import,—but he hath wag'd
New wars 'gainst Pompey; made his will, and read it
To public ear: 5
Spoke scantly of me: when perforce he could not
But pay me terms of honour, cold and sickly
He vented them; most narrow measure lent me:
When the best hint was given him, he not took't,
Or did it from his teeth.

Oct.   O my good lord,   10
Believe not all, or if you must believe,
Stomach not all.   A more unhappy lady,
If this division chance, ne'er stood between,

Scene IV

6, 7. *me: when . . . honour, cold*] Rowe's pointing (approx.); *me, When
. . . Honour: cold* F.   8. *them; most*] Rowe; *then most* F.   8, 9.
measure lent me: When . . . him,] Rowe's pointing (approx); *measure: lent me,
When . . . him:* F.   9. *not took't*] Theobald (Thirlby conj.); *not look't* F;
had look't F 2; *o'er-look'd* Rowe.

Scene IV

3. *semblable*] similar ; as in 2 *H. IV.*
v. i. 72. It sometimes appears as
a noun; so in Day's *English Secretarie* (1599), p. 35 : " whereof no hys-
torie hath the *semblable*, no region the
match," etc.

4, 5. *made his will . . . ear*] In Plutarch it is *Antony's* will which Cæsar
reads. See North, *post,* pp. 272-3. † It
is unlike Shakespeare to desert North
on so specific a point, and I think
there is certainly corruption. The
vagaries of F's punctuation, as well
as other awkwardnesses, suggest an
unusually difficult passage in MS. [R]

9. *not took 't*] The emendation is too
probable to be rejected, although *not
look't* might signify " took no notice."

10. *from his teeth*] Cf. " *Frae the
teeth* forward [Not from the heart] "
(Henderson's *Scottish Proverbs*, ed.
1876, p. 110). Pye quotes *The Wild
Gallant*, IV. i (see Scott's *Dryden*,
1808, ii. 78): " I am confident
she's angry but *from the teeth* out-
wards."

12. *Stomach*] resent. So in Danett's
Comines, book ii. chap. viii : " whereof scoffes arise, which they that are
scoffed *stomacke*." Compare also II.
ii. 9 *ante*.

12-20. Octavia's " situation and
sentiments " are compared with
those of Blanch in *K. J.* III. i. 327 *et
seq.*, and Volumnia in *Coriolanus*, v. iii.
97 *et seq.* Cf. also North, *post*, pp.
268-9.

Praying for both parts:
The good gods will mock me presently,   15
When I shall pray, " O, bless my lord, and husband!"
Undo that prayer, by crying out as loud,
" O, bless my brother!"   Husband win, win brother,
Prays, and destroys the prayer, no midway
'Twixt these extremes at all.

Ant.   Gentle Octavia,   20
Let your best love draw to that point which seeks
Best to preserve it: if I lose mine honour,
I lose myself: better I were not yours
Than yours so branchless.   But, as you requested,
Yourself shall go between's: the mean time, lady,   25
I'll raise the preparation of a war
Shall stain your brother: make your soonest haste;
So your desires are yours.

Oct.   Thanks to my lord.
The Jove of power make me most weak, most weak,
Your reconciler!   Wars 'twixt you twain would be   30
As if the world should cleave, and that slain men
Should solder up the rift.

Ant. When it appears to you where this begins,

16. *pray*] F; *praying* Rowe.   24. *yours*] F 2; *your* F.   30. *Your*]
F 2, *You* F.   32. *solder*] Pope; *soader* F.

15. *presently*] on the instant, immediately, as in II. ii. 159 *ante*.

27. *stain your brother*: i.e. belittle him by comparison, eclipse any preparations in his power. Compare *Tottel's Miscellany*, 1557 (Arber's reprint, p. 163): " one whose face will *staine* you all "; *Robert Laneham's Letter*, ed. Furnivall, 1871, pp. 60, 61: " And, too say truth: what, with myne eyz, az I can amorously gloit it, . . . my deep diapason, my wanton warblz, my running, my tuning, and my twynkling, I can gracify the matters az well az the prowdest of them; and waz yet neuer *stayned*, I thank God "; Churchyard, *The Worthiness of Wales*, 1587 (Repr. 1776, p. 98). " What newe things now, . . . can *staine* those

deedes, our fathers old have done." Boswell's conjecture *stay* has found adopters; but even were the metaphor in the text less common, its source is obvious.

28. *So your desires are yours*] † I suppose simply " So you have what you want." But it could equally well mean " Granted that this is what *you* want, and not something that your brother has instigated you to want." [R]

32. *solder . . . rift*] " I heard that the Earl of Northumberland liues apart againe from his lady now shee hath brought him an heire, which he sayd was the *soder* of their reconcilement: " etc. (*Manningham's Diary*, 1602, Camden Society ed., p. 79).

Turn your displeasure that way, for our faults
Can never be so equal, that your love   35
Can equally move with them.   Provide your going,
Choose your own company, and command what cost
Your heart has mind to.   [*Exeunt.*

[SCENE V.—*The same.   Another room.*]

Enter ENOBARBUS *and* EROS, *meeting.*

Eno. How now, friend Eros?
Eros. There's strange news come, sir.
Eno. What, man?
Eros. Cæsar and Lepidus have made wars upon Pompey.
Eno. This is old, what is the success?   5
Eros. Cæsar, having made use of him in the wars 'gainst
    Pompey, presently denied him rivality, would not
    let him partake in the glory of the action, and not
    resting here, accuses him of letters he had formerly
    wrote to Pompey; upon his own appeal, seizes   10
    him; so the poor third is up, till death enlarge his
    confine.

38. *has*] F 2; *he's* F.

meeting] Capell; not in F.

34-36. *for our faults . . . them*] i.e.
for our faults cannot possibly be so
equally balanced that your love for
the one or the other of us will not
be lessened. (" Spoken resentfully,
these words are his own condem-
nation, and he knows it "—D. W.)

Scene v

5. *success*] issue. See on II. iv. 9
ante.

7. *rivality*] equality, the rank and
rights of a partner. For *rivals* = associates, cf. *Hamlet*, I. i. 13. " The
rivals of my watch."

10. *his own appeal*] his own (Cæsar's)
accusation or impeachment. Cf.
Richard II. I. i. 4: " the boisterous
late *appeal.*"

Scene v

11. *up*] shut up; as appears from
" till death enlarge his confine." Cf.
Brome, *The Antipodes*, IV. xii *ad fin.* :—

" *Ioy.*   Sure your Lordship
          Meanes not to make your
              house our prison.
    Let.   By
          My Lordship but I will for
              this one night.
          See, sir, the keyes are in
              my hand.   Y'are *up*,
          As I am true Letoy."

and Beaumont and Fletcher, *The
Island Princess*, v. i (Camb. VIII. 158)
which is almost a gloss :—

    You hear Armusia's *up*, honest
        Arm :
    Clapt up in prison, . . .

Eno. Then, world, thou hast a pair of chaps, no more,
    And throw between them all the food thou hast,
    They'll grind the one the other.   Where's Antony?   15
Eros. He's walking in the garden—thus, and spurns
    The rush that lies before him; cries, " Fool Lepidus!"
    And threats the throat of that his officer
    That murder'd Pompey.
Eno.   Our great navy's rigg'd.
Eros. For Italy and Cæsar.   More, Domitius, 20
    My lord desires you presently: my news
    I might have told hereafter.
Eno.   'Twill be naught,
    But let it be.   Bring me to Antony.
Eros. Come, sir.   [*Exeunt.*

---

13. *world*] Hanmer; *would* F.   *hast*] Hanmer; *hadst* F.   *chaps,*]
Theobald; no comma F.   15. *the one the other*] Capell (Johnson conject.);
the other F.

Lepidus was compelled to live at
Circeii under strict observation, but
not deprived of his private wealth or
office of Pontifex Maximus.

13-15. *Then, world . . . other*] *chaps*
= jaws. " Cæsar and Antony will
make war on each other, though they
have the world to prey upon between
them " (Johnson). A metaphor re-
lated to that of the " pair of chaps,"
though different, occurs at the close
(III. 487) of Jonson's *Sejanus*, and is
derived from Suetonius, *Tiberius*, cap.
21 :—
    " . . . The Roman race most
        wretched, that should live
    Between so slow jaws, and so long
        a bruising."
16, 17. *spurns The rush*] Cf. *Hamlet*,
IV. v. 6: " Spurns enviously at
straws."
18, 19. *officer . . . Pompey*] Pompey,
defeated in Sicily, escaped to the East,
and there, failing in designs on Antony's provinces, met his fate, in all
probability by Antony's orders, however he might throw the obloquy of
the deed on his lieutenants. See
North, *Cæsar Augustus*, in *The Lives of*

Epaminondas, etc., 1610, pp. 1166/7 :
" Whilst *Antonius* made warre with
the Parthians, or rather infortunately
they made warre with him to his
great confusion: his Lieutenant
Titius found the meanes to lay hands
vpon *Sextus Pompeius* that was fled
into the Ile of Samos, and then fortie
yeares old : whom he put to death
by *Antonius* commandement: for
which fact he was so hated of the
people of Rome, that though he had
giuen them the pastime of certaine
playes at his owne cost and charges,
they draue him out of the Theater."
21. *presently*] at once. See II. ii.
159; III. iv. 15 *ante*.
22, 23. *'Twill be naught, But . . . be*]
Presumably : 'Twill be something of
no consequence he wants me for : but
no matter: unless Enobarbus fore-
sees a disastrous issue of the expedition. Thiselton, I take it, implies
this in giving references here " for
Enobarbus' prescience "; and by
including III. viii. 11 (i.e. III. x. 1 *post* in
the present text) among them, perhaps
intends us to notice the very expression there, " Naught, naught," etc.

[SCENE VI.—*Rome. Cæsar's house.*]

Enter AGRIPPA, MÆCENAS *and* CÆSAR.

Cæs. Contemning Rome he has done all this, and more
In Alexandria: here's the manner of't:
I' the market-place, on a tribunal silver'd,
Cleopatra and himself in chairs of gold
Were publicly enthron'd: at the feet sat   5
Cæsarion, whom they call my father's son,
And all the unlawful issue that their lust
Since then hath made between them.   Unto her
He gave the stablishment of Egypt, made her
Of Lower Syria, Cyprus, Lydia,   10
Absolute queen.
Mæc.   This in the public eye?
Cæs. I' the common show-place, where they exercise.
His sons he there proclaim'd the kings of kings;
Great Media, Parthia, and Armenia,
He gave to Alexander; to Ptolemy he assign'd   15
Syria, Cilicia, and Phœnicia: she
In the habiliments of the goddess Isis
That day appear'd, and oft before gave audience,
As 'tis reported, so.

Scene VI

13. *he there*] Johnson; *hither* F. *kings of kings*] Rowe; *King of Kings* F.
19. *reported, so*] F 2; *reported so* F.

Scene VI
[See North, *post*, p. 271.]
S.D.] † I have no suggestion to make about the odd order of entrance, except the highly conjectural one that there may at some stage have been a brief interchange between Agrippa and Maecenas, covering the entrance and also giving Cæsar a point of departure for his statement, which at present begins somewhat in mid-air. [R]
6. *Cæsarion*] See on II. ii. 228 *ante*.
10. *Lydia*] So North; but Plutarch, *Libya*, which Upton pointed out and Johnson adopted.   Bocchus is king of

Libya in line 69 *post* and in North and Plutarch.
13. *he there*] F's *hither* is, as Dover Wilson points out, very probably a compositor's handling of an MS. *hether* (cf. the frequent printing of *whether* for *whither*) so crowded that the space had disappeared; if so, Johnson's emendation is nearer to the original than at first glance looks likely.
17. *Isis*] See on I. ii. 61 *ante*.
19-21. *As 'tis . . . from him*] †I have retained F's lineation, since Hanmer's regularisation (making the lines *As 'tis . . . thus. Inform'd . . . insolence,*

Mæc.   Let Rome be thus inform'd.

Agr. Who, queasy with his insolence already,   20
    Will their good thoughts call from him.

Cæs. The people knows it; and have now receiv'd
    His accusations.

Agr.   Who does he accuse?

Cæs. Cæsar, and that having in Sicily
    Sextus Pompeius spoil'd, we had not rated him   25
    His part o' the isle.   Then does he say, he lent me
    Some shipping unrestor'd.   Lastly, he frets
    That Lepidus of the triumvirate
    Should be depos'd, and, being, that we detain
    All his revenue.

Agr.   Sir, this should be answer'd.   30

Cæs. 'Tis done already, and the messenger gone.
    I have told him, Lepidus was grown too cruel,
    That he his high authority abus'd,
    And did deserve his change: for what I have
      conquer'd,
    I grant him part: but then in his Armenia,   35
    And other of his conquer'd kingdoms, I
    Demand the like.

Mæc.   He'll never yield to that.

Cæs. Nor must not then be yielded to in this.

Enter OCTAVIA *with her Train.*

Oct. Hail, Cæsar, and my lords!   Hail, most dear Cæsar!

---

23. *Who*] F; *Whom* F 2. 28. *triumvirate*] F 2; *Triumpherate* F.
29. *and, being, that*] *and being, that* Rowe; *And being that,* F. 39. *lords!*] L. F.

Already . . . from him), though adopted by almost all editors but Knight, creates so unnaturally jerky a rhythm that irregularity seems preferable [R].

22. *knows*] See on I. iv. 21 *ante*. *Have now*, etc., appears to show that *people* is not a singular collective here.

25. *rated*] apportioned by estimate, a rare extension of the usual meaning "computed," "valued."   See on III. xi. 69 *post*.

29. *and, being, that*] Boswell (1821 Var.) reads *and, being that*. This, in

sense, corresponds with the reading of F, but makes clumsy both rhythm and construction.

32. *too cruel*] Shakespeare is following North (see p. 271, *post*) but "cruelty is the last vice we should associate with his mild Lepidus" (D.W.).

39. *lords*] † I owe to Dr. Brooks the suggestion that F's *L.* stands for the plural, and not, as most editors take it, for the singular. Octavia thus greets both Maecenas and Agrippa—as

Cæs. That ever I should call thee castaway!   40
Oct. You have not call'd me so, nor have you cause.
Cæs. Why have you stol'n upon us thus? You come not
    Like Cæsar's sister: the wife of Antony
    Should have an army for an usher, and
    The neighs of horse to tell of her approach,   45
    Long ere she did appear. The trees by the way
    Should have borne men, and expectation fainted,
    Longing for what it had not. Nay, the dust
    Should have ascended to the roof of heaven,
    Rais'd by your populous troops: but you are come   50
    A market-maid to Rome, and have prevented
    The ostentation of our love; which, left unshown,
    Is often left unlov'd: we should have met you
    By sea, and land, supplying every stage
    With an augmented greeting.
Oct.   Good my lord,   55
    To come thus was I not constrain'd, but did it
    On my free will. My lord, Mark Antony,
    Hearing that you prepar'd for war, acquainted
    My grieved ear withal; whereon I begg'd
    His pardon for return.

---

42. *have you*] F; *hast thou* F 2.   *us*] F; *me* F 2.

she naturally would—instead of only one of them. [R]

50. *populous*] Similarly used in Hall's *Chronicle* (1548), Richard III, yere ii, fol. xvi. [*b*]: "where the duke not far of lay encamped wyth a *populous* army and a host of great strength and vigor," etc.; and again, *ibid.* yere iii, fol. xxix [*a*].

51. *prevented*] come too soon to allow: or possibly just in the modern sense.

52. *ostentation*] public manifestation, full display. Theobald read *ostent*, and S. Walker conjectured *ostention*, for metrical reasons.

52, 53. *which, left . . . unlov'd*] As it stands the text might conceivably mean: which, if not outwardly manifested, is often left without return, unreciprocated; but it much more probably signifies: a feeling which, if not openly exercised, often ceases to be felt at all. The ungenerous sentiment in a brother must be put down to Cæsar's momentary displeasure, unless we take *our* (line 52) to include Octavia, which much modifies its force. † But Cæsar is displeased, not with Octavia, but with Antony, who has slighted her, and I have no doubt that the required sense is "love which is unshown is often thought to be unfelt," *unlov'd* being a sort of passive construction of a cognate accusative. Along these lines the Collier MS. *held unlov'd*, or, even better, Singer's *felt* (a transposition error), adopted by Hudson, are tempting. But I think the sense is possible even with F's reading, taking *left*=written off as [R].

Cæs.   Which soon he granted,   60
Being an abstract 'tween his lust and him.
Oct. Do not say so, my lord.
Cæs.   I have eyes upon him,
And his affairs come to me on the wind.
Where is he now?
Oct.   My lord, in Athens.
Cæs. No, my most wronged sister, Cleopatra   65
Hath nodded him to her.   He hath given his empire
Up to a whore, who now are levying
The kings o' the earth for war.   He hath assembled
Bocchus, the king of Libya, Archelaus
Of Cappadocia, Philadelphos, king   70
Of Paphlagonia; the Thracian king Adallas;
King Manchus of Arabia, King of Pont,
Herod of Jewry; Mithridates, king
Of Comagene, Polemon and Amyntas,
The kings of Mede and Lycaonia,   75
With a more larger list of sceptres.
Oct.   Ay me most wretched,
That have my heart parted betwixt two friends,

---

61. *abstract*] F; *obstruct* Theobald (Warburton) and most editors.

61. *abstract*] F's *abstract* has found plenty of defenders, beginning with Henley and Steevens.   Knight thinks it refers to Octavia as " something separating him [Antony] from the gratification of his desires."   Schmidt, who calls *obstruct* " an idle conjecture of modern editors," explains *abstract* as " the shortest way for him and his desires, the readiest opportunity to encompass his wishes."   Presumably, this is suggested by the sense of *abstract* as a brief or epitome.   See on I. iv. 9 *ante*.   †It is true that *obstruct* (as Case admitted, while accepting it) is found nowhere else, and that it makes the syntax awkward, since it must refer to Octavia (an absolute construction, " you being an obstruct ") whereas *abstract* refers directly to Octavia's *return*.   But (i) Shakespeare often uses verbs as nouns, e.g. *T.G.V.* IV. iii. 8, " your ladyship's *impose*," 2 *Henry VI.* III. i. 160, " false accuse," and (ii) both sense and elliptical syntax feel to me peculiarly Shakespearean, and I have retained F's reading only on principle, that one should not accept an emendation on mere " preferability ".   [R based on Case's material.]   But it is also possible that *abstract* is being used not in Schmidt's sense, but simply = abstracting, or removal, so that the sense, admittedly compressed, could be, " Your return being the removal of something (which stood in the way between his lust and him). [R]

69-75. Upton points out some confusion of kings and kingdoms here. Cf. North, *post*, p. 273.

72. *Manchus*] so in North; F reads *Mauchus*, and Plutarch *Malchus*.

That does afflict each other!

Cæs.   Welcome hither:
Your letters did withhold our breaking forth
Till we perceiv'd both how you were wrong led,   80
And we in negligent danger.   Cheer your heart;
Be you not troubled with the time, which drives
O'er your content these strong necessities,
But let determin'd things to destiny
Hold unbewail'd their way.   Welcome to Rome,   85
Nothing more dear to me.   You are abus'd
Beyond the mark of thought: and the high gods,
To do you justice, makes his ministers

---

78. *does*] F;   *do* F 2.   80. *wrong led*] F; *wrong'd* Capell and several
editors, reading *perceived* for metre.   88. *makes*] F; *make* F 2.   *his*] F;
them Capell and most edd.;   *their* Theobald.

---

78. *does*] See on i. iv. 21 *ante*.

80. *wrong led*] † I doubt if we are
justified in emending, and Capell's
emendation assumes a compositor's
error not so easy to account for as at
first sight it looks, since, apart from
the error in *perceived* it involves the
supposed insertion by the compositor
of a space and two letters—*two*
letters, both *l* and *e*, since Shakespeare
would not write *wronged* just to produce a feminine ending, but *wrongd*—
and insertions of this kind are less
natural than omissions. On the
other hand it is impossible to be
happy with F's reading. Not only
does it produce a very awkward
rhythm, but it makes it almost impossible to put the stress on *you* which
is demanded by the contrast with *we*
in the next line.

I wonder whether we ought to
consider this alongside the *wrangle*
in *Tempest*, v. i. 174, where the word
must, I think, however slight the
support of dictionaries, mean " play
false." To mis-read *wrangled* as
wrong led would have been much
more natural than so to mis-read
wrongd, though we should still
be left with the need to alter *perceiv'd*.
[R]

81. *negligent danger*] danger through
negligence. For the transferred epithet, compare *The Winter's Tale*, i. ii.
397 ; " In ignorant concealment."

84, 85. *let determin'd . . . their way*]
† Let predestined events go un-
bewailed to their appointed end.
The sentence would not be worth
comment if it were not that some
editors want to take *to destiny* with
determin'd, as " things determined-to-
destiny," i.e. " predestined "—which
seems to me awkward in syntax and
redundant in sense. [R]

87. *Beyond the mark*] Beyond the
reach; probably a metaphor from
archery, as Deighton points out.

88. *makes his*] So F. *Makes* (plural)
is probably correct (see on i. iv. 21
ante), and its identity with the singular
form may be responsible for *his* of the
folios; but if the reading had been *its*
instead of *his*, there would have been
no doubt that Collier (1843), who retained *his*, did right in referring it to
justice instead of to *the high gods*. In
1858, he meekly accepted Singer's rebuke and objection that justice is not
personified here, and that if it were,
his would still be inapplicable (presumably, as not feminine), apparently
not reflecting that if *his* = its, as often

Of us, and those that love you.   Best of comfort,
And ever welcome to us.
Agr.   Welcome, lady.   90
Mæc. Welcome, dear madam.
Each heart in Rome does love and pity you,
Only the adulterous Antony, most large
In his abominations, turns you off,
And gives his potent regiment to a trull,   95
That noises it against us.
Oct.   Is it so, sir?
Cæs. Most certain.   Sister, welcome: pray you,
Be ever known to patience.   My dear'st sister!

            [*Exeunt.*

both objections are invalid: cf. *Hamlet*, IV. v. 124, 125: "treason . . . Acts little of *his* will." Why did F2 alter *makes* and not *his?*

93. *large*] *large* in *Much Ado*, referring to language, II. iii. 217, "*large* jests," and IV. i. 52, "word too *large*" = free, licentious, a sense often attributed here.   More probably it is here = wide, unbounded.   The *O.E.D.* has: 1574, Hellowes, *Guevara's Fam. Ep.* (1577), 63, "It is not a just thing to be *large* in sinning, and short in praying."   See also *Macbeth*, III. iv. 11: "Be *large* in mirth."

95. *regiment*] rule, authority.   Very frequent.   So Jonson, *New Inn*, II. vi. 251:—

  "*Host.* A royal sovereign!
  Lord L. And a rare stateswoman!
   I admire her bearing
  In her new regiment."

trull] harlot: the commonest but not invariable sense of the word. Cf. *The Four Elements* (Hazlitt's *Dodsley*, i. 44):—

 "For to satisfy your wanton lust,
  I shall appoint you a *trull* of trust."

with Phaer and Twyne's *Virgil* (this reference is Steevens's), [book, xi. sig. R 7 in 1607 ed.]:—

 "Pure virgins, with Tarpeia weilding glittring axe in fight
  Italian *trulls*," etc.

96. *noises it*] makes a noise, is clamorous.   Mabbe, *Celestina*, 1631, I. (Tudor Trans. p. 39) has: "Not one stone that strikes against another, but presently *noyseth* out, Old whore"; Milton (*Paradise Regained*, iv. 488) describes certain terrors as "*noising* loud And threatning nigh."

98. *known to patience*] Cf. this circumlocution for "patient" with the scriptural "acquainted with grief."

[SCENE VII.—*Near Actium.   Antony's camp.*]

Enter CLEOPATRA *and* ENOBARBUS.

Cleo. I will be even with thee, doubt it not.

Eno. But why, why, why?

Cleo. Thou hast forspoke my being in these wars,
    And say'st it is not fit.

Eno.   Well, is it, is it?

Cleo. If not denounc'd against us, why should not we   5
    Be there in person?

Scene VII

5. *If . . . denounc'd*] Boswell (Malone conject.);   *If not, denounc'd* F;   *Is't not denounc'd* Rowe;   *If not, denounc't* Malone;   *Is't not? Denounce* Steevens, 1793 (Tyrwhitt conject.)   6. Aside] Johnson.

Scene VII

3. *forspoke*] spoken against.   See North, *post*, p. 272.   The verb commonly = curse, bewitch, as in *Look About You*, 1600, sc. 26 (Hazlitt's *Dodsley*, vii. 465):—

"I think I was *fore-spoken* at the teat,
    This damn'd rogue serv'd me thus!"

but also occurs in senses forbid, speak against, speak evil of.   *O.E.D.* quotes: 1579, J. Stubbes, *Gaping Gulf*, E viij (*b*), "If he should speede (which God *forespeake*); 1611, W. Sclater, *Key* [*to the Key of Scripture*] (1629), 84: "The fashion of most men, in such judgements, is to cry out of ill tongues that have *forespoken* them."

5, 6. *If not denounc'd . . . person*] If the war were not proclaimed against me, why should I not be there in person? i.e. even if the sufficient reason that the war is proclaimed against me —as you well know—did not exist for my presence, what objection could you find to it? I suggest this as at least a possible interpretation of Malone's text, because (1) the simpler

"If the war is not proclaimed against me, why," etc., would contain a hypothesis clean contrary to the fact, the war having been proclaimed against Cleopatra, and, indeed, Cleopatra alone, excluding Antony, as sufficiently appears in North (see *post*, p. 273), and (2) because Malone's own interpretation, "If there be no particular denunciation against me, why should we not be there in person?" obscures the relation of *denounc'd* to *these wars*, tacitly making *denounc'd* impersonal; whereas the uses of *denounce* and *denounce against* make that relation almost inevitable. See, for example, Herbert of Cherbury, *Poems* (ed. Collins, 1881, p. 77): "*Denounce* an open war"; Florio's *Montaigne*, I. v (*Temple Classics*, i. 31): "the custome beareth, that they never undertake a warre, before the same be *denounced*," etc.   The same objections apply to Deighton's further step, in: "If there is no special injunction against my taking part in these wars, why should I not be present in person?" Rowe's reading, "*Is't not denounc'd against us?*" (in Hanmer, ". . . 'gainst us?*") gives an excellent sense, and is adopted in one or the

Eno.   [*Aside*] Well, I could reply:
If we should serve with horse and mares together,
The horse were merely lost; the mares would bear
A soldier and his horse.
Cleo.   What is 't you say?
Eno. Your presence needs must puzzle Antony,   10
Take from his heart, take from his brain, from's time,
What should not then be spar'd.   He is already
Traduc'd for levity, and 'tis said in Rome
That Photinus, an eunuch, and your maids
Manage this war.

14. *Photinus, an*] Delius; no comma in F.

other form by some editors. The
other conjectures *denounc't* and *de-*
nounce need not disturb the folio
comma after *If not*, and depend on
the use of *denounce* as in Turbervile's
translation of Ovid's Epistle from
Phyllis to Demophoon (Steevens's
reference), " *Denounce* to me what I
have doone," etc.; but they, too,
have to infer disconnection between
denounc'd and *wars*. I record Mr.
A. E. Thiselton's explanation of the
exact folio text, retaining the comma,
though unable to accept it. He says
" ' if not ' is equivalent to ' *otherwise*,'
and the meaning is ' it must be fit, for
since the wars are *declared* against us
personally, how can it be improper
for us to take the field in person?'
Cf. lines 16-18."   † The commentators are, I think, almost all too much
preoccupied with the (admittedly
common) association of " denounce "
and " war." If for the moment we
forget that, is not Cleopatra's meaning perfectly clear (as it evidently
was to Deighton)?   " If there is no
express prohibition against my being
in the field, can you give me any
valid reason why I should not be
there?" Enobarbus gives two reasons
one, in an aside, and then one direct
to her, a purely military reason, with
not so much as an allusion to the
question whether the war had been
declared against Cleopatra or not. [R]

7-9. *If we should . . . his horse*]
† Another example of commentators'
silence. I have to admit that I do
not see the precise point of Enobarbus'
(presumable) ribaldry. There is perhaps a play on "serve" in its breeders'
as well as in its military sense, but
this is not very helpful. The critical
word is " bear," which has apparently never had the specific meaning
(" be mounted by ") which is here
needed and which " take " (see
O.E.D.) has had since 1577 (though
that meaning is no doubt *suggested* by
Cleopatra at I. v. 21). (See *O.E.D.*,
but see also *H. V.* III. vii. 50, and
R. and J. I. iv. 94.)   And Shakespeare's bawdry, though sometimes
complicated, is almost always precise.
When one is puzzled it is, I think,
better to admit it than pass over
without comment a passage which
may be puzzling to other readers
besides oneself. [R]

8. *merely*] utterly. So, often. Cf.
Hamlet, I. ii. 137: " things rank . . .
Possess it *merely* ".

14. *Photinus, an eunuch*] If Shakespeare strictly followed the corresponding passage in North, as given, *post*,
p. 273, to which Delius—who is responsible for the comma after Photinus—drew attention, the words " an
eunuch " do not describe Photinus
(the eunuch who was the cause of
Pompey the Great's murder), but
stand for Mardian. Plutarch gives

M

Cleo.   Sink Rome, and their tongues rot 15
That speak against us!   A charge we bear i' the war,
And as the president of my kingdom will
Appear there for a man.   Speak not against it,
I will not stay behind.

Enter ANTONY *and* CANIDIUS.

Eno.   Nay, I have done,
Here comes the emperor.
Ant.   Is it not strange, Canidius,   20
That from Tarentum, and Brundusium
He could so quickly cut the Ionian sea,
And take in Toryne?   You have heard on't, sweet?
Cleo. Celerity is never more admir'd
Than by the negligent.
Ant.   A good rebuke,   25
Which might have well becom'd the best of men,
To taunt at slackness.   Canidius, we
Will fight with him by sea.
Cleo.   By sea, what else?
Can. Why will my lord do so?
Ant.   For that he dares us to't.
Eno. So hath my lord dar'd him to single fight.   30
Can. Ay, and to wage this battle at Pharsalia,
Where Cæsar fought with Pompey.   But these offers,
Which serve not for his vantage, he shakes off,
And so should you.
Eno.   Your ships are not well mann'd,
Your mariners are muleters, reapers, people   35

---

23. *Toryne*] F 2;   *Troine* F.   35. *muleters*] *Muliters* F 2;   *Militers* F.

" Pothinus," as does North in his
life of Cæsar.
   16. *A charge . . . war*] See North,
post, p. 272.
   23. *take in Toryne*] occupy, etc.
Cf. I. i. 23 *ante*. See North, *post*,
p. 274, and for Tarentum and
Brundusium, *ibid.*
   26. *becom'd*] So in *Cymbeline*, v. v.
407 *A Report*, etc., 1591 (*The Revenge*,
ed. Arber, p. 28): " And no man

could haue lesse *becommed* the place
of an Orator for such a purpose, then
this *Morice of Desmond*."
   27. *To taunt at*] " to cast as a
taunt at " (Deighton). The gerun-
dial infinitive.
   30-32. *So hath . . . Pompey*] See
North, *post*, p. 274.
   35. *muleters*] The contemporary
form. Cf. Peele, *Battle of Alcazar*,
IV. i. 8 :—

Ingross'd by swift impress.   In Cæsar's fleet
Are those that often have 'gainst Pompey fought,
Their ships are yare, yours heavy: no disgrace
Shall fall you for refusing him at sea,
Being prepar'd for land.

Ant.   By sea, by sea.   40
Eno. Most worthy sir, you therein throw away
The absolute soldiership you have by land,
Distract your army, which doth most consist
Of war-mark'd footmen, leave unexecuted
Your own renowned knowledge, quite forgo   45
The way which promises assurance, and
Give up yourself merely to chance and hazard,
From firm security.

Ant.   I'll fight at sea.
Cleo. I have sixty sails, Cæsar none better.
Ant. Our overplus of shipping will we burn,   50
And, with the rest full-mann'd, from the head of
      Actium
Beat the approaching Cæsar.   But if we fail,
We then can do 't at land.

51. *Actium*] F 2; *Action* F.

" Three thousand pioners, and a
    thousand coachmen,
  Besides a number almost number-
    less
  Of drudges, negroes, slaves, and
    muleters," etc.
See also, and for the passage gener-
ally, North, *post*, p. 274.

36. *impress*] press-gang work, as in
T. and C. II. i. 107.

38. *yare*] nimble, easily manœuvred.
Cf. II. ii. 211 *ante*, III. xiii. 131, v.
ii. 282 *post*, and Gorges' *Lucan* (1614),
lib. 3, p. 109:—

  " But the *Massilian* gallies are
    Of saile and stirrage much more
      yare,
  Nimble and light to leaue or take,
  And on their staies quick speed
    can make," etc.

(" on their staies . . ." = " come
round quickly " when tacking).

39. *fall*] befall, as in *K. J.* i. i. 78,
" Fair *fall*," etc.

43. *Distract*] *distract* had the senses
" confuse," as now, and " disjoin,"
" divide." See the example on line
76 *post*, and also the participle in
A Lover's Complaint, 231. Schmidt
assigns the latter here, and although
" confuse " sorts suspiciously well with
the ensuing appeal to the nature of
the army, which consisted—as the
soldier says, line 65 *post*—of men who
" Have used to conquer standing on
the earth, And fighting foot to foot,"
the passage in North, *post*, p. 275,
confirms his view. The speech is
there given to Canidius.

44. *leave unexecuted*] give no scope
for the use of.

47. *merely*] utterly, as in line 8 *ante*.

52, 53. *if we fail, We then can do't
at land*] † A dangerous doctrine in war.
We may remember the ill-fated

Enter a Messenger.

                              Thy business?

Mess. The news is true, my lord, he is descried,
    Cæsar has taken Toryne.   55

Ant. Can he be there in person? 'Tis impossible;
    Strange, that his power should be. Canidius,
    Our nineteen legions thou shalt hold by land,
    And our twelve thousand horse. We'll to our ship,
    Away, my Thetis!

Enter a Soldier.

                        How now, worthy soldier?   60

Sold. O noble emperor, do not fight by sea,
    Trust not to rotten planks: do you misdoubt
    This sword, and these my wounds? Let the Egyptians
    And the Phœnicians go a-ducking: we
    Have us'd to conquer standing on the earth,   65
    And fighting foot to foot.

Ant.   Well, well, away!

    [*Exeunt Antony, Cleopatra, and Enobarbus.*

Sold. By Hercules I think I am i' the right.

Can. Soldier, thou art: but his whole action grows
    Not in the power on 't: so our leader's led,
    And we are women's men.

Sold.   You keep by land   70
    The legions and the horse whole, do you not?

---

69. *leader's led*] Theobald; *Leaders leade* F.

---

attempt to force the Gallipoli straits
by sea, and what followed. [R]

57. *power*] forces, as below, line 76,
and commonly.

58, 59. *nineteen legions . . . horse*]
See North, *post*, p. 277.

60. *Thetis!*] " Antony may address
Cleopatra by the name of this sea-
nymph, because she had just promised
him assistance in his naval expedition;
or perhaps in allusion to her voyage
down the Cydnus, when she appeared
like *Thetis* surrounded by the Nereids "
(Steevens, confusing with *Tethys*).

61–66. See North, *post*, p. 275.

64. *a-ducking*] As a result of " rotten
planks " perhaps, though Deighton
explains: " take to the water like
ducks." Cf. Beaumont and Fletcher,
The Scornful Lady, II. ii. 112: " 'Tis
your turn next to sink, you shall
duck twice before I help you."

68, 69. *his . . . power on't*] his course
in the war is shaped without regard
to where his real strength lies, or,
more closely, his action does not spring
from the sources of its possible
strength.

Can. Marcus Octavius, Marcus Justeius,
    Publicola and Cælius, are for sea:
    But we keep whole by land.   This speed of Cæsar's
    Carries beyond belief.
Sold.   While he was yet in Rome,   75
    His power went out in such distractions as
    Beguil'd all spies.
Can.   Who's his lieutenant, hear you?
Sold. They say, one Taurus.
Can.   Well I know the man.

Enter a Messenger.

Mess. The emperor calls Canidius.
Can. With news the time's in labour, and throws forth, 80
    Each minute, some.   [*Exeunt.*

---

72. Can.] Pope; Ven. F.   78. *Taurus*] Theobald; *Towrus* F throughout.
Well I] Rowe (ed. 3); *Well, I* F.   80. *in*] Rowe; *with* F.   *throws*]
throwes F; *throes* Theobald.

72-74. *Marcus Octavius*, etc.] See North, *post*, pp. 275-6; *whole by land*, p. 277.

75. *Carries*] From the language of archery, as Steevens suggests. Compare with the whole passage, Daniel, *A Funerall Poeme Vpon the Earle of Devonshire*, lines 217-20 (*Works*, Grosart, i. 180):—

  " Here is no roome to tell with what
     strange speed
  And secrecy he vsed to preuent
  The enemies designes, nor with
     what heed
  He marcht before report," etc.

78. *Taurus*] In North, *post*, p. 276.
† F's spelling suggests our "modern" pronunciation. (Henslowe, by the way, contrariwise spells Faustus as " Fostus.") [R]

80. *in*] † Rowe's emendation is, I think, so probable as to merit insertion in the text. The compositor would easily pick up and repeat the *with* from five words before, and *with labour* is an almost impossible phrase. [R]

throws] †Theobald's emendation (or rather re-spelling, since *throwe* is common Elizabethan spelling for *throe*) has been almost universally accepted, but is less convincing on examination than at first sight. Steevens quotes in support *Tempest*, II. i. 238 (one of the very rare occurrences of *throe* as a *verb*).

     " a birth indeed
  Which *throes* thee much to yield "

where again F reads *throwes*. But the image here is of a difficult birth, and the object of the verb is the person in labour. Here the object is the thing born, and the image is that of a *series* of births, with no question of difficulty, as of an animal producing a litter. [R]

[SCENES VIII-X.—*A plain near Actium.*]

Enter CÆSAR *and* TAURUS, *with his army, marching.*

Cæs. Taurus!
Taur. My lord?
Cæs. Strike not by land, keep whole, provoke not battle
    Till we have done at sea. Do not exceed
    The prescript of this scroll: our fortune lies   5
    Upon this jump.   [*Exeunt.*

[SCENE IX]

Enter ANTONY *and* ENOBARBUS.

Ant. Set we our squadrons on yond side o' the hill,
    In eye of Cæsar's battle, from which place
    We may the number of the ships behold,
    And so proceed accordingly.   [*Exeunt.*

Scene VIII

Enter . . .] Cambridge edd.; F has no *and Taurus.*

Scene VIII

6. *jump*] hazard. The noun occurs here only in Shakespeare, but the verb in *Macbeth*, I. vii. 7, and elsewhere. *O.E.D.* has *s.v.*: 1601, Holland, *Pliny*, ii. 219, " It [hellebore] putteth the Patient to a *jumpe* or great hazzard."

Scene IX

1-4. Cf. IV. x. 4-9 *post.*
1. *squadrons*] bodies of troops, not necessarily cavalry: cf. *Othello*, I. i. 22-4,
" That never set a squadron in the
    field,
  Nor the division of a battle
    knows,
More than a spinster."

2. *battle*] embattled army, as very often. More particularly it applies to the main body. So in Harington's *Nugæ Antiquæ* (1769), i. 51: " The order was this, Captain Lister led the forlorn hope; Sir Alexander Ratcliffe and his regiment had the vaunt-guard; my Lord of Dublin led the *battle:* Sir Arthur Savage the rear; the horse," etc.

Scene X

[See North, *post*, pp. 276-7.]
S.D.] F, though it has " *Enter Scarrus* " at line 4, also brings him in along with Enobarbus at the opening of the scene. This is probably an example of the not uncommon " anticipatory " S.D. (cf. v. ii. 318 and 327).

[SCENE X]

CANIDIUS *marcheth with his land army one way over the stage,
and* TAURUS, *the lieutenant of* CÆSAR, *the other way. After
their going in, is heard the noise of a sea-fight.*

Alarum. Enter ENOBARBUS.

Eno. Naught, naught, all naught, I can behold no longer:
The Antoniad, the Egyptian admiral,
With all their sixty fly, and turn the rudder:
To see't, mine eyes are blasted.

Enter SCARUS.

Scar.   Gods and goddesses,
All the whole synod of them!
Eno.   What's thy passion?   5
Scar. The greater cantle of the world is lost
With very ignorance, we have kiss'd away
Kingdoms, and provinces.
Eno.   How appears the fight?
Scar. On our side, like the token'd pestilence,

1. *Naught*], i.e. come to naught,
ruined.   D. W.   well   compares
Coriolanus, III. i. 230.

2. *The Antoniad . . . admiral*] See
North, *post*, p. 273. *Admiral* occurs
commonly for the most considerable
ship of a fleet or as the equivalent of
our " flagship." See *A Report*, etc.,
1591 (*The Revenge*, Arber's reprint, p.
18): " The names of her Maiesties
shippes were these as followeth: the
Defiaunce, which was Admirall, the
Reuenge Viceadmirall," etc.; also *1
H. IV.* III. iii. 28.

5. *synod*] Nearly always, as here, of
an assembly of the gods. So in *Coriolanus*, v. ii. 73: " The glorious gods
sit in hourly *synod* about thy particular
prosperity," etc.

6. *cantle*] Originally = corner, and
so portion, piece, etc. Here (see
O.E.D.) " a segment of a circle or

sphere." See also *1 H. IV.* III. i.
101, and *The Magnificent Entertainment*, etc. (Bullen's *Middleton*, vii.
223): " The FOUR ELEMENTS, in
proper shapes, artificially and aptly
expressing their qualities, . . . went
round in a proportionable and even
circle, touching that *cantle* of the
Globe (which was open) to the full
view of his Majesty: " etc.

7. *With*] by, as often. Cf. North,
post, p. 265, l. 25.

9. *token'd pestilence*] Certain red
spots have always been reckoned extremely ominous symptoms in plague,
and, as Steevens tells us, were considered and called " God's tokens " of
speedy death, in Shakespeare's time.
He quotes *L.L.L.* v. ii. 424, and
Two Wise Men, etc., 1619, IV. ii.
See Chapman, *Minor Poems*, etc., ed.
1875, p. 405, col. 1, line 19: " A will

Where death is sure.   Yon ribaudred nag of Egypt,—
Whom leprosy o'ertake!—i' the midst o' the fight,   11
When vantage like a pair of twins appear'd

10. *ribaudred*] F 1-3; *ribauldred* F 4; *ribauld* Rowe, and others.

and a tolling bell are as present death as God's *tokens*." Sylvester (Du Bartas, *The Tropheis*, near the end) calls them " *Tokens* of Terror," and Dekker, *The Bel-man of London*, 1608 (*Temple Classics* ed., p. 241) has: " where the dore of a poore Artificer (if his child had died but with one *Token* of death about him) was close ram'd up," etc. Yet Dr. Forman lived to record in his *Diary*, under 1592: " and the 6 of Julie I toke my bed and had the plague in both my groines, and some moneth after I had the red *tokens* on my feet as brod as halfepence, and yt was 22 wickes before I was well again, the which did hinder me moch."

10. *ribaudred nag*] foul, wanton jade. Malone, Collier (ed. 1), Knight, adopt Steevens' conjecture *ribald-rid*, but " A *ribaudrous* and filthie tongue " —first quoted by Steevens from Baret's *Alvearie*, 1580, and urged by Singer with addition from Horman's *Vulgaria* : " Refrayne fro such foule and rebaudry wordes "—makes *ribaudred* a probable form. Gould's conjecture *ribanded* would else attract, as a natural expression of disgust at the " flying flags " which seem to have impressed Enobarbus (III. xiii. 11 *post*), and because race-horses were decked with ribands, as also, for sale purposes, unserviceable jades. Compare *The Country Captain*, 1649, 1 (*Captain Underwit*, Bullen's *Old Plays*, ii. 333): " What thing's this that looks so like a race Nagg trick'd with *ribbands?* " That the flags deck the ship, not Cleopatra, is of little consequence. Collier (ed. 2) and Singer adopt Tyrwhitt's conjecture, *hag* for *nag*, in view of *magic*, line 19; but *nag* for a runaway, and as applied to women (see *2 H. IV.* II. iv. 207), is too probable. Cf. also *Swetnam the Woman*

Hater, etc. 1620, I. ii: " Those that have good wives ride to Hell Vpon ambling Hackneyes, and all the rest Vpon trotting Iades to the devill." † This last quotation gives some support to Steevens' *ribald-rid* (i.e.— though most of the editors who adopt it are too delicate to explain what the odd word means—" a trollop whom every casual debauchee can 'mount' " —but the objections to it are, I think, two: it is too complicated, though effective, a derogatory image for Scarus' state of mind, and it is feeble in sound, so that no actor, I believe, would hesitate a moment between it and *ribaudred*. Scarus means, I fancy, little more than the modern colloquial " bloody." [R]

11. *leprosy*] Steevens seems to think the word used in a sense appropriate to the stigma in *ribaudred*. See Donne, *Elegy IV*, line 60:—

" By thee the silly amorous sucks
      his death
   By drawing in a *leprous* harlot's
      breath "

and Fairfax, *Eclogue the Fourth* (*The Muses Library*, 1741, p. 373):—

" But such the Issue was of that
      Embrace,
   That deadly Poyson thro' her
      Body spread,
   Rotted her Limbs, and *leprous*
      grew her Face."

As Johnson observes, however, leprosy was " an epidemical distemper of the Ægyptians."   See Sylvester's Du Bartas, *The Furies*, lines 513-16:—

" So *Portugall* hath *Phthisiks* most
      of all,
   Eber Kings-euils ; Arné the *Suddain-
      Fall;*
   Sauoy the *Mumps; West-India,
      Pox;* and *Nyle*
   The *Leprosie:* " etc.

Both as the same, or rather ours the elder,—
The breeze upon her, like a cow in June,
Hoists sails, and flies.   15

Eno. That I beheld:
Mine eyes did sicken at the sight, and could not
Endure a further view.

Scar.   She once being loof'd,
The noble ruin of her magic, Antony,
Claps on his sea-wing, and (like a doting mallard)   20
Leaving the fight in heighth, flies after her:
I never saw an action of such shame;
Experience, manhood, honour, ne'er before
Did violate so itself.

Eno.   Alack, alack!

---

14. *The breeze . . . her*] In parentheses in F.   *June*] F 2 (*Iune*); *Inne* F.
21. *heighth*] F; *height* Theobald and edd.

---

13. *the elder*] Steevens compares
J.C. II. ii. 46:—
    " We are two lions littered in one
        day,
    And I *the elder* and more terrible."
14, 15. *The breeze . . . flies*] † *breeze*
= gadfly, though there may be a pun
on the ordinary sense. The picture
seems clear enough—a gadfly-stung
cow in the heat of summer suddenly charging across a meadow—
but it has provoked a spate of comment and question (rather of the
" When is a cow not a cow? When
it's a nag " variety): is it the nag
that is stung, or the cow? who hoists
sails, the nag, the cow, or Cleopatra?
Staunton proposed a heroic, if un-
wise, cutting of one of the knots by
reading *tail* for *sails*. But the trouble
all arises from failure to realise
Shakespeare's frequent high-handed-
ness with metaphor, and the speaker's
state of mind. Scarus is furiously
angry, and when he gets to the cow
he has forgotten all about his first
derogatory nag—anyway leprosy and
a pair of twins have already intervened. And I suppose that if Enobarbus had been pedantic enough to

challenge his syntax he would have
said that Cleopatra, momentarily
compared to a cow, was the subject
of *hoists*. For the image, cf. Jonson,
The New Inn, v. iii. 3: " Runs like
a heifer, bitten with the brieze."
[R]
    18. *loof'd*] † usually taken, and often
printed, as *luffed*. To luff is to bring
a ship's head up into the wind, and
therefore whether this manœuvre is
preparatory to disengaging, or, as it
well might be, to engaging more
closely, depends entirely on where the
wind is. And I find it hard to believe
that the man who could write the
storm scene of *The Tempest* would ever
use a specific technicality so loosely.
North uses the phrase " to loof off "
as though it meant simply " to dis-
engage," i.e. as though he were
connecting it with " aloof " in the
general sense (whether or not " aloof "
is originally derived from the
technical sense). [R]
    20. *mallard*] wild drake. Rolfe
compares *I H. IV.* II. ii. 111: " there's
no more valour in that Poins than in a
wild-duck," and *ibid.* IV. ii. 21; but
the allusion here is rather to the drake's

Enter CANIDIUS.

Can. Our fortune on the sea is out of breath,   25
    And sinks most lamentably.   Had our general
    Been what he knew himself, it had gone well:
    O, he has given example for our flight,
    Most grossly by his own!
Eno. Ay, are you thereabouts?   Why, then, good-night   30
    Indeed.
Can.   Toward Peloponnesus are they fled.
Scar. 'Tis easy to 't, and there I will attend
    What further comes.
Can.   To Cæsar will I render
    My legions and my horse, six kings already
    Show me the way of yielding.
Eno.   I'll yet follow   35
    The wounded chance of Antony, though my reason
    Sits in the wind against me.   [*Exeunt.*

---

28. *he*] F 2 (*hee*); *his* F.   37. Exeunt] not in F.

aptness to follow the coy female than to his timidity.

27. *Been . . . himself*] It is not very clear whether this is literally, Been what he knew himself to be—another way of saying, acted in character, displayed the courage and skill he consciously possessed—or whether *formerly* is implied in *knew*, as Delius seems to think, and the sense consequently, *either* Been the man he once knew in his own person, *or* Been the man he was once conscious of being. North has, " as if he had not oftentimes proved both the one and the other fortune," etc. (*post*, p. 277).

32, 33. *'Tis easy . . . comes*] † A very odd remark from Scarus. It looks as though it must mean " It's easy enough to get there, and I'll make my way there and watch events." But that is certainly not what Scarus does, and the last thing one would expect him to do. See IV. vii, viii, x and xii *post*. I wonder whether all that really belongs to

Scarus is a scornful aside, " 'Tis easy to 't," and the rest belongs to Canidius, to whose present frame of mind it is perfectly appropriate. [R]

36. *wounded chance*] " broken fortunes " (Malone, comparing v. ii. 173 *post*). *Chance* = fortune is common. Cf. Countess of Pembroke, *Antonie*, 1595, Act v; " Follow we our *chance* "; Churchyard, *A Tragical Discourse of the Vnhappy Man's Life*, stanza 53 (*Chippes*, 1575):—

" This *chaunce* is she some say that
    leads men out
And brings them home, when
    least they looke therefore," etc.

37. *Sits . . . wind*] Shakespeare often uses *sits* of the wind itself, to denote its quarter, as in *M. of V.* I. i. 18: " Plucking the grass, to know where *sits* the wind." We make free with the wind like Enobarbus in the colloquialism, " There's something in the *wind*."

[SCENE XI.—*Alexandria.   Cleopatra's palace.*]

Enter ANTONY *with Attendants.*

Ant. Hark, the land bids me tread no more upon 't,
 It is asham'd to bear me.   Friends, come hither:
 I am so lated in the world that I
 Have lost my way for ever.   I have a ship,
 Laden with gold, take that, divide it; fly,   5
 And make your peace with Cæsar.

All.   Fly? not we.

Ant. I have fled myself, and have instructed cowards
 To run, and show their shoulders.   Friends, be gone,
 I have myself resolv'd upon a course,
 Which has no need of you.   Be gone,   10
 My treasure's in the harbour.   Take it: O,
 I follow'd that I blush to look upon:
 My very hairs do mutiny; for the white
 Reprove the brown for rashness, and they them
 For fear, and doting.   Friends, be gone, you shall 15
 Have letters from me to some friends, that will
 Sweep your way for you.   Pray you, look not sad,
 Nor make replies of loathness; take the hint
 Which my despair proclaims.   Let that be left
 Which leaves itself: to the sea-side straightway; 20
 I will possess you of that ship and treasure.
 Leave me, I pray, a little: pray you now,

Scene XI

19. 20. *that . . . leaves itself*] Capell; *them . . . leaues it selfe* F.

Scene XI

1-24. See North, *post*, p. 276.

3. *lated*] belated, benighted.   So in *Macbeth*, III. iii. 6 " Now spurs the *lated* traveller apace."

8. *show their shoulders*] Cf. Beaumont and Fletcher, *A King and no King*, III. ii. 29: " I was never at battle but once, and there I was running, but *Mardonius* cudgel'd me: yet I got loose at last, but was so afraid that I saw no more than my *shoulders* do," etc.

13-15. *My very hairs . . . doting*] † Cf. IV. viii. 19, 20 *post*, where he is in a very different mood. [R]

19. *that*] Antony himself.

20. *leaves itself*] is no longer itself.

Nay, do so : for indeed I have lost command,
Therefore I pray you: I'll see you by and by. [*Sits down.*

Enter CLEOPATRA *led by* CHARMIAN *and* EROS; IRAS
following.

Eros. Nay, gentle madam, to him, comfort him.   25
Iras. Do, most dear queen.
Char. Do, why, what else?
Cleo. Let me sit down.   O Juno!
Ant. No, no, no, no, no.
Eros. See you here, sir?   30
Ant. O fie, fie, fie!
Char. Madam!
Iras. Madam, O good empress!
Eros. Sir, sir!
Ant. Yes, my lord, yes; he at Philippi kept   35
His sword e'en like a dancer, while I struck

---

23. *for . . . command*] Johnson supposed Antony to refer to his own rising emotion, which does, in fact, become uncontrollable, and is perhaps already indicated by his short-breath'd speech ; and this accords with his request for merely temporary solitude. Steevens's interpretation, however, is probable and generally accepted : " I *entreat* you to leave me, because I have lost all power to *command* your absence." Compare Beaumont and Fletcher, *A King and no King*, I. i. 313 :—

" I pray you leave me, Sirs. I'm proud of this,
    That you will be intreated from my sight."

24-5.] † There has been a general tendency of editors not only to complete F's S.D. by the necessary addition of Iras, but also to change it, by having Cleopatra led in by Charmian and Iras, with Eros following. This, I think, misses the point. Not only is he the first to speak, so that his entry behind the other three is awkward, but he has, one imagines, been instrumental in persuading

Cleopatra to come to comfort his master, and it is therefore appropriate that he should conduct her. [R]

29. *No . . . no*] Perhaps in rejection of Eros' attempt, as Delius says ; but possibly only an audible fragment of Antony's bitter reflections.

35. *Yes, my lord, yes*] To an imaginary collocutor, according to Delius; but Hudson refers it to Cæsar, whom, certainly, Antony might now in bitter irony call " my lord."

35, 36. *he at Philippi . . . dancer*] Steevens explains that Cæsar is charged with wearing his sword for ornament only, undrawn, like a dancer, and compares *Titus Andronicus*, II. i. 38 :—

" Why boy, although our mother unadvis'd
    Gave you a *dancing-rapier* by your side."

Malone added *All*'s *Well*, II. i. 32 :—
    " . . . and no sword worn
    But one to *dance* with."
See also the extracts from " A Paire of Spy-knaves " in the preface to *The*

The lean and wrinkled Cassius, and 'twas I
That the mad Brutus ended: he alone
Dealt on lieutenantry, and no practice had
In the brave squares of war: yet now—No matter.   40
Cleo. Ah, stand by.
Eros. The queen, my lord, the queen.
Iras. Go to him, madam, speak to him,
He is unqualitied with very shame.
Cleo. Well then, sustain me: O!   45
Eros. Most noble sir, arise, the queen approaches,
Her head's declin'd, and death will seize her, but
Your comfort makes the rescue.

44. *He is*] F 2; *Hee's* F.   47. *seize*] F 2; *cease* F.

Four Knaves by S. Rowlands (Percy Society, No. xxxiv, p. xi):—

"Bid him trim up my walking rapier neat,
My *dancing* rapier's pummell is too great;" etc.

On Cæsar at Philippi, see North, *post*, p. 260.

37. *The lean . . . Cassius*; Cf. *J.C.* I. ii. 193, etc.

37, 38. *I . . . mad Brutus ended*] Not to be taken literally. See North, *post*, p. 260. Brutus' high, unselfish aims, and ascription of the like to others, perhaps account for the epithet *mad*.

39. *Dealt on lieutenantry*] "fought by proxy" (Steevens). Cf. III. i. 16, 17 and North, *post*, p. 267. *Dealt on* seems to be = acted *or* proceeded in dependence on, unless it corresponds with our disparaging use of *to deal in, traffic in*. Steevens and Malone quote passages containing *deal upon*, but this in all these = deal with *or* "set to work upon" (*O.E.D.*), as in *R. III.* IV. ii. 75.

39, 40, *no practice . . . squares of war*] Cf. the Countess of Pembroke's *Antonie* (1595), Act III: "A man . . . in Mars' school who never lesson learned"; and again:—

"A man who never saw enlaced pikes

With bristled joints against his stomach bent.
Who fears the field and hides him cowardly
Dead at the very noise the soldiers make."

For *squares* = squadrons, compare *Henry V.* iv. ii. 28: "our *squares* of battle"; Markham's *Sir Richard Grinuile*, 1595 (p. 65 in Arber's repr.):—

"In foure great battailes marcht the *Spanish* hoast,
The first of *Siuill*, led in two great *squares*," etc.

44. *unqualitied*] unmanned, not himself. *Qualited* occurs twice in *The Passionate Morrice*, 1593 (New Shakes. Society, 1876, pp. 82, 85): "They that were wealthy were meanely *qualited*, and they that had many good properties were moniles"; "an exquisite proper *qualited* Squire."

47. *seize*] *cease* for *seize*, as in F, is common. Cf. Marston, *The Dutch Courtesan* (1605), III. i. (III. ii. 30 in Gifford): "mischiefe and a thousand divells *cease* him!"

but] unless. So Peele, *The Battle of Alcazar*, III. iv. 28 "The hellish prince . . . Ding down my soul to hell . . . *But* I perform religiously," etc.

Ant. I have offended reputation,
A most unnoble swerving.
Eros.   Sir, the queen.   50
Ant. O, whither hast thou led me, Egypt?   See,
How I convey my shame out of thine eyes,
By looking back what I have left behind
Stroy'd in dishonour.
Cleo.   O my lord, my lord,
Forgive my fearful sails! I little thought   55
You would have follow'd.
Ant.   Egypt, thou knew'st too well,
My heart was to thy rudder tied by the strings,
And thou shouldst tow me after.   O'er my spirit
Thy full supremacy thou knew'st, and that
Thy beck might from the bidding of the gods   60
Command me.
Cleo.   O, my pardon!
Ant.   Now I must
To the young man send humble treaties, dodge
And palter in the shifts of lowness, who
With half the bulk o' the world play'd as I pleas'd,

---

54. *Stroy'd*] F; *Strow'd* or *Strew'd* Capell conj.   58. *tow*] Rowe (*towe*);
stowe F.   59. *Thy*] Theobald (ed. 2); *The* F.

52-54. *How I convey . . . dishonour*]
See how I take my disgrace out of
your sight by giving myself up to
solitary brooding over the wreck of
my fortunes and my honour. For
stroy'd, compare Sir T. Wyatt, *Of the
meane and sure estate*, etc., line 14:
"And when her store was *stroyed*
with the floode"; *A Collection of . . .
Ballads and Broadsides* (1559-97), 1867,
p. 122 :—

" Let not the wicked thus preuayle,
   To vexe thy church and sayntes;
   But *stroy* them from the head to
   tayle," etc.

Both the infinitives *stroyen* and *des-
troyen* existed in Middle English.
Some print the contraction *'stroy'd*
here. It is used by Henry More,
Philosophicall Poems (1647), p. 111,

line 5 : " For she may deem herself
'stroyed quite," etc.

57. *the strings*] i.e. the heart strings.
Compare the passage in the Countess
of Pembroke's *Antonie* (1595), Act II,
quoted by Steevens, and containing
the lines:—

" Forgetful of his charge (as if his
   soul
   Unto his ladies soul had been en-
   chained)," etc.

62. *treaties*] propositions. So in
K.J. II. i. 480 :—

" Why answer not the double
   majesties
   This friendly *treaty* of our threat-
   en'd town?"

62, 63. *dodge . . . lowness*] shuffle and
hedge in those devices to which the
man who has lost his power is reduced.

Making and marring fortunes.   You did know   65
How much you were my conqueror, and that
My sword, made weak by my affection, would
Obey it on all cause.

Cleo.   Pardon, pardon!

Ant. Fall not a tear, I say, one of them rates
All that is won and lost: give me a kiss,   70
Even this repays me.   We sent our schoolmaster,
Is a' come back?   Love, I am full of lead:
Some wine within there, and our viands!   Fortune
      knows,
We scorn her most, when most she offers blows.

[Exeunt.

65. *Making and marring*] Nothing is commoner than the collocation of *make* and *mar*, and " To make *or* mar " is a proverbial phrase. Yet, in conjunction with " play'd " (line 64), there seems to be an allusion here to a game of some kind. Rushton, *Shakespeare Illustrated by the Lex Scripta* (1870), p. 57, cites : ". . . places for bowling, tennis, dicing, white and black, *making and marring*, and other unlawful games prohibited by the laws and statutes of this realm," . . . " 2 and 3 Philip and Mary, cap. ix."

69. *Fall*] Transitively used, as in *The Tempest*, II. i. 304, and often. Cf. R. Chester, *Love's Martyr*, 1601 (New Shakes. Society, 1878, p. 125):
" *Fall* thou a teare, and thou shalt plainly see,
Mine eyes shall answer teare for teare of thine."

rates] " estimates, expresses the value of, is worth " (Schmidt, who observes that the passage is peculiar). The ordinary meaning (to assess, value) is seen in *Cymbeline*, I. iv. 88: " *Post.* I praised her as I *rated* her: so do I my stone.   *Iach.* What do you esteem it at?"   See also on III. vi. 25 *ante*.

71. *schoolmaster*] Euphronius, the tutor of his children by Cleopatra. See North, *post*, p. 278.

73. *Some wine . . . knows*] † The line is unmetrical, which would be less suspicious if it were not the first line of a concluding couplet. F, which has made an unmetrical jumble of the preceding two lines, gets the couplet " right " by putting *some wine* at the end of the " line " before, and starting the couplet with *Within there*. [R]

[SCENE XII.—*Egypt.   Cæsar's camp.*]

Enter CÆSAR, AGRIPPA, DOLABELLA, *and* THIDIAS, *with others.*

Cæs. Let him appear that's come from Antony.
    Know you him?
Dol.   Cæsar, 'tis his schoolmaster,
    An argument that he is pluck'd, when hither
    He sends so poor a pinion of his wing,
    Which had superfluous kings for messengers,   5
    Not many moons gone by.

Enter Ambassador from Antony.

Cæs.   Approach, and speak.
Amb. Such as I am, I come from Antony:
    I was of late as petty to his ends,
    As is the morn-dew on the myrtle-leaf
    To his grand sea.
Cæs.   Be't so, declare thine office.   10

Scene XII

1. *from*] F; *for* F 2.

Scene XII

See North, *post*, pp. 278-9.
(S.D.) *Agrippa.*   Many editors omit him, on the grounds that he does not speak.   But Shakespeare not infrequently includes a non-speaker, either (perhaps) because he at first intended him to speak and then forgot or changed his mind, or (as more probably here) because it was natural for the character to be there.

5. *kings for messengers*] Cf. III. xiii. 91, and IV. ii. 13 *post.*

10. *To his grand sea*] Tyrwhitt conjectures *this* for *his*, supposing the sea visible from Cæsar's camp, but, as Steevens says, *his* = its, and the sea is the morn-dew's, as being its source, or, I imagine, as being its goal after exhalation by the sun.   This latter would give—besides the usual interpretation, " in comparison with ' the

sea from which the dew-drop is exhaled ' " (Steevens)—an alternative, substituting *to which . . . passes* for *from which . . . is exhaled.*   I have not seen it suggested that the simile may be elliptic, and = as petty to his purposes as the morn-dew to those of the great sea it comes from (i.e. as an insignificant part of it), *or* passes to (i.e. as an insignificant contributor to it).   † I think that Steevens and Case were wrong about *his* meaning " its " here (though it often does), and that the words mean " to the great sea which is Antony." [R] For *grand* = great, cf. III. i. 9 *ante*, and Sylvester's *Du Bartas*, third day, first week, line 184:—

    " Whither the Sea, which we *Atlantick* call,
    Be but a peece of the *Grand Sea* of all "; etc.

Amb. Lord of his fortunes he salutes thee, and
　　　Requires to live in Egypt, which not granted,
　　　He lessens his requests, and to thee sues
　　　To let him breathe between the heavens and earth,
　　　A private man in Athens: this for him.　　　15
　　　Next, Cleopatra does confess thy greatness,
　　　Submits her to thy might, and of thee craves
　　　The circle of the Ptolemies for her heirs,
　　　Now hazarded to thy grace.
Cæs.　　　　　　　　　　　　　For Antony,
　　　I have no ears to his request.　The queen　　20
　　　Of audience nor desire shall fail, so she
　　　From Egypt drive her all-disgraced friend,
　　　Or take his life there.　This if she perform,
　　　She shall not sue unheard.　So to them both.
Amb. Fortune pursue thee!
Cæs.　　　　　　　　　　　Bring him through the bands.

　　　　　　　　　　　　　　　[*Exit ambassador.*

　　　[*To Thidias*] To try thy eloquence, now 'tis time,　26
　　　　despatch;
　　　From Antony win Cleopatra, promise,
　　　And in our name, what she requires; add more,
　　　From thine invention, offers: women are not

---

13. *lessens*] F 2; *Lessons* F.　　　26. To Thidias] Rowe; not in F.

In the preceding day, line 501 *et seq.*, we have the contemporary idea about dew:—

　　" Two sorts of vapours by his heat exhales
　　From floating Deeps, and from the flowry Dales:
　　　.　.　.　.　.
　　And if this vapour fair and softly sty [ascend],
　　Not to the cold Stage of the middle Sky,
　　But 'boue the Clouds, it turneth (in a trice)
　　In *April*, Deaw; in *Ianuary*, Ice."

12. *Requires*] Requests (not " demands ").

13. *lessens*] Thiselton defends *Lessons* of F on the supposition that the initial capital indicates an emphasis scarcely appropriate in the case of *lessens*; and observes: " The fact that the ambassador is on this occasion a schoolmaster should have been sufficient to have warded off the sacrilegious hand of the emendator."

18. *circle*] crown, as in *K.J.* v. i. 2.

19. *Now . . . grace*] The retention of which now depends on your favour.

28, 29. *add . . . offers*] S. Walker conjectures *and more . . . offer*. But, after all, in rapidly worded directions, *offers* comes in naturally enough where it stands in the text. It merely reinforces, by an emphatic word, what has been already expressed. † The most attractive emendation is Hanmer's, *As thine invention offers*. [R]

N

In their best fortunes strong; but want will perjure   30
The ne'er-touch'd vestal: try thy cunning, Thidias;
Make thine own edict for thy pains, which we
Will answer as a law.
Thid.   Cæsar, I go.
Cæs. Observe how Antony becomes his flaw,
And what thou think'st his very action speaks   35
In every power that moves.
Thid.   Cæsar, I shall.   [*Exeunt.*

---

31. *Thidias*] † The name so appears consistently in F. Rowe and Pope were content to leave it. Theobald, on the grounds that North has Thyreus, supplanted Thidias by Thyreus, and almost all editors since, except Dover Wilson, have followed him. But North can have no authority (not even that of Plutarch, who has Thyrsus) against F. Why or how *Thidias* was arrived at is another question. Dover Wilson suggests that Shakespeare made the alteration, because " the Thyreus he found in North was so difficult for the actor to speak." I should have thought that, if anything, it was the other way round; and rhythmically *Thyreus* is surely preferable. [R]

32, 33. *Make . . . law*] Put your own valuation on your services: I will conform to what you decree as to a law. The usual sense of *answer* in connection with law is, " meet the charge," " justify the fact," as in Brome, *The Court Beggar*, IV. ii (Pearson's *Brome*, i. 244):—

" *Doct.* You cannot answer it.
   Gou. Better by *Law* then you can
       the intent
   Of rape upon the Lady."

" Edicts at Rome were rules promulgated by magistrates upon entry into office; and when the practice became common of magistrates adopting the edicts of their predecessors, these edicts practically had the force of ordinary laws " (Deighton).

34. *becomes his flaw*] bears himself as a broken (*or* disgraced, as in line 22 above) man. Cf. the verb in *Henry VIII.* I. i. 95: " For France hath *flaw'd* the league "; and see Day's *English Secretarie*, 1599, part i, p. 76: " Whilst there is yet but one craze or slender *flaw* in the touchstone of thy reputation, peece it up, and new flourish again by a greater excellencie, the square of thy workmanship."

35, 36. *And . . . power that moves*] And what may be augured of his state of mind from a close observation of his behaviour. *Power that moves*, faculty of body or mind that is put in action. Steevens compares *T. and C.* IV. v. 55-57:—

" There's language in her eye, her
       cheek, her lip,
   Nay, her foot speaks; her wanton
       spirits look out
   At every joint and *motion* of her
       body."

See also Sylvester's *Du Bartas*, 1621 ed. (*Babylon*, p. 262):—

" mine eys . . .
   By peece-meal close; all *moving
       powrs* be still;
   From my dull fingers drops my
       fainting quill "; etc.

[SCENE XIII.—*Alexandria. Cleopatra's palace.*]

Enter CLEOPATRA, ENOBARBUS, CHARMIAN, *and* IRAS.

Cleo. What shall we do, Enobarbus?

Eno.   Think, and die.

Cleo. Is Antony, or we, in fault for this?

Eno. Antony only, that would make his will

    Lord of his reason. What though you fled,

    From that great face of war, whose several ranges   5

    Frighted each other? why should he follow?

    The itch of his affection should not then

    Have nick'd his captainship, at such a point,

Scene XIII

1. *Think, and die*] Hanmer read *Drink*, and Tyrwhitt at first proposed *Wink*, on the strength of the bidding *wink and die* in Fletcher's *Sea Voyage*, I. i (Camb. IX. 3). There are other instances, e.g. 2 *H. IV.* I. iii. 33: "winking, leap'd into destruction"; D'Avenant, *To Endymion Porter*, etc. (*Works*, 1673, p. 235): "there I (Scarce griev'd for by my self) would winke and *die*"; Sir R. Howard, *Poems*, 1696, p. 16: "But like a Covvard wink't and fought"; but the question is rather whether to infer from *Think, and die* that death is to be the result of thinking and no other agency (as apparently was later the case with Enobarbus, IV. vi. 35, 36 *post*, on which see), or to be self-inflicted after a melancholy view of a hopeless situation. The former sense, i.e. "Become a prey to melancholy and die of it," is favoured by IV. vi. 35, 36 (see note), but even the passage from *J.C.* (II. i. 186), quoted by Steevens, does not certainly decide the question in its favour:—

"If he love Cæsar, all that he can do
  Is to himself, take thought and
  die for Cæsar."

5. *face of war*] So in Beaumont and Fletcher, *The Queen of Corinth*, IV. iii.

(Camb. VI, 56) : "Fear nothing that this *face of arms* presents."

ranges] the lines of the opposing fleets. For this noun, not elsewhere in Shakespeare, compare Hall's *Chronicle*, 1548, Henry VIII. v. yere, f. xxxiii: "The frenchmen came on in iii *ranges*, xxxvi mens thickness"; *Historie of the Arrivall of Edward IV*, etc. (Camden Society, 1838, p. 20) : "assayled them, in the mydst and strongest of theyr battaile, . . . and, than, turned to the *range*, first on that one hand, and than on that othar hand, in lengthe, and so bet and bare them downe, so that," etc. Fairfax's Tasso, *Godfrey of Bulloigne* (1600), vi. 107: "And breaking through the ranks and *ranges* long."

8. *nick'd*] There are sundry possible sources of this expression, and (1) I seem to be alone in suggesting that of gaming, whence—from a *nick* being a winning throw in the game of hazard —*to nick* came to mean to cheat, or merely *to get the better of*. So, in many passages, e.g.—with a play on words —in *Barnavelt*, v. ii (Bullen's *Old Plays*, ii. 303), where the headsman is said to have "*Nickt* many a worthie gamester"; *Two Wise Men*, etc. (1619), VI. iv (said by an inn-chamberlain of a guest who will order nothing) : "but we'll *nick* him

When half to half the world oppos'd, he being
The mered question. 'Twas a shame no less   10
Than was his loss, to course your flying flags,
And leave his navy gazing.

Cleo.   Prithee, peace.

Enter the Ambassador, with ANTONY.

Ant. Is that his answer?
Amb. Ay, my lord.
Ant. The queen shall then have courtesy, so she   15
Will yield us up.

10. *mered*] *meered* F ; see note.

well enough in his horse-meat and scurvy sheets " ; and Borrow, *The Romany Rye* (1857), II. xiv, p. 213 : " his reverence chated me, and I chated his reverence ; the ould thaif knew every trick that I knew, and one or two more ; but in daling out the cards I *nicked* his reverence ; scarcely a trump did I ever give him, Shorsha, and won his money purty freely." The *Eng. Dial. Dict.* has many examples of the senses " cheat " and " steal." (2) From the simple sense of *nick'd*, i.e. notched, is obtained maimed. So Staunton (emasculated), Deighton (marred, disfigured), Herford (properly cut in notches, here " curtailed "). (3) Steevens, comparing *The Comedy of Errors*, v. i. 175: " His man with scissors *nicks* him like a fool," gives " set the mark of folly on," which has satisfied most editors.

† I have almost no doubt that Case's own interpretation is the right one. *O.E.D.* (which had **not reached** the word when Case wrote his note) gives " cut short," with reference to this passage, as does Onions. But it cites no earlier instance, and none later till 1787—i.e. it derives its meaning from the very passage which is in dispute. On the other hand, for Case's interpretation, besides

quoting *Barnavelt*, it goes back to 1553. [R]

10. *mered question*] whole or sole ground of quarrel, if Mason is correct in supposing a coinage from *mere*. Cf. Middelton, *The Widow*, v. i. 142 :—

" Signor Francisco, whose *mere* object now
   Is woman at these years," etc.

and for *question*, *Hamlet*, I. i. 111. Johnson cites *mere* a boundary, and some make *mered question* = " the matter to which the dispute is limited," comparing Spenser, *Ruins of Rome*, xxii:—

" When that brave honour of the Latin name,
   Which *mear'd* her rule with Africa and Byze," etc.

The boundaries (strips of grass or banks) in the common fields of Shakespeare's day were called *meers*, whence a verb to mark off land, which may appear in extended usage here. Johnson also conjectured *mooted* ; *moved* (often *meued* or *meevid* thirty years or so before this play) is nearer in form and just as probable : " But which part should begin sute : that peace to *moue*," etc. (John Heywood, *The Spider and the Flie*, 1556, Spenser Society ed. p. 370).

Amb.   He says so.

Ant.   Let her know 't.
To the boy Cæsar send this grizzled head,
And he will fill thy wishes to the brim,
With principalities.

Cleo.   That head, my lord?

Ant. To him again, tell him he wears the rose   20
Of youth upon him; from which, the world should note
Something particular: his coin, ships, legions,
May be a coward's, whose ministers would prevail
Under the service of a child, as soon
As i' the command of Cæsar: I dare him therefore   25
To lay his gay comparisons apart
And answer me declin'd, sword against sword,
Ourselves alone.   I'll write it: follow me.

                    [*Exeunt Antony and Ambassador.*

Eno. [*Aside*] Yes, like enough!   High-battled Cæsar will
Unstate his happiness, and be stag'd to the show   30

---

26. *comparisons*] F; *caparisons* Pope.   28. Exeunt . . .] Capell; not in F.
29. Aside] Capell.

20, 21. *rose Of youth*] Cf. *All's Well*,
I. iii. 137: " this thorn Doth to our
rose of youth rightly belong "; and
Hamlet, III. i. 155.

26. *gay comparisons*] the showy supports in which he excels me. Most
editors similarly understand *comparisons* (with Johnson) as = comparative
superiority in fortune, and Malone
quotes *Macbeth*, I. ii. 55 :—

    " Till that Bellona's bridegroom,
        lapp'd in proof,
    Confronted him with *self-compari-
        sons*," etc.

but a few adopt Pope's reading *caparisons*. There is a play on the two words
in *Sir Gyles Goosecappe*, IV. ii (*Old
Plays*, Bullen, iii. 64)   " *Foul*. A my
life a most rich *comparison*. *Goos*.
Never stirre if it be not a richer
Comparison then my Lorde my Cosin
wore at Tilt," etc.   Perhaps it may
support the text to note that *comparisons* are inferred between youth and

age, fortune with its gifts and naked
misfortune ; and that while the gay,
glittering ones, the gifts, can be set
aside, the advantage in years and
flush of success must remain.

27. *declin'd*] i.e. in fortune, and
probably also " into the vale of years "
(*Othello*, III. iii. 266 *q.v.*). In the
Countess of Pembroke's *Antonie*, iii,
A. says he proffered combat :—

    " Though he in prime and I by
        feeble age
    Mightily weakened both in force
        and skill."

The 20th stanza of A. Copley's *A Fig
for Fortune* (1596) begins : " There is
no hell like to *declined* glorie."

29. *high-battled*] master of noble
armies. See on III. ix. 2 *ante*, and
compare *Titus Andronicus*, IV. iv. 35:
" *High-witted* Tamora."

30. *Unstate his happiness*] i.e. strip
it of state and dignity. See *Lear*, I. ii.
110 : " I would *unstate* myself to be

Against a sworder!   I see men's judgements are
A parcel of their fortunes, and things outward
Do draw the inward quality after them,
To suffer all alike, that he should dream,
Knowing all measures, the full Cæsar will   35
Answer his emptiness; Cæsar, thou hast subdued
His judgement too.

Enter a Servant.

Ser.   A messenger from Cæsar.
Cleo. What, no more ceremony?   See, my women,
Against the blown rose may they stop their nose,
That kneel'd unto the buds.   Admit him, sir.   40

[*Exit Servant.*

Eno. [*Aside*] Mine honesty, and I, begin to square.
The loyalty well held to fools does make
Our faith mere folly: yet he that can endure
To follow with allegiance a fall'n lord,
Does conquer him that did his master conquer,   45
And earns a place i' the story.

---

40. Exit . . .] Capell; not in F.   41. Aside] Capell.

in a due resolution " = " give up
my position as a duke, forfeit my
rank and fortune " (Craig).   The
context in both passages supports
this view of *unstate*, which otherwise might merely equal unsettle,
disestablish, as *stated* occurs in the
sense, constituted, firmly fixed.   So
in Felltham's *Resolves* (ed. 1631),
xxiv. : " a soul that is rightly
stated " ; xxvi :—

" Nature is motive in the quest of
ill ;
Stated in mischief," etc.

30, 31. *stag'd . . . sworder*] Henley
notes the allusion to the public
combats of gladiators.   And, as
Kittredge points out, prize fights
with swords were common shows in
London.   With *stag'd*, cf. *M. for M.*
I. i. 67 :—

" I love the people
But do not like to *stage* me to
their eyes " ;

for *sworder*, *2 H. VI.* IV. i. 135 : " A
Roman *sworder* and banditto slave."

32. *A parcel of*] " of a piece with "
(Steevens), literally, a part of.

32-34. *and things outward . . . alike*]
Compare Sonnet cxi :—

" And almost thence my nature is
subdued
To what it works in, like the
dyer's *hand*."

that] † seeing that: the general truth
(*things outward . . .*) is exemplified by
the particular instance. [R]

35. *Knowing all measures*] Being so
good a judge of men's " capacities ".

41. *square*] quarrel.   See on II. i. 45
ante ; and compare our phrase " he
squared up to his opponent."

Enter THIDIAS.

Cleo.   Cæsar's will.
Thid. Hear it apart.
Cleo.   None but friends: say boldly.
Thid. So haply are they friends to Antony.
Eno. He needs as many, sir, as Cæsar has,
    Or needs not us. If Cæsar please, our master   50
    Will leap to be his friend: for us, you know,
    Whose he is, we are, and that is, Cæsar's.
Thid.   So.
    Thus then, thou most renown'd, Cæsar entreats,
    Not to consider in what case thou stand'st
    Further than he is Cæsar.
Cleo.   Go on: right royal.   55
Thid. He knows that you embrac'd not Antony
    As you did love, but as you fear'd him.
Cleo.   O!
Thid. The scars upon your honour, therefore, he
    Does pity, as constrained blemishes,
    Not as deserv'd.
Cleo.   He is a god, and knows   60
    What is most right.   Mine honour was not yielded,
    But conquer'd merely.
Eno.   [*Aside*] To be sure of that,
    I will ask Antony.   Sir, sir, thou art so leaky

---

51. *us, you*] *us you* F; *as you* F 2.   55. *Cæsar*] F 2; Cæsars. F.
56. *embrac'd*] Hudson (Capell conj.); *embrace* F.   62. Aside] Hanmer.

50. *Or needs not us*] Heath: " or
else he needs not even us, whose small
number and want of power render us
incapable, without other assistance,
of being of any service to him ";
Deighton : " or has no *need* for any
friends, i.e. his case is beyond hope."
Is Enobarbus' speech, however, dic-
tated by his meditated defection, and
do these words signify : or does not
need us, for we are among them (viz.
Cæsar's friends) ?   What follows con-
tradicts this if " Whose he is " =
whose friend he is, but not necessarily
if it = whose creature, (i.e. at whose
discretion) he is, in which sense both
commentators understood it.

55. *Further . . . Cæsar*] Beyond the
fact that it is Cæsar, and no harsh
conqueror, with whom you have to do.

57. *as you fear'd him*] † Cleopatra,
in North, during the scene in which
she deludes Cæsar, says the same of
herself (see p. 283).   This may help
to clarify the way in which Cleopatra's *O!* should be delivered. [R]

61. *right*] true.
62. *merely*] utterly.

That we must leave thee to thy sinking, for
Thy dearest quit thee.   [*Exit.*
Thid.   Shall I say to Cæsar   65
What you require of him? for he partly begs
To be desir'd to give.   It much would please him,
That of his fortunes you should make a staff
To lean upon.   But it would warm his spirits
To hear from me you had left Antony,   70
And put yourself under his shroud,
The universal landlord.
Cleo.   What's your name?
Thid. My name is Thidias.
Cleo.   Most kind messenger,
Say to great Cæsar this in deputation:
I kiss his conquering hand: tell him, I am prompt   75
To lay my crown at's feet, and there to kneel:
Tell him, from his all-obeying breath I hear
The doom of Egypt.
Thid.   'Tis your noblest course.

74. *this in deputation:*] *this in disputation,* F; *this; in deputation* Theobald (Warburton), and edd.

66. *require*] request (no hint of demand).

71. *shroud*] shelter. See Kyd, *Works* (ed. Boas), *The Hovsholders Philosophie,* p. 248, line 9: " vnder the shade of a Tree, or *shroude* of a Church " ; *ibid.* p. 240: " ' The wrath of *Fortune* and of mightie me[n] I shun, howbeit I am eftsoones *shrowded* vnder the estate of Sauoy.' ' Vnder a magnanimous, just, and gratious Prince you soiourne then ' (quoth he)."

74. *in deputation:*] in deputed authority, as my representative. I have been guided by the folio punctuation, seeing no necessity for the accepted arrangement due to Warburton, which places the colon after *this,* and makes the sense: " I kiss his conquering hand by proxy."   Other passages hardly favour it.   Cf. *1 H. IV.* iv. iii. 86 :—

" Of all the favourites that the
        absent king
In deputation left behind him
        here," etc.,
ibid. iv. i. 32 :—
" And that his friends by *deputation*
        could not
So soon be drawn."
See also *T. and C.* i. iii. 152. Steevens (pointing as Warburton) believed that F's *disputation* might be retained, suggesting the sense: " I own he has the better in the controversy." The probabilities seem to me, however, in favour of *dis* being a result of the attractive proximity of *this* and *kiss.*

77. *all-obeying*] " which all obey." With *obeying* = obeyed, cf. *Rape of Lucrece,* 993, " unrecalling crime," i.e. crime past recall.

78. *doom of*] judgment on.
Egypt] myself.

Wisdom and fortune combating together,
If that the former dare but what it can,   80
No chance may shake it.   Give me grace to lay
My duty on your hand.

Cleo.   Your Cæsar's father oft,
When he hath mus'd of taking kingdoms in,
Bestow'd his lips on that unworthy place,
As it rain'd kisses.

Enter ANTONY *and* ENOBARBUS.

Ant.   Favours?   By Jove that thunders!   85
What art thou, fellow?

Thid.   One that but performs
The bidding of the fullest man, and worthiest
To have command obey'd.

Eno.   [*Aside*] You will be whipp'd.

Ant. Approach there!   Ah, you kite!   Now, gods and
     devils,
Authority melts from me: of late, when I cried
  " Ho! "   90
Like boys unto a muss, kings would start forth,

88, 94. Aside] Capell.   90. *me: of late, when*] Johnson (*me.   Of*); *me
of late.   When* F.

---

80. *former . . . shake it*] if a man
is wise enough to limit his daring to
the possible, he is secure.

83. *taking . . . in*] Cf. I. i. 23 ; III.
vii. 23, *ante.*

87. *fullest*] Here, I think, not only,
most completely endowed with man's
best qualities, but also with the gifts
of fortune. See line 35 *ante. Full* is
particularly applied in *Othello*, II. i. 36 :
" Like a *full*, [i.e. complete] soldier."
With the rest of the speech, compare Decretas on Antony, v. i. 6, 7
post.

89. *Ah, you kite*] probably addressed to Cleopatra. Mr. Craig
quotes this line on *King Lear*, I. iv. 286,
" Detested kite," and says of *kite:* " a
term of strong opprobrium, when by

Shakespeare applied to women. . . .
Turberville in his *Book of Faulconrie,*
1575, describes kites as ' base, bas-
tardly, refuse, hawks.' " On the
other hand, Thidias might be so
addressed. Compare *Ralph Roister
Doister*, v. v. 9: " Roister Doister that
doughtie *kite* " ; and Sylvester's *Du
Bartas*, ed. 1621, p. 217 (*The Furies*) :—

          " whose *Siren*-notes
     Inchant chaste *Susans*, and like
          hungry *Kite*
     Flie at all game, they *Louers* are
          behight."

91. *a muss*] a scramble. So Jonson,
Bart. Fair, IV. ii. 33: "*Cokes.* Gods so! *a
muss, a muss, a muss, a muss!* [Falls a-
scrambling for the pears]." Cotgrave,
defining another word, has " The

And cry " Your will?"   Have you no ears?
I am Antony yet.

Enter Servants.

       Take hence this Jack, and whip him.
Eno. [*Aside*] 'Tis better playing with a lion's whelp,
   Than with an old one dying.
Ant.   Moon and stars,   95
  Whip him. Were't twenty of the greatest tributaries
  That do acknowledge Cæsar, should I find them
  So saucy with the hand of she here,—what's her
    name,
  Since she was Cleopatra?   Whip him, fellows,
  Till like a boy you see him cringe his face,   100
  And whine aloud for mercy.   Take him hence.
Thid. Mark Antony!

---

93. Enter servants] Dyce; Enter a servant. F, after *him*.   94. Aside]
Capell.

boyish scrambling for nuts, etc., cast
on the ground; a Musse"; and Onions
points out that *muss* = scramble sur-
vives in Leicestershire and Warwick-
shire.   Grey pointed out the inclu-
sion by Rabelais (I. xxii) of *muss*
among the games of Gargantua, and
a mention again, in III. xl, where are
these details : " I found them all [i.e.
the high treasurers of France] re-
creating and diverting themselves at
the play called *musse*, . . . provided
that *hic not.* that the game of the
musse is honest, healthful, ancient,
and lawful, *a Muscho inventore*, . . .
& *muscarii*, such as play and sport it
at the musse, are excusable in and
by law, . . . And at the very same
time was master Tielman Picquet
one of the players of that game of
musse. There is nothing that I
do better remember ; for he laughed
heartily when his fellow-members of
the aforesaid judicial chamber spoiled
their caps in swindging of his
shoulders ": etc. (*Works*, Chatto &

Windus, *n.d.* p. 354). With the succeeding reference to kings, cf. III. xii.
5 *ante*, and IV. ii. 13 *post*.
  93. *Jack*] fellow, impudent rascal.
The frequency of the name led to its
use for clown, peasant, etc. (as now
for sailor), and so in more or less contemptuous senses. Cf. our *Jacks-in-
office*, and with it the corresponding
phrase in " And I may set up for
an *Author*, I hope, among the *Crowd*
. . . where *Licensers*, *Correctors*, and
Criticks, are made but *Jacks* in an
Office" (*The Parliament of Criticks*,
1702, p. 2).
  whip him] See North,*post*, p. 279.
  100. *cringe his face*] *O.E.D.* quotes
for this transitive use of *cringe*, in
addition to the present passage,
Bishop Hall, *Satires*, 1598, IV. ii [ed.
Singer, 1824, p. 85]: " And shake
his head, and *cringe* his neck and side";
Taylor, the Water Poet, *Red Herring*,
circa 1630: " They, *cringing* in their
necks, like rats, smothered in the
hold, poorly replied."

Ant.   Tug him away: being whipp'd
Bring him again: this Jack of Cæsar's shall
Bear us an errand to him.

                              [*Exeunt servants with Thidias.*

You were half blasted ere I knew you: ha?   105
Have I my pillow left unpress'd in Rome,
Forborne the getting of a lawful race,
And by a gem of women, to be abus'd
By one that looks on feeders?

Cleo.   Good my lord,—

Ant. You have been a boggler ever,   110
But when we in our viciousness grow hard—
O misery on't!—the wise gods seel our eyes,

---

103. *this*] Pope; *the* F.   112, 113. *eyes, In our own filth drop*] *eyes:
In our own filth drop* Warburton; *eyes in our owne filth, drop* F.

---

107. *Forborne . . . race*] Not the fact.
See North, *post*, p. 268.

108. *gem*] Headley (*Select Beauties*,
etc. ed. 1810, i. 161) quotes this
passage to illustrate, " My chosen
pheare, my *gem*, and all my joy,"
from G. Gascoigne's *Poems*, p. 141,
1587, 4to. He considers *gem* " An
expression of endearment of great
beauty."

109. *feeders*] servants. Similarly
they are called *cormorants; "* I . . .
forgot to bring one of my *cormorants*
to attend me " (Jonson, *E.M.O.*, v.
i. 8); *beef-eaters:* " Begone yee greedy
beefe-eaters " (*Histriomastix*, III. i. 99);
" *eaters of broken meats* " (*King Lear*,
II. ii. 15); *eaters:* " tall *eaters* in blue
coats " (D'Avenant, *The Wits*, III. i;
Works, 1872, ii. 167; *mouths;* " Where
are all my eaters? my *mouths* now?
[*Enter Servants* " (Jonson, *The Silent
Woman*, III. v. 33). To the last two,
quoted by Steevens, Gifford adds
from Fletcher, *The Nice Valour*, III. i.
(Camb. X, p. 164): " Now servants
he has kept, lusty tall *feeders* "; and in
A.Y.L. II. iv. 100: " I will your
very faithful *feeder* be," the word is
mostly taken as = servant. It is
noteworthy that in none of these

passages are eating propensities *apropos*, so that the terms are general;
and though it is otherwise in *T. of
A.* II. ii. 168: " When all our offices
have been oppress'd With riotous
feeders," the sense of the word is
determined here too, as Steevens
pointed out, by its conjunction with
offices or servants' quarters. The
weight of evidence is wholly against
Delius' and Schmidt's explanation,
parasites. Compare also lines 123,
124, 157 *post*.

110. *boggler*] waverer, shifty one.
See *All's Well*, v. iii. 234: " You
boggle shrewdly," etc.

112. *seel*] The term in falconry for
sewing up a hawk's eyelids temporarily
to prepare it for the use of the hood.
Often used figuratively as here. Cf.
Jonson, *Catiline*, I. 297:—

" Are your eyes yet *unseel'd?* dare
      they look day
    In the dull face?"

The Practice had other uses. Among
amusements provided by Zelmane
(Sidney's *Arcadia*, bk. i. ed. 1725, p.
99) this figures: " Now she brought
them to see a *seeled* dove, who, the
blinder she was, the higher she
strove."

In our own filth drop our clear judgements, make us
Adore our errors, laugh at's while we strut
To our confusion.

Cleo.   O, is't come to this?   115

Ant. I found you as a morsel, cold upon
Dead Cæsar's trencher: nay, you were a fragment
Of Gnaeus Pompey's, besides what hotter hours,
Unregister'd in vulgar fame, you have
Luxuriously pick'd out. For I am sure,   120
Though you can guess what temperance should be,
You know not what it is.

Cleo.   Wherefore is this?

Ant. To let a fellow that will take rewards,
And say, " God quit you!", be familiar with
My playfellow, your hand; this kingly seal,   125
And plighter of high hearts! O that I were
Upon the hill of Basan, to outroar
The horned herd, for I have savage cause,
And to proclaim it civilly, were like
A halter'd neck, which does the hangman thank   130
For being yare about him.

---

113. *In . . . judgements*] Probability and Steevens's illustration from *Henry V.* III. v. 59: " He'll *drop* his heart into the *sink* of fear," negative the pointing of F, to which Knight adheres.

116, 117. *morsel . . . trencher*] Cf. the metaphor for Cleopatra, " his Egyptian dish," II. vi. 123 *ante*, and Cleopatra's own description of herself as " a morsel for a monarch," I. v. 31 *ante*.

117. *fragment*] left scrap or morsel. Cf. the plural in *Cymbeline*, v. iii. 44.

118. *Gnaeus Pompey's*] Compare IV. xii. 13 *post*, and see North, *post*, pp. 261-2.

120. *Luxuriously*] lustfully. So the adjective = lustful, as in *Titus Andronicus*, v. i. 88: " O most insatiate and *luxurious* woman!" and the noun, " lust," as in *Hamlet*, I. v.

83, in Shakespeare and his contemporaries.

124. *quit*] reward. Cf. Browne, *Britannia's Pastorals*, II. iv. 964: " You whose flocks . . . By my protection *quit* your industry."

125. *seal*] So in *M.N.D.* III. ii. 143, 144: " thy hand . . . this *seal* of bliss!"

127, 128. *Basan . . . herd*] Steevens quotes the Prayer-book versions of Psalms lxviii. 15 and xxii. 12: " As the hill of *Basan*, so is God's hill: even an high hill, as the hill of *Basan*"; " Many oxen are come about me: fat bulls of *Basan* close me in on every side." With the inevitable allusion to *horned*, cf. I. ii. 4 *ante*. Antony means that he is the champion cuckold of the world.

131. *yare*] adroit, quick. Cf. II. ii. 211; III. vii. 38 *ante*: v. ii. 282 *post*.

Enter a Servant with THIDIAS.

Is he whipp'd?

Ser. Soundly, my lord.

Ant.   Cried he? and begg'd 'a pardon?

Ser. He did ask favour.

Ant. If that thy father live, let him repent
　　　Thou wast not made his daughter, and be thou sorry
　　　To follow Cæsar in his triumph, since　　　　136
　　　Thou hast been whipp'd for following him: henceforth
　　　The white hand of a lady fever thee,
　　　Shake thou to look on 't.　Get thee back to Cæsar,
　　　Tell him thy entertainment: look thou say　　140
　　　He makes me angry with him.　For he seems
　　　Proud and disdainful, harping on what I am
　　　Not what he knew I was.　He makes me angry,
　　　And at this time most easy 'tis to do 't:
　　　When my good stars, that were my former guides,　145
　　　Have empty left their orbs, and shot their fires
　　　Into the abysm of hell.　If he mislike
　　　My speech, and what is done, tell him he has
　　　Hipparchus, my enfranched bondman, whom
　　　He may at pleasure whip, or hang, or torture,　150
　　　As he shall like to quit me.　Urge it thou:
　　　Hence with thy stripes, begone!　　　*Exit Thidias.*

Cleo. Have you done yet?

---

132. *'a*] *a* F; *he* Capell and most edd.
whipp'd, for Rowe; *whipt. For* F.

137. *whipp'd for*] Theobald;

132. *'a*] For *a* = he in F, compare
II. vii. 90, 133 *ante*.

141-147. *He . . . angry*, etc.] See
North, *post*, p. 279.

142, 143. *what I am . . . was*] Cf.
Arden of Feversham, i. 322, for the
reverse idea: " Measure me *what I
am*, not what I *was*."

144. *do't :*] † so F; most edd. print
a comma. F is right, I think,
marking the pause before he ampli-
fies *this time*. [R]

146. *orbs*] spheres. See on II. vii.

14-16 *ante*, IV. xv. 10 *post*, and *M.N.D.*
II. i. 153.

149. *Hipparchus*] See North, *post*,
pp. 276-7, 279. Antony is not aban-
doning an innocent man thus, but a
revolter.

enfranched] Only here in Shakespeare. *O.E.D.* also cites Marbeck,
Book of Notes (1581), p. 193 : " By
him we be *enfraunched* from the cap-
tivitie and thraldome of the Divell."

151. *quit me*] pay me out, requite
me. Cf. line 124 *ante*.

Ant.   Alack, our terrene moon
Is now eclips'd, and it portends alone
The fall of Antony!
Cleo.   I must stay his time.   165
Ant. To flatter Cæsar, would you mingle eyes
With one that ties his points?
Cleo.   Not know me yet?
Ant. Cold-hearted toward me?
Cleo.   Ah, dear, if I be so,
From my cold heart let heaven engender hail,
And poison it in the source, and the first stone   160
Drop in my neck: as it determines, so
Dissolve my life; the next Cæsarion smite
Till by degrees the memory of my womb,
Together with my brave Egyptians all,
By the discandying of this pelleted storm,   165

---

158. *me?*] F; *me!* Theobald.   162. *Cæsarion smite*] Rowe (*Cæsario*);
Cæsarian smile F.   165. *discandying*] Theobald (Thirlby conj.); *discandering* F.

153, 154. *moon . . . eclips'd . . . portends*] He has already, in his anger, referred to Cleopatra as no longer herself (line 99 *ante*); now similarly, but in softer mood, he figures her as a moon darkened, lustreless, and hence, according to the common superstition, portending evil. See *Lear*, I. ii. 115. Capell supposes him to think of Cleopatra as Isis. See on I. ii. 61 *ante*, and cf. III. vi. 17 *ante*.

155. *stay his time*] be patient till he comes to himself.

157. *one that . . . points*] A contemptuous phrase for a menial, like *feeder*, line 109 *ante*. *Points* were the tagged laces with which the parts of a man's or woman's dress were fastened together. See *1 H. IV.* II. iv. 242; *Kemps nine daies vvonder*, 1600 (Camden Society, 1840, p. 17): "it was the mischaunce of a homely maide, that, belike, was but newly crept into the fashion of long wasted peticotes tyde with *points*," etc.

his] Caesar's.

158. *Cold-hearted towards me?*] † I am inclined to think that Theobald and other editors who follow his reading were right, and that Antony, not yet relenting, is bitterly answering Cleopatra's question: " Yes, only too well I know your cold heart." [R]

161. *determines*] comes to an end, dissolves. See *Coriolanus*, III. iii. 42: " Must all *determine* here?"

162. *Cæsarion*] Cf. III. vi. 6 *ante*.

165. *discandying*] melting. This and *discandy*, IV. xii. 22 *post*, seem to be the only known instances, but the opposite idea is common. Cf. Sylvester's Du Bartas, *The Lawe*, 1621 ed. p. 362:—

" As thick, or thicker then the Welkin pours
His *candi'd* drops vpon the ears of Corn," etc.

The conceit seems to be that the poison in the hail (line 160) is liberated by the melting. The wish which follows resembles that in v. ii. 57-60 *post*.

pelleted] occurs also in *A Lover's Complaint*, 18: " the brine That season'd woe had *pelleted* in tears."

Lie graveless, till the flies and gnats of Nile
Have buried them for prey!

Ant.   I am satisfied.
Cæsar sits down in Alexandria, where
I will oppose his fate.   Our force by land
Hath nobly held, our sever'd navy too   170
Have knit again, and fleet, threatening most sea-like.
Where hast thou been, my heart?   Dost thou hear,
   lady?
If from the field I shall return once more
To kiss these lips, I will appear in blood,
I, and my sword, will earn our chronicle: 175
There's hope in't yet.

Cleo. That's my brave lord!

Ant. I will be treble-sinew'd, hearted, breath'd,
And fight maliciously: for when mine hours
Were nice and lucky, men did ransom lives   180

---

168. *sits*] Johnson; *sets* F.   175. *our*] F; *my* F 2.

166-7. *flies . . . prey*] Deighton well compares *Macbeth*, III. iv. 72, 3: " our monuments shall be the maws of kites."

169. *his fate*] Cf. *Henry V.* II. iv. 64: "and let us fear The native mightiness and *fate* of him."

171. *fleet*] float. Very common ; so T. Hudson, Du Bartas's *Judith*, 1584 (p. 693 in Sylvester, 1621 ed.) :—

" When Seas are calme, and thous-
   and vessels *fleet*
  Vpon the sleeping seas with passage sweet " ; etc.

Selimus, 1594, ed. Grosart, 467 : " a quiet road for *fleeting* ships."

172. *heart*] With Delius, I under-
stand this as courage, spirit, and not as addressed to Cleopatra.

174. *in blood*] Besides the obvious sense, Deighton detects " an allusion to the phrase as used of a stag when in full vigour," and compares *1 H. VI.* IV. ii. 48, and *Coriolanus*, IV. v. 225 : " But when they shall see, sir, his crest up again, and the man *in blood*, they will," etc. See also *Sejanus*, II. 385.

" The way to put
A prince *in blood*, is to present the
  shapes
Of dangers greater than they
  are," etc.

175. *our chronicle*] a record of our deeds. Cf. line 46 *ante*, and Beaumont and Fletcher, *Philaster*, V. iii. 130: " Well, my dear Countrymen, What-
you-lacks, if you continue, and fall not back upon the first broken shin, I'll have you *chronicled* and *chronicled*, and cut and *chronicled*, and all-to-be-
prais'd and sung in Sonnets," etc.

178. *breath'd*] Some print *breathed* and explain " exercised," a frequent sense; but here a treble strength of breath goes with the like of heart and sinews.

180. *nice*] The favoured sense of *nice* here is Warburton's " delicate," or the like (compare Minshew, 1617, " Nice, *or daintie . . . or effeminate* "), and Schmidt well supports with *2 H. IV.* I. i. 145 :—

" Hence, thereafter, thou *nice*
  crutch!

Of me for jests: but now, I'll set my teeth,
And send to darkness all that stop me.   Come,
Let's have one other gaudy night: call to me
All my sad captains, fill our bowls once more;
Let's mock the midnight bell.

Cleo.   It is my birth-day,   185
I had thought t' have held it poor. But since my lord
Is Antony again, I will be Cleopatra.

Ant. We will yet do well.

Cleo. Call all his noble captains to my lord.

Ant. Do so, we'll speak to them, and to-night I'll force   190
The wine peep through their scars.   Come on, my
     queen,

A scaly gauntlet now with joints
     of steel
Must glove this hand : " etc.
A slight objection to this and most
senses suggested, is that as Antony is
speaking of his former *fighting* temper,
his hours, however lucky, could only
have been dainty, etc., in a very relative sense.   Johnson preferred the
modern " just fit for my purpose,
agreeable to my wish " ; and it is perhaps worth remarking that " nice and
lucky " as a colloquialism nowadays
would mean extremely, or satisfactorily, lucky.   Other suggestions are,
" trifling " (Steevens), as in *R. and J.*
v. ii. 18, etc.—and " jests " would
certainly suit hours that were trivial
compared with the present crisis—
" amorous, or wanton," Douce,
who quotes Stowe, of one Mary
Breame in 1583, who " had been
accused by her husband to bee a *nice
woman of her body*." As *nice* comes
from *nescius*, ignorant, this is a probable degradation of the word.   † I
fancy that *nice* has here the sense of
" finicky," " choosy," and that
Antony means " When I was lucky,
I could afford to pick and choose at
my caprice." [R]
183. *gaudy*] festive. Feast days are
still called " gaudy days " at Oxford.
Reed quotes Blount's *Glossographia*
[see for the following, ed. 4, 1674]:

" In the Inns of Court there are four
of these in the year, that is, one in
every Term, viz. *Ascension-day* in
Easter Term, *Midsummer-day* in *Trinity*
Term, *All-Saints-day* in *Michaelmas*
Term, and *Candlemas-day* in *Hillary*
Term; these four are no days in Court,
and on these days double Commons
are allowed, and Musick on *All-Saints*
and *Candlemas-day*, as the first and
last of *Christmas*. The Etymology of
the word may be taken from Judge
Gawdy, who (as some affirm) was the
first institutor of those days or rather
from *gaudium*, because (to say truth)
they are days of *joy*, as bringing good
cheer to the hungry Students.   In
Colledges, they are most commonly
called *Gaudy*, in Inns of Court, *Grand
days*, and at Court, *Coller days*."   See
Bullen's *Middleton*, viii. 43, 44, *The
Black Book*, where " Pierce Pennyless,
exceeding poor scholar, that hath
made clean shoes in both universities"
is spoken of as not " once munching
commons but only upon *gaudy*-days," ;
and, for the general use, Edward
Phillips' *Life of John Milton*, 1694
(Appendix to Godwin's *Lives of
Edward and John Philips*, 1815, p. 365):
" with these gentlemen, he would so
far make bold with his body, as now
and then to keep a *gawdy*-day."
185. *birth-day*] See North, *post*, p.
279.

There's sap in 't yet.   The next time I do fight
I'll make death love me; for I will contend
Even with his pestilent scythe.

[*Exeunt all but Enobarbus.*

Eno. Now he'll outstare the lightning; to be furious   195
Is to be frighted out of fear, and in that mood
The dove will peck the estridge; and I see still,

194. Exeunt . . . Enobarbus] Camb. edd.; Exeunt. F.

193, 194. *contend . . . scythe*] equal
the slaughter of even his scythe of
pestilence (i.e. the plague).

197. *estridge*] goshawk. See on
the word here and in *1 H. IV.* iv. i.
98, Douce (*Illustrations of Shakespeare*,
1807, i. 436), who appeals to *3 H.
VI.* i. iv. 41 : " So doves do peck the
falcon's piercing talons," and quotes
the Romance of Guy of Warwick, of
which the *Early English Text Soc.*
editions, 1883, have (pt. i, p. 12,
lines 175, 176) from Auchinleck MS.

" Michel he coupe of hauk and;
    hounde,
Of *estriche* faucons of gret mounde "

Nares (*Glossary*, 1822) under *Astringer*,
cites Blount's *Tenures*, ed. 1784, p.
166: " A goshawk is in our records
termed by the several names of
osturcum, hostricum, estricium, asturcum,
and *austurcum* " (in which list
estricium is the significant form, while
hostricum suggests a possible reason for
the " ostrich " confusion), and Halliwell (*Dict. Archaic and Provincial
Words*) explains the word in the text
as Douce. Editors have entirely
ignored all this, and are kept in
countenance by *O.E.D.*, in which the
sense " goshawk " is unnoticed, and
our text illustrates that of *ostrich*, for
which *estridge* commonly appears. In
Professor Littledale's re-issue of Dyce's
Glossary to Shakespeare, the correction
is made in the Appendix, but ascribed
to Madden (*Diary of Master William
Silence*, pp. 144, 155, etc.).

† I do not understand why editors
are for the most part so reluctant to
admit that *estridge* can mean goshawk,
as well as ostrich.

Dover Wilson does his best to
support the meaning " ostrich " here
by saying that it is appropriate to
Egypt.   That, to begin with, is not
so, unless the limits of the ostrich's
geographical distribution were in
Shakespeare's day further north
than they are now.   But in any case
would Shakespeare have given a
moment's thought to the geographical
appropriateness of the ostrich—or for
that matter of the goshawk?   He
was concerned with an image, and
an image which he uses elsewhere.
In *Macbeth* (iv. ii. 9-11) the wren, in
defence of her young, will fight
against the owl, and (ii. iv. 12, 13)
a mousing owl hawks at and kills a
falcon.   And the passage quoted
above from *3 H. VI* is seen to be even
more closely relevant to the present
passage when quoted complete, since
it deals with the *mood* in which the
dove will turn upon the bird of prey.

" So cowards fight when they can
    fly no further ;
So doves do peck the falcon's
    piercing talons."

Suppose for a moment that *estridge*
had been a ἅπαξ λεγόμενον, occurring
in this passage only.   Would any
commentator with the other Shakespearean passages before him have
doubted that it meant some kind of
bird of prey, or, with the " estriche "
and " estricium " passages before
him, that it probably meant specifically a goshawk? [R]

o

A diminution in our captain's brain
Restores his heart; when valour preys on reason,
It eats the sword it fights with: I will seek   200
Some way to leave him.   [*Exit.*

199. *preys on*] Rowe; *prayes in* F.   201. Exit] Rowe; Exeunt. F.

ACT IV

[SCENE I.—*Before Alexandria.   Cæsar's camp.*]

Enter CÆSAR, AGRIPPA, *and* MÆCENAS, *with his Army;*
CÆSAR *reading a letter.*

Cæs. He calls me boy, and chides as he had power
　　To beat me out of Egypt.   My messenger
　　He hath whipp'd with rods, dares me to personal
　　　combat.
　　Cæsar to Antony: let the old ruffian know,
　　I have many other ways to die; meantime　　　　　　5
　　Laugh at his challenge.
Mæc.　　　　　　　　　　　　Cæsar must think,
　　When one so great begins to rage, he's hunted
　　Even to falling.   Give him no breath, but now
　　Make boot of his distraction: never anger
　　Made good guard for itself.
Cæs.　　　　　　　　　　　　Let our best heads　　10
　　Know, that to-morrow the last of many battles
　　We mean to fight.   Within our files there are,
　　Of those that serv'd Mark Antony but late,

Scene 1

3, 4. † I think F's punctuation very probably right. *Cæsar to Antony* is then the opening of his reply (as though he was dictating a letter). But for *to* (awkward in modern idiom) meaning " versus," cf. *1 H. VI.* I. ii. 47, " Blue coats to tawny coats." [R]

6. *Cæsar must think*] † Apart from the halting rhythm, this is an oddly third-personal way for Maecenas to address Cæsar (which he is clearly doing, and not delivering a comment aside). Should we perhaps read *Cæsar, we must think?* [R]

9. *Make boot of*] Take advantage of. See on II. v. 71 *ante.*

12. *files*] " It must be added that the file was, in those days, the unit (to use a modern phrase) in which the strength of an army was expressed. Men took their places in the *files*, not in the *ranks* of an army " (*Shakespeare's England*, Oxford, 1916, I. iv, p. 114.

Enough to fetch him in.   See it done,
And feast the army;   we have store to do 't,   15
And they have earn'd the waste.   Poor Antony!

                               [*Exeunt.*

[SCENE II.—*Alexandria.   Cleopatra's palace.*]

Enter ANTONY, CLEOPATRA, ENOBARBUS, CHARMIAN, IRAS,
                ALEXAS, *with others.*

Ant. He will not fight with me, Domitius?
Eno.   No.
Ant. Why should he not?
Eno. He thinks, being twenty times of better fortune,
He is twenty men to one.
Ant.   To-morrow, soldier,
By sea and land I'll fight: or I will live,   5
Or bathe my dying honour in the blood
Shall make it live again.   Woo't thou fight well?

<hr>

Scene II

1. *Domitius?*] *Domitius.* Rowe and others; Domitian? F.

14. *fetch him in*] capture him, as in *Cymbeline*, IV. ii. 140: " and swear He 'ld *fetch us in.*"

16. *waste*] needless expenditure.

Scene II

[See North, *post*, p. 280.]

5. *or*] either.

6. *Or bathe . . . blood*] Perhaps an allusion to baths of blood as a remedy. Mr. C. Crawford refers me to Jonson's *Discoveries*, line 1058 : " *Morbi.* The Body hath certaine diseases, that are with lesse evil, tolerated, then remov'd. As if to cure a Leprosie a man should *bathe* himselfe with the warme *blood* of a murthered Child, so," etc., on which Professor Schelling refers, *inter alia*, to " *Gesta Romanorum*, ed. Osterley, No. 230, in which a girl afflicted with leprosy, only to be cured by her *bathing* in royal *blood*, accepts the sacrifice of her royal lover, who allows so much blood to be taken from him that it causes his death." In a citation of Carlyle's (*French Rev.* I. i. 2) from Lacretelle, *Histoire de France*, etc., occurs : " an absurd and horrid rumour rises among the people ; it is said that the doctors have ordered a Great Person to take *baths* of young human *blood* for the restoration of his own, all spoiled by debaucheries."

7. *Woo 't*] A common form = *wilt.* Cf. IV. xv. 59 *post ; Hamlet*, V. i. 298 ; S. Rowlands, *The Knave of Clubbs* (Percy Society, 1843, No. xxxiv, pp. 9-12 *passim*) : " Why doe and *t' woot,*" etc.

Eno. I'll strike, and cry " Take all."

Ant.   Well said, come on,
Call forth my household servants, let's to-night

Enter three or four Servitors.

Be bounteous at our meal.   Give me thy hand,   10
Thou hast been rightly honest;—so hast thou,—
Thou,—and thou,—and thou: you have serv'd me
     well,
And kings have been your fellows.

Cleo.   [*Aside to Eno.*] What means this?

Eno. [*Aside to Cleo.*] 'Tis one of those odd tricks which
     sorrow shoots
Out of the mind.

Ant.   And thou art honest too.   15
I wish I could be made so many men,
And all of you clapp'd up together in
An Antony; that I might do you service,
So good as you have done.

All.   The gods forbid!

Ant. Well, my good fellows, wait on me to-night: 20
Scant not my cups, and make as much of me
As when mine empire was your fellow too,
And suffer'd my command.

Cleo.   [*Aside to Eno.*] What does he mean?

Eno. [*Aside to Cleo.*] To make his followers weep.

13, 14. Aside . . .] Capell.   23, 24. Aside . . .] Capell.

8. " *Take all* "] Johnson : " Let the survivor *take all*. No composition ; victory or death." No doubt the expression comes, as Collier says, from the language of gaming. See *A Warning for Faire Women*, ii. 683 (Simpson, *School of Shakspere*, ii. 295) : " *Yong San.* Come, Harrie, shall we play a game? *Har.* At what? *Yong San.* Why, at crosse and pile. *Har.* You have no Counters. *Yong San.* Yes, but I have as many as you. *Har.* Ile drop with you ; and he that has most, *take all.*" A proverbial expression, " the

longer liver *take all*," occurs in *R. and J.* i. v. 19, and elsewhere.

9-10. S.D.] † The majority of editors from Dyce onwards have put this S.D. after " meal," a good example of the difference in placing S.D.s required by the different depths of the Elizabethan and modern stages. F's placing avoids the awkward pause which, on the deep Elizabethan stage would have intervened between the entry and Antony's " Give me thy hand." [R]

13. kings . . . fellows] Cf. III. xii. 5 and xiii. 91 *ante*.

Ant.   Tend me to-night;

May be it is the period of your duty,   25
Haply you shall not see me more, or if,
A mangled shadow.   Perchance to-morrow
You'll serve another master.   I look on you,
As one that takes his leave.   Mine honest friends,
I turn you not away, but like a master   30
Married to your good service, stay till death:
Tend me to-night two hours, I ask no more,
And the gods yield you for't!

Eno.   What mean you, sir,

To give them this discomfort? Look, they weep,
And I, an ass, am onion-ey'd; for shame,   35
Transform us not to women.

Ant.   Ho, ho, ho!

Now the witch take me, if I meant it thus!
Grace grow where those drops fall, my hearty friends;

---

38. *fall, my . . . friends;*] *fall (my . . . Friends)* F; *fall! My . . . friends,*
Theobald.

---

25. *period*] end (full stop), as in
IV. xiv. 107 *post*.

30, 31. *but like a master . . . stay till
death*] † I suppose this must mean
"You have served me well and I
will remain your master till I die,"
but I think that the *like* is slightly
awkward, and that the natural sense
(though it cannot be extracted from
the text) would be " I ask you to stay
with me till I die " (which, the whole
context implies, will be soon).   It is
perhaps worth considering a " transposed pointing " so that the passage
will read:—

  I turn you not away, but like a
    master
  Married to your good service: stay
    till death,
  Tend me. . . .

Then, taking *but* = except, the lines
will mean " I am not turning you
away except as any master would
warn loyal servants of his approaching death : stay with me till death
comes." [R]

33. *yield*] pay, requite, the original

sense. Cf. *A.Y.L.*, III. iii. 81. " God
'*ild* you for your last company," etc.

35. *And I . . . onion-ey'd*] Cf. I. ii.
166.

36. *Ho, ho, ho*] After his brief indulgence in sentiment and pathos,
Antony laughs it off. Holt White
seriously produces many instances of
a single *ho* = stop, to show that *stop*
or *desist* is the sense here.

37. *the witch take me*] may I be be-
witched! For *take* = bewitch, exert
a malignant influence on, cf. *Hamlet*,
I. i. 163 " No fairy *takes*, nor witch
hath power to charm "; *M.W.W.*
IV. iv. 33, of Herne the hunter : "And
then he blasts the tree and *takes* the
cattle," etc. ; *Gammer Gurton's Needle*
(1575), I. ii. 26: " As though they
had ben *taken* with fairies, or els with
some il sprite."

38. *Grace grow . . . fall*] Steevens
quotes *R. II* [III. iv. 104, 105]:—

  " Here did she fall a tear ; here in
    this place
  I'll set a bank of rue, sour herb of
    grace."

You take me in too dolorous a sense,
For I spake to you for your comfort, did desire you   40
To burn this night with torches: know, my hearts,
I hope well of to-morrow, and will lead you
Where rather I'll expect victorious life,
Than death, and honour.   Let's to supper, come,
And drown consideration.   [*Exeunt.* 45

[SCENE III.—*The same.   Before the palace.*]

Enter a Company of Soldiers.

First Sold. Brother, good night: to-morrow is the day.
Sec. Sold. It will determine one way: fare you well.
     Heard you of nothing strange about the streets?
First Sold. Nothing: what news?

---

44. *death, and honour*] refers to IV. ii.
6 *ante.*

Scene III

† I have retained throughout the
scene the stage directions and speech-
headings of F, except immediately
after the entry of the " other soldiers "
where one of the two speeches (given
by F to " 2 " and " 1 " respectively)
must, I think, be given to one of the
newcomers. I can see no valid reason
elsewhere for joining in the game of
musical chairs played by the eighteenth century editors with the rest
of the speeches. Capell up to a
point saw, I think, what is supposed
to be happening. His stage-directions are *Enter two Soldiers, to their
guard:* then *Enter two other Soldiers.*
Shakespeare, I think, meant there to
be four or five soldiers in each group,
even though only two in each are
vocal, and his " *they meet* " indicates
that the second group come in by
the other door. But Capell then
obscures the situation by giving,
instead of " *They place themselves
. . . ,*" " *The two first go to their posts,*"
rather as though they went off-stage
to their posts—which, from his
own subsequent stage-directions, they
clearly do not. He saw, however,
that all the soldiers are on guard.
Dover Wilson complicates matters
further by saying that the dialogue
makes it plain that the first two are
going off guard and the second pair
coming on (though he retains F's
stage-directions) and therefore has to
accept Capell's redistribution of
speeches in lines 9-12. But Shakespeare's intentions are, I suggest,
perfectly clear.   A number of sentries
meet, as they go on their way to their
posts, and exchange greetings. They
then distribute themselves to their
posts, which are, by the space-
destroying conventions of the Elizabethan stage, improbably close
together (cf. the tents of Richard and
Richmond in *Richard III*, v. iii).
Thus they are in a position not only
to hear the music, which in fact they
could have done, but to interchange
comments on it, which in fact they
could not. [R]

Sec. Sold. Belike 'tis but a rumour, good night to you.   5
First Sold. Well, sir, good night.

They meet other Soldiers.

Third Sold.   Soldiers, have careful watch.
First Sold. And you: good night, good night.
            [*They place themselves in every corner of the stage.*
Sec. Sold. Here we: and if to-morrow
        Our navy thrive, I have an absolute hope
        Our landmen will stand up.
First Sold.   'Tis a brave army,   10
        And full of purpose.
                    [*Music of the hautboys is under the stage.*
Sec. Sold.   Peace, what noise?
First Sold.   List, list!
Sec. Sold. Hark!
First Sold.   Music i' the air.
Third Sold.   Under the earth.
Fourth Sold. It signs well, does it not?
Third Sold.   No.
First Sold.   Peace, I say:
        What should this mean?
Sec. Sold. 'Tis the god Hercules, whom Antony lov'd,   15
        Now leaves him.
First Sold.   Walk, let's see if other watchmen
        Do hear what we do.

5. *Belike*] probably, as in I. ii. 35 *ante.*

11. *noise*] possibly = music here, as understood in *Macbeth*, IV. i. 106: " and what *noise* is this? [*Hautboys*.";but the word in North (see *post*, p. 280) applies generally, including the cries and sounds of a multitude, as well as music, and the marginal note is, " Strange *noises* heard, and nothing seene."

13. *signs well*] signifies good luck.

15. *Hercules . . . lov'd*] See on I. iii. 84 *ante.* Upton and Capell note that Shakespeare varies from Plutarch here (see extracts, *post*, p. 280) in sub-stituting Hercules, Antony's supposed ancestor, for Bacchus, the object of his " singular devotion," etc. In re-counting the signs and wonders ante-cedent to Actium, Plutarch says (North, *Tudor Trans.* vi. 63) : " And at the citie of Athens also, . . . the statue of Bacchus with a terrible winde was throwen downe in the Theater. It was sayd that Antonius came of the race of Hercules, as you have heard before, and in the manner of his life he followed Bacchus : and therefore he was called the new Bacchus." Cf. also North extracts, *post*, p. 262.

Sec. Sold.　　　　　How now, masters? [*Speak together.*
All.　　　　　　　　　　How now?
How now? do you hear this?
First Sold.　　　　　　　Ay, is 't not strange?
Third Sold. Do you hear, masters? do you hear?
First Sold. Follow the noise so far as we have quarter.　20
　　Let's see how it will give off.
All.　　　　　　　Content. 'Tis strange.
　　　　　　　　　　　　　[*Exeunt.*

[SCENE IV.—*The same. A room in the palace.*]

Enter ANTONY *and* CLEOPATRA, CHARMIAN, *and others
attending.*

Ant. Eros! mine armour, Eros!
Cleo.　　　　　　Sleep a little.
Ant. No, my chuck. Eros! come, mine armour, Eros!

Enter EROS *with armour.*

Come, good fellow, put thine iron on:
If fortune be not ours to-day, it is
Because we brave her. Come.

Scene III

17. S.D. and All] Speak together. Omnes. F; All [Speaking together]
most edd.

Scene IV

Enter . . .] Malone; Enter Anthony and Cleopatra, with others. F.
　2. (S.D.) with armour] added by Capell.　3. *thine*] F; *mine* Hanmer and
many other edd.

17. Speak together] Another " imperatival " S.D. Cf. II. v. 73.
　20. *as . . . quarter*] as the post assigned to us (i.e. our watch) extends.
Cf. *K. J.* v. v. 20 : " Well : keep good
quarter and good care to-night."
　21. *give off*] cease (in modern
northern dialect " give over ").

Scene IV

S.D.] F's omission of Charmian
may be just an oversight, but
it may suggest that Charmian's

few words and Cleopatra's two words
of rejoinder (l. 35) were an after-
thought.
　2. *chuck*] This term of fondness
(= chick) was used of either sex. So
Mistress Potluck in Cartwright's
Ordinary, 1651, I. ii: " Thou must
keep nothing from thy Rib, good
Chuck." And cf. *Macb.* III. ii. 45.
　3. *thine iron*] † I see no justification
for changing F, but some at least of
the editors who retain it adduce a
weak reason, namely that a third *mine*

Cleo.   Nay, I'll help too.   5
What's this for?
Ant.   Ah, let be, let be! thou art
The armourer of my heart: false, false; this, this.
Cleo. Sooth, la, I'll help: thus it must be.
Ant.   Well, well,
We shall thrive now.   Seest thou, my good fellow?
Go, put on thy defences.
Eros.   Briefly, sir.   10
Cleo. Is not this buckled well?
Ant.   Rarely, rarely:
He that unbuckles this, till we do please
To daff't for our repose, shall hear a storm.
Thou fumblest, Eros, and my queen's a squire
More tight at this than thou: despatch. O love,   15

5-8. *Nay . . . must be*] As Malone (Capell's suggestion); in F all assigned to Cleo. reading *Nay, I'll help too*, Anthony. (See note.)   13. *daff't*] Dyce; *daft* F; *doft* F 2.

---

would be repetitive. Why not? But Antony is, I think, being slightly humorous: "Come on, Eros, put your whole ironmonger's shop on me." [R]

5-8. † I think Capell's suggestion must be, in the main, right. F reads:—

> *Cleo.* Nay, Ile helpe too, *Anthony.*
> What's this for? Ah let be, let be, thou art
> The Armourer of my heart : False, false : This, this,
> Sooth-law Ile helpe : thus it must bee.

It is quite clear that this does not all belong to Cleopatra, and fairly clear that from " Ah let be " down to at any rate " False, false," and probably to " This, this " belongs to Antony, while the italic *Anthony* was a speech heading, and not a proper name, in the text, but found its way into the wrong place. Dover Wilson suggests that Antony's speech was added in the margin, which is possible enough, but does not, I think go far enough, since if we then take what remains for Cleopatra it is awkward, running:—

> *Cleo.* Nay, Ile helpe too, what's this for?
> Sooth-law Ile helpe : thus it must be.

I suggest that " Sooth-law Ile helpe " was also part of the addition, with the appropriate speech-heading for Cleopatra, and that her speech originally stood simply:—

> *Cleo.* Nay, Ile helpe too, what's this for? Thus it must bee. [R]

6, 7. *thou . . . heart*] " your work is to steel my *heart* with courage, not," etc. (Deighton).

7. *false, false* ; " That is all wrong " (Deighton).

10. *Briefly*] in a moment.

13. *daff't*] doff it, put it off. For the form, cf. *Much Ado*, II. iii. 187 ; v. i. 78.

15. *tight*] deft, adroit. So the adverb in Massinger, *The Picture*, v. iii. 58 " You shall see I am experienced at the game, And can play it *tightly* " ; and Spence's *Lucian* (1684), i. 70 : " *Vulcan.* [To Jupiter] Take heed we don't commit some Absurdity, for I

That thou couldst see my wars to-day, and knew'st
The royal occupation, thou shouldst see
A workman in't.

Enter an armed Soldier.

　　　　Good morrow to thee, welcome:
Thou look'st like him that knows a warlike charge:
To business that we love, we rise betime,　　　20
And go to't with delight.
Sold.　　　　　　　　　　　A thousand, sir,
Early though 't be, have on their riveted trim,
And at the port expect you. [*Shout.　Trumpets flourish.*

Enter Captains, and Soldiers.

Capt. The morn is fair: good morrow, general.
All. Good morrow, general.
Ant.　　　　　　　　　　'Tis well blown, lads.　　　25
This morning, like the spirit of a youth
That means to be of note, begins betimes.

24. Capt.] Rowe; Alex. F.

shall not manage you so *tightly* as a
Midwife wou'd." *Tight* sometimes
improperly represents the adverb *tite*
= quickly.

18. *A workman*] a real craftsman.

22. *riveted trim*] *trim* = any kind of
dress or finery (cf. Sonnet xcviii)
(† but surely there is here something
of the sense in which a ship or her
sails are "trimmed," i.e. properly
adjusted. [R]) See *Jack Drum's
Entertainment*, 1616, v (Simpson's *School
of Shakspere*, ii. 200) and *Henry V.* iv.
prol. 13:—

　"The armourers, accomplishing
　　the knights,
　With busy hammers closing rivets
　　up,"
on which Douce: "This does not
solely refer to the business of *riveting*
the plate armour before it was put on,
but as to part when it was on. Thus,"
etc. See *Illustrations of Shakespeare*,

1807, or *Henry V* (*Arden Shakespeare*),
ad. loc.

23. *port*] gate. So in *2 H. IV.* iv.
v. 23: "the *ports* of slumber," and
Chapman's Hesiod, *Georgics*, i. p. 216,
col. 1, note: "He calls this seven-
ported Thebes, to distinguish it from
that of Egypt, that had a hundred
ports," etc. See also on i. iii. 46 *ante*.

24. Capt.] Rowe's necessary substitution for F Alex. See iv. vi. 12 *post*.

25. *'Tis well blown*] Delius and
Rolfe refer this to the trumpets (which
blow a "Good Morrow": see
Othello, iii. i. 2, *Arden Shakespeare*),
Hudson and Deighton to the morn-
ing; "the metaphor being employed
of night blossoming into day"
(Hudson). The former explanation
is simple and unforced, the latter
forced: yet, as it has some excuse
in lines 26, 27, it at least demands
record.

So, so; come, give me that: this way; well said.
Fare thee well, dame, whate'er becomes of me:
This is a soldier's kiss: rebukeable,   [*Kisses her.*   30
And worthy shameful check it were, to stand
On more mechanic compliment; I'll leave thee
Now like a man of steel.   You that will fight,
Follow me close, I'll bring you to't.   Adieu.

    [*Exeunt Antony, Eros, Captains, and Soldiers.*

Char. Please you retire to your chamber?
Cleo.   Lead me: 35
He goes forth gallantly: that he and Caesar might
Determine this great war in single fight!
Then Antony—; but now—Well, on.   [*Exeunt.*

---

28. *well said*] F 2; *well-sed* F.   30. Kisses her] Johnson; not in F.
34. Exeunt . . .] Capell (substantially); Exeunt. F.

---

28. *So, so . . . said*] Antony is still putting on his armour, and the "that" is a piece of it. "Well said" signalises the completion of the arming.

well said] well done; as often in Shakespeare, approving action, not speech; "Well said, Hal! to it, Hal! (*1 H 4*, V. iv. 75, where Hal is not saying anything but fighting for his life), "Well said, i'faith, Wart. *2 H 4*, III. ii. 298, Wart not having opened his mouth), "Now masters, draw. (*They shoot*).   O ! well said, Lucius!" (Tit., IV. iii 63).   The phrase is, in fact, just the equivalent of "Attaboy!"

32. *mechanic*] From the contemptuous application to artisans, as in v. ii. 208 *post*, "mechanic slaves," the word came to mean "vulgar," "common"; and this sense, or "journeyman-like," is assigned here.   It does not seem altogether satisfactory; I should prefer to take " to stand on more mechanic compliment " as = to stand on ceremony, were evidence forthcoming for the early use of *mechanic* for unspontaneous, and so ceremonious or conventional.

[SCENE V.—*Alexandria. Antony's camp.*]

Trumpets sound. Enter ANTONY *and* EROS ; *a Soldier meeting them.*

Sold. The gods make this a happy day to Antony!

Ant. Would thou, and those thy scars had once prevail'd
To make me fight at land!

Sold.   Hadst thou done so,
The kings that have revolted, and the soldier
That has this morning left thee, would have still   5
Follow'd thy heels.

Ant.   Who's gone this morning?

Sold.   Who?
One ever near thee; call for Enobarbus,
He shall not hear thee, or from Cæsar's camp
Say " I am none of thine."

Ant.   What sayest thou?

Sold.   Sir,
He is with Cæsar.

Eros.   Sir, his chests and treasure   10
He has not with him.

Ant.   Is he gone?

Sold.   Most certain.

Scene v

a Soldier meeting them] Theobald; not in F.   1. Sold.] Theobald
(Thirlby conj.); Eros. F.   3, 6. Sold.] Eros. F.

Scene v

S.D. and speech-headings] † There is some confusion here, and confusion for which it is not easy to account. One might suppose that Shakespeare had intended to operate with only Antony and Eros, but found that later he wanted another speaker, and hurriedly inserted a soldier. But this will not account for the opening lines since " those thy scars " makes it certain that this is the soldier of III. vii. 61, with his " these my wounds,"

and the second speech which F attributes to Eros must therefore from the outset have been the soldier's. [R]

1. *happy*] lucky.

2, 3. *Would . . . land*] See III. vii. 61-66 *ante.*

7. *Enobarbus*] In Plutarch (see North, *post,* p. 274-5) Enobarbus deserts prior to Actium. It is the brave man-at-arms whom Antony calls Scarus in scenes vii and viii *post* who presently decamps with his reward; see North, p. 279.

Ant. Go, Eros, send his treasure after, do it,
    Detain no jot, I charge thee: write to him—
    I will subscribe—gentle adieus, and greetings;
    Say, that I wish he never find more cause   15
    To change a master.   O, my fortunes have
    Corrupted honest men.   Despatch.—Enobarbus.

                                                    [*Exeunt.*

            [SCENE VI.—*Alexandria.   Cæsar's camp.*]

    Flourish.   Enter AGRIPPA, CÆSAR, *with* ENOBARBUS,
                    and DOLABELLA.

Cæs. Go forth, Agrippa, and begin the fight:
    Our will is Antony be took alive;
    Make it so known.
Agr. Cæsar, I shall.   [*Exit.*
Cæs. The time of universal peace is near: 5
    Prove this a prosperous day, the three-nook'd world
    Shall bear the olive freely.

17. *Dispatch.—Enobarbus*] See note.

                        Scene VI
    4. Exit] not in F.

16, 17. *O, my fortunes . . . men*] See
note on III. xiii. 32-34 *ante*.

17. *Despatch.—Enobarbus*] F has
Dispatch Enobarbus; F 2 *Dispatch Eros,*
whence Pope, *Dispatch my Eros*;
Steevens, 1793 (Ritson conj.) *Eros,
despatch*.   Steevens (1773) reads *Dispatch. Enobarbus!* Capell *Dispatch.
—O Enobarbus!* Thiselton says the
reading of F means "Get fully quit of
Enobarbus by sending his belongings
after him," a sense which would need
much softening to put it in harmony
with what precedes.   For Antony's
conduct, compare North, *post*,
pp. 274-5. According to Plutarch,
Cæsar similarly treated Labienus on
his desertion to Pompey (*Life of
Julius Cæsar*).

                        Scene VI
    S.D.] † The placing of Agrippa first
may be due to mere carelessness,
but does it perhaps indicate that
Agrippa is to enter by a different door
(on his return from seeing that the
troops are ready for action, or the
like)? [R]

6. *three-nook'd*] three cornered; alluding, perhaps, to the world's having
been divided between the Triumvirs.
See also *J.C.*, IV. i. 14. A trine
aspect of the world was familiar to
contemporary poets apart from such
associations. See Pearson's *Heywood*,
iii. 242 (*The Brazen Age*): "Il'e make
her Empresse ore the *triple* world";
Locrine, III. iv. 36: "Stout Hercules
. . . That tam'd the monsters of the

Enter a Messenger.

Mess.   Antony
    Is come into the field.

Cæs.   Go charge Agrippa,
    Plant those that have revolted in the vant,
    That Antony may seem to spend his fury   10
    Upon himself.   *[Exeunt all but Enobarbus.*

Eno. Alexas did revolt; and went to Jewry on
    Affairs of Antony, there did dissuade
    Great Herod to incline himself to Cæsar,
    And leave his master Antony. For this pains,   15
    Cæsar hath hang'd him; Canidius and the rest
    That fell away, have entertainment, but

---

9. *vant*] F; *van* F 2 and edd.   11. Exeunt . . .] Exeunt. F.   13.
dissuade] F (*disswade*); *persuade* Rowe.

---

three-fold world "; *ibid.* v. iv. 5:
" The great foundation of the *triple*
world, Trembleth," etc. In such
cases the phrase was probably caught
from the *triplex mundus* of Ovid,
Metam. xii. 40, involving sky, land
and sea. Du Bartas (Sylvester,
1621 ed.) speaks of the earth as
divided " in *three* vnequall Portions "
by the sea and its arms (p. 49) and
again (p. 268), of " this spacious
Orb " as parted by the Creator
" Into *three* Parts," east, south and
west, " Twixt *Sem*, and *Cham*, and
Japheth."

7. *bear*] bring forth. Cf. *2 H. IV.*
iv. iv. 87: " But Peace puts forth
her olive everywhere." Mason—in
favour of *bear* = carry—ignores metaphor in objecting that Augustus'
success " could not make the olive-
tree grow without culture in all
climates "; but Schmidt also explains
wear. So D'Avenant sings in *The first
dayes entertainment at Rutland House* :—
    " Did ever war so cease
      That all might olive *wear?* "

9. *vant*] The old form of the word,
short for *vantwarde*, whence *vanguard*
and so *van*.

12. *and*] † ? '*a* (= he). Alexas
clearly did not revolt *before* he went
to Jewry. [R]

13. *dissuade*] Johnson thought *dissuade* of F probably right. North
(*post*, p. 278) has *persuaded*, but it is
not impossible that the thought of
dissuasion from Antony's service
determined the word here. When
King John's emissary pander, in
Drayton's *Legend of Matilda*, becomes
threateningly persuasive, the heroine
does not describe herself, during her
hesitation, as by fear *persuaded*, but
" By fear disswaded, menaced by
murder " (stanza 74), not thinking
of persuasion to unchasteness—the
natural sequence—but dissuasion from
chastity. *Dissuade* can be followed
by the infinitive: *O.E.D.* quotes
Camden's *Remains*, ed. 1637, p.
246: " Some *disswaded* him to hunt
that day."

17. *entertainment*] employment. Cf.
All's Well, iv. i. 16: " He must think
us some band of strangers i' the
adversary's *entertainment* "; *A Report*,
etc., 1591 (*The Revenge*, ed. Arber, p.
27): " A notable testimonie of their
rich *entertainment* and great wages.' '

No honourable trust: I have done ill,
Of which I do accuse myself so sorely,
That I will joy no more.

Enter a Soldier of CÆSAR'S.

Sold.   Enobarbus, Antony   20
Hath after thee sent all thy treasure, with
His bounty overplus. The messenger
Came on my guard, and at thy tent is now
Unloading of his mules.
Eno.   I give it you.
Sold. Mock not, Enobarbus,   25
I tell you true: best you saf'd the bringer
Out of the host; I must attend mine office,
Or would have done't myself. Your emperor
Continues still a Jove.   [*Exit.*
Eno. I am alone the villain of the earth,   30
And feel I am so most.   O Antony,
Thou mine of bounty, how wouldst thou have paid
My better service, when my turpitude
Thou dost so crown with gold! This blows my
    heart:
If swift thought break it not, a swifter mean   35
Shall outstrike thought, but thought will do't, I feel.

---

20. *more*] F 2; *mote* F.   36. *do't, I feel.*] Rowe; *doo't. I feele* F.

23. *on my*] while I was on.
26. *true : best*]   † ? *'twere* has dropped out before *best,* by confusion with *true.* [R]
saf'd] conducted safely. Cf. Chapman's *Homer, Odyssey,* iv (ed. Shepherd, p. 332*b*): " Neptune . . . *Saft* him unwrack'd to the Gyræan isle."   *Safe* = make safe, occurs in I. iii. 55 *ante.*
31. *And feel . . . most*] And am he who most realises it.
32. *mine of bounty*] Cf. *1 H. IV.* III. i. 167 " as bountiful As *mines* of India."
34. *blows*] swells, " makes it full to bursting " (Schmidt). Cf. *blown* = swollen, v. ii. 347 *post* (if that is what

it means there), and Jonson, *Catiline,* IV. 18: " It is our base petitionary breath That *blows* 'em to this greatness."
    † But may it not mean simply " beats upon "? [R]
35. *mean*] See on III. ii. 32 *ante.*
35, 36. *thought*] melancholy. See on III. xiii. 1 *ante,* and cf. " in great trowble, *thought,* and hevines " (p. 13) with " right great trowble, sorow, and hevines " (p. 17) in *Historie of the Arrivall of Edward IV* etc. (Camden Society, 1838). Cf. *Hamlet,* IV. v. 187 and Brome, *A mad Couple well Match'd* (Pearson's *Brome,* i. 16): " And can you be so mild? " then

I fight against thee? No, I will go seek
Some ditch, wherein to die: the foul'st best fits
My latter part of life.   [*Exit.*

[SCENE VII.—*Field of battle between the camps.*]

Alarum.   Drums and trumpets.   Enter AGRIPPA *and others.*

Agr. Retire, we have engag'd ourselves too far:
Cæsar himself has work, and our oppression
Exceeds what we expected.   [*Exeunt.*

Alarums.   Enter ANTONY, *and* SCARUS *wounded.*

Scar. O my brave emperor, this is fought indeed!
Had we done so at first, we had droven them home   5
With clouts about their heads.
Ant.   Thou bleed'st apace.
Scar. I had a wound here that was like a T,
But now 'tis made an H.   [*Retreat afar off.*
Ant.   They do retire.

Enter . . . others.] Steevens, 1778; Enter Agrippa. F.   2. *and our*
oppression] F; *our opposition* Hanmer.   8. Retreat afar off] Capell; *Far*
off. (after *heads*, l. 6) F.

farwell *thought*," the exclamation of a husband whose wife has inquired into the cause of his melancholy and forgiven its offensive nature when confessed.

Scene VII

2. *our oppression*] † our difficulties— —but Hanmer's *opposition* is tempting. [R]

4. *Scarus*] As Capell notes, the name is not from Plutarch, the hero of this sally being merely " one of his [Antony's] men of armes." The character, as he further says, was a necessity, in order to fill up the place about Antony left vacant by Enobarbus.

6. *clouts*] cloths, bandages. The sug-

gested " cuffs," or " blows " is not bloodthirsty enough for Scarus or for the wounds of the scene, received and meditated (line 12).

8. *an H*] Scarus's jocular allusion to the enlargement of his wound is supposed to include a play on *H* and *ache*, once often pronounced alike. Cf. *Much Ado*, III. iv. 55. There would be more confidence about it if we could find any particular reason for selecting T just before. († But a T with an extra stroke (wound) at the bottom *is* an H on its side, if we are thinking of printed capitals. And see Dover Wilson's note *ad loc.* giving Maunde Thompson's comment on the minuscule letters in " secretary " hand. [R]

P

Scar. We'll beat 'em into bench-holes, I have yet
    Room for six scotches more.   10

Enter EROS.

Eros. They are beaten, sir, and our advantage serves
    For a fair victory.
Scar.   Let us score their backs,
    And snatch 'em up, as we take hares, behind,
    'Tis sport to maul a runner.
Ant.   I will reward thee
    Once for thy spritely comfort, and ten-fold   15
    For thy good valour. Come thee on.
Scar.   I'll halt after.
                                            [*Exeunt.*

[SCENE VIII.—Under the walls of Alexandria.]

Alarum. *Enter* ANTONY *again, in a march;* SCARUS, *with others.*

Ant. We have beat him to his camp: run one before,
    And let the queen know of our gests: to-morrow
    Before the sun shall see's, we'll spill the blood
    That has to-day escap'd. I thank you all,

---

13. *hares, behind*] Theobald; *Hares behinde* F.

Scene VIII

2. *gests*] Theobald (Warburton); *guests* F.

9. *bench-holes*] holes of privies. Cf. *North-ward Hoe*, 1607, v (Pearson's *Dekker*, iii. 78): "The Trab [i.e. *drab*] will driue you (if she put you before her) into a *pench hole*"; Fletcher, *Woman Pleased*, IV. iii. (Camb. VII. 291):—

> "That I were a Cat now,
> Or anything could run into a
>   *Bench-hole.*

Malone quotes Cecil's *Secret Correspondence* (ed. Lord Hailes, 1766): a . . . I will leave it like an abort in "*bench-hole.*"

15. *spritely*] Cheerful, high-spirited. It has a "solider" connotation than our modern rather effervescent one. Cf. IV. xiv. 52 *post, our sprightly port.*

Scene VIII

Scene VIII. [See North, *post*, p. 279.]
2. *gests*] deeds. So Heywood, *The Exemplary Lives . . . of Nine, the most worthy Women of the World* 1640, sig. **3: "Of History there be foure species, either taken from place, as Geography; from time, as Chronologie; from Generation, as Genealogie; or from *gests* really done," etc.

For doughty-handed are you, and have fought   5
Not as you serv'd the cause, but as't had been
Each man's like mine: you have shown all Hectors.
Enter the city, clip your wives, your friends,
Tell them your feats, whilst they with joyful tears
Wash the congealment from your wounds, and kiss   10
The honour'd gashes whole.   *Enter* CLEOPATRA.
        [*To Scarus*]   Give me thy hand;
To this great fairy I'll commend thy acts,
Make her thanks bless thee.   O thou day o' the world,
Chain mine arm'd neck, leap thou, attire and all,
Through proof of harness to my heart, and there   15
Ride on the pants triumphing!

Cleo.   Lord of lords,
O infinite virtue, com'st thou smiling from
The world's great snare uncaught?

Ant.   My nightingale,
We have beat them to their beds.   What, girl,
        though grey

---

11. To Scarus] Rowe; not in F.

18. *My*] F 2; *Mine* F.

8. *clip*] hug; as frequently. So in
Coriolanus, I. vi. 29: " O let me *clip*
ye," etc.

12. *fairy*] enchantress.   Used of
Venus by Sylvester, Du Bartas, *The
Magnificence*, ed. 1621, p. 461: " But
O, fair *Faëry*, who art thou? ";
by Braithwaite, of a courtesan,
Strappado for the Diuell, 1615, *The
Conyburrow* :—

    " Now my (prodigious *faery*) that
        canst take
    Vpon occasion a contrary shape,"

In Shirley's *The Brothers*, II. i (*Works*,
1833, i. 217), Carlos says of a girl :
" Ha! turn away That *fairy*, she's a
witch, the count talks with her."
Delius says Cleopatra is so called as
dispenser of the good fortune which
Scarus had deserved by his valour,
such being the light in which the
fairies were regarded in Shakespeare's
time.

15. *proof of harness*] proof-armour,
in which sense *proof* alone usually

appears.   Cf. *R. and J.*, I. i. 216:
" And in strong *proof* of chastity well
arm'd."

16. *Ride . . . triumphing*] Fletcher
imitates this in *The False One*, IV. ii.
126 :—

    " *Cleo.* . . . I love with as much
            ambition as a Conqueror,
    And where I love, will triumph.
    Cæsar. So you shall;
    My heart shall be the chariot
        that shall bear ye," etc.

For the accentuation, *triumphing*,
cf. *R. III.* III. iv. 88.

17. *virtue*] valour (the Latin *virtus*),
as in *Lear*, v. iii. 104: " Trust to
thy single *virtue*," etc.

18. *world's great snare*] " i.e. the
war " (Steevens).   († less limited,
I think, and nearer to " all the snares
the world can set." [R])

19, 20. *though grey . . . brown*]
† in his present mood he can laugh
about his greying hair : cf. III. xi.
13-15 *ante*. [R]

Do something mingle with our younger brown,
    yet ha' we   20
A brain that nourishes our nerves, and can
Get goal for goal of youth. Behold this man,
Commend unto his lips thy favouring hand:
Kiss it, my warrior: he hath fought to-day
As if a god in hate of mankind had   25
Destroy'd in such a shape.
Cleo.   I'll give thee, friend,
An armour all of gold; it was a king's.
Ant. He has deserv'd it, were it carbuncled
Like holy Phœbus' car. Give me thy hand,
Through Alexandria make a jolly march,   30
Bear our hack'd targets like the men that owe them.
Had our great palace the capacity
To camp this host, we all would sup together,
And drink carouses to the next day's fate,

---

23. *favouring*] Theobald; *savouring* F.

22. *Get goal . . . youth*] " At all plays of barriers, the boundary is called a *goal;* to *win a goal* is to be a superior in a contest of activity " (Johnson).

25. *mankind*] " Accented mostly on the last syllable in *Timon of Athens*, on the first in the other plays" (Schmidt).

28, 29. *carbuncled . . . car*] Cf. *Cymbeline*, v. v. 190, " a *carbuncle* of Phœbus' wheel." In the description in Ovid, *Metam.* ii, which probably suggests the simile, the yoke of Phœbus' chariot is set with chrysolite and gems, his palace with carbuncles. See also Fairfax's *Tasso*, 1600, xvii. 34 :—
    " Her chariot like *Auroraes* glorious waine,
        With *Carbuncles* and *Iacinthes* glistred round."

30. *jolly*] Professor Warwick Bond credits the word here with an approach to the " sense of proud bearing," in a note on *T. of S.* iii. ii. 215 (Arden ed.), where he gives examples of *jolly* = arrogant, over-bearing. This is possible ; but the ordinary sense, as in " Be jolly, lords," ii. vii. 59 *ante*, is, I think, more likely here

31. *owe*] own, as very often. The whole line admits of two senses ; Johnson's straightforward : " Bear . . . with spirit and exultation, such as becomes the brave warriors that own them," and Warburton's interpretation of " hack'd targets," etc., as = " hack'd as much as the men to whom they belong." Abbot (*Shakespearian Grammar*, § 419 a) includes the line as a probable case of such transposition of adjectival phrases.

34. *drink carouses*] drain bumpers. A German adverb *garaus* = right out is the ultimate source of *carouse*, etc., and underwent little or no modification at first as English adverb, verb, noun. See, e.g. Fynes Moryson, *An Itinerary*, 1617, pt. iii, p. 90 : " did at the very beginning of supper, drinke great *garausses*," etc. B. Rich, *The Irish Hubbub* (see p. xix. Introduction to *The Honestie of this Age*, Percy

Which promises royal peril.   Trumpeters,   35
With brazen din blast you the city's ear,
Make mingle with our rattling tabourines,
That heaven and earth may strike their sounds
   together,
Applauding our approach.   [*Exeunt.*

Society, 1844) begins a description of
" *Healths* " thus : " In former ages
they had no conceits whereby to draw
on drunkennesse ; their best was, I
drinke to you, and I pledge yee, till
at length some shallow-witted drunk-
ard found out the *Carowse*, which
shortly afterwards was turned into a
hearty draught."   Each of the company drank a full cup quite out, or a
carouse, in turn, after much ceremony
and then, turning the cup bottom
upward, " in ostentation of his
dexteritie," filliped it " to make it cry
Twango." " Hearty draught " was
a new name mockingly employed by

the convivial, since *Quaffing* and
Carowsing were reprobated.   See Gascoigne, *A Delicate Diet for daintie
mouthde Droonkardes*, 1576.

37. *tabourines*] Cf. *T. and C.* IV. v.
277.   The commentators very naturally explain, " small drums," but the
tabourine appears to have been
" the full-sized military drum, corresponding to the modern side-drum,"
while the tabor was a little drum,
chiefly devoted to peaceful amusements. See Naylor, *Shakespeare and
Music*, 1896, pp. 161, 2, and Cowling,
Music on the Shakespearian Stage (1913),
c. iii, p. 42.

[SCENE IX.—*Cæsar's camp.*]

Enter a Sentry and his company; ENOBARBUS *follows.*

Sent. If we be not reliev'd within this hour,
    We must return to the court of guard: the night
    Is shiny, and they say we shall embattle
    By the second hour i' the morn.
First Watch.   This last day was
    A shrewd one to's.
Eno.   O bear me witness, night—   5
Sec. Watch. What man is this?
First Watch.   Stand close, and list him.

Scene IX

Scene IX]. † I have retained the stage-directions and speech-headings of F throughout the scene, with the exception of F's spelling " *Centerie*," and the additions of " *dies* " and " *with the body*," though indeed the latter is so clearly implied in the text that it is hardly needed. The usual stage-directions, deriving from Capell and Malone, are an amusing example of what was apt to happen when the eighteenth century editors really got to work. Capell started off with *Sentinels upon their posts*, distributed the speeches as he thought best among three " *soldiers* " (giving the first speech, oddly enough, to the third), but adhered to F by giving *Enter Enobarbus* at the beginning of the scene, instead of, like later editors, bringing him in just before his opening words in line 5.

Now, in the first place, *Sentinels upon their posts* is an impossible stage-direction for the Elizabethan curtain-less stage, which precluded ringing up on actors already in position, and on which everyone must " enter." In the second place, Shakespeare did not bring on just any three soldiers, but rather an N.C.O. and the two men who with him were to form the

sentry-group, and it is moderately clear from his speeches that the " Sentry " is the leader. Lastly, Enobarbus' entry in line 5 is awkward, partly because he too patently enters merely to deliver his farewell speeches, and partly because an abrupt entry after the watchmen are more or less in position ought to be the occasion for a challenge. Shakespeare brought him wandering in almost on the heels of the group, so that when he begins to speak they might have fancied that he had been there before them. [R]

2. *court of guard*] guard-room, or other place of muster, as in *1 H. VI.* II. i. 4; Heywood, ΓΥΝΑΙΚΕΙΟΝ, 1624, p. 408 : " his officers leave the *court of guard* and come to know the matter "; and cf. *Othello*, II. iii. 218. According to *O.E.D.*, a perversion of *Corps de garde*, which came to mean guard-room, as well as the guard itself. In the original sense, it occurs several times in Greene's *Orlando Furioso* (*Works*, Dyce, ed. 1883, pp. 94-96), e.g. " The *court-of-guard* is put unto the sword." The forms *court de (du) guard* also occur.

5. *shrewd*] ill, curst; the old sense. So in *All's Well*, III. v. 68 : " *a shrewd* turn."

Eno. Be witness to me, O thou blessed moon,
    When men revolted shall upon record
    Bear hateful memory: poor Enobarbus did
    Before thy face repent.
Sent.   Enobarbus?
Sec. Watch.   Peace!   10
    Hark further.
Eno. O sovereign mistress of true melancholy,
    The poisonous damp of night disponge upon me,
    That life, a very rebel to my will,
    May hang no longer on me.   Throw my heart   15
    Against the flint and hardness of my fault,
    Which being dried with grief, will break to powder,
    And finish all foul thoughts.   O Antony,
    Nobler than my revolt is infamous,
    Forgive me in thine own particular,   20
    But let the world rank me in register
    A master-leaver, and a fugitive:
    O Antony! O Antony!   *[Dies.*
First Watch.   Let's speak to him.
Sent. Let's hear him, for the things he speaks
    May concern Cæsar.
Sec. Watch.   Let's do so; but he sleeps.   25
Sent. Swoons rather, for so bad a prayer as his
    Was never yet for sleep.
First Watch.   Go we to him.
Sec. Watch. Awake, sir, awake, speak to us.
First Watch.   Hear you, sir?
Sent. The hand of death hath raught him.
          [Drums afar off.]   Hark, the drums

---

23. Dies] Rowe; not in F.

12. *O . . . melancholy*] The moon; so apostrophized for her " wanne " face, and supposed influence in mental disease.

13. *disponge*] drop, as from a sponge. Browne, *Brit. Pastorals*, I. ii. 239, has : " The hand of Heaven his *spongy* clouds doth strain," etc.

20. *in . . . particular*] as far as you

yourself are concerned. Cf. I. iii. 54 *ante.*

22. *master-leaver*] it was a serious offence for an apprentice, or servant, to abscond.

fugitive] deserter, as in Latin.

27. *for*] a prelude to.

29. *raught*] = *reached*, but here most likely used in the further sense of

Demurely wake the sleepers. Let us bear him   30
To th' court of guard: he is of note: our hour
Is fully out.
Sec. Watch. Come on then, he may recover yet.

[Exeunt with the body.

[SCENES X-XII.—*Between the two camps.*]

Enter ANTONY *and* SCARUS, *with their Army.*

Ant. Their preparation is to-day by sea,
We please them not by land.
Scar.   For both, my lord.
Ant. I would they'ld fight i' the fire, or i' the air,
We'ld fight there too.   But this it is; our foot
Upon the hills adjoining to the city   5
Shall stay with us (order for sea is given,

---

33. with the body] added by Capell.

Scene x

6, 7. *ıs* (*order . . . haven*)] *vs. Order . . . Hauen:* F.

snatched away. So 2 *H. VI.* II. iii. 43,
and Middleton, *Mayor* of *Queen-*
borough, IV. ii. 154 :—

      " I was surpris'd
By villains, and so *raught.*"

30. *Demurely*] solemnly (Warburton), soberly, gravely (Schmidt), in a
subdued manner (*O.E.D.*). Perhaps the soldier inconsistently treats
the mellowed sound, that reaches him
at a distance, as if it were similarly
heard by those in camp. Hanmer
reads *din early wakes*; Collier MS.
and ed. 2, *Do early wake*; Dyce conjectures *Do merrily wake.*

31. *court of guard*] See on line 2
above.

Scene x

† Just as a reminder of the vexa-
tiousness of modern scene-divisions,
with their " Between the two camps "
—" Another part of the same "—
" Another part of the same," I have
bracketed the scene indications of xi

and xii and omitted any further
indication of place. [R]

6, 7. (*order . . . haven*),] Most
editors consider line 7 incomplete,
and some out of many rash conjectures have even appeared in the text,
as; *Further on,* Rowe; *Let's seek a*
spot, Malone;—*forward, now,* Dyce,
etc. If *Where* (line 8) has the force
of *Whither,* as most of them assume,
the sense might be: They have . . .
haven, *to a place where* we may best
observe their array and watch their
efforts; but *best* would be improbably applied save to Antony's choice
of a vantage-point for observation,
and bearing in mind that the situation is very like that in III. ix *ante,*
Where in line 8, here, seems to
refer to *hills* (line 5) almost as inevitably as *from which place* to *yond*
side o' the hill in that passage. Like
Staunton, who, nevertheless, believed
line 7 incomplete, I tentatively adopt
the parenthesis of Knight, Collier and

They have put forth the haven),
Where their appointment we may best discover,
And look on their endeavour.   [*Exeunt.*

[SCENE XI]

Enter CÆSAR, *and his Army.*

Cæs. But being charg'd, we will be still by land,
Which, as I take it, we shall, for his best force
Is forth to man his galleys. To the vales,
And hold our best advantage.   [*Exeunt.*

[SCENE XII]

Alarum afar off, as at a sea-fight.

Enter ANTONY *and* SCARUS.

Scene XII

S.D. **Alarum . . .**] F; placed later in scene by most edd. (see note).

Singer, as affording a plain sense in a practically undisturbed text.

† R. G. White, though he used the reference to justify an insertion, refers I think decisively *against* the need for insertion, to the relevant passage in North (*post*, p. 280) " he went to set those few footemen he had in order upon the hills adjoyning unto the citie; and there he stoode to behold his gallies which departed from the haven." [R]

Scene XI

1, 2. *But . . . shall*] Except being charged, etc., i.e. Unless we are assailed, we will remain quiescent by land, which I expect we shall be left to do. Cf. *but* as a preposition in such phrases as " We were all *but* killed *or* being killed."

4. *hold . . . advantage*] occupy the best position we can.

Scene XII

(S.D.) **Alarum . . .**] † Most editors have felt it necessary to transpose this S.D., either (as Dover Wilson) to just after Antony's exit at line 3, or (as Steevens and most others, but,

I think, less happily) to just before his re-entry in line 9, on the grounds that it is an awkward opening to the scene, particularly in view of Antony's first words. Dover Wilson suggests that it may have been written " somewhat indefinitely " in the margin. This is no doubt possible, but since it is also quite possible that its position represents Shakespeare's intention, it is worth examining the point, not least because it well illustrates the troubles that are sometimes created by the post-Elizabethan division into scenes. F prints as follows:—

. . . our best advantage.   *exeunt.*
Alarum afarre off, as at a Sea-fight.
Enter Anthony, and Scarrus.

Ant. Yet they are . . .

That is to say, the S.D. does not belong to either " scene," but occupies the empty-stage interval between *exeunt* and *Enter.* And we may, if we like, assume that the producer faded out the alarum just before Antony's entrance, so that his opening words are not absurd, but the audience knows that he is wrong, which has a certain effectiveness. [R]

Ant. Yet they are not join'd: where yond pine does stand,
    I shall discover all: I'll bring thee word
    Straight, how 'tis like to go.   [*Exit.*
Scar.   Swallows have built
    In Cleopatra's sails their nests. The augurers
    Say, they know not, they cannot tell, look grimly,
    And dare not speak their knowledge. Antony
    Is valiant, and dejected, and by starts
    His fretted fortunes give him hope and fear
    Of what he has, and has not.

Re-enter ANTONY.

Ant.   All is lost:
    This foul Egyptian hath betrayed me: 10
    My fleet hath yielded to the foe, and yonder
    They cast their caps up, and carouse together
    Like friends long lost. Triple-turn'd whore, 'tis thou

---

4. *augurers*] Capell; *Auguries* F.

1. *pine*] The conspicuous tree probably supplies Antony with the metaphor for himself in line 23 below, as Thiselton notes. His further deductions I cannot follow.

3. *Swallows*, etc.] This omen is transferred from before Actium. See North, *post*, p. 273; and for the rest of the scene, p. 280.

4. *augurers*] † I have adopted the usual emendation of F's *auguries*. There are no doubt plenty of places in Shakespeare where an abstract is used for a concrete, but seldom, I think, where the abstract is immediately followed by a run of verbs which seem to demand a concretely personal subject. But I rather suspect that the true reading is *augures*, a Latin plural, like "pyramides " in v. ii. 61. [R]

8. *fretted*] chequered. To *fret* is to interlace, and the noun *fret*—originally, a grille or grating—signifies heraldic or architectural ornament partaking of the nature of trelliswork. Hence the figurative use in the text to express mingled or varied fortune, a sense which the context seems to indicate in preference to that of *harassed, impaired*, from the verb *fret* = gnaw, corrode. In *J.C.* II. i. 104:—
    " and yon grey lines
    That *fret* the clouds are messengers
        of day "
we encounter the word in the like, though not figurative, sense of chequer, variegate.

8, 9. *hope, and fear, Of . . . not*] i.e. probably, hope of keeping and fear of losing the power he still has, and hope of recovering and fear of not recovering what he has no longer. It seems better not to apply hope and fear separately, that is to *has not* and *has* respectively, supposing an irregular correspondency as in IV. xv. 25, 26 *post*.

13. *Triple-turn'd*] Cf. III. xiii. 116-18 *ante*. Staunton's acuteness reconciled this epithet with the fact that Cleopatra had more than three lovers, if Octavius was to be reckoned as one. He says: " From Julius Cæsar to

Hast sold me to this novice, and my heart
Makes only wars on thee.   Bid them all fly: 15
For when I am reveng'd upon my charm,
I have done all.   Bid them all fly, be gone.

[Exit Scarus.

O sun, thy uprise shall I see no more,
Fortune and Antony part here, even here
Do we shake hands. All come to this? The hearts   20
That spaniel'd me at heels, to whom I gave
Their wishes, do discandy, melt their sweets
On blossoming Cæsar: and this pine is bark'd,
That overtopp'd them all.   Betray'd I am.
O this false soul of Egypt! this grave charm,   25

---

17. Exit Scarus] Capell; not in F.   20. *hands.*] Capell; *hands?* F.
21. *spaniel'd* Hanmer; *pannelled* F.

Cneius Pompey, from Pompey to Antony, and, as he suspects now, from
him to Octavius Cæsar." Previous
commentators had disputed as to
whether Pompey or Octavius was to
be left out of the application.

16. *charm*] Abstract for concrete,
charmer or enchantress. Cf. *charmer*
= enchantress in *Othello*, III. iv. 58,
and *charm*, line 25, *spell*, line 30,
post.

21. *spaniel'd*] In support of this
emendation of Hanmer's, Tollet
urges the frequent spelling *spannel* for
spaniel [see, e.g. *spannell* in Lyly's
Campaspe, v. i.] and quotes *M.N.D.*
II. i. 203 *et seq.* : " I am your *spaniel*,"
etc. Halliwell supplies an example
closely resembling the text, from
Copley's *Fig for Fortune*, 1596, p. 64:
" I *spanield* after Catechrysius' foot."
Cf. also *The Buggbears*, II. i. 19, 20
(*Early Plays from the Italian*, 1911,
R. Warwick Bond, p. 99): " . . .
they shold not run & lackie like
spaniells at my stirrop, but shold ride
everye iornye," etc.; and Pepys'
Diary, May 26, 1660 : " My Lord
dined with the Vice-Admiral to-day
(who is as officious, poor man! as any
spaniel can be.") Upton defended F
pannelled on the ground that a panel

of wainscot, being inset, comes behind
the main surface; and Theobald,
more reasonably, adopted Warburton's conjecture *pantler'd me*
for " ran after me like footmen or
pantlers," comparing the contemptuous application of the noun in
Cymbeline, II. iii. 129. But, as has
been observed, *pantler* does not mean
servant or footman, and therefore
one likely to follow at heel, but the
servant who has the care of bread.

22. *discandy*] See on III. xiii. 165
ante.

23. *bark'd*] stripped, and so destroyed.

25. *grave charm*] Steevens: " deadly
or destructive piece of witchcraft."
Pope changed the epithet to *gay*, but
grave in the above or some allied sense
is far more beautiful and appropriate
than this or other suggestions, as *great*
(Collier MS.), *grand* (Singer, ed. 2),
brave (Deighton conj.). In support of
it Steevens adduces two passages from
Chapman's Homer, viz. *Iliad*, xix,
and *Odyssey*, xxii [see Herne Shepherd's ed., 1875, pp. 237*b*, 510*b*],
containing " thy *grave* ruin " and
" Their *grave* steel " respectively. It
is also possible, especially in view of
the next line, that the word = potent

Whose eye beck'd forth my wars, and call'd them
    home;
Whose bosom was my crownet, my chief end,
Like a right gipsy, hath at fast and loose
Beguil'd me, to the very heart of loss.
What, Eros, Eros!

or commanding. Chapman (*Odyssey*, xxii, *ibid.* p. 509*b*] makes Minerva say to Ulysses : " Priam's broad way'd town By thy *grave* parts was sack'd and overthrown."

27. *crownet*] i.e. coronet: the object and reward of my toils. Cf. the use of *crown*, in various senses of fulfilment and superlativeness, in IV. xv. 63 *post*; Chapman's Homer (Steevens's reference), *Iliad*, II [ed. Herne Shepherd, 1875, p. 33*a*]: " and all things have their *crown* "; *ibid.* p. 29*b*: " We fly, not putting on the *crown* of our so long held war." The form *crownet* recurs in V. ii. 91 *post*; in Peele, *Arraignment of Paris*, I. i. 76: " Her robes, her lawns, her *crownet*, and her mace "; and often.

28, 29. *Like a right . . . of loss*] † An interesting example of differences of punctuation. The accepted modern punctuation is

> *Like a right gipsy, hath, at fast and loose,*
> *Beguil'd me to the very heart of loss.*

I think that F, throwing heavier emphasis on to the last six words, is more effective. [R]

28. *right*] true, typical.

gipsy] Hawkins notes " a kind of pun . . . arising from the corruption of the word *Ægyptian* into *gipsy*." The gipsies were falsely supposed from Egypt: hence this name *via* Middle English *Egyptien*, and *Gipsen*, instanced by Skeat, *Etymol. Dict.*, from Spenser, *Mother Hubbard's Tale*, line 86. See *Othello*, III. iv. 57, and Jonson, *The Gipsies Metamorphos'd*, First Song (line 124): " Thus the Ægyptians throng in clusters "; and other passages, as line 60: " Gaze upon them, as on the offspring

of Ptolemy, begotten upon several Cleopatras," and

> " And Queene *Cleopatra*,
>   The *gipsyes* grand-matra "

(the Patrico's speech, line 173). Egyptian may still be heard for gipsy among the lower classes.

fast and loose] A cheating game thus described by Sir I. Hawkins (1821 Variorum): " A leathern belt is made up into a number of intricate folds, and placed edgewise upon a table. One of the folds is made to represent the middle of the girdle, so that whoever should thrust a skewer into it would think he held it fast to the table; whereas, when he has so done, the person with whom he plays may take hold of both ends, and draw it away." There is a play on the game and hanging in Whetstone's *1 Promos and Cassandra*, II. v:—

> " Heare are new ropes: how are my
>   knots? I faith syr, slippery.
>   At *fast or loose* with my Giptian, I
>   mean to have a cast ";

and again in Harvey's *The Trimming of Thomas Nashe Gentleman*, etc., 1597, near the end. The name was applied to any trick of apparent knots, and its figurative use is as familiar to-day as ever. Cf. also *L.L.L.* I. ii. 162, III. i. 109; and Suckling, " Upon my Lord Brohall's Wedding " :—

> " How weak is lover's law!
> The bonds made there (like gipsies'
>   knots) with ease
> Are *fast and loose*, as they that
>   hold them please."

29. *heart of loss*] So Jonson, *Sejanus*, I. 250:—

> " I do not know
> The *heart* of his designs."

Enter CLEOPATRA.

                    Ah, thou spell!   Avaunt!   30
Cleo. Why is my lord enrag'd against his love?
Ant. Vanish, or I shall give thee thy deserving,
And blemish Cæsar's triumph.   Let him take thee,
And hoist thee up to the shouting plebeians,
Follow his chariot, like the greatest spot   35
Of all thy sex.   Most monster-like be shown
For poor'st diminutives, for dolts, and let
Patient Octavia plough thy visage up
With her prepared nails.   [*Exit Cleopatra.*
                    'Tis well th' art gone,
If it be well to live.   But better 'twere   40
Thou fell'st into my fury, for one death
Might have prevented many.   Eros, ho!

34. *plebeians*] The accent is similarly on the first syllable in *Coriolanus*, I. ix. 7; v. iv. 40.

35. *spot*] Cf. Bunyan, *The Pilgrim's Progress*: "They say you are a spot among Christians, and that Religion fareth the worse."

36. *monster-like*] like a "curiosity" (fat woman, child with six toes, etc.) at a travelling show. Cf. *Tempest*, II. ii. 29-36; *Macbeth*, v. vii. 54: "We'll have thee, as our rarer monsters are, Painted upon a pole, and underwrit, 'Here may you see the tyrant.'"

37. *For . . . diminutives, for dolts*]. To poor undersized weaklings, to fools. Though some who accept Thirlby's ingenious *doits* for *dolts* also explain *diminutives* thus, with most editors the change involves interpreting *diminutives* as small pieces of money, for which no instance is adduced; whereas as applied to persons, we have "Such a *diminutive?*" (Chapman, *Byron's Conspiracy*, v. i. 88), *diminutives of nature* (*T. and C.* v. i. 38). The change also rather interrupts the sequence of ideas, which seems wholly concerned with (1) the triumph; (2) the vengeance of Octavia, as is the case also in later reminiscences of the passage; one in general terms, IV. xv. 23-29 *post*, and two in particular, v. ii. 52-57, and 207 *et seq. post*, all of which persuade that the showing is in the procession and in that only, maugre a reference in the last to puppet-shows, of which —as Gifford says—shows of monsters were the constant concomitants. Certain passages alone cause hesitation, viz. *The Tempest*, II. ii. 29-35, concluding: "when they will not give a doit to relieve a lame beggar, they will lay out ten to see a dead Indian"; and this new one (Chapman, *Bussy D'Ambois*, III. i. 26):—

  "the sly charms
Of the witch Policy makes him [i.e. sin] like a monster
Kept only to show men for servile money:" etc.
This passage immediately follows that which corresponds with IV. xiv. 2-7 *post* (see note there), and increases the probabilities in favour of *doits*; but such do not justify tampering with a text clear and reasonable in sense as it stands.

39. *prepared*] "Suffered to grow for this purpose," as Warburton says, or, may be, sharpened.

The shirt of Nessus is upon me, teach me,
Alcides, thou mine ancestor, thy rage.
Let me lodge Lichas on the horns o' the moon,   45
And with those hands that grasp'd the heaviest club,
Subdue my worthiest self.   The witch shall die,
To the young Roman boy she hath sold me, and I fall
Under this plot: she dies for 't.   Eros, ho!   [*Exit.*

43. *shirt of Nessus*] Hercules shot the centaur Nessus with a poisoned arrow. Nessus gave Deianira, Hercules' wife, a shirt soaked with his poisoned blood for use at need as a love charm.   Sent to Hercules later, it caused his torture and self-destruction.   See on 45 *infra*.

44. *mine ancestor*] See on I. iii. 84 *ante*.

45. *Let . . . Lichas . . . moon*] Lichas, who innocently brought the shirt to Hercules, was flung skyward by his infuriated master, and fell into the sea, after being turned into pebble-stone by the force of his despatch.   See Golding, Ovid's *Metam.* bk. ix, and for a dramatization of the story, Heywood's *Brazen Age*.   In *The Actor's Vindication*, n.d. p. 30.   Heywood relates the story of Julius Cæsar's realistic personation of Hercules, even to the actual slaying of the representative of Lichas.   Cf. for the hyperbole in the text for extreme height, *Coriolanus*, I. i. 219, and Fletcher, *The Sea Voyage*, I. i. 5: "I saw a Dolphin hang i' the *horns o' th' moon*, Shot from a wave," etc.   Warburton thought it derived in this case from Seneca's *Hercules Oetæus*.   John Studley translates :—

" With Lycas thus his labours end
     throwne vp to heauen they say,
  That with his dropping bloud the
     cloudes he stayned all the way"
(*Seneca, His Tenne Tragedies*, etc., 1581, p. 201).

47. *worthiest*] Rolfe explains " *worthiest* of being *subdued* or destroyed "; but Antony in lines 45-47 expresses the fury he seeks to show, in terms of the actions of his ancestor, the last of which was to destroy himself.   His own " worth " (i.e. his heroic nature) is, therefore, that of Hercules : but, apart from that, there is no reason why he should not assert it in a passage expressive of rage and resentment, and not of humiliation.

48. *young Roman boy*] † The line is hypermetric, and though it is possible to regularize it by a slurring rapidity of delivery, that seems not consonant with the rest of the speech. We should perhaps omit *young*, conjecturing that Shakespeare first wrote *young boy*, then saw that it was redundant, and that *Roman boy* would give a double point (betrayal to one who was both an enemy and a mere boy), wrote in *Roman* but did not make clear his deletion of *young*. [R]

[SCENE XIII.—*Alexandria.   Cleopatra's palace.*]

Enter CLEOPATRA, CHARMIAN, IRAS, MARDIAN.

Cleo. Help me, my women!   O, he's more mad
          Than Telamon for his shield, the boar of Thessaly
          Was never so emboss'd.
Char.   To the monument,
          There lock yourself, and send him word you are
          dead.

Scene XIII

1. *he's*] F (*hee's*); *he is* F 2.

Scene XIII

2. *Telamon*] Ajax Telamon, who went mad and slew himself when Ulysses, and not he, was awarded the armour and famous shield of Achilles as bravest of the Greeks. Heywood treats the story in *The Iron Age*, pt. i, Act v.

    boar of Thessaly] The boar—whose "eies did glister bloud and fire" (Golding, Ovid's *Metam.* bk. viii.)—sent by Diana in revenge for omitted sacrifices to ravage the territories of the king of Caledon, and slain by his son Meleager, the brother of Deianira. The story is one of the themes of Heywood's *Brazen Age*.

    3. *emboss'd*] A term of the chase, sometimes used merely for "driven to extremity," sometimes to signify that the quarry showed signs of exhaustion by foaming at the mouth. Cf. *1 King Edward IV* (Pearson's *Heywood*, i. 40) : "*Dutch.* Cam'st thou not downe the wood? *Hobs.* Yes mistriss ; that I did. *Dutch.* And sawest thou not the deere *imbost?*" with Lyly, *Midas*, IV. iii. 26 : "*Pet.* There was a boy leasht on the single because when he was *imbost*, he tooke soyle. *Licio.* What's that? *Pet.* Why, a boy was beaten on the taile with a leathern thong, bicause when he fomde at the mouth with running, he went into the

water"; and P. Fletcher, Psalm xlii (*Poems*, ed. Grosart, iii. 248) :—

> "Look as an hart with sweat and bloud embrued
> Chas'd and *embost*, thirsts in the soil to be."

In our text are meant the similar tokens of rage. The term is often applied to animals other than the quarry, and to men, in the sense of "spent," "visibly heated by exertion." So in *T. of S. Induc.* i. 17, "the poor cur is emboss'd" and *Albumazar*, v. ii. 12 (Hazlitt's *Dodsley*, xi. 406) :—

> "I am *emboss'd*
> With trotting all the streets to find Pandolfo";

and *Swetnam the Woman Hater* (1620), I. ii :—

> "Hast thou been running for a wager, Sirrah?
> Thou art horribly *imbost*."

While both senses at the head of this note are thought to derive from a verb whose primary sense is "to take shelter in a wood," the second of the two is probably influenced by another verb *emboss*, to form protuberances, or bosses, to which blobs of foam have some resemblance. See *O.E.D.*, s.v.

    3, 4. *To the monument*, etc.] See North, *post*, p. 280.

The soul and body rive not more in parting   5
Than greatness going off.

Cleo.   To the monument!
Mardian, go tell him I have slain myself:
Say, that the last I spoke was " Antony,"
And word it, prithee, piteously.   Hence, Mardian,
And bring me how he takes my death to the
    monument.   10

                                            [*Exeunt.*

[SCENE XIV.—*The same.   Another room.*]

Enter ANTONY *and* EROS.

Ant. Eros, thou yet behold'st me?
Eros.   Ay, noble lord.
Ant. Sometime we see a cloud that's dragonish,
    A vapour sometime, like a bear, or lion,
    A tower'd citadel, a pendent rock,
    A forked mountain, or blue promontory   5

---

10. *death to the monument.*] F(*to' th'*); *death; To the monument!* Pope.

                    Scene XIV

4. *tower'd*] Rowe; *toward* F.

5, 6. *The soul . . . off*] Malone compares *Henry VIII* [II. iii. 12-16]. The
idea in line 5 also occurs in *Arden of
Feversham*, III. i. 19, 20, and Chapman, *Bussy D'Ambois*, II. ii (Parrott
I. 564*b*):—

        " I must utter that
    That will in parting break more
        strings in me,
    Than death when life parts ; " etc.

10. † I have, with some hesitation,
retained F's punctuation. It makes
good sense, but Pope's emendation
does undoubtedly provide a more
emphatic exit. [R]

                Scene XIV

2-7. *Sometime we see,* etc.] Several
passages have been suggested as the
source of this fancy, but its beautiful
and striking use to illustrate man's
unstable hold of his very entity seems
to occur here only.   The passages are
Aristophanes, *Nubes,* 346 [in Theobald's version, *The Clouds,* 1715, p. 20:
" In looking upon the Sky, have you
never seen a Cloud resemble a
Centaur, a Leopard, a Wolf or a
Bull? "] (Sir W. Rawlinson) ; Holland's Pliny, *Natural History,* II. iii,
where the shapes are of chariot, bear,
bull (Steevens); Chapman's *Monsieur
D'Olive,* II. ii. 91:—

        " our great men
    Like to a mass of clouds that now
        seem like
    An elephant, and straightways
        like an ox,
    And   then   a   mouse," etc.
        (Steevens);

With trees upon 't, that nod unto the world,
And mock our eyes with air.   Thou hast seen these
   signs,
They are black vesper's pageants.
Eros.   Ay, my lord.
Ant. That which is now a horse, even with a thought
   The rack dislimns, and makes it indistinct   10
   As water is in water.

10. *dislimns*] Theobald; *dislimes* F.

where, indeed, as in the text, the dwindling of the great is expressed; Chapman's *Bussy D'Ambois*, III. i. 23-5, where the shapes are dragons, lions, elephants (Malone); *A Treatise of Spectres*, etc. 4to, 1605: "The *cloudes* sometimes will seem to be monsters, *lions*, bulls, and wolves; painted and figured albeit . . . nothing but a *moyst humour mounted in the ayre,*" etc. (Malone). I have met with passages anterior to these last in Sylvester's Du Bartas (1598), *The Imposture* (in 1621 ed. p. 189) :—

  "For, as the Air, with scattred
    clouds bespred,
  Is heer and there black, yellow,
    white and red,
  Resembling Armies, Monsters,
    Mountains, Dragons,
  Rocks, fiery Castles, Forrests,
    Ships, and Wagons,
  And such to vs through glass
    transparent clear
  From form to form varying it
    doth appear : " etc. :

and Fairfax's *Tasso*, 1600, bk. xvi. st. 69 :—

  "As oft the clouds frame shapes of
    castles great
  Amid the aire, that little time do
    last,
  But are dissolu'd by winde or
    Titans heat ; " etc.

Examples later than *Antony and Cleopatra* occur in Ford, etc., *The Witch of Edmonton*, v. i. 15; *The City Nightcap*, IV. i (Bullen's *Davenport*, p. 150).

8. *pageants*] The following from Whetstone's *2 Promos* and *Cassandra*, 1578, I. v (Nichols, *Six Old Plays*, 1779, p. 65), explains the allusion :—
  "*Phallax.*   With what strange
    showes doo they their *Pageaunt*
    grace?
  Bedell.   They have *Hercules* of
    monsters conquerying,
  Huge great *Giants* in a forest
    fighting
  With *Lyons, Beares, Wolves, Apes,
    Foxes,* and *Grayes,*
  Baiards, Brockes, &c.*"

According to Singer, Boswell somewhere (not in 1821 Variorum) cites "the following apposite passage from a sermon by Bishop Hall " : " I feare some of you are like the *pageants* of your great solemnities, wherein there is a show of a solid body, whether of a lion, or elephant, or unicorne ; but if they be curiously look'd into, there is nothing but cloth, and sticks, and ayre." Pageants were originally the movable stages on which Miracle plays were represented, then the plays themselves, and so moving shows or spectacles in general.

9. *even with a thought*] as fast as thought. So in *J.C.* v. iii. 19: " I will be here again, *even with a thought.*"

10. *The rack dislimns*] The drifting clouds efface. Cf. Jonson, *Masque of Hymen:* " Here the upper part of the scene, which was all of clouds, and made artificially to swell, and ride like the *rack*, began to open : "

Q

Eros.   It does, my lord.

Ant. My good knave Eros, now thy captain is
  Even such a body: here I am Antony,
  Yet cannot hold this visible shape, my knave.
  I made these wars for Egypt, and the queen,   15
  Whose heart I thought I had, for she had mine:
  Which whilst it was mine, had annex'd unto't
  A million moe, now lost: she, Eros, has
  Pack'd cards with Cæsar, and false-play'd my glory
  Unto an enemy's triumph.   20

---

18. *moe*] F; *more* Rowe and many edd.   19. *Cæsar*] Rowe; *Caesars* F.

---

etc. *Dislimns* reverses *limns* (i.e.
paints), and is not found elsewhere till
imitated in the nineteenth century.
See *O.E.D.*

12. *knave*] boy, servant, as often;
the former is the original meaning.

15. *Egypt*] Cleopatra. So in I. iii.
41, 78 *ante*, etc.

18. *moe*] more *in number*, while *more*
referred to degree.   Originally an adverbial comparative.

19. *Pack'd . . . Cæsar*] Ensured
good hands for herself and Cæsar by
false dealing, i.e. treacherously con-
spired with Cæsar. Cf. Cartwright,
The Ordinary, 1651, II. iii, p. 28:
" For Cards you may . . . without
the cut or shuffle, Or the *packt* trick,
have what you will yourself ";
Southey, *Commonplace Book*, 4th series,
1850, p. 275: " The Lady Cheatabell,
playing at hunt the Knave out of
town, *packed* the cards, and gave herself the Knave of Hearts, being Jack";
and for a figurative use, as in the
text, *The Parliament of Criticks*, 12mo,
1702, p. 16: " The *Cards* are *pack'd*
by Authority, and Dominion turns
up what *Trump* it pleases." We still
speak of *packing* a jury. Thiselton
observes that " knave " and "queen"
(lines 14, 15) possibly suggested the
metaphor from cards.

19, 20. *false-play'd . . . triumph*]
Warburton was probably right in seeing in *triumph*—as well as the obvious
sense—an allusion to the trump card,

or *triumph* as it was originally called.
Cf. French *triomphe*. Halliwell cites
Cotgrave, who has " Triomphe: f.
The card-game called Ruffe, or
Trump; also the Ruffe, or Trump at
it " [1660 ed.] ; and Warburton's
reference to Latimer's *Sermons on the
Card* yields : " The game that we will
play at shall be called the *triumph*,"
etc. (Parker Society ed. p. 8) : " Let
therefore every christian man and
woman play at these cards, that they
may have and obtain the *triumph*;
you must mark also that the *triumph*
must apply to fetch home unto him
all the other cards, whatsoever suit
they be of " (pp. 8, 9). Later on
he employs " trump " (pp. 12, 13),
but so that we may identify it with
the triumph, that fetches " home the
other cards " : " Now turn up your
trump, your heart (hearts is trump,
as I said before), and cast your trump,
your heart, on this card " ; etc.
The objection of Malone and others
that playing false to an *adversary's*
trump would be meaningless here,
does not hold. Cæsar, in Antony's
view, is only *in show* Cleopatra's
adversary. Ostensibly Antony's partner, Cleopatra not only unfairly helps
Cæsar to secure good cards, but *false-
plays* those in her own power (involving Antony's glory) to encounter
them. The form *triump* occurs in
The Interlude of Youth (Hazlitt's
Dodsley, II. 34) : "Also at the cards

Nay, weep not, gentle Eros, there is left us
Ourselves to end ourselves.

Enter MARDIAN.

                  O, thy vile lady!
She has robb'd me of my sword.

Mar.   No, Antony.
My mistress lov'd thee, and her fortunes mingled
With thine entirely.

Ant.   Hence, saucy eunuch, peace!   25
She hath betray'd me, and shall die the death.

Mar. Death of one person can be paid but once,
And that she has discharg'd.   What thou wouldst do
Is done unto thy hand: the last she spake
Was " Antony! most noble Antony! "   30
Then in the midst a tearing groan did break
The name of Antony; it was divided
Between her heart, and lips: she render'd life
Thy name so buried in her.

Ant.   Dead, then?

Mar.   Dead.

Ant. Unarm, Eros, the long day's task is done,   35

---

35. *Unarm*] *Vnarme* F; *Unarm me* Rowe and many edd.

I can teach you to play, At the *triump* and one-and-thirty, Post, pinion, and also aums-ace," etc. Whiter quotes Jonson, *The Fortunate Isles*, line 362 : " Except the four knaves entertained for the guards, Of the kings and the queens that *triumph* in the cards."

26. *die the death*] See on *Cymbeline* IV. ii. 96, and *M.N.D.* I. i. 65, in *Arden Shakespeare*.

31-34. *Then in the midst*, etc.] The like of this is cleverly ridiculed by Sheridan in *The Critic*, near the end :—

" *Whisk. . . .* And Whiskerandos quits this bustling scene
  For all eter——
Beef.   ——nity—he would have added, but stern death

Cut short his being, and the noun at once!"
and cf. *1 H. IV.* v. iv. 86.

35. *Unarm*] See North, *post*, p. 280.
Unarm, Eros] † It is one of the curiosities of editing that so many editors (Dover Wilson indeed, though erroneously, says " all editors ") have followed Rowe in reading *Unarm me, Eros,* and even more remarkable that the arguments pro and con have been almost entirely metrical. The emendation is, of course, graphically easy, and the intrusive *me*, though I think it produces a rhythm less suiting to the context, is metrically quite defensible (it is more awkward if we are pronouncing the name as Ērŏs rather than Ĕrōs). But it changes

And we must sleep. [*To Mar.*] That thou depart'st
    hence safe
Does pay thy laboru richly; go.   [*Exit Mardian.*
                        Off, pluck off,
The seven-fold shield of Ajax cannot keep
The battery from my heart.   O, cleave, my sides!
Heart, once be stronger than thy continent,   40
Crack thy frail case!   Apace, Eros, apace!
No more a soldier: bruised pieces, go,
You have been nobly borne.   From me awhile.
                              [*Exit Eros.*

36. To Mar.] Globe; not in F.

the force of Antony's words. They
are more general (like the echo,
the bright day is done, in v. ii. 192)
than a command to unarm *him*.
He is saying " All is over; our
' occupation's gone '." [R]
   38. *seven-fold shield of Ajax*] The
shield of brass, backed with seven
folds of ox-hide, which defied the
lance of Hector (Homer, *Iliad*, vii.
222, 245, etc.) :—
   " Six folds th' untamed dart strook
        through, and in the *seventh*
        tough hide
   The point was check'd "
(see Chapman's *Homer*, 1598, ed.
R. H. Shepherd, 1875, pp. 95, 96).
See also Ovid, *Metam.* xiii. 2 : " The
owner of the *seauenfold shield*, to these
did Ajax rise " (Golding, ed. 1593).
   39. *The battery . . . heart*] The sense
generally received here is Boswell's :
" the battery proceeding from my
heart, which is strong enough to break
through the seven-fold shield of
Ajax," which depends on the ensuing
" O cleave," etc. However probable, it is, nevertheless, as I think,
unconvincing. The sense of oppression from the heart's agitation would
explain " Off, pluck off " if it stood
alone, but it is natural to suppose it
repeats the thought in " Unarm,
Eros," etc., line 35, the source of
which is entirely different. If that
be so, it is as safe to interpret " No

external arms—even the strongest—
can defend me from the assault of
such a calamity as this," regarding
line 35 and disregarding line 39
(" O cleave," etc.), as to regard the
latter and disregard the former with
Boswell. Cf. Kyd, *The Spanish Trag-
edie*, I. iii. 57 " My *hart* growne hard
gainst mischiefes *battery*." A shield,
moreover, is not so placed as to curb
inward batteries. We should rather
expect a reference to armour, as in I.
i. 6-8 *ante*, and Marston, *1 Antonio
and Mellida*, v. i. 311, where
Andrugio, entering " in armour,"
says : " And twere not hoopt with
steele, my brest wold break."
   40, 41. *Heart . . . case*] For this
appeal, cf. *Lear*, II. iv. 200 : " O sides,
you are too tough." † Antony is not
asking his heart to break (as in
Lear, v. iii. 314) but to have for once
the strength to break out into freedom
from the confining body. [R]
   40. *thy continent*] what contains
thee. So *Lear*, III. ii. 57 :—
                " close pent-up guilts
   Rive your concealing *continents*,"
   etc.
Sandys, *A Paraphrase*, etc., 1638, *Job*,
chap. xxxii, p. 41 :—
   " My Bowels boyle like wine that
        hath no vent ;
   Ready to breake the swelling *Con-
        tinent*."

I will o'ertake thee, Cleopatra, and
Weep for my pardon.   So it must be, for now   45
All length is torture: since the torch is out,
Lie down and stray no farther.   Now all labour
Mars what it does: yea, very force entangles
Itself with strength: seal then, and all is done.
Eros!—I come, my queen:—Eros!—Stay for me,   50
Where souls do couch on flowers, we'll hand in hand,
And with our sprightly port make the ghosts gaze:
Dido, and her Æneas, shall want troops,
And all the haunt be ours.   Come, Eros, Eros!

Re-enter EROS.

46. *length*] i.e. of time *or* life, duration. So in *R. II.* v. i. 94: . . . " there is such length in grief," etc.

torch] i.e. the light of his life's travel, Cleopatra.

48, 49. *very force . . . strength*] even the power of strength serves only to embarrass it.   Dover Wilson well compares Sonnet XXIII, lines 3-4, 7-8.

49. *seal then*, etc.] For the metaphor from sealing and thus *completing* agreements, compare *Henry V.* IV. vi. 26 ; *Hamlet*, III. ii. 41 ; Daniel, *Cleopatra*, IV, line 1024 (*Works*, ed. Grosart, vol. iii): " My blood must *seale* th' assurance of his state."

51. *Where souls . . . flowers*, etc.] So in a delightful passage depicting " deaths Ioyes " in *Nero*, 1624, IV. [Scene vii] (Bullen's *Old Plays*, i. 81) :—

" Mingled with that faire company
    shall we
On bankes of *Violets* and of *Hia-
    cinths*,
Of loves devising, sit and gently
    sport " ; etc.

With *couch*, cf. *Much Ado*, III. i. 45 : " as fortunate a bed, As even Beatrice shall *couch* upon."

52. *sprightly*] High-spirited, full of vitality—stronger and more dignified than our " spritely."   Cf. IV. vii. 15 *ante*.

53. *Dido and her Æneas*] Successive

commentators tell us that Shakespeare forgot that Virgil (*Æneid*, vi. 467-74) consorts Dido with her husband, Sichæus, in Hades, and makes her repel Æneas during his visit to the shades.   But Shakespeare was not likely, any more than others, to uncouple a famous pair of lovers for a pedantic scruple.   Theobald long ago quoted the jailor's daughter in *The Two Noble Kinsmen*, IV. iii. 16 : " For in the next world will *Dido* see *Palamon*, and then will she be out of love with *Æneas.*"   The ingenious author of *Nero*, in the passage quoted in the last note, even reconciles Lucrece and Tarquin in Elysium ; and Thomas May, *Antony and Cleopatra*, v. 1639, sig. D 12, makes Antony say :—

                " I'll follow thee,
And beg thy pardon in the other
    world.
All crimes are there for evermore
    forgot.
There *Ariadine* pardons *Theseus*
    falsehood.
Dido forgives the perjur'd Prince
    of Troy,
And *Troilus* repentant *Cressida.*"

54. *all the haunt be ours*] not " we shall possess all the region," but " we shall be the people run after."

Re-enter *Eros*] For the rest of the scene, compare North, *post*, p. 281.

Eros. What would my lord?

Ant.   Since Cleopatra died,   55
I have liv'd in such dishonour that the gods
Detest my baseness.   I, that with my sword
Quarter'd the world, and o'er green Neptune's back
With ships made cities, condemn myself, to lack
The courage of a woman, less noble mind   60
Than she which by her death our Cæsar tells
" I am conqueror of myself."   Thou art sworn, Eros,
That when the exigent should come, which now
Is come indeed: when I should see behind me
The inevitable prosecution of   65
Disgrace and horror, that, on my command,
Thou then wouldst kill me.   Do't, the time is come:
Thou strik'st not me, 'tis Cæsar thou defeat'st.
Put colour in thy cheek.

Eros.   The gods withhold me,
Shall I do that which all the Parthian darts,   70
Though enemy, lost aim, and could not?

Ant.   Eros,
Wouldst thou be window'd in great Rome, and see
Thy master thus with pleach'd arms, bending down

---

60. *less noble mind*] Probably in apposition with *I*, line 57, in which case there is scarcely need to suppose any ellipse, as is usual if it be made to depend on *condemn myself* or *to lack.* Rowe, Pope, Dyce, for *mind* read *minded*, but the corresponding passage in North supports the noun. See *post*, p. 281. Malone, comparing, e.g. *The Winter's Tale*, III. ii. 55-58, supposes an inaccurate use of *less* after *to lack*, making Antony say " that he is *destitute of a less noble mind* than Cleopatra," when he meant to " acknowledge he *has* a less noble mind than she."

63. *exigent*] exigency, emergency. Cf. *J.C.* v. i. 19 ; Sidney's *Arcadia*, bk. ii. (ed. 1725, i. 169) : " Now was *Zelmane* brought to an *exigent*," etc.

65. *inevitable prosecution*] pursuit admitting no escape. For *inevitable*, cf.

S. Marmion, *Cupid and Psyche*, 1637 (reprint 1820, p. 72) :—

   " What darkness can protect me?
      what disguise
   Hide **me** from her *inevitable*
      eyes?"

68. *defeat'st*] frustratest. Cf. v. i. 65 *post*. Some—I think unnecessarily—explain by *destroyest*, comparing such passages as *Othello*, IV. ii. 160 : " And his unkindness may *defeat* my life."

71. *enemy*] Here an adjective as in *Coriolanus*, IV. iv. 24 : " This *enemy* town " ; *Lear*, v. iii. 222 : " Follow'd his *enemy* king."

73. *pleach'd*] folded or intertwined. Cf. *Much Ado*, I. ii. 12 : " a thick-*pleached* alley " ; III. i. 7 : " the *pleached* bower," etc. Delius suggests that Antony thus indicates the together-bound arms of a captive. With the whole passage Steevens

His corrigible neck, his face subdued
To penetrative shame; whilst the wheel'd seat   75
Of fortunate Cæsar, drawn before him, branded
His baseness that ensued?

Eros.   I would not see't.

Ant. Come then: for with a wound I must be cur'd,
Draw that thy honest sword, which thou hast worn
Most useful for thy country.

Eros.   O, sir, pardon me!   80

Ant. When I did make thee free, swor'st thou not then
To do this when I bade thee?   Do it at once,
Or thy precedent services are all
But accidents unpurpos'd.   Draw, and come.

Eros. Turn from me then that noble countenance,   85
Wherein the worship of the whole world lies.

Ant. Lo thee!   [*Turning from him.*

Eros. My sword is drawn.

Ant.   Then let it do at once
The thing why thou hast drawn it.

87. Turning . . .] Rowe; not in F.

compares Kyd, *Cornelia*, III. ii.
12-15:—

> " Now shalt thou march (thy hands
>   fast bound behind thee),
> Thy head hung downe, thy cheeks
>   with teares besprent,
> Before the victor ; Whyle thy
>   rebell sonne,
> With crowned front, tryumphing
>   followes thee."

In this passage, unlike that in the text,
the proper order of captives (" Before
the victor ") in a Roman triumph is
observed.

74. *corrigible*] "submissive to correction." *O.E.D.* cites 1583, Babington,
Commandm., iii (1637), 28: " If hee
be *corrigible*, not euen in the Lords
cause should I curse my brother."
It is used in an active sense = " corrective " in *Othello*, I. iii. 330.

75. *penetrative*] penetrating. The *Century Dict.* cites Sir T. Elyot, *Castle of
Health*, ii : " The rayne water . . . if

it be receyued pure and cleane, it is
most subtyl and *penetrative* of any
other waters " ; Sir H. Wotton,
Reliquiæ Wottonianæ [1672], p 7 :
" . . . the Aire . . . That it be not
too *gross*, nor too *penetrative*."

76, 77. *branded . . . ensued*] rendered
conspicuous, as by a brand, the ab-
ject condition of him who followed.
With *ensued*, cf. Queen Elizabeth,
Translation out of Seneca, Nugæ Antiquæ
(1769), i. 137 : " The cleare daies
followes the darck clowdes ; the
rowghest seas *insues* the greattest
calmes."

81. *swor'st thou not*, etc.] Cf. the
inferior scene between Cassius and
Pindarus in *J.C.* v. iii. 36-50.

86. *worship . . . world*] that majesty
which the whole world reveres as a
god's. Johnson's " dignity, authority," scarcely give the force of
worship here.

87. *Lo thee*] So in *H. VIII.* I. i. 202 :
" *Lo*, you, my lord," etc.

Eros.   My dear master,
   My captain, and my emperor: let me say   90
   Before I strike this bloody stroke, farewell.
Ant. 'Tis said, man, and farewell.
Eros. Farewell, great chief.   Shall I strike now?
Ant.   Now, Eros.
Eros. Why, there then: thus I do escape the sorrow
   Of Antony's death.   [*Kills himself.*
Ant.   Thrice-nobler than myself,   95
   Thou teachest me, O valiant Eros, what
   I should, and thou couldst not; my queen and Eros
   Have by their brave instruction got upon me
   A nobleness in record.   But I will be
   A bridegroom in my death, and run into't   100
   As to a lover's bed.   Come, then; and, Eros,
   Thy master dies thy scholar; to do thus

                [*Falling on his sword.*

  I learnt of thee.   How, not dead? not dead?
  The guard, ho!   O, despatch me!

---

65. *Kills* . . .] Opposite Eros, line 93, in F.   102. *Falling* . . .] Rowe;
not in F.   104. *ho!*] Theobald; *how?* F. Enter . . .] Enter a Guard. F.
See note.

98, 99. *Have . . . record*] Have, as
my tutors in courage, *or*, by teaching
me a lesson in bravery, won for themselves [from me] a noble place in
story. Perhaps "got upon me"
would justify the comparative, "a
nobler place." Rolfe's "forestalled
me in gaining" is a very attractive
explanation, for which he compares
"win upon me" in II. iv. 9 *ante*.
But the case does not strike me as
parallel, and I should rather compare Milton, *Samson Agonistes*, 470
"all these boasted trophies won on
me."

  104. *ho*] The F spelling (*how* for
ho) is frequent. Cf. I. ii. 110 *ante*, and
"Peace, *how*, peace! I charg you,
keep the peace!" (*Sir Thomas More*,
p. 25, Shakes. Society, 1844), on
which Dyce comments: "One of a

hundred passages in old plays, which
shew how improperly the two latest
editors [Knight and Collier] of
Shakespeare have followed the folios
in printing, 'The guard!—*how?*'
Ant. and Cleop., act IV. sc. 12."

  (S.D.) Enter . . .] † F has only *Enter
a Guard*. We clearly have to get
Decretas on at some point, and the
usual method has been to give
"Enter Decretas (or Dercetas or
Dercetus) and Guard " but that rather
suggests that he is in command of the
guard, which he pretty clearly is not.
We can bring him in after the guard's
exit at line 110, but that makes his
first speech abrupt—he needs a short
while in which to take in the situation.
I suggest therefore that he comes in
behind the guard (like Enobarbus in
IV. viii), and watches and listens. [R]

Enter a Guard; DECRETAS *following them.*

First Guard.　　　　　　　　　　What's the noise?

Ant. I have done my work ill, friends: O make an end　105
　　Of what I have begun.

Sec. Guard.　　　　　　　　　The star is fall'n.

First Guard. And time is at his period.

All.　　　　　　　　　　　　Alas, and woe!

Ant. Let him that loves me, strike me dead.

First Guard.　　　　　　　　　Not I.

Sec. Guard. Nor I.

Third Guard.　　Nor any one.　　　[*Exeunt Guard.* 110

Dec. Thy death and fortunes bid thy followers fly.
　　This sword but shown to Cæsar with this tidings,
　　Shall enter me with him.

Enter DIOMEDES.

Dio. Where's Antony?

Dec.　　　　　　There, Diomed, there.

Dio.　　　　　　　　　　　Lives he?
　　Wilt thou not answer, man?　　[*Exit Decretas.* 115

Ant. Art thou there, Diomed? Draw thy sword, and
　　give me
　　Sufficing strokes for death.

Dio.　　　　　　　Most absolute lord,
　　My mistress Cleopatra sent me to thee.

Ant. When did she send thee?

Dio.　　　　　　Now, my lord,

Ant.　　　　　　　　　Where is she?

Dio. Lock'd in her monument; she had a prophesying fear
　　Of what hath come to pass: for when she saw—　121
　　Which never shall be found—you did suspect
　　She had dispos'd with Cæsar, and that your rage

---

110. Exeunt Guard] Pope; Exeunt. F.　　111. Dec.] Dercetus. F.
114. Dec.] Decre. F.　　115. Exit Decretas] no exit in F.

Decretas] for the variations in this character's name, see note on v. i. 3 *post.*
　107. *period*] end, full stop, as in IV. ii. 25 *ante.*
　114. Dover Wilson adds a good stage-direction for Decretas, *hiding the sword in his cloak.*
　123. *dispos'd*] made arrangements *or* dispositions, come to terms. The sole example in *O.E.D.*

Would not be purg'd, she sent you word she was dead;
But fearing since how it might work, hath sent   125
Me to proclaim the truth, and I am come,
I dread, too late.
Ant. Too late, good Diomed: call my guard, I prithee.
Dio. What ho; the emperor's guard, the guard, what ho!
Come, your lord calls.   130

Enter four or five of the Guard of ANTONY.

Ant. Bear me, good friends, where Cleopatra bides,
'Tis the last service that I shall command you.
First Guard. Woe, woe are we, sir, you may not live to wear
All your true followers out.
All.   Most heavy day!
Ant. Nay, good my fellows, do not please sharp fate   135
To grace it with your sorrows: bid that welcome
Which comes to punish us, and we punish it
Seeming to bear it lightly.   Take me up;
I have led you oft, carry me now, good friends,
And have my thanks for all.   140

[Exeunt, bearing Antony.

[SCENE XV.—*The same.   A monument.*]

Enter CLEOPATRA *and her maids aloft, with* CHARMIAN
and IRAS.

Cleo. O Charmian, I will never go from hence.
Char. Be comforted, dear madam.

124. *purg'd*] expelled [by assertions of innocence].   See on I. iii. 53 *ante*. The figure is perhaps continued in *work*, next line.

136. *To grace*] a gerund = by gracing.   So in *R. II.* II. ii. 95 : " But I shall grieve you to report the rest." See Abbott (*Shakes. Gram.*, § 356).

bid] the not uncommonly imperative-conditional—" if we bid . . . we punish it."

Scene xv

Scene xv] See North, *post*, pp. 281-2, and for the staging see Appendix IV.

aloft] i.e. to the balcony at the rear, which was a special feature of the old stage.   A well-known sketch of the interior of the Swan Theatre in 1596 (?) by a Dutch traveller, reproduced in Mr. Ordish's *Early London Theatres* and *Shakespeare's London*, represents it as a sort of stage box divided

Cleo.   No, I will not:
All strange and terrible events are welcome,
But comforts we despise; our size of sorrow,
Proportion'd to our cause, must be as great   5
As that which makes it.

Enter, below, DIOMEDES.

How now? is he dead?
Dio. His death's upon him, but not dead.
Look out o' the other side your monument,
His guard have brought him thither.

Enter, below, ANTONY, *borne by the Guard.*

Cleo.   O sun,
Burn the great sphere thou mov'st in, darkling stand   10
The varying shore o' the world. O Antony,
Antony, Antony! Help, Charmian, help, Iras, help:
Help, friends below, let's draw him hither.

6. Enter . . .] Collier; Enter Diomed. F.   9. Enter . . .] Collier;
Enter Anthony, and the Guard. F.

by five pillars, occupying the length
of the tiring house—at some height
above its doors—at the back of the
stage.

7. Steevens thought that respect
for the questioner, as well as metre,
necessitated the insertion of *madam*
after *him*; Keightly reads "but *he is*
not dead."

10, 11. *Burn the great sphere . . .
world*] See on II. vii. 14-16 *ante.* In
the system there described, "the sun
was a planet, and was whirled round
the earth by the motion of a solid
sphere in which it was fixed.—If the
sun therefore was to set fire to the
sphere, so as to consume it, the consequence must be, that itself, for want of
support, must drop through, and wander in endless space; and in this case
the earth would be involved in endless
night" (Heath). For *darkling*, i.e. in
darkness, cf. *Lear*, I. iv. 240. War-

burton explains *The varying shore o'
the world* as the shore " of the *earth,*
where light and darkness made an
incessant *variation.*" Hudson applauds and adopts a conjecture of
Staunton's (*Athenæum*, 1873) of *star*
(*starre*) for *shore*, making " the varying
star " = the changing moon. He observes that Shakespeare uses *star*, with
some epithet, such as *moist* or *watery*,
for the moon; but that is not the same
thing as calling it " the varying star *o'*
the world." If " darkling stand," etc.
is a consequence, Cleopatra would
make it apply to the orb that held
herself and Antony rather than to the
moon.

12, 13. *Help . . . hither*] † Dover
Wilson regards this line and a half
as "indubitable interpolation"; in
the region of conjecture "indubitable" is an unduly positive word,
against which a reader rightly reacts

Ant.   Peace!
Not Cæsar's valour hath o'erthrown Antony,
But Antony's hath triumph'd on itself.   15
Cleo. So it should be, that none but Antony
Should conquer Antony, but woe 'tis so!
Ant. I am dying, Egypt, dying; only
I here importune death awhile, until
Of many thousand kisses, the poor last   20
I lay upon thy lips.
Cleo.   I dare not, dear,

unfavourably, but he makes a strong case (see pp. 128-30 of his edition). If the words stand here, then lines 30, 31 are awkwardly repetitive, whereas they are effective if they propose, *for the first time*, the drawing of Antony up as the alternative to Cleopatra coming down. Further, Antony's *Peace!* at the end of line 13 follows more naturally on Cleopatra's repeated *Antony!* if nothing else intervenes. Dover Wilson accounts for the "interpolation" by assuming that the passage originally ran as we have it, but without this line and a half, and that then a proposed cut was indicated from line 13, *Peace!* to line 31, *good friends:* but the cutter, finding that he had now no text left to correspond to the drawing up of Antony, wrote in the substance of lines 30, 31 at lines 12, 13 in a version of his own. (It is just worth remark that Cleopatra's triple *Antony!* in lines 11, 12 is all in one line in F, so that *Help, Charmian* starts a new line.) The weakness of the argument (unless I misunderstand the details of it) is that it posits an unskilful, and even silly, cutter, who gave himself more trouble than there was any need for. Why did he not simply stop his cut at the end of line 29 (*Antony*), and relieve himself of the job of rewriting Shakespeare for the insertion at line 12. But there is another possibility, which is, I think, more likely, namely, that Shake-

speare, having brought Antony in, and written Cleopatra's impassioned greeting (line 9, *O sun* down to the third *Antony* in line 12), first intended to have Antony immediately hoisted up, and wrote the appropriate lines for Cleopatra; that he then saw the advantages of a brief interchange before the hoisting up, and wrote lines 13 (*Peace!*)—31 (*good friends*); and that either he forgot to delete the now worse than unwanted *Help, Charmian . . . hither*, or his indications of deletion were neglected. (Something of the same kind almost certainly happened in *L.L.L.* IV. iii, where a speech of twenty-two lines (296-317) is immediately followed by an elaborated version of the same speech (318-54), where it is reasonable to assume that the deletion of the first version was either forgotten or neglected.) We shall still need the cutter to account for the repetition of Antony's *I am dying, Egypt, dying* (if we are determined to be rid of its second occurrence—see note on line 41 below), but at least he need no longer be a fool. [R]

16, 17. *that none . . . Antony*] Cf. Ovid, *Metam.* xiii. 390: "That none may Ajax overcome save Ajax" (Golding's Ovid), and *J.C.* v. v. 56.

19. *importune death awhile*] *importune* seems to be used with much latitude here. Johnson explains: "I *solicit* death to delay *or* I trouble death by keeping him in waiting."

Dear my lord, pardon: I dare not,
Lest I be taken: not the imperious show
Of the full-fortun'd Cæsar ever shall
Be brooch'd with me, if knife, drugs, serpents, have   25
Edge, sting, or operation.   I am safe:
Your wife Octavia, with her modest eyes,
And still conclusion, shall acquire no honour
Demuring upon me: but come, come, Antony,—
Help me, my women,—we must draw thee up: 30
Assist, good friends.

Ant.   O quick, or I am gone.

Cleo. Here's sport indeed!   How heavy weighs my lord!

---

22. *dare not*] F; *dare not descend* Malone; *dare not open* D. Wilson.

---

22. *dare not*] † The line halts and though completion is not essential the sense is improved if Cleopatra makes plain what it is she " dare not," and Malone's *descend* is as easy an addition as any.   But I am not sure that the improvement in sense, and metre, is not bought with a loss in effectiveness.   There is a compression, or ellipse, in Cleopatra's words as they stand: it is not that she dare not take his last kiss—though that is what she says—but that even for that she dare not come down [R].

25. *brooch'd*] adorned; a brooch being always an ornament, as Ritson observes.   Cf. *Hamlet*, IV. vii. 93: " he is the *brooch* indeed And gem of all the nation."   Steevens cites Jonson, *The Staple of News*, III. ii. 265: " The very *brooch* o' the bench, gem o' the city "; *The Magnetic Lady*, I. vii. 33: " The *brooch* to any true state-cap in Europe."   In the last passage, the brooch is the last of several ornaments, to which " the jewel Of all the court, close Master Bias " is compared, and the prevailing mode of wearing a brooch in the front of the cap or hat is alluded to, as also in *The Poetaster*, I. ii. 161: " honour's a good *brooch* to wear in a man's hat, at all times."

26. *sting, or operation*] Hanmer reads

operation, or sting to correspond in order with *drugs, serpents*; but for disregard of such nicety, cf. *Hamlet*, III. i. 160.

28. *still conclusion*] composed and silent censure, quiet formation of opinion.   The idea seems to be one of disapproval following on inspection, instinctively felt by its object, maugre silence and " modest eyes " or demure looks.   Cf. v. ii. 54 *post*.

29. *Demuring upon me*] Looking demurely upon me, with an air of innocence. *Demuring* is not found elsewhere.   It is just possible that it may be from *demur* (see *O.E.D. demur*), and thus used to indicate the leisurely consideration of Octavia, the deliberation, as of one doubtful, with which she would appear to draw her conclusions.   Cf. Sir John Harington, *Epigrams* (ed. 1633, bk. i. 37) :—

" Once, by mishap, two Poets fell a
     squaring,
The Sonnet and our Epigram
     comparing ;
And *Faustus* having long *demur'd*
     upon it,
Yet at the last gave sentence for
     the Sonnet," etc.

32. *Here's sport indeed*] The grim humour of this exclamation was lost on Johnson, who took it for a rebuke of trifling efforts! and others have

Our strength is all gone into heaviness,
That makes the weight.   Had I great Juno's power,
The strong-wing'd Mercury should fetch thee up,   35
And set thee by Jove's side.   Yet come a little,
Wishers were ever fools, O, come, come, come.
      [*They heave Antony aloft to Cleopatra.*
And welcome, welcome!   Die when thou hast liv'd,
Quicken with kissing: had my lips that power,
Thus would I wear them out.

All.   A heavy sight!   40
Ant. I am dying, Egypt, dying.
      Give me some wine, and let me speak a little.
Cleo. No, let me speak, and let me rail so high,
That the false huswife Fortune break her wheel,
Provok'd by my offence.

---

33. *heaviness,*] F; *heaviness;* Cambridge edd.   **38.** *when*] F; *where* Pope.

positively suggested emendations. Possibly, as Malone suggests, there is a thought of their former fishing diversions. Cf. II. v. 13-15 *ante*:—

> " and, as I draw them up,
> I'll think them every one an Antony,
> And say, ' Ah, ha! you're caught.' "

33. *heaviness*] Malone "equivocally for sorrow and weight." See the passages cited on IV. vi. 36 *ante*. Cf. for the thought, Daniel, *Cleopatra*, 1607 (*Works*, ed. Grosart, III. 8) : " Whose surcharg'd heart more then her body wayes."

37. *Wishers . . . fools*] This sounds like a proverb. In Ray's collection occurs, " Wishers and woulders are never good householders."

38. *when*] † Few commentators (Rowe and Dover Wilson among them) have adhered to F's *when,* but I think they are right. The sense is then " live once more before you die," and a point is given to *Quicken with kissing* which it otherwise awkwardly lacks. [R]

39. *Quicken*] gain life or vitality. Cf. *Othello*, III. iii. 277.

40. *A heavy*] † Perhaps *Ah, heavy*; (Rowe emends to *Oh*). [R]

41. *I am dying, Egypt, dying*] † This also Dover Wilson regards as an interpolation (see note to lines 12, 13 of this scene), arguing that the cutter, feeling that he had left Antony's dying condition insufficiently stressed, lifted a significant phrase from the cut (line 18) and inserted it.   If one accepts the general hypothesis of the cut, this seems convincing.   The exact repetition of the famous phrase weakens it, and further, the lines which follow its first occurrence are so immeasurably more effective than those which follow its second [R].

44. *housewife*] Here, as often, *huswife* has a bad sense : jilt, wanton, etc. Cf. *Henry V.* v. i. 85 : " Doth Fortune play the *huswife* with me now?" *Huswiverie* is similarly used, e.g. mistrust in husbands is said to " plante newe trickes of *huswiuerie* in their wiues consciences " (*Tell-Trothes New-yeares Gift*, 1593, New Shakes. Soc., 1876, p. 22).   In this speech, lines 43-45, Cleopatra seems to strike a false note.   The like of line 44, which Johnson calls " this despicable

Ant.   One word, sweet queen: 45
     Of Cæsar seek your honour, with your safety.   O!
Cleo. They do not go together.
Ant.   Gentle, hear me,
     None about Cæsar trust but Proculeius.
Cleo. My resolution, and my hands, I'll trust,
     None about Cæsar.   50
Ant. The miserable change now at my end
     Lament nor sorrow at: but please your thoughts
     In feeding them with those my former fortunes
     Wherein I liv'd: the greatest prince o' the world,
     The noblest; and do now not basely die,   55
     Not cowardly put off my helmet to
     My countryman: a Roman, by a Roman
     Valiantly vanquish'd.   Now my spirit is going,
     I can no more.
Cleo.   Noblest of men, woo't die?
     Hast thou no care of me, shall I abide   60
     In this dull world, which in thy absence is
     No better than a sty?   O, see, my women:
     The crown o' the earth doth melt.   [*Antony dies.*]
                              My lord?

---

54. *liv'd: the*] *liued. The* F; *liv'd the* Theobald.   63. Antony dies]
Capell, after *women*, line 62; Rowe after *more*, line 59; not in F.

line," is in keeping in *A.Y.L.* i. ii.
34 ; here it savours of uncouth early
dramas.
     † But perhaps Shakespeare knew
better than his editors how men and
women talk under stress : cf.
Malcolm's surprising " O by whom?"
in *Macbeth*, ii. iii. 107. [R]
     54-7. *liv'd: countryman:*] F's full-
stops are disconcerting to the modern
reader, since they are syntactically
very awkward, and he is used to
syntactical punctuation. They may,
of course, be mere blunders, and
many editors have emended them.
But they may, I think more probably,
come from the original, and if so, the
colons of the present text (lightening
F's colon after *noblest*, to maintain the
distinction in length of pause) perhaps come as near as modern nota-

tion will permit to representing
Shakespeare's intention without un-
due distraction to the reader. Antony
is, literally, at the last gasp, and his
utterance is broken, with heavy
pauses.
     56-8. *Not cowardly put*, etc.] See
North, *post*, pp. 281-2. Rowe placed
a comma after *cowardly* with F 4, thus
connecting it with *die*, and changed
not to *nor*. This is defensible ; but
surely those who, with Pope, read *Nor
cowardly put off* . . . weaken the connection of the negative with *cowardly :*
to which alone it applies and not to
put off, etc.
     59. *woo 't*] See on iv. ii. 7 *ante*.
     63. *crown*] Cf. next note, and
see on iv. xii. 27 *ante*.
     S.D.] † I have inserted the usual
S.D. for Antony's death, though at a

O, wither'd is the garland of the war,
The soldier's pole is fall'n: young boys and girls   65
Are level now with men: the odds is gone,
And there is nothing left remarkable
Beneath the visiting moon.   [*Faints.*
Char.   O quietness; lady!
Iras. She's dead too, our sovereign.
Char.   Lady!
Iras.   Madam!
Char. O madam, madam, madam!
Iras.   Royal Egypt: 70
        Empress!   [*Cleopatra stirs.*
Char. Peace, peace, Iras!

---

68. Faints.] She Faints. Rowe; not in F.   71. Cleopatra stirs] D.
Wilson (she stirs); not in F.

place slightly later than the usual.
But I am not clear that we should not
do better to follow F and dispense
with it altogether. Antony's death
occurs, presumably, somewhere between Cleopatra's " woo't die? "
and her " O, wither'd . . .", and
the precise instant of it matters very
little. [R]
64. *garland of the war*] Cf. *Coriolanus*, I. i. 189: " And call . . .
Him vile that was your *garland* ";
Quarles. *Argalus and Parthenia*, bk. i.
(ed. 1701, p. 35):—
        " he that is the crown
Of prized virtue, honour and re-
        nown.
The flower of Arts, the *Cyprian*
        living story,
Arcadia's Garland, and great
        Greece's glory "
†But surely, as Deighton and Furness
saw, there is a suggestion of the may-
pole. [R]
65. *pole*] perhaps standard, which
the aptitude of the metaphor supports.
Boswell gets the credit of the suggestion, really Beckett's (*Concordance*,
1787, p. 445). Schmidt and the
Temple and Eversley editors explain
by " lodestar," and, certainly, the
second guard in IV. xiv. 106 *ante* says

" The star is fall'n," while the use of
pole in simile or metaphor is common.
Cf. Richard James (1592-1638), *Poems*
ed. Grosart, 1880, p. 124: " This
[i.e. Faith and True Religion] was
the *Pole*, the Pillar, and the light,"
etc.
66. *the odds is gone*] There is no
distinction left between great and
small, cf. *T. and C.* iii. 23-28, 83-126;
and *No-body and Some-body*, lines 107,
108 (Simpson's *School of Shakspere*, p.
281): " if your highnesse note his leg
and mine, there is *ods*; and for a foot,
I dare compare."
67. *remarkable*] Staunton receives
credit for observing that this word had,
when this play was written, a more
impressive sense, far worthier of the
occasion, than the present one of
merely " observable or noteworthy,"
but he had the remark from Gifford.
See the latter's *Massinger*, 1805, i. 157,
note on *The Unnatural Combat*, II. i.
Malone compares with lines 66-68,
Macbeth, II. iii. 99-103:—
        " from this instant
There's nothing serious in mor-
        tality:" etc.
69-73. † There are various small
points in these lines. Rowe's S.D.
is clearly justified, since otherwise

Cleo. No more but e'en a woman, and commanded
　　By such poor passion as the maid that milks,
　　And does the meanest chares.　It were for me　　75
　　To throw my sceptre at the injurious gods,
　　To tell them that this world did equal theirs,
　　Till they had stol'n our jewel.　All's but naught:
　　Patience is sottish, and impatience does
　　Become a dog that's mad:　then is it sin,　　80
　　To rush into the secret house of death,
　　Ere death dare come to us?　How do you, women?
　　What, what, good cheer!　Why, how now, Charmian?
　　My noble girls!　Ah, women, women.　Look,
　　Our lamp is spent, it's out.　Good sirs, take heart,　　85

---

73. *e'en*] Johnson; *in* F.　　　83. *what, good cheer!*] *what good cheere?* F.

---

there is no point of reference for Iras's first speech, and so is Wilson's, as the occasion for Charmian's *Peace, peace, Iras!* (if that should be hers). I think that Charmian's *O quietness is addressed* to Iras, and her *Lady!* to Cleopatra, like her own and Iras's subsequent exclamations, and I have punctuated accordingly. I think that Cleopatra's *No more but e'en a woman* is a correction of Iras's *Empress!*, and if so Charmian's *Peace, peace, Iras!* must be given as a rapid aside. But it is very tempting to attribute the words to Cleopatra herself, comparing her *Peace, peace!* at v. ii. 307 *post*, where also the words check an excited address. [R]

73. *No more but e'en a woman*] As Malone observes, this responds to the words of Iras, without noticing those of Charmian. But is the sense, as he takes it—placing with most editors (Johnson's conjecture) a comma after *more*—No more (i.e. no longer) an empress, but just a woman; or merely No more than just a woman, as Hudson evidently interprets? One can only be guided here by an instinctive preference, and specious as the first explanation is, my impulse is to read with Hudson, as in the text above.

The words seem to me not so much an answer to Iras, as the outcome of a train of thought suggested by Iras.

e'en] † In support of Johnson's emendation, cf. F's frequent *bin* for *been*. [R]

75. *chares*] tasks. A *char* or *chare* is a turn, and hence, a turn of work. Cf. *char-woman*. The word is used by Shakespeare only in this play but was very common in his time. See Peele, *Edward I*, vi. 119: "Why, so, this *chare* is chared"; (again in v. ii. 230 *post*).

79. *sottish*] foolish, mere stupidity. Not elsewhere in Shakespeare, but common; so in The Epistle Dedicatorie, *Mirour for Magistrates*, 1587: " not coūted wise, righteous, and constant, but *sottish*, rude and desperate."

79, 80. *does Become*] is characteristic of.

85. *Our lamp*] one of the many echoes of which the play is full; cf. the preceding scene, line 46, *the torch is out.*

Good sirs] To the women. Cf. *Sirrah Iras*, v. ii. 228 *post*, and Whetstone, *1 Promos and Cassandra*, IV. vii. 6 :—

　" *Grimball* . . . kysse me for acquaintaunce.

R

We'll bury him: and then, what's brave, what's noble,
Let's do it after the high Roman fashion,
And make death proud to take us.   Come, away,
This case of that huge spirit now is cold.
Ah, women, women! come, we have no friend   90
But resolution, and the briefest end.

> [*Exeunt; those above bearing off Antony's body.*

87. *do it*] Pope; *doo't* F.   91. Exeunt . . .] Capell (substantially);
Exeunt, bearing of Anthonies body. F.

Dalia. If I lyke your manhoode, I
may do so perchaunce.
[*She faynes to looke in his basket.*
Grimball. Bate me an ase, quoth
Boulton : Tush your minde I
know :

Ah *Syr*, you would, belike, let my
cocke sparrowes goe."
Dyce quotes examples from Beaumont
and Fletcher, *A King and no King*, II. i.
250 ; *Philaster*, IV. iii. 54.

ACT V

[SCENE I.—*Alexandria.   Cæsar's camp.*]

Enter CÆSAR, AGRIPPA, DOLABELLA, MÆCENAS, GALLUS,
   PROCULEIUS, *and others, his council of war.*

Cæs. Go to him, Dolabella, bid him yield.
   Being so frustrate, tell him, he mocks
   The pauses that he makes.
Dol.   Cæsar, I shall.   [*Exit.*

Enter DECRETAS, *with the sword of* ANTONY.

ACT V

Scene 1

Enter . . .] Globe;   Enter Cæsar, Agrippa, Dolabella, Menas, with his
Counsell of Warre. F.   3. Exit] not in F.

Scene 1

Scene 1 [see North, *post*, p. 282].

Enter . . . *Mæcenas* . . .] Theobald (Thirlby conj.) first substituted *Mæcenas* for *Menas* of F, pointing out that the speeches of the character are marked *Mec.* in the margin, and that though *Menas* died a partisan of Cæsar, it was five years before Antony's death.

2. *frustrate*] baffled. So *The Tempest*, III. iii. 10 : " Our *frustrate* search on land." Perhaps pronounced as a trisyllable. Compare *mistress*, II. v. 27 *ante*.

2, 3. *he mocks . . . makes*] his delays are mere mockery. Steevens suggested this very probable sense, which seems capable of being deduced from the text. I can imagine a phrase " to mock pauses " as equivalent to " to make mocking pauses," i.e. pauses mocking either the maker or another, according to the sense required by the context ; and perhaps

" to mock " here is a condensation for something like " to make ineffectually," or " to make ridiculously." Malone evaded the difficulty by reading " *mocks* us by."

† Cæsar's meaning is, I think, plain (and Malone therefore is on the wrong tack) : " tell him his pauses— i.e. his shifts, evasions, attempts to postpone the moment of surrender— are idle," which is substantially Case's interpretation, but not very easy to elicit from the text as it stands. [R]

3. (S.D.) † *Decretas*. I do not know that it matters much what we call this unimportant character, but I think that Dover Wilson's note about him merits a moment's consideration. He says : " I follow Shakespeare and read ' Decretus,' which is the form he gives to Plutarch-North's ' Dercetaeus ' at 4.4.111, and not like Pope and later editors ' Dercetas ', which lies half way between North and the

Cæs. Wherefore is that? and what art thou that dar'st
    Appear thus to us?

Dec.   I am call'd Decretas,   5
    Mark Antony I serv'd, who best was worthy
    Best to be serv'd: whilst he stood up, and spoke,
    He was my master, and I wore my life
    To spend upon his haters.   If thou please
    To take me to thee, as I was to him   10
    I'll be to Cæsar, if thou pleasest not,
    I yield thee up my life.

Cæs.   What is't thou say'st?

Dec. I say, O Cæsar, Antony is dead.

Cæs. The breaking of so great a thing should make
    A greater crack.   The round world   15
    Should have shook lions into civil streets,
    And citizens to their dens.   The death of Antony
    Is not a single doom, in the name lay
    A moiety of the world.

Dec.   He is dead, Cæsar,
    Not by a public minister of justice,   20
    Nor by a hired knife, but that self hand
    Which writ his honour in the acts it did,

---

spelling ' Decretas ' that crops up in
F at 5.1.3 (S.D.) and 5.1.5, and is in
fact the sort of conflation that pre-
Pollardian editors loved." I think
this is somewhat misleading.   The
facts are these : the name occurs in
full three times, once in a speech-
heading (IV. xiv. 111) as Dercetus,
once in a stage-direction (V. i. 3)
as Decretas, and once in the text
(V. i. 5) also as Decretas; an abbreviated form occurs four times, at
IV. xiv. 114 (Decre.) and v. i. 5, 13,
19 (Dec.). Admittedly a confusion
between the two forms of the name
would be easy enough, but I think
that we are more likely to be " following Shakespeare " if we accept the
6-1 majority of F in favour of
Decretas. [R]
    5. *thus*, i.e. as Delius observes, with
a naked, bloody sword.

6, 7. *who best . . . serv'd*] **Cf.**
Thidias on Cæsar, III. xiii. 87, 88 *ante.*

    15. An omission has been generally
suspected here, and made the subject
of many conjectures. Steevens suggested : " A greater crack than this :
the ruin'd world." As the sense is
plain, may not the short line have
been intentional? a pause here would
be natural and impressive. For the
thought, cf. *J.C.* I. iii. 3, 4, 20-22.

    19. *moiety*] half, the strict sense of
the word, as in *All's Well*, III. ii. 69.
Often merely = share, portion, as in
Lear, I. i. 7.

    21. *self*] same, as in *The Comedy of
Errors*, v. i. 10: " that *self* chain
about his neck," *Lear*, IV. iii. 36,
etc. Cf. also *The Three Lords*, etc.
(Hazlitt's *Dodsley*, vi. 376) : " Not
all our ships do sail for one *self*
haven."

Hath, with the courage which the heart did lend it,
Splitted the heart.   This is his sword,
I robb'd his wound of it: behold it stain'd   25
With his most noble blood.
Cæs.   Look you sad, friends?
The gods rebuke me, but it is a tidings
To wash the eyes of kings.
Agr.   And strange it is,
That nature must compel us to lament
Our most persisted deeds.
Mæc.   His taints and honours   30
Wag'd equal with him.
Agr.   A rarer spirit never
Did steer humanity: but you gods will give us
Some faults to make us men.   Cæsar is touch'd.
Mæc. When such a spacious mirror's set before him,
He needs must see himself.
Cæs.   O Antony,   35
I have follow'd thee to this, but we do launch
Diseases in our bodies.   I must perforce
Have shown to thee such a declining day,

---

26. *Look . . . sad, friends?*] Hanmer; *sad friends;* Theobald; *Looke you sad friends,* F; *Look you, sad friends,* F 3.   27. *is a tidings*] F 2 (*Tydings*); *is Tydings* F.   28, 31. Agr.] Theobald; Dol. F.   31. *Wag'd*] F ; *way* F 2; *weigh'd* Rowe, and many others.   36. *launch*] F; *lance* Theobald and edd.

24. *Splitted*] Cf. *2 H. VI.* III. ii. 411; *The Comedy of Errors*, I. i. 103 ; v. i. 309 :—

  " O time's extremity,
Hast thou so crack'd and *splitted*
  my poor tongue," etc.

27. *a tidings*] † F's rhythm is so awkward that we may without much compunction, I think, accept F 2, particularly since a too grammatically-minded compositor might easily, thinking *a Tydings* a solecism, have dropped the *a* in the interest of supposed correctness. [R]

28-30. *And strange . . . deeds*] Cf. III. ii. 58 *ante*.

31. *Wag'd equal*] Steevens : " were an equal match, i.e. were opposed to each other in just proportions, like the counterparts of a wager." This explanation is confirmed by *Pericles*, IV. ii. 34 : " The commodity *wages not* with the danger."

36. *launch*] *launch* or *lanch* is the old and common form of "lance". Cf. Nashe, *Christ's Tears* (McK. II. 156, line 19) : " and even as *Archabius* the Trumpeter had more giuen him to cease then to sound (the noise that he made was so harsh) so wil they giue them more . . to corrupt them then to make them sound, to feede their sores than to *launch* them " ; and see note on *Lear*, II. i. 52 (*Arden Shakespeare*).

Or look on thine: we could not stall together,
In the whole world.   But yet let me lament   40
With tears as sovereign as the blood of hearts,
That thou my brother, my competitor,
In top of all design; my mate in empire,
Friend and companion in the front of war,
The arm of mine own body, and the heart   45
Where mine his thoughts did kindle;—that our stars,
Unreconciliable, should divide
Our equalness to this.   Hear me, good friends,—
But I will tell you at some meeter season,
The business of this man looks out of him,   50
We'll hear him what he says.   [*Enter an Egyptian.*
                         Whence are you?
Egyp. A poor Egyptian yet; the queen my mistress,
Confin'd in all she has, her monument,
Of thy intents desires instruction,

---

52. *Egyptian yet*; *the*] Rowe (ed. 3); *Egyptian yet, the* F; Hunter, followed by
D. Wilson, reads *Egyptian, yet the*.

---

39. *stall*] dwell.   See Whetstone, *2 Promos and Cassandra*, iii. ii (Nichols, *Six Old Plays*, 1779, p. 83) :—

> " Well, ere I leave, my poorest subjects shall
> Both lyve and lyke, and by the richest *stawl*."

41. *sovereign . . . blood*] See on iv. ii. 6 *ante*, the thought being, perhaps, of a sovereign remedy.

42. *competitor*] Perhaps here = friendly rival, [thou] who viedst with me, rather than merely—as in i. iv. 3 and ii. vii. 70 *ante*—associate.

43. *In top . . . design*] " In top of " means " in height of," and expresses the superlative degree of whatever is in question, as in *A Lover's Complaint*, 55 : " This said, *in top of* rage the lines she rents," etc.   Hence, possibly, it may be allowable to paraphrase here : " in the daring (*or* supreme) conception and conduct of all enterprise."

46. *Where . . . kindle*] No one seems to find a difficulty here.   *His*, of course = its, but does " Where my heart did kindle its thoughts " = Where I found inspiration, or merely indicate the close commune of friends ?

47, 48. *divide . . . this*] sunder us, who were thus equal associates in everything, so widely and so fatally.

50. *The business . . . him*] Cf. *Cymbeline*, v. v. 23 : " There's business in these faces " ; and *Macbeth*, i. ii. 47: " What a haste looks through his eyes!"

52. *A poor Egyptian yet*] Taken in connection with what follows, this reply seems equivalent to : " From what is yet Egypt, till your intents pronounce its fate."   Johnson's explanation is : " Yet a servant of the Queen of Egypt, though soon to become a subject of Rome."   A new suggestion is made by Deighton, viz. : " one who, though conquered, still boasts himself an Egyptian."   Schmidt prefers the F reading, explaining " A poor Egyptian yet, the queen," as " My queen, who is now no more than a poor Egyptian."

That she preparedly may frame herself   55
To the way she's forc'd to.
Cæs.   Bid her have good heart;
She soon shall know of us, by some of ours,
How honourable, and how kindly we
Determine for her.   For Cæsar cannot live
To be ungentle.
Egyp.   So the gods preserve thee!   [*Exit.*   60
Cæs. Come hither, Proculeius.   Go and say
We purpose her no shame: give her what comforts
The quality of her passion shall require,
Lest, in her greatness, by some mortal stroke
She do defeat us.   For her life in Rome   65
Would be eternal in our triumph: go,
And with your speediest bring us what she says,
And how you find of her.
Pro.   Cæsar, I shall.   [*Exit.*
Cæs. Gallus, go you along.   [*Exit Gallus.*]   Where's Dola-
bella,
To second Proculeius?
All.   Dolabella!   70

---

56. *to*] F 2 ; *too* F.   59. *live*] Rowe (ed. 3) and Southern MS.; *leaue* F;
learn Dyce (Tyrwhitt conj.).   60. *ungentle*] F; *gentle* Capell, reading *Leave*
transferred to this line.   69. Exit Gallus] Theobald; not in F.

59, 60. *live to be ungentle*] † The
Southern-Rowe emendation has been
almost universally accepted. It is
fairly easy graphically (especially if
we accept Dover Wilson's suggestion
of a MS. *leue*, a spelling which would
account for F's *love* for *leave* in I. ii.
177) and even easier auditorily ; and
it makes quite adequate sense. None
the less *leave* has to me a more Shakespearean " feel," with the sense
" stop being gentle " or even more
nearly " stop being himself so as to
become ungentle." But the first
involves an almost impossible (in
spite of Capell) emendation, and the
second an almost impossible ellipse
[R].
     65, 66. *her life . . . triumph*] Not
"her abode in Rome would perpetuate

my triumph," but " her presence,
alive, at my triumph in Rome, would
make it everlastingly memorable."
The sense of *life* is not here " continuous existence," but merely contains the idea of life, as opposed to
that of death involved in " some
mortal stroke." We may, perhaps,
regard *eternal* here as having become
merely intensive, and explain : " her
presence . . . would contribute in the
highest degree to my triumph."
Expressions like " an eternal swindle"
may be heard nowadays. See also
an *eternal villain* in *Othello*, IV. ii. 130
(*Arden Shakespeare*). Cf. North, *post*,
p. 282.
     67. *with your speediest*] as quickly as
you can. Cf. " *with your earliest*,"
Othello, II. iii. 7.

Cæs. Let him alone: for I remember now
    How he's employ'd: he shall in time be ready.
    Go with me to my tent, where you shall see
    How hardly I was drawn into this war,
    How calm and gentle I proceeded still   75
    In all my writings. Go with me, and see
    What I can show in this.   [*Exeunt.*

[SCENE II.—*Alexandria. A room in the monument.*]

Enter CLEOPATRA, CHARMIAN, *and* IRAS.

Cleo. My desolation does begin to make
    A better life: 'tis paltry to be Cæsar:
    Not being Fortune, he's but Fortune's knave,
    A minister of her will: and it is great
    To do that thing that ends all other deeds,   5
    Which shackles accidents, and bolts up change;
    Which sleeps, and never palates more the dung,
    The beggar's nurse, and Cæsar's.

Scene II

7. *dung*] F ; *dug* Theobald (*dugg*) and many other edd.   8. (S.D.), Enter Proculeius] F; Enter, to the gates of the monument, Proculeius, Gallus, and Soldiers. Capell.

Scene II

For the staging of this scene see Appendix IV.

S.D. Enter *Cleopatra . . .*] † F brings in Mardian also. Much as I dislike tinkering with F's S.D.s, I think that he must be omitted. (a) He says nothing throughout the scene ; not a strong argument, in view of Agrippa in III. xi. (b) North (see p. 284) stresses the absence of everyone but the two waiting-women ; a trifle stronger, but not at all decisive. (c) There is no place that I can see where we can restore a supposedly omitted " Exit Mardian ", so that if he is to be there we must imagine him as a silent spectator throughout. But there are two points at which, if he is there,

one would expect some notice to be taken of him, first at the moment of Cleopatra's farewell (l. 291), second after Cæsar's entry (l. 332), where he would naturally be questioned. I fancy that Shakespeare intended to include him in the dialogue, but then found that the scene was better without him, and forgot to delete his entry [R].

2. *A better life,* i.e. a life in which Fortune's gifts are rightly estimated and despised, and the contemplation of one crowning and emancipating deed restores a sense of confidence, and superiority over Fortune's minion.

3. *knave*] servant, as in IV. xiv. 12.

7, 8. *Which . . . Cæsar's*] Fortune's favour has just been scorned : it remains to decry life, which Cæsar and

Enter PROCULEIUS.

Pro. Cæsar sends greeting to the Queen of Egypt,
And bids thee study on what fair demands　　　　10
Thou mean'st to have him grant thee.
Cleo.　　　　　　　　　　　　　What's thy name?
Pro. My name is Proculeius.
Cleo.　　　　　　　　　Antony
Did tell me of you, bade me trust you, but
I do not greatly care to be deceiv'd
That have no use for trusting. If your master　　　15
Would have a queen his beggar, you must tell him,
That majesty, to keep decorum, must
No less beg than a kingdom: if he please
To give me conquer'd Egypt for my son,
He gives me so much of mine own, as I　　　　20
Will kneel to him with thanks.
Pro.　　　　　　　　　　　Be of good cheer:
Y'are fall'n into a princely hand, fear nothing,

---

the beggar must retain by the same means. "Which sleeps," etc. (line 7), is a bold equivalent for: Which is a sleep, emancipated from need of the base food on which depends as much the life of Cæsar as a beggar's. Johnson says: "The difficulty of the passage, if any difficulty there be, arises only from this, that the act of suicide, and the state which is the effect of suicide, are confounded. Voluntary death, says she, is an act *which bolts up change*; it produces a state . . . which has no longer need of the gross and terrene sustenance, in the use of which Cæsar and the beggar are on a level. The speech is abrupt, but perturbation in such a state is surely natural." For *palates* = tastes, cf. *T. and C.* IV. i. 59: "Not *palating* the taste of her dishonour." A little earlier (IV. xv. 62) Cleopatra has described the world as now "No better than a sty," and in I. i. 35-37 *ante*, Antony contrasts the nobleness

of life in love with kingship over clay: "our dungy earth alike," he says, "feeds beast as man": and as the play is full of reminiscences, we have probably one such here. And it is probably the attraction of an inoffensive for an unpleasant idea, repulsive to modern refinement, rather than the association with the word *nurse*, which has caused so many editors to read *dug* for *dung* with Warburton.

8. Enter . . . *Proculeius* . . .] With what follows, to line 46, cf. North, *post*, p. 282. And see Appendix IV.

14. *care to be deceiv'd*] i.e. care whether I am deceived or not (Delius).

20. *as*] = that, after *so*. Cf. *R. III.* III. iv. 37 (Q).

And finds the testy gentleman so hot,
　As he will lose his head ere give consent," etc.

and see Abbott (*Shakes. Gram.*, § 109).

Make your full reference freely to my lord,
Who is so full of grace, that it flows over
On all that need.   Let me report to him   25
Your sweet dependency, and you shall find
A conqueror that will pray in aid for kindness,
Where he for grace is kneel'd to.

Cleo.   Pray you, tell him
I am his fortune's vassal, and I send him
The greatness he has got.   I hourly learn   30
A doctrine of obedience, and would gladly
Look him i' the face.

Pro.   This I'll report, dear lady.
Have comfort, for I know your plight is pitied
Of him that caus'd it.

                    Enter GALLUS *and soldiers behind.*

Gal. You see how easily she may be surpris'd: 35
     [*To Proculeius and the Guard*] Guard her till Cæsar come.
                                                   [*Exit.*

34. S.D.] not in F. See App. IV.   35. Gal.] Malone; Pro. F; Char. F 2.
See note.

23. *make your . . . reference*] refer
your case.
27. *pray in aid*] A legal term, as
Hanmer pointed out.   Here, with
the context, equivalent to, beg your
assistance in order that he may omit
no kindness.   " This word (Ayde) is
also particularly used in matter of
Pleading, for a Petition made in
Court for the calling in of help from
another that hath an interest in the
cause in question, and is likely both
to give strength to the Party that
prayeth in ayd of him, and also to
avoid a prejudice growing toward his
own right, except it be prevented."
So Cowel's *Interpreter,* enlarged by
Manley, ed. 2, 1684, under *Ayde.*
The meaning of the term seems to
admit of the above " beg *your* assistance " instead of merely " seek assistance," and in lines 185, 186 *post,*
Cæsar says :—

" For we intend so to dispose you as
     Yourself shall give us counsel."
The simpler sense occurs in Bacon's
essay " Of Friendship " : " But yet
without *praying in aid* of alchemists,"
etc.
29. 30. *I send . . . got*] Johnson :
" I allow him to be my conqueror ; I
own his superiority with complete
submission."
35, 36. Gal. *You . . . come*] Theobald was the first to see, by reference
to Plutarch, that line 35 belongs to
Gallus.   Line 36, however, " Guard
her," etc., he left to Proculeius, inserting a corresponding stage-direction
after line 34 : " Here Gallus, and
Guard, ascend the Monument by a
ladder, and enter at a back-window."
See *post,* p. 282, for the passage in
North which justifies Malone in assigning line 36 also to Gallus, by showing
that Proculeius, with two of his men,

Iras. Royal queen!

Char. O Cleopatra, thou art taken, queen.

Cleo. Quick, quick, good hands.   [*Drawing a dagger.*

Pro.   Hold, worthy lady, hold:

                   [*Seizes and disarms her.*

Do not yourself such wrong, who are in this   40
Reliev'd, but not betray'd.

Cleo.   What, of death, too,
That rids our dogs of languish?

Pro.   Cleopatra,
Do not abuse my master's bounty, by
The undoing of yourself: let the world see
His nobleness well acted, which your death   45
Will never let come forth.

Cleo.   Where art thou, death?
Come hither, come; come, come, and take a queen
Worth many babes and beggars!

Pro.   O, temperance, lady!

Cleo. Sir, I will eat no meat, I'll not drink, sir,—
If idle talk will once be necessary,—   50

---

36. To Proculeius . . .] Malone.   Exit] Exit Gallus. Malone; F has
neither.   39. Drawing . . .] Theobald.   Seizes . . .] Malone. F
has neither.   42. *languish*] F; *anguish* Johnson conj.   49, 50. *sir,—*
. . . necessary,—] See note; *sir, . . . necessary* F.

was now within the monument in presence of Cleopatra, while Gallus remained without.

† See Appendix IV. I have left the original note standing, as an example. of the dangers of equating North and Shakespeare. There is nothing in Shakespeare to show that Proculeius ever had two or any other number of men with him, or that he is now anywhere else than he has been throughout. [R]

42. *languish*] the miserable drooping condition caused by disease or injury. See *R. and J.* i. ii. 50. A late example is cited in *O.E.D.*: "A long record of perishable *languish*" (H. Coleridge, *Poems*, 1851, i. 118).

50. *If . . . necessary,* —] I prefer to regard this line as parenthetical, with Singer and Kinnear. Most editors point, *sir; If . . . necessary, I'll neither:* F has no stop save comma after *sir* and full stop after *neither.* Hitherto (and she reverts to this course in her interview with Cæsar) Cleopatra has silently nursed her purpose and deceived her conquerors. Now, shaken out of her self-possession, she reveals it in threats, idle talk, as she calls them by contrast with her settled and previously dissembled purpose. "Words," says Daniel's Cleopatra, "are for them that can complaine and liue" (*Works*, Grosart, iii. 73, *Cleopatra*, IV. line 1154). The line will then mean: "If for once I must weakly deal in words": and it seems more naturally to follow the first threats than to be confined to that

I'll not sleep neither.   This mortal house I'll ruin,
Do Cæsar what he can.   Know, sir, that I
Will not wait pinion'd at your master's court,
Nor once be chastis'd with the sober eye
Of dull Octavia.   Shall they hoist me up,   55
And show me to the shouting varletry
Of censuring Rome?   Rather a ditch in Egypt
Be gentle grave unto me, rather on Nilus' mud
Lay me stark-nak'd, and let the water-flies
Blow me into abhorring; rather make   60
My country's high pyramides my gibbet,
And hang me up in chains.

Pro.   You do extend
These thoughts of horror further than you shall
Find cause in Cæsar.

Enter DOLABELLA.

Dol.   Proculeius,
What thou hast done thy master Cæsar knows,   65

56. *varletry*] *Varlotry* F 2; *Varlotarie* F.

of not sleeping.   Steevens suggested :
" If it be necessary, for once, to talk of
performing impossibilities, why, I'll
not sleep neither."   Malone and Ritson
believed a line to be lost after *necessary*,
such as—according to the former—
" I'll not so much as syllable a word."
Hanmer has *accessary*, and so, too, the
Collier MS. and Staunton, the last
named explaining : " and if idle talk
will for the nonce be assistant, I'll not
sleep."   Capell reads *speak* for *sleep*.
The omission of the line (50), as one
cancelled by Shakespeare but retained
by the printer, has also been suggested
With Cleopatra's threats, cf. :—
" I neuer will nor eate, nor drinke,
      nor taste
   Of any Cates that may preserue
      my life
   I neuer will nor smile, nor sleepe,
      nor rest."
A Woman Kilde with Kindnesse, 1607
(Pearson's *Heywood*, ii. 151).

52-57. Cf. IV. xii. 33-39 *ante*,
and v. ii. 207 *et seq. post.*

53. *pinioned*] with wings clipped (not
" manacled ").

58-60. Cf. the wish in III. xiii.
166, 167 *ante*.

61. *high pyramides*] Though *pyra-
mids* occurs in *Macbeth*, IV. i. 57, the
classical and quadrisyllabic plural
was the prevalent form. Cf. e.g.
Locrine, III. iv. 32 :—
            " the high *pyramides*,
   Which with their top surmount
      the firmament "
and Heywood, *The Actor's Vindication*,
N.D. London, by G. E. for W. C. p.
7 : " Hercules . . . on his high *Pyramides* writing *Nil ultra*," etc.

64. Enter *Dolabella*] In North (see
post, p. 283) it is Epaphroditus who is
sent at this stage. For *Dolabella*, see
ibid. pp. 283-4, the source of lines
196, 206 *post*.

And he hath sent for thee: for the queen,
I'll take her to my guard.
Pro.   So, Dolabella,
It shall content me best: be gentle to her;
[*To Cleo.*] To Cæsar I will speak what you shall please,
If you'll employ me to him.
Cleo.   Say, I would die.   70

> [*Exit Proculeius.*

Dol. Most noble empress, you have heard of me?
Cleo. I cannot tell.
Dol.   Assuredly you know me.
Cleo. No matter, sir, what I have heard or known:
You laugh when boys or women tell their dreams,
Is't not your trick?
Dol.   I understand not, madam.   75
Cleo. I dreamt there was an Emperor Antony.
O such another sleep, that I might see
But such another man!
Dol.   If it might please ye,—
Cleo. His face was as the heavens, and therein stuck
A sun and moon, which kept their course, and lighted 80
The little O, the earth.
Dol.   Most sovereign creature,—
Cleo. His legs bestrid the ocean, his rear'd arm
Crested the world: his voice was propertied

---

66. *for the queen*] F; *as for . . .* F 2.   69. To Cleo.] Hanmer
71. *me?*] Capell; *me.* F.   81. *O, the*] Steevens; *o' th'* F: *O o'th'* Theobald.

70. Exit Proculeius] This in F is after *to him*, an interesting illustration of the time which an exit (like an entrance) took on the Elizabethan stage. Cleopatra speaks to him as he moves to the door.

71. *empress*] " It owns her Antony's widow and ignores Octavia " (Barker).

81. *O, the earth*] This reading squares with Shakespeare's use of O for anything circular, as in *Henry V*, prol. 13: " Within this wooden *O*,", for the first Globe theatre, a round building. See also *M.N.D.* III. ii. 188 *L.L.L.* v. ii. 45. Hanmer has

" orb *o' th' earth*," as in *Coriolanus*, v. v. 127.

82. *His legs . . . ocean*] Cf. *J.C.* I. ii. 134:—
" Why man, he doth bestride the narrow world
Like a Colossus," etc.
and Webster, *Appius and Virginia*, III. i. 84 : " The high Colossus that bestrides us all."

83. *Crested the world*] Percy : " Alluding to some of the old crests in heraldry, where a raised arm on a wreath was mounted on the helmet."

83, 84. *was propertied . . . spheres*] was as musical in quality as, etc.

As all the tuned spheres, and that to friends:
But when he meant to quail, and shake the orb,   85
He was as rattling thunder.   For his bounty,
There was no winter in 't: an autumn 'twas

87. *autumn 'twas*] Thirlby conj.; Theobald, independently; Anthony *it was* F.

" Pythagoras (saith Censorinus) asserted, that this whole World is made according to musical proportion, and that the seven Planets, betwixt Heaven and the Earth, which govern the Nativities of Mortals, have a harmonious motion, and Intervals correspondent to musical Diastemes, and render various sounds, according to their several heights, so consonant, that they make most sweet melody ; but to us inaudible, by reason of the greatness of the noise, which the narrow passage of our Ears is not capable to receive " (Stanley, *History of Philosophy*, ed. 3, 1701, p. 393, pt. ix, sect. iv, chap. iii). See also on II. vii. 14-16 *ante*.   This sphere-music is the subject of a poetical scene (the last of Act III.) in *Lingua* (Hazlitt's *Dodsley*, ix. 406-10) and recurs constantly in Elizabethan poetry.   For *propertied*, cf. *The English Traveller*, I. i (Pearson's *Heywood*, iv. 9):—

    " This approues you,
To be most nobly *propertied*, that,"
    etc.

84. *and that to friends*] Theobald read *when that* with no advantage. Anon. conj. *addrest* ; Staunton, *and sweet* ; Elze, *and soft*.   Cf. Middleton's *The Roaring Girl*, IV. ii. 109 :—

    " when *friends* meet,
The music of the spheres sounds
    not more sweet
Than does their conference."

85. *quail*] Often, as here, transitive ; cow, overpower.   Cf. *The Three Ladies of London*, 1584 (Hazlitt's *Dodsley*, vi. 266): " She cannot *quail* me, if she came in likeness of the great devil."

87. *an autumn 'twas*] † This brilliant emendation is graphically easy (no

more than the rectification of two minim errors) if (but only if) we assume, with Dover Wilson, an MS. spelling *Automne*, misread by the compositor as *Antonie*.

There is no doubt that *autumn* gives admirable sense, and that the turn of imagination is thoroughly Shakespearean, whereas *Antony* gives no sense at all.   For the word, Jonson's use of it in *Volpone*, v. vi. 18 is illustrative

    " You should ha' some would swell
        now, like a wine-fat,
    With such an *Autumn*—Did he
        gi' you all, Sir?"

while for the thought, and particularly the coupling of *bounty* with the idea of autumn, Malone's quotation from Sonnet LIII brings one near to conviction

    " Speak of the spring, and foison of
        the year;
    The one doth shadow of your
        beauty show,
    The other as your bounty doth
        appear."

The real trouble about the emendation is implied in " but only if " above.   The evidence of F is strong that, unless we are to suppose that he altered the spelling of the name every time he came to it, what the compositor had in front of him in his copy was regularly *Anthony* (very occasionally *Anthonie*).   And easy though the *Automne-Antonie* confusion would be, to misread *Automne* as a word containing (probably) *y*, and (almost certainly) distinctive long-tailed *h*, would be much less natural. Further, if, whatever the normal spelling, the copy (whether Shakespeare's autograph or transcript)

That grew the more by reaping: his delights
Were dolphin-like, they show'd his back above
The element they lived in: in his livery　　　90
Walk'd crowns and crownets: realms and islands were
As plates dropp'd from his pocket.

Dol.　　　　　　　　　　　　　Cleopatra!

indicated proper names for italicization, the absence of such indication for the hypothetical *Automne*
ought to have made the compositor
suspicious. However, as Dr. Brooks
points out, F's reading at III. xiii. 162,
where the compositor apparently took
Cæsarion as an adjective, suggests that
the copy was at least not consistent
in such indication. And, for what it
is worth, there is no such indication
in the " three pages " of *Sir Thomas
More.*

But graphical considerations have
much stronger positive than negative
force. To show that a blunder was
graphically easy is cogent support for
an emendation; but to show that it
was not easy is slender evidence
against an emendation which on other
grounds is convincing. Experience of
the vagaries of compositors, modern as
well as Elizabethan, makes one
progressively surer that no blunder is
" impossible "—a word, I think, too
readily used in dismissing an emendation on graphical grounds. And I
have little doubt that *Automne* is what
Shakespeare wrote. [R]

88-90. *his delights . . . in*] This
seems to mean that not even the sea
of pleasure in which he lived could
conceal the strength and greatness of
the man, which his very pastimes displayed. Delius explains that Antony
was not submerged in his pleasures,
but knew how to keep himself always
above them. By reading *their back*
for *his back* Hanmer made the delights
into consistent dolphins but spoiled
the sense. With the image, Steevens
compares a poem [" Being Absent
from his Mistresse," etc.] from Lodge's
William Longbeard, 1593 (see *Glaucus*

and Scylla, etc., Chiswick Press, 1819,
p. 115):—
> " Oh, faire of fairest, dolphin-like,
> Within the riuers of my plaint,
> With labouring finnes the waue
> I strike," etc.

In the explanation of the frontispiece
to a work on the " Law of Drinking," quoted in Braithwaite's *Barnabee's Journal* (ed. Hazlitt, 1876, pp.
44, 45 *note*), occurs : " Next adjoyning
stands the signe of the Dolphin with a
bush and upon the signe this impreze,
TEMULENTIS LÆTOR IN UNDIS."

91. *crownets*] coronets, as in IV. xii.
27 *ante*, q.v. Crowns and crownets
are put for their wearers, as often
drum for drummer and the like.

92. *plates*] silver coins or pieces, a
sense derived from the Spanish form
(*plata*) of *plate*. Cf. *Christmas Carols*,
from a collection " probably printed
between 1546 and 1552 " (*Bibliographical Miscellanies*, Oxford, 1813,
p. 51:—
> " For .xxx. *plates* of money
> His mayster had he solde," etc.

Steevens quotes Marlowe, *Jew of
Malta*, line 865 :—
> " What, can he steale that you de-
> mand so much?
> Belike he has some new tricke for
> a purse
> And if he has, he is worth 300
> *plats*."

And again, immediately after :—
> " Ratest thou this Moore but at
> 200 *plats*?"

The Spanish original reappears in
Tom Cringle's Log, 1834, chap. xiii :
" and last of all we got two live land-
crabs from the servants, by dint of
persuasion and a little *plata*, and
clapped one into each stocking foot."

Cleo. Think you there was, or might be such a man
  As this I dreamt of?
Dol.   Gentle madam, no.
Cleo. You lie up to the hearing of the gods.   95
  But if there be, or ever were one such,
  It's past the size of dreaming: nature wants stuff
  To vie strange forms with fancy, yet to imagine
  An Antony were nature's piece, 'gainst fancy,
  Condemning shadows quite.
Dol.   Hear me, good madam:
  Your loss is as yourself, great; and you bear it 101
  As answering to the weight: would I might never
  O'ertake pursued success, but I do feel,
  By the rebound of yours, a grief that smites
  My very heart at root.

---

96. *or*] F 3; *nor* F, F 2.   104. *smites*] Capell; *suites* F; *shoots* Pope.

---

96. *or*] Mr. Thiselton thinks *nor* of F, F 2 " has been unwarrantably changed to *or*, owing to its being overlooked that this line is in direct contrast with the preceding, and that *nor* implies an ellipsis of *neither* or *not*." " Cleopatra would ask," he says, ' But assuming for the moment you are right how came I to dream of such a one? ' " This is ingenious, but Shakespeare's ellipses of *neither* are always unmistakable and cause no ambiguity.

97. *It's past . . . dreaming*] No dream can come up to the reality. The thought is not unlike *Othello*, II. i. 63-65 (F as usually emended):—
 " One that excels the quirks of blazoning pens,
 And in the essential vesture of creation
 Does tire the ingener."
Cf. " size of words," *T. of A.* v. i. 71.

98. *To vie . . . fancy*] To compete with fancy in the creation of strange forms. " To vie " in gaming was to stake or counter-stake, originally (see Skeat, *Etymol. Dict.*) " to draw on or invite a game " by staking a sum, *vie* and *invite* being different forms of one

original. Cf. *T. of S.* II. i. 303, and *Swetnam the Woman Hater*, 1620, IV. iii, where the tying of Misogynus to a post and pricking him with pins is jocularly treated as a game of Post and Pair : " *Scold.* First, stake. *Mis.* Oh, oh, oh, oh. . . . *Aur.* Againe, for me too, I will *vye* it " : also Braithwaite, *Strappado for the Diuell*, 1615 (reprint 1878), p. 146 :—
 " from his eyes
 Her teares by his finde their renew'd supplies,
 Both *vie* as for a wager, which to winne," etc.

99, 100. *were nature's piece . . . quite*] would be a masterpiece of conception which would entirely discredit the unsubstantial creations of fancy. For *piece*, see on III ii. 28 *ante*, and cf. Mabbe, *Celestina*, 1631, IV. (Tudor Trans. p. 97) : " Not a woman that sees him, but praiseth Nature's workemanship, whose hand did draw so perfect a *piece* " ; etc.

102, 103. *would I might . . . but I do*] may I never achieve my aim if I do not . . .

104. *smites*] Pope's reading (shoots), which Malone and Boswell adopt,

Cleo.   I thank you, sir: 105
　 Know you what Cæsar means to do with me?
Dol. I am loath to tell you what, I would you knew.
Cleo. Nay, pray you, sir,—
Dol.   Though he be honourable,—
Cleo. He'll lead me then in triumph.
Dol. Madam, he will, I know 't.   110
[*Flourish and shout within,* " Make way there: Cæsar! "

　　　 Enter Proculeius, Cæsar, Gallus, Mæcenas, *and
　　　　　　　 others of his Train.*

Cæs. Which is the Queen of Egypt?
Dol. It is the emperor, madam.   [*Cleopatra kneels.*
Cæs. Arise, you shall not kneel:
　 I pray you, rise, rise, Egypt.
Cleo.   Sir, the gods
　 Will have it thus, my master and my lord   115
　 I must obey.

---

109. *triumph.*] F; *triumph?* Pope 110.　　110. S.D.s]   See note.

relying on the once similar pronunciation of *suits* and *shoots,* is further supported by Mr. Thiselton's reference
to *Coriolanus,* v. i. 45 : " grief-shot
With his unkindness." But it does
not agree with " at root," as *smites*
does, † and also produces an impossible assonance. [R]   Cf. *smites me,*
line 170 *post.*

110-11. Enter *Proculeius,* etc] With
what follows, down to line 189, cf.
North, *post,* p. 283.

S.D.s] † F reads here as follows:—
Dol. Madam, he will, I know't.
　　　　　　　　　　　 Flourish.
*Enter Proculeius, Cæsar, Gallus,
Mecenas, and others of his Traine.*
All. Make way there *Cæsar.*
This is all puzzling.   In the first
place, one feels that the " Make
way " must surely precede Cæsar's
entry.   And in the second place
what is Proculeius doing apparently
leading the procession?   The usual
modern method of dealing with it has
been to have a " shout within "

along with the flourish, and to demote
Proculeius to a humbler place.
This will serve, and perhaps gives the
modern reader (and producer) as
near as we can get to what was intended. But it is not wholly satisfying,
and one or two observations fall to be
made. First, on the Elizabethan stage
the " Make way " would need to
precede Cæsar's appearance at the
entrance door by very little, if at all.
He still has to make his way some
distance down stage, and a certain
amount of noise and bustle would not
be amiss. Second, the guard have
presumably, from the time of Cleopatra's capture, been lining the back
of the stage, guarding the exits, and it
is they who have to make way. Is it
possible that Proculeius does in fact
enter first, perhaps with a few soldiers,
as a kind of advance party, and that
the " Make way " comes from the
guard, clearing the doors under his
instructions, and not from " voices
off "? [R]

S

Cæs.   Take to you no hard thoughts;
    The record of what injuries you did us,
    Though written in our flesh, we shall remember
    As things but done by chance.
Cleo.   Sole sir o' the world,
    I cannot project mine own cause so well   120
    To make it clear, but do confess I have
    Been laden with like frailties, which before
    Have often sham'd our sex.
Cæs.   Cleopatra, know,
    We will extenuate rather than enforce:
    If you apply yourself to our intents,   125
    Which towards you are most gentle, you shall find
    A benefit in this change, but if you seek
    To lay on me a cruelty, by taking
    Antony's course, you shall bereave yourself
    Of my good purposes, and put your children   130
    To that destruction which I'll guard them from,
    If thereon you rely.   I'll take my leave.
Cleo. And may through all the world: 'tis yours, and we
    Your scutcheons, and your signs of conquest shall
    Hang in what place you please.   Here, my good lord.

120. *project*] frame or set forth. The projector of Shakespeare's day was the promoter of ours, one who framed or planned a scheme and set it forth to the best advantage.   The extension of the sense from *plan* to *set forth* seems, therefore, natural, but I have not met with another example of the latter. The former is common.   Cf. Nabbes, *Covent Garden*, IV. iii (*Works*, Bullen, i. 67): "A countrey Gentleman to sell his land, is as it were to change his copie : leave his knowne trade to *project* a better profit "; and Quarles, *Argalus and Parthenia*, book i. (ed. 1701, p. 14):—
    " *Projects* and casts about which way to find
        The progress of young Parthenia's heart."
121. *clear*] clear of blame.
124. *enforce*] press home, emphasize

[frailties].   Cf. II. ii. 99 *ante* ; and *J.C.* III. ii. 42: "his glory not extenuated, wherein he was worthy, nor his offences *enforced*, for which he suffered death."

125. *If . . . intents*] If you conform yourself to my intentions, fall in with my designs.

133. *And may . . . world*] As Delius remarks, Cleopatra takes *leave* in a wider sense than Octavius.   She tells him that liberty to do his will is now his without restriction of place ; or, perhaps, says, as Deighton puts it : "the whole world is yours and therefore you are free to go through it from end to end."

134. *scutcheons*] shields, or representations of them, showing the armorial bearings.   Cf. *1 H. IV.* v. i. 142: "Honour is a mere *scutcheon* "; *L.L.L.* v. ii. 565.

Cæs. You shall advise me in all for Cleopatra.   136

Cleo. [*handing a paper.*] This is the brief: of money, plate, and jewels,
    I am possess'd of, 'tis exactly valued,
    Not petty things admitted.   Where's Seleucus?

Enter SELEUCUS.

Sel. Here, madam.   140

Cleo. This is my treasurer, let him speak, my lord,
    Upon his peril, that I have reserv'd
    To myself nothing.   Speak the truth, Seleucus.

Sel. Madam,
    I had rather seel my lips, than to my peril   145
    Speak that which is not.

---

145. *seel*] F (*seele*), Johnson, and some others; *seal* F 3 (*seale*) and most edd.

137. S.D.] † Craig added the useful " *Giving a scroll* " at this point, Dover Wilson " *she proffers a paper* " two lines earlier. I think Craig is right. " Here, my good lord " is said as Cleopatra gets ready to hand the paper, and Cæsar's line, which has nothing to do with the paper but is an anticipation of lines 185-6, really interrupts continuous speech and action on her part. [R]

brief] concise list, schedule. See *M.N.D.* v. i. 42 : " There is a *brief* how many sports are ripe," etc. Also in sense of *abstract* or *summary*, as in *Edward III.* II. i. 82:—
" Whose body as an abstract or a *brief*,
    Contains each general virtue in the world " ;
Jonson, *A Tale of a Tub*, v. ii. 52 : " Give me the *brief* of your subject."

139. *admitted*] Because Cleopatra immediately calls Seleucus to witness that she has reserved nothing, Theobald reads, " Not petty things *omitted* " ; " for this declaration," he says, " lays open her falsehood ; and makes her angry when her treasurer detects her in a direct lie." But her anger, as Johnson observes, is because

" she is accused of having reserved more than petty things." Warburton, Hanmer, and Capell read as Theobald.

Enter *Seleucus*] † Capell, followed by most editors since, brought on Seleucus in Cæsar's train at line 110. But what is he doing there? And if he had already gone over to Cæsar why does Cleopatra here explain who he is? For the episode which follows, see p. 283. [R]

145. *seel*] † *seel* in its technical sense is to close a hawk's eyelid by a stitch. I see no reason for deserting F, and some for retaining it.   (i) Out of the seventy-one occurrences in Shakespeare of *seal* (verb or noun), in the ordinary sense or a metaphorical sense derived from it, there is not a single instance of the spelling with *ee* (apart from one misprint *steale* and one *seal* it appears always as *seale* or *Seale*), and the same is true of the twenty-six occurrences of the past participle. It seems a gratuitous assumption that this is the one instance of error out of 100.   (ii) The emendation (for it is an emendation, and not, as the above count shows, merely a matter of accepting one of

Cleo.   What have I kept back?
Sel. Enough to purchase what you have made known.
Cæs. Nay, blush not, Cleopatra, I approve
        Your wisdom in the deed.
Cleo.   See, Cæsar! O behold,
How pomp is follow'd! mine will now be yours,   150
And should we shift estates, yours would be mine.
The ingratitude of this Seleucus does
Even make me wild.   O slave, of no more trust
Than love that's hir'd?   What, goest thou back?
        thou shalt
Go back, I warrant thee: but I'll catch thine eyes   155
Though they had wings.   Slave, soulless villain, dog!
O rarely base!
Cæs.   Good queen, let us entreat you.
Cleo. O Cæsar, what a wounding shame is this,
That thou vouchsafing here to visit me,
Doing the honour of thy lordliness   160
To one so meek, that mine own servant should
Parcel the sum of my disgraces, by

---

156. *soulless villain*] Pope (*soul-less*); *Soule-lesse, Villain* F.

two spellings commonly confused) is usually supported by the statement that *seel* is used only of the eyes. This statement—unless it means that the word in its technical sense is only so used, which is so obvious as to be hardly worth stating—is just not true. Of the four occurrences of *seele* or *seeling* in F three have to do with the eyes, but in the fourth, *Othello*, I. iii. 270, the speculative and offic'd instrument which (if we accept F rather than Q as giving us Shakespeare's word) is to be *seelcd* is much more than the eyes.   And in any case if we are going to confine Shakespeare's metaphorical use of a word to the limits of its everyday use we are going to find ourselves in deep waters. (iii) In the matter of appropriateness to the context, *seal* makes Seleucus say, in effect, " I would rather keep my mouth shut than tell lies," a

sufficiently vapid remark, whereas *seel* allows him to say " I would rather submit to a painful operation than tell lies ". [R]
   150. *mine*, i.e. my followers.
   154-156. *What, goest thou back? thou shalt*, etc.] Said as Seleucus recoils before Cleopatra's threatening advance.
   156. *soulless villain*] †F's *Soule-lesse, Villain*, can no doubt be defended, but it seems to weaken the crescendo of invective from a creature despicable but still human, through something barely human, to something not human at all. [R]
   161, *meek*] Malone: " tame, subdued by adversity . . . Cleopatra, in any other sense, was not eminent for meekness."
   162, 163. *Parcel . . . envy*] O.E.D. observes that the verb here has not been satisfactorily explained, and

Addition of his envy.   Say, good Cæsar,
That I some lady trifles have reserv'd,
Immoment toys, things of such dignity   165
As we greet modern friends withal, and say
Some nobler token I have kept apart
For Livia and Octavia, to induce
Their mediation, must I be unfolded
With one that I have bred?   The gods! it smites me   170
Beneath the fall I have.   [*To Seleucus*] Prithee go hence,
Or I shall show the cinders of my spirits

171. To Seleucus] Johnson;   not in F.

cites the versions of Johnson " (To
make up into a mass ") and Schmidt
(" To enumerate by items, specify ").
Johnson does not explain how he
takes *addition*, on which much depends
and, in any case, if *parcel* means what
he says, *sum* is rather unnecessary.
Schmidt, like Delius, takes *addition* as
" the summing up of numbers,"
which suits his sense of *parcel* and
yields, practically, " reckons up my
disgraces by his malicious adding up
or counting."   But Seleucus had not
done this : what he did was to increase the number of disgraces by one
more, a sense at least met by Malone
—whom most editors follow—with
" add one more parcel or *item* to the
sum of my disgraces, namely, his own
malice."   The difficulty is the doubtful possibility of Malone's interpretation of " parcel by addition."   After
the morris dance in Nashe's *Summer's
Last Will* (III. p. 240, line 209) Ver
says : " May it please my lord, this
is the grand capitall summe : but
there are certayne parcels behind, as
you shall see," to which *Summer*
rejoins : " Nay, nay, no more : for
this is all too much."   The participle
parcell'd occurs in *R. III.* II. ii. 81, but
in sense, distributed, severally assigned : " Their woes are parcell'd,
mine are general."

† Since *piece* can mean " piece out,"
extend by adding pieces, as in II. xi.
45, *ante*, may not *parcel* mean " extend

by adding ' parcels,' " i.e. extra
items? [R]

165. *Immoment*] Of no moment or
consequence.   No other example of
the word is known.

166. *modern*] ordinary, common.
Cf. *Othello*, I. iii. 109 ; *Macbeth*, IV. iii.
170 :—
> " where violent sorrow seems
>   A *modern* ecstasy."

See also Jonson, *The Poetaster*, v.
iii. 280: " Alas! that were no *modern*
consequence," etc., and *A.Y.L.* II.
vii. 156, *modern* instances."   The
present-day sense was also in use.
It is probably the sense in Marston's
Scourge of Villanie, ix. 45 : " O what a
tricksie, lerned, nicking strain Is this
applauded, senseless, *modern* vain " ;
and certainly in *Jack Drum's Entertainment*, 1601, iv. 37 (*School of Shakspere*,
1878, II. 183) : " Brother, how like you
of our *modern* wits?   How like you
the new Poet *Mellidus?* "   In the
same play, IV. 100 (*ibid.* 185) : " Indeed
I yeeld, 'tis *moderne* policie, To kisse
euen durt that plaisters vp our
wants," the sense is as likely, or more
so, to be " common."

168. *Livia*] Cæsar's wife.

169, 170. *unfolded With*] exposed by.
Unfold has a similar sense in *Othello*,
IV. ii. 141 : v. i. 21.   For *with* = by,
see *The Winter's Tale*, v. i. 113 ; v.
ii. 68 *Lear*, II. iv. 308, etc.

172, 173. *cinders . . . chance*] The
metaphor from fire concealed under

Through the ashes of my chance: wert thou a man,
Thou wouldst have mercy on me.

Cæs.   Forbear, Seleucus.

                                        [*Exit Seleucus.*

Cleo. Be it known, that we, the greatest, are misthought
        For things that others do; and when we fall,   176
        We answer others' merits in our name,
        Are therefore to be pitied.

---

174. Exit . . .] Capell; not in F.
merits, in our name F.

177. *merits in our name,*] Johnson;

---

ashes is very frequent. See ii. ii. 13
ante ; Sidney's *Arcadia*, ii. (1725 ed.
i, p. 202) : " so truly the cold ashes
laid upon my fire, did not take the
nature of fire from it. Full often
hath my breast swollen with keeping
my sighs imprisoned," etc. ; R.
Tailor's *The Hog hath lost his Pearle*, i. i.
(Hazlitt's *Dodsley*, xi. 431) :—

" I am that spark, sir, though now
      raked up in ashes ;
    Yet when it pleaseth fortune's
      chaps to blow
Some gentler gale upon me, I may
      then
    From forth of embers rise and
      shine again."

Jonson uses it very nobly in *Sejanus*,
i. 97-101. Cleopatra says that the
fires of her nature are within an ace
of showing that they are not utterly
overwhelmed by the ashes to which
her power and prosperity (see on
chance, iii. x. 36 *ante*) have been
reduced ; in plain English, that her
misfortunes have not subdued her
past a dangerous resentment. Dr.
Hudson, however, adopts *spirit* (S.
Walker conj. and Collier MS.) for
spirits (used iii. xiii. 69 *ante*)—an unnecessary change—and Dr. Ingleby's
" correction " (*Shakespeare Hermeneu-
tics*, 1875, p. 158) of *glance* for *chance*,
on the ground that " neither *my
chance*, nor *mischance* [Hanmer], nor
my change [S. Walker conj.], appears to answer the occasion or the

speaker's mood : we seem," he says,
" to need some word referring directly
to Cleopatra's own person or personal
appearance." Why?

174. *Forbear*] equivalent to " withdraw." Cf. *Forbear me*, i. ii. 118 *ante*.

175. *misthought*] misjudged. Cf.
3 H. VI. ii. v. 107 : " How will the
country . . . *Misthink* the king and
not be satisfied!"

177. *We answer . . . name*] We
answer (are accountable) in our own
names for the demerits (or misdeeds)
of others. Cf. *Stukeley*, line 1126
(Simpson's *School of Shakspere*, i.
204) : " No sir I will not, and will
answer it." The observation is general,
or Cleopatra has forgotten that she has
practically acknowledged the particular delinquency. Delius separates
" in our name " from " answer,"
and makes " others' merits in our
name " = what others have misdone
in our name; but the connection
with " answer " is too probable to be
lightly dismissed, admitting this ex-
pansion to be possible, *Merits* and
demerits were used interchangeably.
Cf. Braithwaite, *Strappado for the
Diuell*, 1615 (reprint 1878, p. 174) :—

" That those which wil not labour
      they should sterue,
    For rightly so their *merits* do
      deserue," etc.,

with *Coriolanus*, i. i. 277 : " Opinion
. . . shall Of his *demerits* rob Comin-
ius," and *Othello*, i. ii. 22.

Cæs.   Cleopatra,
Not what you have reserv'd, nor what acknowledg'd,
Put we i' the roll of conquest: still be 't yours,   180
Bestow it at your pleasure, and believe
Cæsar's no merchant, to make prize with you
Of things that merchants sold.   Therefore be cheer'd,
Make not your thoughts your prisons: no, dear queen,
For we intend so to dispose you, as   185
Yourself shall give us counsel: feed, and sleep:
Our care and pity is so much upon you,
That we remain your friend, and so adieu.

Cleo. My master, and my lord!
Cæs.   Not so: adieu.
            [*Flourish.   Exeunt Cæsar and his Train.*
Cleo. He words me, girls, he words me, that I should not   190
Be noble to myself.   But hark thee Charmian.
                              [*Whispers Charmian.*
Iras. Finish, good lady, the bright day is done,
And we are for the dark.
Cleo.   Hie thee again,
I have spoke already, and it is provided,
Go put it to the haste.
Char.   Madam, I will.   195

191. Whispers . . .] Theobald; not in F.

182. *make prize with you*] This usually escapes comment, but Deighton explains " with you " as " together with you," quoting *R. III.* III. vii. 184: " widow . . . Made *prize* and purchase of his wanton eye." Schmidt, however, explains *prize* as *estimation*, quoting *Cymbeline*, III. vi. 76, *Lear*, II. i. 122, leaving us to speculate whether he takes " make," etc., as make estimation " like you " (as Deighton understands him), *or* (referring to the goods), in the same category with you, *or*, finally, make estimation along with you, i.e. enter into the question of reservations with you (" whether 'tis exactly valued, Not petty things admitted "), a tempting sense if *prize* can really equal estimation in the sense of valuation.

† But prize can also mean a contest—see *M. of V.* III. ii. 142, " Like one of two contending in a prize," and though *O.E.D.* does not give an example of " make prize " = " engage in a contest " it seems a quite possible phrase, and is certainly the natural sense here required, " to haggle ". [R]

184. *Make not . . . prisons*] Johnson : " Be not a prisoner in imagination, when in reality you are free." Cf. Bacon, *Device on the Queen's Day* (1595), " The Hermit's Speech in the Presence " ; " there is no *prison* to the *prison* of the thoughts, which are free under the greatest tyrants."

195. *the haste*] Cf. *i' the haste* for " in great haste " (*Lear*, II. i. 26).

Re-enter DOLABELLA.

Dol. Where's the queen?
Char.   Behold, sir.   [*Exit.*
Cleo.   Dolabella!
Dol. Madam, as thereto sworn, by your command
    (Which my love makes religion to obey),
    I tell you this: Cæsar through Syria
    Intends his journey, and within three days   200
    You with your children will he send before:
    Make your best use of this.   I have perform'd
    Your pleasure, and my promise.
Cleo.   Dolabella,
    I shall remain your debtor.
Dol.   I your servant.
    Adieu, good queen, I must attend on Cæsar.   205
Cleo. Farewell, and thanks.   [*Exit Dolabella.*
                    Now, Iras, what think'st thou?
    Thou, an Egyptian puppet shall be shown
    In Rome as well as I: mechanic slaves
    With greasy aprons, rules, and hammers shall

---

196. Exit] not in F; Exit Charmian placed here by Capell, line 195
Theobald.   206. Exit . . .] Capell; Exit. F, after *Cæsar.*   207. shall] F;
shalt F 2 and edd.

196-206. *Dolabella!* . . .] Cf.
North, *post*, pp. 283-4.
  196. Exit] † another example of
Elizabethan exit, not easy to indicate,
as the discrepancy between Theobald
and Capell interestingly shows.
Charmian begins to move off on
Madam, I will, and meets Dolabella
on her way to the door. [R]
  207. *an Egyptian puppet*] An allusion
to the innumerable puppet shows of
the time, which drew their subjects
from contemporary events, as well as
popular plays, and history, sacred and
profane. See Jonson, *Bartholomew
Fair,* v. i. 6: "O the motions, that I
Lanthorn Leatherhead have given
light to, in my time, since my Master
Pod died! Jerusalem was a stately
thing ; and so was Nineveh, and the

City of Norwich, and Sodom and Go-
morrah ; with the rising of the pren-
tices ; and pulling down the bawdy-
houses there, upon Shrove-Tuesday ;
but the *Gunpowder-plot,* there was a
get-penny!" etc.   With what follows,
cf. IV. xii. 33 *et seq.* and v. ii. 55-57
ante.
  209. *rules*] Instruments for ruling
straight lines, and measuring short
lengths, used by carpenters, etc. Cf.
J.C I. i. 7: " Where is thy leather
apron and thy *rule?* " and Sylvester's
Du Bartas, *The Magnificence,* 1621 ed.
p. 447 :—

  " Where e'r she [Wisdom] go, she
      never goes without
  Compasse and *Rule,* Measure and
      weights about."

Uplift us to the view. In their thick breaths,   210
Rank of gross diet, shall we be enclouded,
And forc'd to drink their vapour.

Iras.   The gods forbid!

Cleo. Nay, 'tis most certain, Iras: saucy lictors
Will catch at us like strumpets, and scald rhymers
Ballad us out o' tune. The quick comedians   215
Extemporally will stage us, and present
Our Alexandrian revels: Antony
Shall be brought drunken forth, and I shall see
Some squeaking Cleopatra boy my greatness
I' the posture of a whore.

Iras.   O the good gods!   220

Cleo. Nay, that's certain.

---

215. *Ballad*] F 2; *Ballads* F.   *o'* Theobald; *a* F.   219. *squeaking Cleopatra boy*] F (*Boy*); *speaking-Cleopatra-Boy* F 2.

212. *drink*] inhale. Cf. Jonson, *E.M.I.* III. v. 137: "The most divine tobacco that ever I drunk", or (in case that suggests a Robinson Crusoe decoction), Purchas, *Pilgrimage*, IX. i. 820, "after they have drunke the smoke of a certain herbe."

213. *lictors*] As Dover Wilson points out, Shakespeare is probably equating lictors with beadles, who officially dealt with strumpets, cf. *Lear*, IV. vi. 166.

214. *scald*] scabbed, scurvy. So in *Henry V*. v. i. 5: "the rascally, *scald*, beggarly, lousy, pragging knave, Pistol," etc.

215. *Ballad us*] Cf. *Andromana*, v. ii (Hazlitt's *Dodsley*, xiv. 267):—

"I shall be grown discourse for grooms and footboys,
  Be *balladed*, and sung to filthy tunes."

Massinger deplores the plague of ballads at the end of *The Bondman*, in a longer passage containing these lines:

"Let but a chapel fall, or a street be fired,
A foolish lover hang himself for pure love,

Or any such like accident, and, before
They are cold in their graves, some damn'd ditty's made," etc.

quick] Malone: "lively, inventive, quick-witted," for Johnson's "gay inventive."

216. *stage us, and present*] So Jonson, *Poetaster*, III. iv. 197: "I hear you'll bring me o' the *stage* there; you'll play me, they say; I shall be presented by a sort of copper-laced scoundrels of you: life of Pluto! an you *stage* me, stinkard," etc.

219. *boy*] English, unlike Continental practice, confined female parts to boys or young men on public stages, till a clause in the patent granted to D'Avenant in Jan. 1662-63 provided: "That, whereas the women's parts in plays have hitherto been acted by men in the habits of women, at which some have taken offence, we permit and give leave for the time to come, that all women's parts be acted by women." See D'Avenant, *Works*, 1872, I. lxvii (*Prefatory Memoir*). In 1656, he had already experimented by giving the part of Ianthe in his musical piece, *The Siege of Rhodes*, to Mrs. Coleman. See *ibid.* lxiv.

Iras. I'll never see't! for I am sure my nails
    Are stronger than mine eyes.
Cleo.   Why, that's the way
    To fool their preparation, and to conquer
    Their most absurd intents.

Re-enter CHARMIAN.

                         Now, Charmian!   225
Show me, my women, like a queen: go fetch
My best attires.   I am again for Cydnus,
To meet Mark Antony.   Sirrah Iras, go
(Now noble Charmian, we'll dispatch indeed),
And when thou hast done this chare, I'll give thee
    leave   230
To play till doomsday: bring our crown, and all.

          [*Exeunt Charmian and Iras.   A noise within.*
Wherefore's this noise?

Enter a Guardsman.

Guard.   Here is a rural fellow,
    That will not be denied your highness' presence,
    He brings you figs.
Cleo. Let him come in.   [*Exit Guardsman.*

---

222. *my*] F 2; *mine* F.   224. *to conquer* F; *conquer* F 2.   225. *absurd*] F;
assur'd Theobald; *abhorr'd* Kinnear; *obscene* D. Wilson conj.   228, 229.
go (*Now . . . indeed,*)] F; Rowe removed parentheses.   231. S.D.]
F has no exit; Exit Iras. Malone; Exit Iras. Charmian falls to adjusting
Cleopatra's Dress. Noise within. Capell. See Appendix IV.

---

225. *absurd*] †Why this desire for emendation? *Absurd* is surely triumphantly proleptic, "the intents that I am going to make look silly"; cf. *ass, unpolicied* in lines 306, 7. [R]

227. *I . . . Cydnus*] See II. ii. 187 *et. seq., ante.*

228. *sirrah*] Women were often addressed thus. Cf. *Ralph Roister Doister*, IV. viii. 2: "Ah sirrha now, Custance," etc. Philippa calls Violetta *sirrah* in Middleton's *The Widow*,

III. ii. 28. See also on IV. xv. 85 *ante*, and examples in Pearson's *Dekker*, ii. 383, illustrating *Westward Hoe*, p. 292.

230. *chare*] See on IV. xv. 75 *ante*, and cf. *Sir Thomas More* (Shakes. Society 1844, p. 37): "This *charre* being charde, then all our debt is payd."

S.D. Exeunt] See Appendix IV.

232. etc. *Here . . . rural fellow . . .*] See North *post*, p. 284.

> What poor an instrument   235
May do a noble deed! he brings me liberty:
My resolution's plac'd, and I have nothing
Of woman in me: now from head to foot
I am marble-constant: now the fleeting moon
No planet is of mine.

Re-enter Guardsman, with Clown bringing in a basket.

Guard.   This is the man.   240
Cleo. Avoid, and leave him.   [*Exit Guardsman.*
Hast thou the pretty worm of Nilus there,
That kills and pains not?
Clown. Truly I have him: but I would not be the party
that should desire you to touch him, for his biting is 245
immortal: those that do die of it, do seldom or
never recover.
Cleo. Remember'st thou any that have died on 't?
Clown. Very many, men and women too. I heard of
one of them no longer than yesterday, a very 250
honest woman, but something given to lie, as a
woman should not do, but in the way of honesty,
how she died of the biting of it, what pain she felt:
truly, she makes a very good report o' the worm:
but he that will believe all that they say, shall 255

---

235. *What*] F; *How* F 2.   239. *marble-constant*] hyphened by Capell.
240. Re-enter . . .] Globe; Enter Guardsman, and Clowne. F; with a
Basket. added by Rowe.

235. *What poor an instrument*] Abbot
(*Shakes. Gram.* § 422) treating of transposition of the article, observes on this
passage that " we can say ' how poor
an instrument,' regarding ' how ' as
an adverb, and ' how poor ' as an ad-
verbialised expression, but not ' what
poor an instrument,' because ' what '
has almost lost with us its adverbial
force."

239. *marble-constant*] Philoclea, in
Sidney's *Arcadia*, bk. ii, inscribed her
vows of chastity on marble ; but sub-
sequently blaming her love for
Zelmane, composed other verses to
subjoin to the former, confessing
" how ill agree in one, A woman's
hand with *constant marble* stone."

fleeting moon] As at III. xiii. 153,
154 *q.v.*, Capell thinks that Cleopatra's imitation of the goddess Isis,
the moon goddess, is alluded to. The
suggestion here is originally Warburton's.

242. *worm*] snake ; an old and common sense. So in *Cymbeline*, III. iv.
37 ; " outvenoms all the *worms* of
Nile "; Jonson, *Sejanus*, v. 47 : " T'express a *worm*, a snake!"

249. *of*] from.

never be saved by half that they do: but this is
most falliable, the worm's an odd worm.

Cleo. Get thee hence, farewell.

Clown. I wish you all joy of the worm.

[Setting down his basket.

Cleo. Farewell.   260

Clown. You must think this, look you, that the worm
will do his kind.

Cleo. Ay, ay, farewell.

Clown. Look you, the worm is not to be trusted, but in
the keeping of wise people: for indeed, there is no 265
goodness in the worm.

Cleo. Take thou no care, it shall be heeded.

Clown. Very good: give it nothing, I pray you, for it is
not worth the feeding.

Cleo. Will it eat me?   270

Clown. You must not think I am so simple but I know
the devil himself will not eat a woman: I know,
that a woman is a dish for the gods, if the devil
dress her not. But truly, these same whoreson
devils do the gods great harm in their women: for 275
in every ten that they make, the devils mar five.

Cleo. Well, get thee gone, farewell.

Clown. Yes, forsooth: I wish you joy o' the worm.   [*Exit.*

Re-enter CHARMIAN *and* IRAS *with a robe, crown, and
other jewels.*

Cleo. Give me my robe, put on my crown, I have

---

257. *falliable*] F; *fallible* F 2 and edd.   259. Setting . . .] Capell; not
in F.   278. (S.D.) Re-enter . . . jewels] no S.D. in F; Re-enter Iras with
a robe, crown, etc. Malone, followed by most other edd.   See Appendix IV.

257. *falliable*] Editors read *fallible*
with F 2, but the odd form may be as
intentional as the positions of *all* and
half in the preceding clause, which
Warburton wished to transpose. Cf.
infalliable in Kirk, *Secret Commonwealth*, etc., 1691, ed. Lang, 1893,
p. 48; and, in general, the grave-
diggers in *Hamlet*.
    262. *his kind*] what his nature dic-
tates. Cf. "the deed of *kind*"

(*M. of V.* i. iii. 86); Jonson, *The
New Inn*, iii. ii. 250: " She did her
kind, according to her latitude ";
Fuller, *The Profane State*, v. xviii,
1648, p. 477: " Diseases do but their
kind, if they kill, and an evil expected,
is the lesse evil: but no such Torment
as to die of the remedie," etc.
    278. (S.D.). See Appendix IV.
    279. *robe, . . . crown*] Compare
North, *post*, p. 285.

Immortal longings in me.　Now no more　　280
The juice of Egypt's grape shall moist this lip.
Yare, yare, good Iras; quick: methinks I hear
Antony call.　I see him rouse himself
To praise my noble act.　I hear him mock
The luck of Cæsar, which the gods give men　　285
To excuse their after wrath.　Husband, I come:
Now to that name, my courage prove my title!
I am fire, and air; my other elements
I give to baser life.　So, have you done?
Come then, and take the last warmth of my lips.　290
Farewell, kind Charmian, Iras, long farewell.
　　　　　　　　[*Kisses them.　Iras falls and dies.*
Have I the aspic in my lips?　Dost fall?

291. Kisses . . .] Malone; Kissing them. Hanmer; Kissing them. Iras falls. Capell; not in F.

280. *Immortal longings*] longings for immortality.

282. *Yare, yare*] deftly.

286. *their after wrath*] nemesis, disaster sent to punish arrogance resulting from excessive good luck.

288. *my other elements*] i.e. earth and water, as man was thought to be composed of the four elements, whose relative proportions determined his character in each case. Cf. *Henry V.* III. vii. 22 of the Dauphin's horse : " he is pure air and fire ; and the dull *elements* of earth and water never appear in him "; *Twelfth Night*, II. iii. 10; *J.C.*, v. v. 73. There is a full discussion of the matter in Sylvester's *Du Bartas*, week 1, day 2, pp. 20-22 in 1621 ed., from which is :—

" For, in our Flesh, our Bodie's Earth remains:
　Our vitall spirits, our Fire and Aire possess:
　And last, our Water in our humours rests."

289. *I give . . . life*] According to Deighton, " I leave to be eaten by worms." I doubt the idea's being so definite. " Fire and air " are that part of Cleopatra which she supposes to escape through death to immortal life : her other elements she leaves with the *baser* conditions she is quitting, baser whether compared with the new life or with death, by which that is to be nobly attained. In my view it is simply life in a general sense, the abstract idea of life as opposed to death, that is implied.

291. *Charmian, Iras*] So the folio ; with the result in sound of slow, unbroken movement befitting farewells and in sense, of uniting both women in the long adieu. The usual separative pointing, *Charmian ; Iras,* gains nothing but a paltry contrast of the halves of the line.

292. *aspic*]. The form of the word used by North (see *post*, pp. 278, 285) and others. So in *Othello*, III. iii. 451.

Dost fall] Steevens : " Iras must be supposed to have applied an asp to her arm while her mistress was settling her dress, or I know not why she should fall so soon." I am rather inclined to agree with Delius that Iras is meant to die of grief at parting from her mistress. After all, the improbability is little, if any, greater than that connected with the death of Enobarbus.

If thou and nature can so gently part,
The stroke of death is as a lover's pinch,
Which hurts, and is desir'd.   Dost thou lie still?   295
If thus thou vanishest, thou tell'st the world
It is not worth leave-taking.
Char. Dissolve, thick cloud, and rain, that I may say,
The gods themselves do weep!
Cleo.   This proves me base :
If she first meet the curled Antony,   300
He'll make demand of her, and spend that kiss
Which is my heaven to have.   Come, thou mortal
    wretch,

        [*To an asp, which she applies to her breast.*
With thy sharp teeth this knot intrinsicate
Of life at once untie: poor venomous fool,
Be angry, and despatch.   O, couldst thou speak,   305
That I might hear thee call great Cæsar ass,
Unpolicied!

---

302. [To . . .] Capell (substantially); To the Serpent. Pope; not in F.
306, 307. *ass, Unpolicied*] F; most edd. omit comma.

† But Dover Wilson, I think
rightly, says that *This* in line 299
surely implies a self-sought death. [R]

300. *curled*] Probably she thinks of
Antony as she first saw him, " barber'd
ten times o'er " (II. ii. 224 *ante*), again
set off to the best advantage for this
meeting, as she herself will be (lines
226-228 *ante*) in " her best attires,"
" again for Cydnus, To meet Mark
Antony." Shakespeare alludes to the
fashion of his own day, as in *Othello*,
I. ii. 68 " The wealthy *curled* darlings
of our nation." Cf. Lyly, *Midas*,
III. ii. 40: " A lowe *curle* on your
head like a Bull or dangling lock like
a spaniel? . . . your love-lockes
wreathed with a silken twist, or
shaggie to fall on your shoulders?"

301. *He'll make demand . . . kiss*]
Johnson : " He will enquire of her
concerning me, and kiss her for giving him intelligence." (†A kindly
explanation ; but Shakespeare's Cleo-

patra knew her Antony better than
Johnson did. [R])

302. *mortal*] deadly. Similarly used
of a creature in 2 *H. VI.* III. ii. 263
(" The *mortal* worm "), and elsewhere
in Shakespeare.

wretch] merely = creature. Cf.
Othello, III. iii. 90 : " Excellent
wretch !"

303. *intrinsicate*] intricate. The
word, as has been pointed out, is
ridiculed as a " new-minted epithet "
in Marston's preface to his *Scourge of
Villanie*, 1598, and affectedly used by
Amorphus in Jonson's *Cynthia's Revels*
(in the 1616 folio additions), v. ii.
14 : " Yet there are certain *puntilioes*,
or (as I may more nakedly insinuate
them) certaine *intrinsecate* strokes, and
wardes, to which your actiuitie is not
yet amounted." See *Lear*, II. ii. 80,
for *intrinse* in same sense:
    " Such smiling rogues as these,
Like rats, oft bite the holy cords a-twain
Which are too intrinse to unloose."

Char.   O eastern star!

Cleo.   Peace, peace!

Dost thou not see my baby at my breast,

That sucks the nurse asleep?

Char.   O, break! O, break!

Cleo. As sweet as balm, as soft as air, as gentle.   310

O Antony! Nay, I will take thee too.

                           [Applying another asp to her arm.

What should I stay—   *[Dies.*

Char. In this vile world? So fare thee well.

Now boast thee, death, in thy possession lies

A lass unparallel'd. Downy windows, close,   315

And golden Phœbus, never be beheld

Of eyes again so royal! Your crown's awry,

I'll mend it, and then play.

---

311. Applying . . .] Theobald; not in F.   313. *vile*] Capell; *wilde* F.
317. *awry*] Rowe, ed. 3; *away* F.   318. *play.*] Capell; *play*—F.

308. *baby*] In Peele's *Edward I*, xvi. 20-26, the same idea occurs to Queen Elinor, when she cruelly kills the Mayoress by applying a serpent to her breast : " Why, so ; now she is a nurse.—Suck on, sweet *babe*." See also *Christ's Tears*, etc., 1593-94 (Grosart's *Nashe*, prose, iv, pp. 211, 212) : " At thy breasts (as at Cleopatraes) aspisses shall be put out to nurse."

311. [*Applying another . . . arm*] One aspic (biting the arm only, not the breast) is mentioned in Plutarch, though some Latin writers speak of two : see *post*, p. 285 ; and Sir T. Browne, *Vulgar and Common Errors*, v. xii, " Of the Picture describing the death of Cleopatra," speaking of the breast being indicated as the place in some writers, says : " But herein the mistake was easy, it being the custom in capital malefactors to apply them unto the breast ; as the author *De Theriaca ad Pisonem*, an eye-witness hereof in Alexandria, where Cleopatra died, determineth ; ' I beheld,' saith he, ' in Alexandria, how suddenly these ser-

pents bereave a man of life ; for when any one is condemned to this kind of death, if they intend to use him favourably, that is, to despatch him suddenly, they fasten an asp unto his breast, and bidding him walk about, he presently perisheth thereby.' " Halliwell (folio ed.) quotes this passage.

312. *What*] *Why*, as in *Lear*, II. iv. 264, 266.

313. *vile*] F *wilde* is probably a misprint of *vilde*, a very common form of *vile ;* but some editors retain *wild* = desert, savage. Cf. " *vilde* lady! " IV. xiv. 22 *ante*. Here I respect Capell's modernization.

315. *windows*] eyelids, as in *R. and J.*, IV. i. 100 : " thy eyes' *windows* fall"; *Cymbeline*, II. ii. 22, and elsewhere.

317. *awry*] †A few editors have attempted to justify F's *away*, Furness on the very strange grounds that *away* is " more smooth and liquid than the crooked, harsh " *awry* (a good example of the dangers of looking at a word instead of hearing it). But the emendation is graphically easy (the comparatively frequent

Enter the Guard, rustling in.

First Guard. Where's the queen?
Char.   Speak softly, wake her not.
First Guard. Cæsar hath sent—
Char.   Too slow a messenger.   320
                                          [*Applies an asp.*
  O, come apace, despatch, I partly feel thee.
First Guard. Approach ho, all's not well: Cæsar's beguil'd.
Sec. Guard. There's Dolabella sent from Cæsar; call him.
First Guard. What work is here, Charmian? Is this well
    done?
Char. It is well done, and fitting for a princess   325
    Descended of so many royal kings.
    Ah, soldier!   [*Dies.*

Re-enter DOLABELLA.

Dol. How goes it here?
Sec. Guard.   All dead.
Dol.   Cæsar, thy thoughts
    Touch their effects in this: thyself art coming
    To see perform'd the dreaded act which thou   330
    So sought'st to hinder.
                            [*Within* " A way there, a way for Cæsar!"

Enter CÆSAR *and all his Train, marching.*

Dol. O sir, you are too sure an augurer;
    That you did fear, is done.

---

319. *Where's*] F; *Where is* Hanmer.   320. Applies . . .] not in F;
Charmian and Iras apply the asp. Rowe.   324. *here, Charmian? Is*] *heere*
Charmian? *Is* F; *here?—Charmian, is* Capell and most edd.

a : r confusion), and I think that   duces a better rhythm, and, for what
Dover Wilson's apposite quotation   it is worth, a closer approximation to
from Daniel's *Cleopatra*, v. ii. 268-9,   North; but I am not clear that we
" in her sinking down shee wryes   are therefore justified in deserting F.
The Diadem " is decisive. [R]   [R]
  318. *play*] a touching reference to   327. S.D.] F brings Dolabella in
her mistress's words, line 231 *ante*.   with the guard at 318, as well as
  320 ad *fin.*] *Cæsar hath sent*—] See   giving him an entry here. Cf. III. x
North, *post*, pp. 284-5.   (S.D.).
  324. *What work* . . .] † Capell's   329. *Touch their effects*] Meet with
emendation, usually accepted, pro-   realization. Cf. *Lear*, IV. ii. 14.

Cæs.　　　　　　　　　　　　Bravest at the last,
　She levell'd at our purposes, and being royal
　Took her own way: the manner of their deaths?　335
　I do not see them bleed.
Dol.　　　　　　　　　　Who was last with them?
First Guard. A simple countryman, that brought her figs:
　This was his basket.
Cæs.　　　　　　　　　Poison'd then.
First Guard.　　　　　　　　　　O Cæsar;
　This Charmian lived but now, she stood and spake:
　I found her trimming up the diadem　　　　340
　On her dead mistress; tremblingly she stood,
　And on the sudden dropp'd.
Cæs.　　　　　　　　O noble weakness!
　If they had swallow'd poison, 'twould appear
　By external swelling: but she looks like sleep,
　As she would catch another Antony　　　345
　In her strong toil of grace.
Dol.　　　　　　　　　Here on her breast,
　There is a vent of blood, and something blown,
　The like is on her arm.
First Guard. This is an aspic's trail, and these fig-leaves

---

334. *levell'd at*] guessed correctly; a tropical sense from levelling a weapon to take aim, which also occurs in *M. of V.* i. ii. 41. It means *aimed at* in *Nobody and Somebody* (Simpson's *School of Shakspere*, i. 298): "My thoughts are *leveld* at a bloody end"; and for the concrete sense, cf. Sylvester's *Du Bartas*, ed. 1621, week 1, day 7, lines 22, 23: "A skilfull Gunner with his left eye winking, *Levels* directly at an oak hard by."

337. *simple*] of humble degree. Cf. *Lear*, IV. vi. 156: "yond *simple* thief."

344. *external swelling*] Cf. North, *post*, p. 285, and see on line 311 *ante*. There are many allusions to the painlessness of the death caused by asps; in Sylvester's Du Bartas, *The Lawe* (p. 350 in 1621 ed.), the absence of swelling is also noted:—

"So th' Aspick pale . . . doth spet
　.　　.　　.　　.　　.
A drowzy bane, that inly creeps,
　and burns
So secretly, that without sense of
　pain,
Scar, wound, or swelling, soon
　the Partie's slain."

347. *blown*] † This is usually explained as "swollen," which I find very hard to accept. No doubt *blown* can mean "swollen," but it does not appear to suit the context. It will be observed that the Guard does not say "*Here* is an aspic's trail," as though he was looking elsewhere about the room, but "*This* is," presumably referring to whatever Dolabella has discovered on breast and arm. I think therefore that *blown* must refer to something like the track of a snail. [R]

T

    Have slime upon them, such as the aspic leaves   350
    Upon the caves of Nile.

Cæs.   Most probable
    That so she died: for her physician tells me
    She hath pursued conclusions infinite
    Of easy ways to die.   Take up her bed,
    And bear her women from the monument;   355
    She shall be buried by her Antony.
    No grave upon the earth shall clip in it
    A pair so famous: high events as these
    Strike those that make them: and their story is
    No less in pity than his glory which   360
    Brought them to be lamented.   Our army shall
    In solemn show attend this funeral,
    And then to Rome.   Come, Dolabella, see
    High order, in this great solemnity.   *[Exeunt.*

---

351. *caves*] *caues* F; *canes* Barry conj.

351. *caves*]† Though I have not ventured to promote it to the text, I think Barry's emendation almost certain. No doubt there were caves by the Nile, and no doubt " aspics " may have left slime in them. But " upon the caves " is an odd expression for the natural " in the caves " or " upon the walls of the caves," whereas the parallel between the *canes* and the fig-leaves is appropriate. The misreading of *n* as *u* is easy. [R]

353. *conclusions*] experiments, as in *Hamlet*, III. iv. 195; *Cymbeline*, I. v. 18, etc. So Braithwaite, *His Odes*, 1621, No. 7, verse 6 :—

  " *These, conclusions* try on man,
    Surgeon and Physician," etc.

For the physician's information, cf. North, *post*, p. 278.

357. *clip*] clasp. See on IV. viii. 8 *ante*.

359. *Strike . . . make them*] Afflict those whose actions have caused them. A reflection corresponding with v. i. 36 *et seq.*, *ante*: " I have follow'd thee to this, . . . but yet let me lament," etc.

360, 361. *No less . . . lamented*] Apparently elliptical for: and the tale of these events is as pitiful as the renown of him who caused their lamentable nature is glorious. But in an uncritical perusal, the mind—and perhaps rightly after all—may refer *their* in *their story* to *A pair so famous*, and understand: and there is as much to pity in their story as glory for him who made them objects of pity.

APPENDIX 1

"An arm-gaunt steed" (i. v. 48).

In favour of *arm-gaunt*, or at least its first syllable, are (1) the frequent application to *horse* or *steed* of epithets from arms, as war-apparelled, barbed, harnessed, all-armed, as in Drayton's *Baron's War*, vi. 85 (ed. Morley, p. 158) " Why fell I not from that all-armed horse On which I rode before the gates of Gaunt," etc., (2) the existence of like compounds, as the Chaucerian *arm-greet* (as great as one's arm), *arm-strong* (strong of arm: *Locrine*, I. i; III. i; III. iv), etc.; and the fact that *arm* was not restricted to the limbs of man (see *O.E.D.*, *s.v.*). (*a*) From *gaunt* = lean, we have suggested meanings: worn lean by much service in war (Warburton), gaunt by bearing arms (Collier), thin-shouldered (Seward, pref. to *Beaumont and Fletcher*: in 1778 ed. p. lxxi, note), thin as one's arm (Halliwell, who compares *arm-greet*, as above), having lean fore-limbs (*Temple Shakespeare*)? with gaunt limbs (*O.E.D.*). The following from Sylvester's Du Bartas (*The Handycrafts*, p. 227 in 1621 ed.) favours the latter meanings in giving some characteristics of " a gallant Horse ":—

> With Pasterns short, vpright (but yet in mean);
> Dry sinewie shanks; strong, flesh-less knees, and lean;
> With Hart-like legs, etc.

(*b*) From derived senses of *gaunt*: looking fierce in armour (Boswell: who conjectures a sense " fierce " for *gaunt* from its being used of animals made savage by hunger), hungry for battle (Thiselton; relying on Jonson, *Catiline*, III. i. 199: " and let His own [*i.e.* Jove's] gaunt Eagle flie at him, to tire," a reference of Staunton's). In *O.E.D.* under sense *hungry, greedy*, etc., I find: Smollett, *Reproo₃*, 125, " Gorg'd with our plunder, yet still gaunt for spoil," etc. (*c*) From *gaunt* as = gaunted, *i.e.* gloved, armour-gloved (Nicholson), gloved in arms (Schmidt). No evidence of the sense is adduced: *Gaunters* occurs for Glovers in the list of crafts and plays, dated 1415, pr. in *York Plays*, ed. Toulmin Smith, 1881. (*d*) Schmidt suggests also: completely armed, harnessed; *or rather* lusty in arms, full of life and martial spirits, from another *gaunt* found in Old English, the German *ganz*, signifying " whole," " healthful," " lusty." The *English Dialect Dict.* (Wright) has *ganty* (of a horse) = frisky (Sussex), and I find in Braithwaite, *Barnabee's Iournall*, pt. 3 (ed. Hazlitt, 1876, sig. H 3), presumably in a somewhat similar sense:—

> Where were dainty Ducks, and gant ones,
> Wenches that could play the wantons, etc.

In the following, however, *gaunte* seems to mean slenderness in a maid: " hur medyll ys bothe gaunte and small " (*Anglia*, 10 Aug. 1908, p. 315, *Songs* temp. *Henry VIII*, from Rawlinson MS. c. 813).

The chief emendations proposed are: *arm-girt* (Hanmer) *termagaunt* (Mason) *war-gaunt* (Jackson) *arrogaunt* (Boaden) *rampaunt* (Lettsom). As to *arm-girt*, *guirt* is a common spelling of *girt*, and the word (which Hudson adopts) retains the article *an* of the text. Singer urges this advantage on behalf of *arrogant* (adopted by himself, Delius, and Deighton), and cites " el cavallo arrogante " from Lope de Vega's *Auraco Domado*. In the *Times Literary Supplement*, 29 April, 1920, Dr. John Sampson proposed to read *armigerent*, as possibly coined by Shakespeare, " intending to call up a picture of the horse's trappings, emblazoned with the armorial bearings of his master." (†But challenge any actor to deliver the line as thus emended! [R])

APPENDIX II

MISLINEATION

Here are some examples of F's mislineation, taken from
II. ii. (I have modernized the spelling but retained the
punctuation.)

II. ii. 8-14

> I would not shave't to day.
> *Lep.* 'Tis not a time for private stomaching.
> *Eno.* Every time serves for the matter that is then born in't.
> *Lep.* But small to greater matters must give way.
> *Eno.* Not if the small come first.
> *Lep.* Your speech is passion : but pray you stir
> No embers up.   Here comes the noble *Antony.*
> > *Enter Antony and Ventidius*
> *Eno.* And yonder *Cæsar.*

It may be observed that Lepidus' speeches will do very
well as they are.   But unless Enobarbus, who has hitherto
been talking unmistakable verse, suddenly lapses into prose,
his first complete " line " (" Every time . . .") will not do at
all, and to cure it involves a general reshuffle, so that modern
editors, probably rightly, print

> > I would not shave't to-day.
> *Lep.*   'Tis not a time
> For private stomaching.
> *Eno.*   Every time
> Serves for the matter that is then born in't.
> *Lep.* But small to greater matters must give way.
> *Eno.* Not if the small come first.
> *Lep.*   Your speech is passion:
> But, pray you, stir no embers up.   Here comes
> The noble Antony.
> > *Enter Antony and Ventidius*
> *Eno.*   And yonder, Cæsar.

II. ii. 118-24

> *Agri.* Thou hast a sister by the mother's side, admir'd
> *Octavia?*   Great *Mark Antony* is now a widower.
> *Cæsar.* Say not, say *Agrippa* ; if *Cleopater* heard you, your
> proof were well deserved of rashness.
> *Ant.* I am not married Cæsar : let me hear *Agrippa*
> further speak.

This is a curious passage. An oasis of prose cannot have been intended in the middle of a straight run of regular verse (which the compositor set quite correctly). All one can say is that the compositor, for whatever reason, whether difficulty with his copy (but why should the copy have been more difficult here than just before or just after?) or from a temporary fit of drowsiness, struck a bad patch, since not only does he set verse as prose, but he makes certainly two blunders (a second " say " for " so ", with transposed comma, and *Cleopater*) and perhaps two more (a question mark and " proof " for " reproof "). This is usually regularized thus:—

> *Agri.* Thou hast a sister by the mother's side,
> Admir'd Octavia: great Mark Antony
> Is now a widower.
> *Cæs.* Say not so, Agrippa;
> If Cleopatra heard you, your reproof
> Were well deserv'd of rashness.
> *Ant.* I am not married, Cæsar: let me hear
> Agrippa further speak.

It is worth notice that the passage, even when regularized, contains two incomplete lines. I see no other way of dividing the lines, but this suggests that in other places there may be more than one readjustment possible, as in the next example.

II. ii. 29-37

> *Ant.* I learn, you take things ill, which are not so:
> Or being, concern you not.
> *Cæs.* I must be laugh'd at, if or for nothing, or a little, I
> Should say myself offended, and with you
> Chiefly i' the world. More laugh'd at, that I should
> Once name you derogately: when to sound your name
> It not concern'd me.
> *Ant.* My being in Egypt *Cæsar*, what was't to you?
> *Cæs.* No more than my residing here at Rome. . . .

Up to a point this is plain enough; Cæsar's first five words are clearly the completion of the preceding line, and Rowe's cure has been universally accepted

> *Ant.* I learn, you take things, ill that are not so,
> Or being, concern you not.
> *Cæs.* I must be laugh'd at,
> If, or for nothing or a little, I
> Should say myself offended, and with you
> Chiefly i' the world : more laugh'd at that I should
> Once name you derogately,

but after this things are much less plain. Almost all editors, even those who are elsewhere earnestly and even sometimes fussily determined to extort more or less metrical lines from the most unpromising material, happily accept F's " Once name . . . your name " as a line, and follow Capell in redistributing the rest thus:—

> Once name you derogately, when to sound your name
> It not concern'd me.
> *Ant.*   My being in Egypt, Cæsar,
> What was't to you?
> *Cæs.* No more than my residing here in Rome. . . .

On this one may observe that the F line can be made metrical only by an awkwardly slurring rapidity of delivery which will reduce the six syllables " you derogately when " to the value of two feet instead of three, and, further, that whatever we do we are going to be left with an incomplete line somewhere, so that two other redistributions are possible, one of them, I think, preferable to Capell's:—

> Once name you derogately, when to sound
> Your name it not concern'd me.
> *Ant.*   My being in Egypt,
> Cæsar, what was't to you?
> *Cæs.* No more than . . . .

or

> Once name you derogately, when to sound
> Your name it not concern'd me.
> *Ant.* My being in Egypt, Cæsar, what was't to you?
> *Cæs.* No more than . . . .

II. ii. 158-63

> At heel of that, defy him.
> *Lepi.* Time calls upon's,
> Of us must *Pompey* presently be sought,
> Or else he seeks out us.
> *Anth.* Where lies he?
> *Cæsar.* About the Mount-Misena.
> *Anth.* What is his strength by land?
> *Cæsar.* Great, and increasing:
> But by sea he is an absolute master.
> *Anth.* So is the fame.

This is a good example of the results of the practice of starting each new speech with a new line. It looks like prose, and one might also be tempted to think that Shakespeare had intended this staccato interchange to be prose, if it were not for Lepidus'

one complete line, which is unmistakable verse. The operations of the early editors were surprisingly tentative. Some
adhered to F, and even Theobald produced the odd " line "
" Great and increasing, but by sea." But from Hanmer onwards the accepted distribution has been

> At heel of that, defy him.
> *Lep.*   Time calls upon's:
> Of us must Pompey presently be sought,
> Or else he seeks out us.
> *Ant.*   Where lies he?
> *Cæs.* About the Mount Misena.
> *Ant.*   What's his strength
> By land?
> *Cæs.*   Great and increasing, but by sea
> He is an absolute master.
> *Ant.*   So is the fame.

(Hanmer made a further, and attractive, change by attributing
" By land " to Cæsar.   See the notes, *ad loc.*)

II. ii. 193-5

> Purple the sails: and so perfumed that
> The winds were love-sick.
> With them the oars were silver,
> Which to the tune of flutes kept stroke, and made
> The water . . . .

This is an example of a type of mislineation rare in this
play, namely of unmistakable mislineation (and incidentally
of mispunctuation) occurring in the middle of a continuous
piece of verse otherwise correctly set.   It may be that Shakespeare had here made some alterations in the copy which confused the compositor, or simply that the correct line was too
long for the narrow column and the compositor arbitrarily
divided it, getting his punctuation wrong in the process.   I
give (in F's spelling) the next longest line in the passage, which
just fills the width of the column, for purposes of comparison.

> With diuers coulour'd Fannes whose winde did seeme,
> The Windes were Loue-sick.   With them the Owers were Silver,

[It may have been expected that on this question of mislineation
I should have at least referred to the views of Dr. R. Flatter, set
out in *Shakespeare's Producing Hand* (1948).   I shall have a good
deal to say about them later, so far as they bear upon *Othello*,
on the textual problems of which Dr. Flatter has views both

decided and remarkable, and from which he adduces a considerable number of his instances. But he adduces few from *Antony
and Cleopatra*, as is indeed natural, since the problems of this play
are in the main not ones to which his views are helpfully applic-
able. And I will therefore for the moment content myself with
a brief comment. Dr. Flatter is a scholar and knows Shakespeare. But I do not believe that anyone, however scholarly and
however well read, can appreciate the prosodic subtleties of a
language other than his own, since he has not, in the nature
of the case, the indispensable native ear. When therefore Dr.
Flatter is dealing with metrical considerations, and basing
his arguments upon them, he seems to me almost uniformly
wide of the mark, and wandering in a region which he does not
begin to understand. When, on the other hand, he is dealing
with points of dramatic effectiveness and verisimilitude (for
example, and especially, his point that, when a new speaker
has had no chance of hearing what the last speaker said, it would
be unreasonable for him to open with a metrical completion of an
unfinished line), then I think he has a great deal that is of interest,
and something that is of value, to say.]

APPENDIX III

PUNCTUATION

(*a*) I. v. 59-78. F has two misprints in words (*mans* for *man* in 61 and *Parago nagaine* for *Paragon againe*); it prints some verse as prose (63-7); and in punctuation it has one intrusive colon (after *againe* in 71) and a probably intrusive comma (after *say* in 75). The rest of the punctuation, though far from modern, is certainly not impossible. But Case, Craig, and Dover Wilson make respectively 15, 14, and 13 alterations in punctuation. They agree in deleting three commas and a colon, in inserting at least four commas (Case six), in replacing one comma by colon or full stop, and one comma and one full stop by exclamation marks. (*b*) III. xiii. 182-201. F has one misprint (*in* for *on* in 199) and a comma (after *lightning* in 195) where even on Elizabethan principles a heavier stop would probably be better. Case, Craig and Dover Wilson make 15, 14 and 7 changes in punctuation. Case and Craig, apart from the usual insertions and deletions of commas, replace a comma by a heavier stop five times, and semi-colon or colon by the next heavier stop twice; but in the other direction they lighten a full stop or colon to semi-colon or comma three times. (*c*) v. ii. 345-64. F has one misprint (*Solmemnity* for *Solemnity* in 364), one possible misprint (*caues* for, perhaps, *canes* in 351), a comma after *monument* in 355 where a heavier stop would be more natural, and a comma after *show* in 362 but no comma after *shall* at the end of the line before. Case, Craig and Dover Wilson make 13, 13 and 10 changes. They all insert two commas and delete two; Case and Craig replace four commas by heavier stops (Dover Wilson only two); but Case and Craig both replace a full stop and a colon by the next lighter stop.

There follow some further examples of the different effect produced by the two types of punctuation.

Examples of Folio punctuation.

(I have throughout taken the original Arden edition's punctuation as typical of the " usual " modern text.)

I. iii. 71-3
(Arden)

> *Cleo.*   Cut my lace, Charmian, come;
> But let it be: I am quickly ill, and well,
> So Antony loves.

(F)

> *Cleo.*   Cut my Lace, *Charmian* come,
> But let it be, I am quickly ill, and well,
> So *Anthony* loues.

V. ii. 193-5
(Arden)

> *Cleo.*   Hie thee again:
> I have spoke already, and it is provided;
> Go put it to the haste.

(Craig, by the way, even adds a comma after " Go ").

(F)

> *Cleo.*   Hye thee againe,
> I haue spoke already, and it is prouided,
> Go put it to the haste.

In both these examples the light punctuation of F is tanta-
mount to a stage-direction, in the first *Cleo. (in agitation)*, in
the second, *Cleo. (with hurried urgency)*. She has no time for
semi-colons.

I. iv. 12
(Arden)

> His faults in him seem as the spots of heaven,

(F)

> His faults in him, seeme as the Spots of Heauen,

Where the F comma, I think, throws the required emphasis
on to *him*—in a lesser man, Lepidus means, the faults would
darken all the goodness. I have made this yet plainer in the
present edition by inserting the second comma which the modern
reader expects, before *in.*

II. ii. 151-3
(Arden)

> let her live
> To join our kingdoms and our hearts; and never
> Fly off our loves again!

(F)

> Let her liue
> To ioyne our kingdomes, and our hearts, and neuer
> Flie off our Loues againe.

The comma after *kingdomes* points the distinction between
the official union and the personal concord.

II. vii. 101, 102

(Arden)

> but I had rather fast from all four days
> Than drink so much in one.

(F)

> but I had rather fast from all, foure dayes, then
> drinke so much in one.

The F commas emphasize the duration of the fast (in modern American idiom " Yes, and I mean ' fast ' ").

III. iv. 11, 12

(Arden)

> Believe not all ; or, if you must believe,
> Stomach not all.

(F)

> Beleeue not all, or if you must beleeue,
> Stomacke not all.

Almost no one in speech would make the pause suggested by the " logical " comma after *or*. And the same difference between speech and thought is shown in the next two examples.

IV. xiv. 62-4

(Arden)

> Thou art sworn, Eros,
> That, when the exigent should come,—which now
> Is come indeed,—

(F)

> Thou art sworne *Eros*,
> That when the exigent should come, which now
> Is come indeed :

IV. xiv. 85

(Arden)

> Turn from me, then, that noble countenance. . . .

(F)

> Turne from me then that Noble countenance. . . .

IV. xii. 9-20, an example of the greater rapidity of delivery suggested by F's punctuation.

(Arden)

> *Ant.*   All is lost;
> This foul Egyptian hath betrayed me:
> My fleet hath yielded to the foe;   and yonder
> They cast their caps up and carouse together
> Like friends long lost.   Triple-turn'd whore! 'tis thou

Hast sold me to this novice; and my heart
Makes only wars on thee.   Bid them all fly;
For when I am revenged upon my charm,
I have done all.   Bid them all fly; begone.
O sun, thy uprise shall I see no more:
Fortune and Antony part here; even here
Do we shake hands.   All come to this? . . .

(F)

 Ant. All is lost:
This fowle Egyptian hath betrayed me:
My Fleete hath yeelded to the Foe, and yonder
They cast their Caps vp, and Carowse together
Like Friends long lost.   Triple-turn'd Whore, 'tis thou
Hast sold me to this Nouice, and my heart
Makes onely Warres on thee.   Bid them all flye:
For when I am reueng'd vpon my Charme,
I haue done all.   Bid them all flye, be gone.
Oh Sunne, thy vprise shall I see no more,
Fortune, and *Anthony* part heere, euen heere
Do we shake hands?   All come to this?

V. ii. 7, 8
(Arden)

Which sleeps, and never palates more the dung,
The beggar's nurse and Cæsar's.

(F)

Which sleepes, and neuer pallates more the dung,
The beggers Nurse, and *Cæsars*.

The comma after *Nurse* surely points the ironic levelling-
down of Cæsar.

V. ii. 158-163
(Arden)

O Cæsar, what a wounding shame is this,
That thou, vouchsafing here to visit me,
Doing the honour of thy lordliness
To one so meek, that mine own servant should
Parcel the sum of my disgraces by
Addition of his envy!

(F)

O *Cæsar*, what a wounding shame is this,
That thou vouchsafing heere to visit me,
Doing the Honour of thy Lordlinesse
To one so meeke, that mine owne Seruant should
Parcell the summe of my disgraces, by
Addition of his Enuy.

This is an interesting example. The modern punctuation, whatever else may be said of it, is as a rule grammatical. But here the inserted comma after *thou* in the second line wrecks the syntactical structure by leaving *thou* a nominative hanging over a vacuum. If a comma was to be inserted at all it should have been after *That,* since it is plain that *thou vouchsafing . . . doing* is an " absolute " construction (" when you vouchsafe . . .").

V. ii. 286, 7
(Arden)

> Husband, I come:
> Now to that name my courage prove my title!

(F)

> Husband, I come:
> Now to that name, my Courage proue my Title.

The slight pause after *name* is surely as oratorically masterly as it is logically indefensible.

APPENDIX IV

SCENES IV. xv AND V. ii.

THE staging of these scenes is discussed by Granville Barker, *Prefaces to Shakespeare*, second series, pp. 162-6, by Adams, *The Globe Playhouse*, pp. 263-8, and by Jenkin in the *Review of English Studies*, xxi, pp. 1-14. All three assume the use of the inner stages, the upper for IV. xv and the lower for V. ii. But Dover Wilson points out that in both scenes dead bodies have to be carried off (the operation is explicit in the F stage-direction at the end of IV. xv *Exeunt, bearing of Anthonies body*, and implicit in the text of V. ii. 355), and that this carrying off would not be necessary with the curtainable inner stage (cf. the end of *Othello*). He therefore suggests that a temporary monument was devised, "a square painted wooden structure, with a barred gate in front" to conform with North (see page 282 *post*) "and a flat roof" and that this structure was "erected by servitors at the end of IV. xiv. on the outer stage over the central trap (through which Cleo. etc., could enter and thence climb to the roof by a concealed stair)." Antony's body would then be "borne off down the stair at the end of IV. xv." and the structure would "remain in position during the brief interval scene (V. i.), be inexpensive to make, and quick to erect."

This highly ingenious suggestion seems to me to create more, and more difficult, problems than it solves. (*a*) What is the audience, keyed up by Antony's attempted suicide, and waiting for his arrival "where Cleopatra bides," supposed to be doing between the end of scene xiv and the opening of xv? Watching servitors at work on a bit of stage carpentry? "Quick" is a relative term, and even five minutes of "quick erection" would surely be fatally dislocating. (*b*) Would any manager or producer in his senses, having a ready built-in structure with which the two scenes can be adequately staged, go to the nuisance and expense of cluttering up his main stage with a temporary erection? (*c*) I say "cluttering up" be-cause V. i, cheerfully dismissed by Dover Wilson as a "brief interval scene", has in fact seventy-seven lines, only fourteen fewer than IV. xv, and a much fuller stage, since besides five speaking characters (and Gallus, who is there only to receive an order) on the stage till a few lines from the end, the F stage-direction brings on also Caesar's *Counsell of Warre*. There are

247

also two entries, one of which, that of Decretas with Antony's sword, is a dramatic moment. Imagine the Elizabethan stage, with the audience round three sides of it, and this temporary structure in the centre. No part of the audience can get an uninterrupted view of the whole stage, and the only part of the stage that will be visible to all the audience will be a narrow strip in the front. The problems of the producer—to dispose a minimum of ten characters in this restricted space, and to make Decretas' entry effective—are surely insoluble.

Nor does Dover Wilson's argument appear, on examination, particularly cogent. It rests on an unwarranted assumption. It is true that the removal of dead bodies was *unnecessary* when the regular inner stage was in use, since it could be curtained off ; but it does not at all follow that the removal was therefore always *undesirable*. In *Othello* there would be no dramatic gain, and some loss, in such a removal; so the tragic lodging of the bed is covered, and Othello is left alone with his wife and her faithful attendant. But in *Antony and Cleopatra* there is every possible reason why " royal Egypt " should pass from the stage, like Hamlet, with full ceremonial honours, and there is neither mechanical nor any other reason why the bearers should not start as well from the inner as from the outer stage. Dover Wilson, driven by his fixed idea, takes Cæsar's words near the end (v. ii. 354-5) : " Take up her bed, And bear her women from the monument " and comments " This instruction proves that the deaths take place on the outer stage." Clearly the instruction *proves* nothing of the kind, and unless the whole stage, outer as well as inner, is by now to be thought of as inside the monument, it *implies* exactly the reverse.

Anyhow, the presence or absence of the temporary structure is irrelevant to the end of the play, except in so far as its presence would be a practical nuisance for the producer in staging the final procession. Would its presence help at any other point in either scene ? I think not. (*a*) There is one point in IV. xv where it might at first sight seem to help, and oddly enough Dover Wilson does not adduce this, by far the strongest bit of supporting evidence which the text offers him. At line 8 Diomedes says " Look out o' the other side your monument." It is quite true that a structure such as Dover Wilson posits would have more obviously an " other side " than the permanent " above ". But I think that this is more than counterbalanced by the fact that the entry of the guard with Antony would be obscured from some of the audience. And there is no real difficulty in staging the episode with the existing stage. Diomedes enters by one door, and talks up to Cleopatra standing at one end of "above". On Diomedes' direction she moves to the other end and sees Antony, who has been carried in by the other door. (b) The *ad hoc* structure would, so far as I can see, do less than nothing to help with some supposed difficulties in the earlier part of v. ii, and in any case these difficulties are more apparent than real. Let us, for the moment neglecting North, examine what happens, according to F. In the first sixty-four lines of the scene, down to the entry of Dolabella, there are no stage-directions except for the entry of Cleopatra, Charmian, Iras and Mardian at the opening, and of Proculeius at line 8. Cleopatra and her attendants are perhaps in the inner stage, and she talks to Proculeius, who enters on the outer stage. At one point two successive speeches (lines 32-4, "This I'll report . . . caus'd it" and lines 35, 36, "You see . . . Cæsar come") are both credited to Proculeius, the speech-heading *Pro.* being repeated, and it is moderately certain that the second of these should be attributed to someone else, presumably (see later) Gallus. At line 35, while listening to Proculeius, Cleopatra is taken unawares by the entry of Cæsar's men behind her ; she attempts to stab herself and is prevented by Proculeius. There is no indication in the text where the "guards" have come from, nor does it particularly matter. It is natural, though not essential, to suppose from earlier indications that Cleopatra is locked in her monument (this is explicit in North, but I am trying for the moment to do without North), and that therefore there is a barred gate across the opening of the inner stage, through which she talks to Proculeius, and which the guard after their entry unbar from inside so that Proculeius can enter. That, I think, is all fairly plain sailing, though no doubt some stage-directions from Shakespeare would have made it plainer. The early editors, beginning with Theobald, followed by Warburton and Johnson, and later elaborated by Malone, vexed in particular by the unaccounted for appearance of the guard, went to work to remedy Shakespeare's (or F's) omissions, and called North to their aid. Here is North (see p. 282):

For Proculeius came to the gates that were very thicke and strong, and surely barred, but yet there were some cranewes through the which her voyce might be heard, and so they without understoode, that Cleopatra demaunded the kingdome of Ægypt for her sonnes : and that Proculeius aunswered her, that she should be of good cheere, and not be affrayed to referre all unto Cæsar. After he had viewed the place verie well, he came and reported her aunswere unto Cæsar.

Who immediately sent Gallus to speake once againe with her, and bad
him purposely hold her with talke, whilest Proculeius did set up a
ladder against that highe windowe, by the which Antonius was trised
up, and came downe into the monument with two of his men hard
by the gate, where Cleopatra stoode to heare what Gallus sayd unto
her.   One of her women which was shut in her monuments with her,
saw Proculeius by chaunce as he came downe, and shreeked out :
O, poore Cleopatra, thou art taken.   Then when she sawe Proculeius
behind her as she came from the gate, she thought to have stabbed
her selfe in with a short dagger she ware of purpose by her side.   But
Proculeius came sodainly upon her, and taking her by both the
hands, said unto her :

From this Hanmer brought in Gallus along with Proculeius
at line 8, and at line 35 Theobald read *Here Gallus, and Guard,
ascend the Monument by a Ladder, and enter at a back-window,* and
Malone *Here Proculeius, and two of the guard, ascend the Monument
by a Ladder placed against a window, and having descended, come
behind Cleopatra.   Some of the guard unbar and open the gates.*   Now
the first thing to be observed about these directions, whatever
their intrinsic merits, and whether it is to be Gallus or Proculeius
who leads the storming party, is that, if they are placed where
their authors placed them, there is no time for these scaling-
ladder operations.   They would take an appreciable time,
during which Cleopatra must be held in talk by someone—
in North it is Gallus, but Shakespeare, compressing two episodes
into one, has committed himself to Proculeius.   Dover Wilson,
seeing this, greatly improves matters as follows: at line 8,
Enter PROCULEIUS.   *As he speaks with* CLEOPATRA *through the
bars,* GALLUS *and soldiers enter, unseen by those within, mount to the
top with ladders, and go down into the monument,* and after line 34,
*The doors are suddenly flung open, showing a richly furnished room,
with* GALLUS *and soldiers standing behind* CLEOPATRA *and her
women.*
    Gallus.   You see how easily . . . .
    Now, if Gallus and the guard have to come on to the outer
stage at all, that is the way to do it.   They have plenty of time
to get into the monument, and the audience has the pleasure
of suspense while it waits for their appearance behind Cleopatra.
And for this entry the temporary monument would be undeniably convenient.   It is true that the unobserved escalade could
be conducted on the ordinary stage, so long as Cleopatra and
her attendants were kept well back on the inner stage, since to
an actor even 4 or 5 feet back on the inner stage there are two
segments of the outer stage which are invisible.   But it would

I think be unconvincing, whereas if conducted at the rear or one side of the hypothetical structure it would be natural enough.

But is there any reason for having Gallus and the guard on the stage at all until their sudden entry at lines 34-5? If not, F's entry for Proculeius alone at line 8 is justified, and we get rid at one sweep of most of the elaborate additions to the stage-directions. All we need will be at line 34, *Gallus and three or four soldiers enter behind Cleopatra* (and we may have to add *and unbar the gate*, to allow Proculeius to enter the inner stage, but this is a point to be considered later). The sudden irruption is effective, it has the advantage of making line 35 (otherwise a trifle awkward) more natural, as a sort of " cover " line, explaining their arrival, and the audience will simply assume that they have broken in somewhere at the back of the monument. It is worth quoting some excellent common-sense from Furness. " I have not quoted in the Textual notes all the stage-directions given by the early editors in their vain reachings after those which would satisfy all requirements ; nor have I recorded all the minor variations of the modern editors. For my own part, I see no need of any stage-direction at all. It is, at least for me, quite sufficient to see that the Romans rush in and seize the queen. In these thrilling moments, how they got in, I neither know nor care. Nor does any one in the audience ever know how they entered, and would not know, unless the stage-manager came forward and read aloud Plutarch, or Malone's directions."

We now come to the last main problem in the staging of v. ii, one which is of considerable intrinsic importance, and the consideration of which, I think, finally demolishes the temporary structure. Where, for the first thirty-five lines of the scene, are Cleopatra and her attendants supposed to be? Malone assumed that they were on the inner stage, with a barred gate across the opening. That is all very well for the dialogue with Proculeius, and it is according to North. But it is very far from well for Cleopatra's opening speech. We do not want that to come from a sort of disembodied voice of an imperfectly visible actress. Nor does it make effective the entry of the guard, who would be even less visible. Some editors, seeing this difficulty, bring in Cleopatra *aloft*. This has, for the moment, obvious advantages. It gives Cleopatra a prominent position on the stage, she talks to Proculeius with a barrier between them, though it is one of height, not of a barred gate, and the irruption of the guard—so long as they now appear

for the first time—can be made as well on the upper level as
on the lower. (Some editors who add *aloft* also retain at line
35 the climb of the guard, watched apparently by Cleopatra
with quiet interest.)   But these momentary advantages are paid
for too high by difficulties later.   How does Proculeius arrive
where he can prevent Cleopatra's attempt at suicide—unless
he joins in the absurd climb of the guard?   And at what point
does Cleopatra come down from aloft for the scene with Cæsar,
which must, I think, occur on the main stage?   In any case,
this insertion of *aloft* has no authority, and textual evidence is
against it, since F's stage-direction for iv. xv specifies an entry
aloft, and as there is no *aloft* in the v. ii stage-direction it is a
reasonable inference that Shakespeare did not intend there
to be one, but wished the scene to be played throughout on
the lower level, whether or not the inner stage was to be used.
The difficulties caused by a gate across the opening of the
inner stage have already been glanced at ; but consider the
much greater difficulties created by a temporary monument.
It is, *ex hypothesi*, a square structure, standing in the middle
of the stage, with a gate on the side towards the front of the
stage.   Not only therefore will that part of the audience which
faces it see Cleopatra imperfectly (as with the gated inner stage)
but about half the audience will not see her at all, but will be
looking frustratedly at one or other blank side of the structure.
Which, I think, is absurd.   The only solution would be to have
the structure open—though with bars—on three sides, so that
Cleopatra and her attendants would appear like animals in
the Zoo, or like Bajazeth in *Tamburlaine*.   Which is yet more
absurd.   I think that the structure must be dismantled, along
with other ingenious, but not fully thought-out, hypotheses.

    If, then, we dismiss both an entry aloft and a temporary
monument, how is the scene to be presented ?   There has
been an almost universal insistence by editors (except those
who make the first entry *aloft*) from Capell downwards that
Cleopatra's entry is to a barred inner stage, which is unbarred
at line 35.   And stage-direction after stage-direction (none of
them in F), differing in detail but concurring in general sense,
have been devoted to emphasizing this picture.   I have pointed
out certain weaknesses which this method of staging involves,
and I said earlier " unless the whole stage, outer as well as
inner, is by now to be thought of as inside the monument."
I want to hazard the heterodox suggestion that the whole stage
should be so thought of, and that if it is many of the difficulties
melt into thin air.

Why, then, in the first place, such concurrence of the editors ? To this there are, I think, two answers. First, they paid very natural, but excessive, attention to North. It happens that the relevant North passage is not only detailed but pictorially vivid, with the gates very thick and strong, and surely barred, and with their " cranewes." And it was naturally felt that Shakespeare, who elsewhere follows North so closely, must have followed him here also, in spite of F. But if Shakespeare had found matter in North which was undramatic or difficult of presentation on his stage, surely he would have jettisoned him without a second thought. (As it is he compresses two episodes of North into one, and the compression has caused part of the editorial troubles.) Second, I think that, accustomed to their own stage with scenery and properties, the editors failed to reckon with the readiness of the Elizabethan audience to change their imaginative conception of what their bare stage was at any moment supposed to represent. It is quite true that in iv. xv " aloft " is the monument which Cleopatra dare not leave, and the outer stage, on which Antony is carried in, is the outer world. But it does not follow that this must be permanently so. And it is clear that at some point (if not from the start) in v. ii the outer stage has become a room inside the monument. Apart from the scene with Cæsar, which demands a full stage, there is the episode of the " clown " with the figs, which is, I think, decisive. The F stage-directions are here explicit. Cleopatra is interrupted in her orders to Charmian by " *A noise within* " (i.e. off-stage). " *Enter a Guardsman*," announcing the arrival of " a rural fellow." " Let him come in," says Cleopatra. " *Exit Guardsman.*" " *Enter Guardsman, and Clowne.*" " *Exit Guardsman.*" The implications are, I think, inescapable. Cleopatra, the means of self-destruction being presumably removed, is under guard in the monument. But the guard is off-stage, not on the outer stage. Therefore the outer stage is now part of a room in the monument.

Suppose we push this conception of " locality " back to the opening of the scene. Cleopatra and her attendants enter (I think through the curtains of the inner stage, to mark that they come from another room in the monument). She delivers her first speech in full view of the audience. *Enter Proculeius.* Here is, I think, the one real difficulty, a difficulty which some readers may think insuperable. It is that Cleopatra expresses no surprise at his entry. One rather expects her to say, in effect, " And how, by Isis, did you get in?" I suggest, however, that if one is troubled about the problem at all, which many spectators would not be, one may assume that Cleopatra, hearing that a single emissary has come from Cæsar, has given orders for him to be admitted. (It is reasonable to suppose that Cleopatra still has servants besides her immediate attendants—the Egyptian in v. i proves that she had at least one—and that some of them were on duty at the outer gates.) This makes it natural enough that he, and not she, opens the conversation, and that she asks as it were for his credentials— what is his name?—with perhaps the hope that he may be the one man whom Antony told her to trust. At line 35 the guards break in from behind, either through the curtains or through the ordinary doors. On these lines the scene plays straight-forwardly from beginning to end, and we are relieved of the temptation to add elaborate stage-directions to those of F. Down to the entry of Cæsar at line 110 we need add only the entry of Gallus and the guard at line 34, Gallus's exit at line 36, and perhaps (though the necessary action is clear from the text) Cleopatra's drawing the dagger and Proculeius' removing it from her.

There remains only the minor problem (which has nothing to do with the major one of staging) of Gallus and the muddled speech-heading at line 35. It is, I think, a prime mistake to add Gallus to F's entry of Proculeius alone at line 8. Cæsar's orders to Gallus in v. i. 69 come, according to F's stage-direction, after Proculeius' exit, so that Proculeius supposes himself to be the sole emissary. Further, it seems to me flat contrary to the expectation created by Antony's verdict on Proculeius that we should now find him party to a design to capture the queen. Nor do his speeches feel like those of a man dishonestly playing for time, but rather like those of a man honestly presenting his master's attitude. But Gallus must, I think, be introduced somewhere, not because of North, but because Cæsar gave him orders, and it is bad craftsmanship (though Shakespeare is elsewhere guilty of it, as in *M. of V.*) to create an expectation which is not fulfilled, and also because we must have someone to take the news to Cæsar (see line 65), and as Gallus enters with Cæsar later it is natural to suppose that he has been the someone. Hence I think it right to cut out the second *Pro.* speech-heading for line 35 ("You see how easily . . .") and give the speech to Gallus, but I suggest that the erroneous speech-heading was not just a matter of careless substitution, but rather of the transference of a proper name from text to speech-heading, and that the lines should run thus:

Pro.   This I'll report, dear lady
              Have comfort, for I know your plight is pitied
              Of him that caus'd it.   *Enter Gallus and guard behind.*
Gal.   *Proculeius,*
              You see how easily she may be surpris'd
              Guard her till *Caesar* come.   *Exit Gallus.*

v. ii. 231, 278, *stage-directions.* Since F has no stage-directions, editors are free to insert what they consider most consonant with the text and theatrically effective. It has been universally accepted that Capell was right in leaving Charmian on the stage. I am doubtful whether this was Shakespeare's intention and I am sure that the point is profitably arguable, since the determination of it makes a considerable difference to a dramatic moment in the play.

The argument for Iras' exit alone must rest entirely on Cleopatra's words in lines 225-31, and possibly on line 282. (Between lines 232 and 278 there is nothing in the text to indicate whether Charmian is present or absent, nor anything in line 279 to indicate whether the re-entry is of one or both attendants.) Now it is true that Iras alone is specifically ordered to " go " (line 228), and that if we take F's brackets in line 229 to indicate a *parenthesis* the " thou " in line 230 must be addressed to Iras, and further that if " yare " is taken to mean no more than " quick " the first five words of line 282 may be taken as no more than a somewhat repetitive direction to Iras to bring robe and crown more quickly from the entry door to where Cleopatra is standing.

But let us examine the two passages a little more in detail. In the first place, if lines 225-6 stood alone no one would have had any hesitation.

              Show me, my women, like a queen: go fetch
              My best attires

is clearly an instruction to *both* her attendants to bring all her royal array, and editors would inevitably, and rightly, have inserted after it, *Exeunt Charmian and Iras.* It also creates the expectation that if there are to be further instructions they will be addressed to both attendants, and not to one only. And so I think they are. It will be noticed, by the way, that if " thou " in line 230 is Iras, the half-ironic effectiveness of the echo in line 317 (Charmian's " Your crown 's awry, I'll mend it, and then play ") is sadly weakened. As to " Yare, yare, good Iras, quick," I doubt whether it is relevant one way or the other. " Yare," I think, has almost never the

meaning merely of " quick " ; there is a notion of deftness
as well as that of speed.   (A ship that is yare is one that is easily
manœuverable, not so much a fast sailer, but quick on the
helm ; see III. vii. 38 of this play, and *Tempest* v. i. 226.   But
compare especially II. ii. 211 of this play, " yarely frame the
office.")   And I take it that the remark to Iras comes after
the robing has begun, telling her to show her usual skill in
adjusting the robe, and to be quick about it.

To return then to the crucial seven lines.   As to Cleopatra's
" Now, Charmian," we can either follow Capell and others, read
a question mark for F's full stop, and take it that Cleopatra is
asking whether Charmian has been successful in the mission on
which she was despatched at line 195, or take the words as a
statement that she knows from Charmian's return that she has
been successful and that all is in order.   The first is perhaps a
trifle the more effective, but I doubt whether the emendation
is justified.   The real crux is F's brackets, which certainly
mean something, and cannot just be neglected and replaced by
commas, as is mostly done (though it would, of course, greatly
strengthen my case if they could).   I think that they represent
not a grammatical *parenthesis*, but an *aside*, addressed to Charmian
alone, apropos her confidential mission to secure the asps, and
followed up, as she waves Charmian to follow Iras, by the rest
of the speech aloud, but addressed to Charmian.

Here, along these lines, is the passage with full stage-
directions, giving first the alternative with Capell's emendation :

> *Cleo.*   Now, Charmian ?
> > *Charmian nods*
> (*triumphant*) Show me . . .

or

> *Cleo.* (*knowing from Charmian's return that all is ready, and exultant*)
> Show me, my women, like a queen: go fetch
> My best attires.   I am again for Cydnus,
> To meet Mark Antony.   Sirrah Iras, go.
> > *Iras moves towards the door*
> (*sotto voce to Charmian*) Now, noble Charmian, we'll
> > dispatch indeed,
> (*waves Charmian to follow Iras and speaks aloud to her*
> *as she moves away*)
> And when thou hast done this chare, I'll give thee leave
> To play till doomsday: bring our crown and all.
> > *Exeunt Iras and Charmian.   Cleopatra is left alone.*
> > *Noise within.*
> Wherefore's this noise ?

Cleopatra is thus left alone on the stage for her interview with the clown. This, I think, has two dramatic advantages. First, her few lines (235-40) in which she stiffens her resolution are, I feel, more naturally delivered in soliloquy (like Juliet's before she drinks the drug) than to an audience even of one. (This, I admit, may be countered by saying that Cleopatra likes an audience, and that if I am right this is the only time in the play at which she is even for a moment alone.) Second, her apprehension of interruption, which makes her impatient with the clown (she makes three ineffective attempts to get rid of him) more strongly compels the audience to share it if she is for the moment without the support of even one of her women. And this is perhaps true also of " Wherefore's this noise?", since she cannot be certain that this is only the arrival of her means of freedom.

Finally, as to the re-entry. Cleopatra's " and all " rather suggests that there is more to be brought than a crown and robe—perhaps more jewels from the regalia—even though later she mentions those only. And I feel that the entry of both her women, equipped to array their mistress for her last imperial exit, is more dignified and more effective than that of a solitary and perhaps somewhat overburdened Iras.

APPENDIX V

EXTRACTS FROM NORTH'S *PLUTARCH* (1579)

Antonius shape and presence.

BUT besides all this, he had a noble presence, and shewed a countenaunce of one of a noble house : he had a goodly thicke beard, a broad forehead, crooke nosed, and there appeared such a manly looke in

The house of the Antonii discended from Hercules.

his countenaunce, as is commonly seene in Hercules pictures, stamped or graven in mettell. Now it had bene a speeche of old time, that the familie of the Antonii were discended from one Anton, the sonne of Hercules, whereof the familie tooke name. This opinion did Antonius seeke to confirme in all his doings : not onely resembling him in the likenes of his bodye, as we have sayd before, but also in the wearing of his garments. For when he would openly shewe him selfe abroad before many people, he would alwayes weare his cassocke gyrt downe lowe upon his hippes, with a great sword hanging by his side, and upon that, some ill favored cloke. Furthermore, things that seeme intollerable in other men, as to boast commonly, to jeast with one or other, to drinke like a good fellow with every body, to sit with the souldiers when they dine, and to eate and drinke with them souldierlike : it is incredible what wonderfull love it wanne him amongest them. And furthermore, being given to love : that made him the more desired, and by that meanes he brought many to love him. For he would further every mans love, and also would not be angry that men should merily tell him of those he loved. But besides all this, that which most pro-

Antonius liberalitie.

cured his rising and advauncement, was his liberalitie, who gave all to the souldiers, and kept nothing for him selfe : and when he was growen to great credit, then was his authoritie and power also very great, the which notwithstanding him selfe did overthrowe by a thowsand other faults he had.

· · · · · · · · · · ·

Antonius byeth Pompeys house.

Afterwards when Pompeys house was put to open sale, Antonius bought it : but when they asked him money for it, he made it very straung, and was offended with them, and writeth himself that he would not goe with Cæsar into the warres of Africk, bicause he was not well recompenced for the service he had done him before. Yet Cæsar did somewhat bridle his madnes and insolencie, not suffering him to passe his faulte so lightly away, making as though he sawe them not. And

Antonius married Fulvia, Clodius widow.

therefore he left his dissolute manner of life, and married Fulvia that was Clodius widowe, a woman not so basely minded to spend her time in spinning and housewivery, and was not contented to master her husband at home, but would also rule him in his office abroad,

Fulvia ruled Antonius, at home, and abroad.

and commaund him, that commaunded legions and great armies : so that Cleopatra was to give Fulvia thankes for that she had taught

258

Antonius this obedience to women, that learned so well to be at their commaundement. Nowe, bicause Fulvia was somewhat sower, and crooked of condition, Antonius devised to make her pleasaunter, and somewhat better disposed: and therefore he would playe her many prety youthfull partes to make her mery.

. . . .

Now thinges remayning in this state at Rome, Octavius Cæsar the younger, came to Rome, who was the sonne of Iuslius Cæsars Nece, as you have heard before, and was left his lawefull heire by will, re-mayning at the tyme of the death of his great Unkle that was slayne, in the citie of Apollonia.

. . . .

This young Cæsar seeing his doings, went unto Cicero and others, which were Antonius enemies, and by them crept into favor with the Senate: and he him selfe sought the peoples good will every manner of way, gathering together the olde souldiers of the late deceased Cæsar, which were dispersed in divers cities and colonyes. Antonius being affrayd of it, talked with Octavius in the capitoll, and became his friend. But the very same night Antonius had a straunge dreame, who thought that lightning fell upon him, and burnt his right hand. Shortly after word was brought him, that Cæsar lay in waite to kil him. Cæsar cleered himselfe unto him, and told him there was no such matter: but he could not make Antonius believe the contrary. Whereuppon they became further enemies than ever they were: in-somuch that both of them made friends of either side to gather together all the old souldiers through Italy, that were dispersed in divers townes: and made them large promises, and sought also to winne the legions of their side, which were already in armes. Cicero on the other side being at that time the chiefest man of authoritie and estimation in the citie, he stirred up al men against Antonius: so that in the end he made the Senate pronounce him an enemy to his contry, and appointed young Cæsar Sergeaunts to cary axes before him, and such other signes as were incident to the dignitie of a Consul or Prætor: and moreover sent Hircius and Pansa, then Consuls, to drive Antonius out of Italy. These two Consuls together with Cæsar, who also had an armye, went against Antonius that beseeged the citie of Modena, and there overthrew him in battell: but both the Consuls were slaine there. Antonius flying upon this overthrowe, fell into great miserie all at once: but the chiefest want of all other, and that pinched him most, was famine. Howbeit he was of such a strong nature, that by pacience he would overcome any adversitie, and the heavier fortune lay upon him, the more constant shewed he him selfe. Every man that feleth want or adversitie, knoweth by vertue and discretion what he should doe: but when in deede they are overlayed with extremitie, and be sore oppressed, few have the harts to follow that which they praise and commend, and much lesse to avoid that they reprove and mislike. But rather to the contrary, they yeld to their accustomed easie life:

(marginal notes)

Octavius Cæsar joyned in friendship with Cicero.

Antonius and Octavius be-came friends.

Antonius dreame.

Antonius judged an enemy by the Senate.

Hircius and Pansa Con-suls.

Antonius overthrowen in battell by the citie of Modena.

Antonius patient in adversitie.

and through faynt hart, and lacke of corage, do chaunge their first
mind and purpose. And therefore it was a wonderful example to
the souldiers, to see Antonius that was brought up in all fineness and
superfluitie, so easily to drinke puddle water, and to eate wild frutes
and rootes : and moreover it is reported, that even as they passed the
Alpes, they did eate the barcks of trees, and such beasts, as never man
tasted of their flesh before.

.   .   .   .

Now the government of these Triumviri grewe odious and hatefull
to the Romanes, for divers respects : but they most blamed Antonius,
bicause he being elder then Cæsar, and of more power and force than
Lepidus, gave him selfe again to his former riot and excesse, when he
left to deale in the affaires of the common wealth. But setting aside
the ill name he had for his insolencie, he was yet much more hated in
respect of the house he dwelt in, the which was the house of Pompey
the great : a man as famous for his temperaunce, modestie, and civill
life, as for his three triumphes. For it grieved them to see the gates
commonly shut against the Captaines, Magistrates of the citie, and
also Ambassadors of straunge nations, which were sometimes thrust
from the gate with violence : and that the house within was full of
tomblers, anticke dauncers, juglers, players, jeasters, and dronkards,
quaffing and goseling, and that on them he spent and bestowed the
most parte of his money he got by all kind of possible extorcions, briberie
and policie.

Antonius
riot in his
Trium-
virate.

The praise
of Pompey
the great.

.   .   .   .

Octavius Cæsar perceiving that no money woulde serve Antonius
turne, he prayed that they might devide the money betwene them, and
so did they also devide the armie, for them both to goe into Macedon
to make warre against Brutus and Cassius : and in the meane time they
left the government of the citie of Rome unto Lepidus. When they
had passed over the seas, and that they beganne to make warre, they
being both camped by their enemies, to wit, Antonius against Cassius,
and Cæsar against Brutus : Cæsar did no great matter, but Antonius
had alway the upper hand, and did all. For at the first battell Cæsar
was overthrowen by Brutus, and lost his campe, and verie hardly saved
him selfe by flying from them that followed him. Howebeit he writeth
himselfe in his *Commentaries*, that he fled before the charge was geven,
bicause of a dreame one of his frends had. Antonius on the other side
overthrewe Cassius in battell, though some write that he was not there
him selfe at the battell, but that he came after the overthrowe, whilest
his men had the enemies in chase. So Cassius at his earnest request
was slaine by a faithfull servaunt of his owne called Pindarus, whom
he had infranchised : bicause he knew not in time that Brutus had
overcomen Cæsar. Shortly after they fought an other battell againe,
in the which Brutus was overthrowen, who afterwardes also slue him
selfe. Thus Antonius had the chiefest glorie of all this victorie, specially
bicause Cæsar was sicke at that time.

The valiant-
nes of Anto-
nius against
Brutus.

The death
of Cassius.

Brutus slue
him selfe.

.   .   .   .

For he understoode not many of the thefts and robberies his officers committed by his authoritie, in his treasure and affaires : not so muche bicause he was carelesse, as for that he over-simply trusted his men in all things. For he was a plaine man, without suttletie, and there- fore overlate founde out the fowle faultes they committed against him : but when he heard of them, he was muche offended, and would plainly confesse it unto them whome his officers had done injurie unto, by countenaunce of his authoritie. He had a noble minde, as well to punish offendors, as to reward well doers : and yet he did exceede more in geving, then in punishing. Now for his outragious manner of railing he commonly used, mocking and flouting of everie man : that was remedied by it selfe. For a man might as boldly exchaunge a mocke with him, and he was as well contented to be mocked, as to mock others. But yet it oftentimes marred all. For he thought that those which told him so plainly, and truly in mirth : would never flatter him in good earnest, in any matter of weight. But thus he was easely abused by the praises they gave him, not finding howe these flatterers mingled their flatterie, under this familiar and plaine manner of speach unto him, as a fine devise to make difference of meates with sharpe and tart sauce, and also to kepe him by this franke jeasting and bourding with him at the table, that their common flatterie should not be troublesome unto him, as men do easely mislike to have too muche of one thing : and that they handled him finely thereby, when they would geve him place in any matter of waight, and follow his counsell, that it might not appeare to him they did it so muche to please him, but bicause they were ignorant, and understoode not so much as he did. Antonius being thus inclined the last and extreamest mischiefe of all other (to wit, the love of Cleopatra) lighted on him, who did waken and stirre up many vices yet hidden in him, and were never seene to any : and if any sparke of goodnesse or hope of rising were left him, Cleopatra quenched it straight, and made it worse then before. The manner how he fell in love with her was this. Antonius going to make warre with the Parthians, sent to commaunde Cleopatra to appeare personally before him, when he came into Cilicia, to aunswere unto suche accusacions as were layed against her, being this : that she had aided Cassius and Brutus in their warre against him. The messenger sent unto Cleopatra to make this summons unto her, was called Dellius : who when he had thoroughly considered her beawtie, the excellent grace and sweetnesse of her tongue, he nothing mistrusted that Antonius would doe any hurte to so noble a Ladie, but rather assured him selfe, that within few dayes she should be in great favor with him. Thereupon he did her great honour, and perswaded her to come into Cilicia, as honorably furnished as she could possible, and bad her not to be affrayed at all of Antonius, for he was a more curteous Lord, then any that she had ever seene. Cleopatra on thother side beleving Dellius wordes, and gessing by the former accesse and credit she had with Julius Cæsar, and Cneus Pompey (the sonne of Pompey the great) only for her bewtie : she began to have good hope that she

Antonius simplicity.

Antonius maners.

Antonius love to Cleopatra whom he sent for into Cilicia.

might more easely win Antonius. For Cæsar and Pompey knew her
when she was but a young thing, and knew not then what the worlde
ment : but nowe she went to Antonius at the age when a womans

The wonder-
full sumptu-
ousnes of
Cleopatra,
Queene of
Ægypt, going
unto
Antonius.
beawtie is at the prime, and she also of best judgement. So, she
furnished her selfe with a world of gifts, store of gold and silver, and
of riches and other sumptuous ornaments, as is credible enough she
might bring from so great a house, and from so wealthie and rich a
realme as Ægypt was. But yet she caried nothing with her wherein
she trusted more then in her selfe, and in the charmes and inchaunt-
ment of her passing beawtie and grace. Therefore when she was
sent unto by divers letters, both from Antonius him selfe, and also
from his frendes, she made so light of it, and mocked Antonius so
much, that she disdained to set forward otherwise, but to take her barge

Cydnus fl.
in the river of Cydnus, the poope whereof was of gold, the sailes of purple,
and the owers of silver, which kept stroke in rowing after the sounde
of the musicke of flutes, howboyes, citherns, violls, and such other
instruments as they played upon in the barge. And now for the person
of her selfe : she was layed under a pavillion of cloth of gold of tissue,
apparelled and attired like the goddesse Venus, commonly drawen in
picture : and hard by her, on either hand of her, pretie faire boyes
apparelled as painters doe set forth god Cupide, with little fannes in
their hands, with the which they fanned wind upon her. Her ladies
and gentlewomen also, the fairest of them were apparelled like the
nymphes Nereides (which are the mermaides of the waters) and like
the Graces, some stearing the helme, others tending the tackle and
ropes of the barge, out of the which there came a wonderfull passing
sweete savor of perfumes, that perfumed the wharfes side, pestered
with innumerable multitudes of people. Some of them followed the
barge all alongest the rivers side : others also ranne out of the citie
to see her comming in. So that in thend, there ranne such multitudes
of people one after an other to see her, that Antonius was left post
alone in the market place, in his Imperiall seate to geve audience :
and there went a rumor in the peoples mouthes, that the goddesse
Venus was come to play with the god Bacchus, for the generall good
of all Asia. When Cleopatra landed, Antonius sent to invite her to
supper to him. But she sent him word againe, he should doe better
rather to come and suppe with her. Antonius therefore to shew him
selfe curteous unto her at her arrivall, was contented to obey her, and

The sumptu-
ous prepara-
tions of the
suppers of
Cleopatra
and
Antonius.
went to supper to her : where he found such passing sumptuous fare,
that no tongue can expresse it. But amongest all other thinges, he
most wondered at the infinite number of lightes and torches hanged
on the toppe of the house, geving light in everie place, so artificially
set and ordered by devises, some round, some square : that it was
the rarest thing to behold that eye could discerne, or that ever books
could mencion. The next night, Antonius feasting her, contended
to passe her in magnificence and finenes : but she overcame him in
both. So that he him selfe began to skorne the grosse service of his
house, in respect of Cleopatraes sumptuousnes and finenesse. And

when Cleopatra found Antonius jeasts and slents to be but grosse, and souldier like, in plaine manner : she gave it him finely, and without feare taunted him throughly. Now her beawtie (as it is reported) was not so passing, as unmatchable of other women, nor yet suche, Cleopatraes as upon present viewe did enamor men with her : but so sweete was beawtie. her companie and conversacion, that a man could not possiblie but be taken. And besides her beawtie, the good grace she had to talke and discourse, her curteous nature that tempered her words and dedes, was a spurre that pricked to the quick. Furthermore, besides all these, her voyce and words were marvelous pleasant : for her tongue was an instrument of musicke to divers sports and pastimes, the which she easely turned to any language that pleased her. She spake unto few barbarous people by interpreter, but made them aunswere her self, or at the least the most parte of them : as the Æthiopians, the Arabians, the Troglodytes, the Hebrues, the Syrians, the Medes, and the Parthians, and to many others also, whose languages she had learned. Whereas divers of her progenitors, the kings of Ægypt, could scarce learne the Ægyptian tongue only, and many of them forgot to speake the Macedonian. Nowe, Antonius was so ravished with the love of Cleopatra, that though his wife Fulvia had great warres, and much a doe with Cæsar for his affaires, and that the armie of the Parthians (the which the kings Lieutenauntes had geven to the onely leading of Labienus) was now assembled in Mesopotamia readie to invade Syria : yet, as though all this had nothing touched him, he yeelded him selfe to goe with Cleopatra into Alexandria, where he spent and lost in childish sports, (as a man might say) and idle pastimes, the most pretious thing a man can spende, as Antiphon sayth : and that is, time. For they An order set made an order betwene them, which they called Amimetobion (as up by An- much to say, no life comparable and matcheable with it) one feasting tonius and ech other by turnes, and in cost, exceeding all measure and reason. Cleopatra. And for proofe hereof, I have heard my grandfather Lampryas report, The excessive that one Philotas a Physition, born in the citie of Amphissa, told him expences of that he was at that present time in Alexandria, and studied Physicke : Antonius and and that having acquaintance with one of Antonius cookes, he tooke Cleopatra in him with him to Antonius house, (being a young man desirous to see Ægypt. things) to shew him the wonderfull sumptuous charge and preparation of only one supper.—When he was in the kitchin, and saw a world of diversities of meates, and amongst others, eight wilde boares rosted Eight wilde whole : he began to wonder at it, and sayd, Sure you have a great boares rosted number of ghests to supper. The cooke fell a laughing and answered whole. him, No (quoth he) not many ghests, nor above twelve in all : but yet all that is boyled or roasted must be served in whole, or else it would be marred straight. For Antonius peradventure will suppe presently, or it may be a pretie while hence, or likely enough he will deferre it longer, for that he hathe dronke well to day, or else hath had some other great matters in hand : and therefore we do not dresse one supper only, but many suppers, bicause we are uncerteine of the houre he will suppe in.

. . . .

But now againe to Cleopatra. Plato wryteth that there are foure
kinds of flatterie: but Cleopatra devided it into many kinds. For
she, were it in sport, or in matter of earnest, still devised sundrie new
delights to have Antonius at commaundement, never leaving him
night or day, nor once letting him go out of her sight. For she would
play at dyce with him, drinke with him, and hunt commonly with
him, and also be with him when he went to any exercise or activity of
body. And sometime also, when he would goe up and downe the
citie disguised like a slave in the night, and would peere into poore
mens windowes and their shops, and scold and brawle with them within
the house: Cleopatra would be also in a chamber maide array, and
amble up and downe the streets with him, so that oftentimes Antonius
bare away both mockes and blowes. Now, though most men misliked
this maner, yet the Alexandrians were commonly glad of this jolity,
and liked it well saying verie gallantly, and wisely: that Antonius
shewed them a commicall face, to wit, a merie countenaunce: and
the Romanes a tragicall face, to say, a grimme looke. But to reckon
up all the foolishe sportes they made, revelling in this sorte: it were
too fond a parte of me, and therefore I will only tell you one among
Antonius
fishing in
Ægypt.
the rest. On a time he went to angle for fish, and when he could take
none, he was as angrie as could be, bicause Cleopatra stood by.
Wherefore he secretly commaunded the fisher men, that when he cast
in his line, they should straight dive under the water, and put a fishe
on his hooke which they had taken before: and so snatched up his
angling rodde, and brought up fish twise or thrise. Cleopatra found
it straight, yet she seemed not to see it, but wondred at his excellent
fishing: but when she was alone by her selfe among her owne people,
she told them howe it was, and bad them the next morning to be on
the water to see the fishing. A number of people came to the haven,
and got into the fisher boates to see this fishing. Antonius then threw
in his line and Cleopatra straight commaunded one of her men to
dive under water before Antonius men, and to put some old salte
fish upon his baite, like unto those that are brought out of the contrie
of Pont. When he had hong the fish on his hooke, Antonius thinking
he had taken a fishe in deede, snatched up his line presently. Then
they all fell a laughing. Cleopatra laughing also, said unto him:
Leave us (my Lord) Ægyptians (which dwell in the contry of Pharus
and Canobus) your angling rodd: this is not thy profession: thou
must hunt after conquering of realmes and contries. Nowe Antonius
delighting in these fond and childish pastimes, verie ill newes were
The warres
of Lucius
Antonius
and Fulvia,
against
Octavius
Cæsar.
brought him from two places. The first from Rome, that his brother
Lucius, and Fulvia his wife, fell out first betwene them selves, and
afterwards fell to open warre with Cæsar, and had brought all to nought,
that they were both driven to flie out of Italie. The second newes, as
bad as the first: that Labienus conquered all Asia with the armie of the
Parthians, from the river of Euphrates, and from Syria, unto the
contries of Lydia and Ionia. Then began Antonius with much a doe,
a litle to rouse him selfe as if he had bene wakened out of a deepe

sleepe, and as a man may say, comming out of a great dronkennes. So, first of all he bent him selfe against the Parthians, and went as farre as the contrie of Phœnicia: but there he received lamentable letters from his wife Fulvia. Whereuppon he straight returned towards Italie with two hundred saile: and as he went, tooke up his frendes by the way that fled out of Italie, to come to him. By them he was informed, that his wife Fulvia was the only cause of this warre: who being of a peevish, crooked, and troublesome nature, had purposely raised this uprore in Italie, in hope thereby to withdraw him from Cleopatra. But by good fortune, his wife Fulvia going to meete with Antonius, sickened by the way, and dyed in the citie of Sicyone: and therefore Octavius Cæsar, and he were the easelier made frendes together. For when Antonius landed in Italie, and that men saw Cæsar asked nothing of him, and that Antonius on the other side layed all the fault and burden on his wife Fulvia: the frendes of both parties would not suffer them to unrippe any old matters, and to prove or defend who had the wrong or right, and who was the first procurer of this warre, fearing to make matters worse betwene them: but they made them frendes together, and devided the Empire of Rome betwene them, making the sea Ionium the bounds of their division. For they gave all the provinces Eastward, unto Antonius: and the countries Westward, unto Cæsar: and left Africke unto Lepidus: and made a law, that they three one after another should make their frendes Consuls, when they would not be them selves. This seemed to be a sound councell, but yet it was to be confirmed with a straighter bonde, which fortune offered thus. There was Octavia the eldest sister of Cæsar, not by one mother, for she came of Ancharia, and Cæsar him self afterwards of Accia. It is reported, that he dearly loved his sister Octavia, for in deede she was a noble Ladie, and left the widow of her first husband Caius Marcellus, who dyed not long before: and it seemed also that Antonius had bene widower ever since the death of his wife Fulvia. For he denied not that he kept Cleopatra, but so did he not confesse that he had her as his wife: and so with reason he did defend the love he bare unto this Ægyptian Cleopatra. Thereuppon everie man did set forward this mariage, hoping thereby that this Ladie Octavia, having an excellent grace, wisedom, and honestie, joined unto so rare a beawtie, that when she were with Antonius (he loving her as so worthy a Ladie deserveth) she should be a good meane to keepe good love and amitie betwext her brother and him. So when Cæsar and he had made the matche betwene them, they both went to Rome about this mariage, although it was against the law, that a widow should be maried within tenne monethes after her husbandes death. Howbeit the Senate dispensed with the law, and so the mariage proceeded accordingly. Sextus Pompeius at that time kept in Sicilia, and so made many an inrode into Italie with a great number of pynnasies and other pirates shippes, of the which were Captaines two notable pirats, Menas, and Menecrates, who so scoored all the sea thereabouts, that none durst peepe out with a sayle. Furthermore,

The death of Fulvia Antonius wife.

All the Empire of Rome devided betwene the Triumviri.

Octavia, the halfe sister of Octavius Cæsar, and daughter of Ancharia which was not Cæsar's mother.

A lawe at Rome for marying of widowes. Antonius maried Octavia, Octavius Cæsar's halfe sister.

x

Sextus Pompeius had delt verie frendly with Antonius, for he had curteously received his mother, when she fled out of Italie with Fulvia: and therefore they thought good to make peace with him. So they met all three together by the mount of Misena, upon a hill that runneth farre into the sea: Pompey having his shippes ryding hard by at ancker, and Antonius and Cæsar their armies upon the shoare side, directly over against him. Now, after they had agreed that Sextus Pompeius should have Sicile and Sardinia, with this condicion that he should ridde the sea of all theeves and pirats, and make it safe for passengers, and withall that he should send a certaine [quantity] of wheate to Rome: one of them did feast an other, and drew cuts who should beginne. It was Pompeius chaunce to invite them first. Whereupon Antonius asked him: And where shall we suppe? There, said Pompey, and shewed him his admirall galley which had six bankes of owers: That (sayd he) is my fathers house they have left me. He spake it to taunt Antonius, bicause he had his fathers house, that was Pompey the great. So he cast ankers enowe into the sea, to make his galley fast, and then built a bridge of wodde to convey them to his galley, from the heade of mount Misena: and there he welcomed them, and made them great cheere. Now in the middest of the feast, when they fell to be merie with Antonius love unto Cleopatra: Menas the pirate came to Pompey, and whispering in his eare, said unto him: Shall I cut the gables of the ankers, and make thee Lord not only of Sicile and Sardinia, but of the whole Empire of Rome besides? Pompey having pawsed a while upon it, at length aunswered him: Thou shouldest have done it, and never told it me, but now we must content us with that we have. As for my selfe, I was never taught to breake my faith, nor to be counted a traitor. The other two also did likewise feast him in their campe, and then he returned into Sicile. Antonius after this agreement made, sent Ventidius before into Asia to stay the Parthians, and to keepe them they should come no further: and he him selfe in the meane time, to gratefie Cæsar, was contented to be chosen Iulius Cæsars priest and sacrificer, and so they joyntly together dispatched all great matters, concerning the state of the Empire. But in all other maner of sportes and exercises, wherein they passed the time away the one with the other: Antonius was ever inferior unto Cæsar, and always lost, which grieved him much. With Antonius there was a soothsayer or astronomer of Ægypt, that coulde cast a figure, and judge of mens nativities, to tell them what should happen to them. He, either to please Cleopatra, or else for that he founde it so by his art, told Antonius plainly that his fortune (which of it selfe was excellent good, and very great) was altogether bleamished and obscured by Cæsars fortune: and therefore he counselled him utterly to leave his company, and to get him as farre from him as he could. For thy Demon, said he, (that is to say, the good angell and spirit that kepeth thee), is affraied of his: and being coragious and high when he is alone, becometh fearefull and timerous when he commeth neere unto the other. Howsoever it was, the events

Antonius and Octavius Cæsar, doe make peace with Sextus Pompeius.

Sextus Pompeius taunt to Antonius.

Sextus Pompeius being offered wonderfull great fortune: for his honestie and faithes sake, refused it.

Antonius told by a Soothsayer, that his fortune was inferior unto Octavius Cæsar.

ensuing proved the Ægyptians words true.   For, it is said, that as often as Antonius
they two drew cuts for pastime, who should have any thing, or whether unfortunate
they plaied at dice, Antonius alway lost.   Oftentimes when they were in sport and
disposed to see cocke-fight, or quailes that were taught to fight one against
with an other : Cæsars cockes or quailes did ever overcome.   The which Octavius
spighted Antonius in his mind, although he made no outward shew Cæsar.
of it : and therefore he beleved the Ægyptian the better.   In fine, he
recommended the affaires of his house unto Cæsar, and went out of
Italie with Octavia his wife, whom he caried into Græce, after he had
had a daughter by her.   So Antonius lying all the winter at Athens,
newes came unto him of the victories of Ventidius, who had overcome
the Parthians in battel, in the which also were slaine, Labienus, and
Pharnabates, the chiefest Captaine king Orodes had.   For these good Orodes king
newes he feasted all Athens, and kept open house for all the Græcians, of Parthia.
and many games of price were plaied at Athens, of the which he him
selfe would be judge.

.   .   .   .

In the meane time, Ventidius once againe overcame Pacorus, Ventidius
(Orodes sonne king of Parthia) in a battell fought in the contrie of notable vic-
Cyrrestica, he being come againe with a great armie to invade Syria : torie of the
at which battell was slaine a great number of the Parthians, and among Parthians.
them Pacorus, the kings owne sonne slaine.   This noble exploit as The death of
famous as ever any was, was a full revenge to the Romanes, of the Pacorus, the
shame and losse they had received before by the death of Marcus king of Par-
Crassus : and he made the Parthians flie, and glad to kepe them selves thiaes sonne
within the confines and territories of Mesopotamia, and Media after
they had thrise together bene overcome in severall battells.   Howbeit Ventidius durst not undertake to follow them any further, fearing
least he should have gotten Antonius displeasure by it.

.   .   .   .

Ventidius was the only man that ever triumphed of the Parthians Ventidius
untill this present day, a meane man borne, and of no noble house the only man
nor family : who only came to that he attained unto, through Antonius of the Ro-
frendshippe, the which delivered him happie occasion to achieve to manes, that
great matters.   And yet to say truely, he did so well quit him selfe in for the
all his enterprises, that he confirmed that which was spoken of Antonius Parthians.
and Cæsar : to wit, that they were alway more fortunate when they
made warre by their Lieutenants, then by them selves.   For Sossius,
one of Antonius Lieutenauntes in Syria, did notable good service :
and Canidius, whom he had also left his Lieutenaunt in the borders Canidius
of Armenia, did conquer it all.   So did he also overcome the kinges conquests.
of the Iberians and Albanians, and went on with his conquests unto
mount Caucasus.   By these conquests, the fame of Antonius power Newe dis-
increased more and more, and grew dreadfull unto all the barbarous pleasures
nations.   But Antonius notwithstanding grewe to be marvelously betwext An-
offended with Cæsar, upon certaine reportes, that had bene brought tonius and
unto him : and so tooke sea to go towards Italie with three hundred Octavius
Cæsar.

saile. And bicause those of Brundusium, would not receive his armie
into their haven, he went further unto Tarentum. There his wife
Octavia that came out of Græce with him, besought him to send her
unto her brother: the which he did. Octavia at that time was great
with child, and moreover had a second daughter by him, and yet she
put her selfe in jorney, and met with her brother Octavius Cæsar by
the way, who brought his two chiefe frendes, Mæcenas and Agrippa
The wordes
of Octavia
unto
Mæcenas
and Agrippa. with him. She tooke them aside, and with all the instance she could
possible, intreated them they would not suffer her that was the happiest
woman of the world, to become nowe the most wretched and un-
fortunatest creature of all other. For now, said she, everie mans
eyes doe gaze on me, that am the sister of one of the Emperours and
wife of the other. And if the worst councell take place, (which the
goddes forbidde) and that they growe to warres: for your selves, it is
uncertaine to which of them two the goddes have assigned the victorie,
or overthrowe. But for me, on which side soever victorie fall, my
Octavia
pacifieth the
quarrell be-
twixt An-
tonius, and
her brother
Octavius
Cæsar. state can be but most miserable still. These words of Octavia so
softned Cæsars harte, that he went quickely unto Tarentum. But it
was a noble sight for them that were present, to see so great an armie
by lande not to sturre, and so many shippes aflote in the roade, quietly
and safe: and furthermore, the meeting and kindenesse of frendes,
lovinglie imbracing one an other. First, Antonius feasted Cæsar,
which he graunted unto for his sisters sake. Afterwardes they agreed
together, that Cæsar should geve Antonius two legions to go against
the Parthians: and that Antonius should let Cæsar have a hundred
gallies armed with brasen spurres at the prooes. Besides all this,
Octavia obteyned of her husbande, twentie brigantines for her brother:
and of her brother for her husbande, a thowsande armed men. After
they had taken leave of eache other, Cæsar went immediately to make
warre with Sextus Pompeius, to gette Sicilia into his handes. Antonius
also leaving his wife Octavia and litle children begotten of her, with
Cæsar, and his other children which he had by Fulvia: he went directlie
into Asia. Then beganne this pestilent plague and mischiefe of Cleopatraes love (which had slept a longe tyme, and seemed to have bene
utterlie forgotten, and that Antonius had geven place to better counsell)
againe to kindle, and to be in force, so soone as Antonius came neere
Plato calleth
concupis-
cence: the
horse of the
minde. unto Syria. And in the ende, the horse of the minde as Plato termeth
it, that is so hard of rayne (I meane the unreyned lust of concupiscence)
did put out of Antonius heade, all honest and commendable thoughtes:
for he sent Fonteius Capito to bring Cleopatra into Syria. Unto
Antonius
sent for
Cleopatra
into Syria. whome, to welcome her, he gave no trifling things: but unto that
she had already, he added the provinces of Phœnicia, those of the
nethermost Syria, the Ile of Cyprus, and a great parte of Cilicia, and
that contry of Iurie where the true balme is, and that parte of Arabia
Antonius
gave great
provinces
unto
Cleopatra. where the Nabatheians doe dwell, which stretcheth out towardes the
Ocean. These great giftes muche misliked the Romanes. But now,
though Antonius did easely geve away great seigniories, realmes, and
mighty nations unto some private men, and that also he tooke from

other kings their lawfull realmes: (as from Antigonus king of the Antigonus king of Iurie, the first king beheaded by Antonius.
Iewes, whom he openly beheaded, where never king before had suffred
like death) yet all this did not so much offend the Romanes, as the
unmeasurable honors which he did unto Cleopatra. But yet he did
much more aggravate their malice and il wil towards him, bicause
that Cleopatra having brought him two twinnes, a sonne and a daughter, Antonius twinnes by Cleopatra, and their names.
he named his sonne Alexander, and his daughter Cleopatra, and gave
them to their surnames, the Sunne to the one, and the moone to the
other. This notwithstanding, he that could finely cloke his shamefull
deedes with fine words, said that the greatnes and magnificence of the
Empire of Rome appeared most, not where the Romanes tooke, but
where they gave much: and nobility was multiplied amongest men,
by the posterity of kings, when they left of their seede in divers places:
and that by this meanes his first auncestor was begotten of Hercules,
who had not left the hope and continuance of his line and posterity,
in the wombe of one only woman, fearing Solons lawes, or regarding
the ordinaunces of men touching the procreacion of children: but
that he gave it unto nature, and established the fundacion of many
noble races and families in divers places.

．　　．　　．　　．　　．　　．　　．　　．　　．

Now whilest Antonius was busie in this preparation, Octavia his
wife, whome he had left at Rome, would needes take sea to come unto
him. Her brother Octavius Cæsar was willing unto it, not for his
respect at all (as most authors doe report) as for that he might have
an honest culler to make warre with Antonius if he did misuse her,
and not esteeme of her as she ought to be. But when she was come Octavia, Antonius' wife, came to Athens to meete with him.
to Athens, she received letters from Antonius, willing her to stay there
untill his comming, and did advertise her of his jorney and determination. The which though it grieved her much, and that she knewe
it was but an excuse: yet by her letters to him of aunswer, she asked
him whether he would have those thinges sent unto him which she
had brought him, being great store of apparell for souldiers, a great
number of horse, summe of money, and gifts, to bestow on his friendes
and Captaines he had about him: and besides all those, she had two
thowsand souldiers chosen men, all well armed, like unto the Prætors
bands. When Niger, one of Antonius friends whome he had sent
unto Athens, had brought these newes from his wife Octavia, and withall
did greatly prayse her, as she was worthy, and well deserved: Cleopatra
knowing that Octavia would have Antonius from her, and fearing also
that if with her vertue and honest behavior, (besides the great power
of her brother Cæsar) she did adde thereunto her modest kind of
love to please her husband, that she would then be too stronge for her,
and in the end winne him away: she suttelly seemed to languish The flickering enticements of Cleopatra unto Antonius.
for the love of Antonius, pyning her body for lacke of meate. Further-
more, she every way so framed her countenaunce, that when Antonius
came to see her, she cast her eyes upon him, like a woman ravished
for joy. Straight againe when he went from her, she fell a weeping
and blubbering, looked rufully of the matter, and still found the

meanes that Antonius should oftentymes finde her weeping: and
then when he came sodainely uppon her, she made as though she
dryed her eyes, and turned her face away, as if she were unwilling
that he should see her weepe. All these tricks she used, Antonius
being in readines to goe into Syria, to speake with the king of Medes.
Then the flatterers that futhered Cleopatraes mind, blamed Antonius,
and tolde him that he was a hard natured man, and that he had small
love in him, that would see a poore Ladye in such torment for his sake,
whose life depended onely upon him alone. For, Octavia, sayd they,
that was maryed unto him as it were of necessitie, bicause her brother
Cæsars affayres so required it: hath the honor to be called Antonius
lawefull spowse and wife: and Cleopatra, being borne a Queene of
so many thowsands of men, is onely named Antonius Leman, and
yet that she disdayned not so to be called, if it might please him she
might enjoy his company, and live with him: but if he once leave her,
that then it is unpossible she should live. To be short, by these their
flatteries and enticements, they so wrought Antonius effeminate mind,
that fearing least she would make her selfe away: he returned againe
unto Alexandria, and referred the king of Medes to the next yeare
following, although he receyved newes that the Parthians at that tyme
were at civill warres amonge them selves. This notwithstanding, he
went afterwardes and made peace with him. For he maried his
Daughter which was very younge, unto one of the sonnes that Cleopatra had by him: and then returned, beeing fully bent to make warre
with Cæsar. When Octavia, was returned to Rome from Athens,
Cæsar commaunded her to goe out of Antonius house, and to dwell
by her selfe, bicause he had abused her. Octavia aunswered him
againe, that she would not forsake her husbands house, and that if
he had no other occasion to make warre with him, she prayed him
then to take no thought for her: for sayd she, it were too shamefull
a thinge, that two so famous Captaines should bringe in civill warres
among the Romanes, the one for the love of a woman, and the other
for the jelousy betwixt one an other. Now as she spake the worde, so
did she also performe the deede. For she kept still in Antonius house,
as if he had bene there, and very honestly and honorably kept his
children, not those onely she had by him, but the other which her
husband had by Fulvia. Furthermore, when Antonius sent any of
his men to Rome, to sue for any office in the common wealth: she
received him very curteously, and so used her selfe unto her brother,
that she obtained the thing she requested. Howbeit thereby, thinking
no hurt, she did Antonius great hurt. For her honest love and regard
to her husband, made every man hate him, when they sawe he did
so unkindly use so noble a Lady: but yet the greatest cause of their
malice unto him, was for the division of lands he made amongst his
children in the citie of Alexandria. And to confesse a troth, it was too
arrogant and insolent a part, and done (as a man would say) in derision
and contempt of the Romanes. For he assembled all the people in
the show place, where younge men doe exercise them selves, and there

The occasion of civil warres betwixt Antonius and Cæsar.

The love of Octavia to Antonius her husband, and her wise and womanly behavior.

upon a high tribunall silvered, he set two chayres of gold, the one for him selfe, and the other for Cleopatra, and lower chaires for his children : then he openly published before the assembly, that first of all he did establish Cleopatra Queene of Ægypt, of Cyprus, of Lydia, and of the lower Syria, and at that time also, Cæsarion king of the same Realmes. This Cæsarion was supposed to be the sonne of Iulius Cæsar, who had left Cleopatra great with child. Secondly he called the sonnes he had by her, the kings of kings, and gave Alexander for his portion, Armenia, Media and Parthia, when he had conquered the contry : and unto Ptolomy for his portion, Phenicia, Syria, and Cilicia. And there-withall he brought out Alexander in a long gowne after the facion of the Medes, with a high copped tanke hat on his head, narrow in the toppe, as the kings of the Medes and Armenians doe use to weare them : and Ptolomy apparelled in a cloke after the Macedonian manner, with slippers on his feete, and a broad hat, with a royall band or diademe. Such was the apparell and old attyre of the auncient kinges and successors of Alexander the great. So after his sonnes had done their humble duties, and kissed their father and mother : presently a company of Armenian souldiers set there of purpose, com-passed the one about, and a like company of the Macedonians the other. Now for Cleopatra, she did not onely weare at that time (but at all other times els when she came abroad) the apparell of the goddesse Isis, and so gave audience unto all her subjects, as a new Isis. Octavius Cæsar reporting all these thinges unto the Senate, and oftentimes accusing him to the whole people and assembly in Rome : he thereby stirred up all the Romanes against him. Antonius on thother side sent to Rome likewise to accuse him, and the chiefest poyntes of his accusations he charged him with, were these : First, that having spoyld Sextus Pompeius in Sicile, he did not give him his parte of the Ile. Secondly, that he did deteyne in his hands the shippes he lent him to make that warre. Thirdly, that having put Lepidus their companion and triumvirate out of his part of the Empire, and having deprived him of all honors : he retayned for him selfe the lands and revenues thereof, which had bene assigned unto him for his part. And last of all, that he had in manner devided all Italy amongest his owne souldiers, and had left no part of it for his souldiers. Octavius Cæsar aunswered him againe : that for Lepidus, he had in deede deposed him, and taken his part of the Empire from him, bicause he did overcruelly use his authoritie. And secondly, for the conquests he had made by force of armes, he was contented Antonius should have his part of them, so that he would likewise let him have his part of Armenia. And thirdly, that for his souldiers, they should seeke for nothing in Italy, bicause they possessed Media and Parthia, the which provinces they had added to the Empire of Rome, valiantly fighting with their Em-peror and Captaine. Antonius hearing these newes, being yet in Armenia, commaunded Canidius to goe presently to the sea side with his sixteene legions he had : and he him selfe with Cleopatra, went unto the citie of Ephesus, and there gathered together his gallies and

Antonius arrogantly devideth divers provinces unto his children by Cleopatra, Cæsarion, the supposed sone of Cæsar, by Cleopatra. Alexander and Ptolomy, Antonius sonnes by Cleopatra.

Accusasion, betwixt Oc-tavius Cæsar, and Antonius.

shippes out of all parts, which came to the number of eight hundred,
reckoning the great shippes of burden: and of those, Cleopatra
furnished him with two hundred, and twenty thowsand talents besides,
and provision of vittells also to mainteyne al the whole army in this
warre. So Antonius, through the perswasions of Domitius, commaunded Cleopatra to returne againe into Ægypt, and there to
understand the successe of this warre. But Cleopatra, fearing least
Antonius should againe be made friends with Octavius Cæsar, by
the meanes of his wife Octavia: she so plyed Canidius with money,
and filled his purse, that he became her spokes man unto Antonius,
and told him there was no reason to send her from this warre, who
defraied so great a charge: neither that it was for his profit, bicause
that thereby the Ægyptians would then be utterly discoraged, which
were the chiefest strength of the army by sea: considering that he
could see no king of all the kings their confederats, that Cleopatra
was inferior unto, either for wisedome or judgment, seeing that longe
before she had wisely governed so great a realme as Ægypt, and
besides she had bene so long acquainted with him, by whom she had
learned to manedge great affayres. These fayer perswasions wan him:
for it was predestined that the government of all the world should
fall into Octavius Cæsars handes. Thus, all their forces being joyned
together, they hoysed sayle towards the Ile of Samos, and there gave
them selves to feasts and sollace. For as all the kings, Princes, and
communalties, peoples and cities from Syria, unto the marishes Mæo-
tides, and from the Armenians to the Illyrians, were sent unto, to send
and bringe all munition and warlike preparation they could: even
so all players, minstrells, tumblers, fooles, and jeasters, were commaunded to assemble in the Ile of Samos. So that, where in manner
all the world in every place was full of lamentations, sighes and teares:
onely in this Ile of Samos there was nothing for many dayes space,
but singing and pyping, and all the Theater full of these common
players, minstrells, and singing men. Besides all this, every citie sent
an oxe thither to sacrifice, and kings did strive one with another who
should make the noblest feasts, and give the richest gifts. So that
every man sayd, What can they doe more for joy of victorie, if they
winne the battell? when they make already such sumptuous feasts
at the beginning of the warre?

Antonius came with eight hundred saile against Octavius Cæsar.

Antonius carieth Cleopatra with him to the warres, against Octavius Cæsar: and kept great feasting at the Ile of Samos together.

.   .   .   .

Furthermore, Titius and Plancus (two of Antonius chiefest friends
and that had bene both of them Consuls) for the great injuries Cleopatra did them, bicause they hindered all they could, that she should
not come to this warre: they went and yelded them selves unto Cæsar,
and tolde him where the testament was that Antonius had made,
knowing perfitly what was in it. The will was in the custodie of the
Vestall Nunnes: of whom Cæsar demaunded for it. They aunswered
him, that they would not give it him: but if he would goe and take
it, they would not hinder him. Thereuppon Cæsar went thither,
and having red it first to him self, he noted certaine places worthy

Titius and Plancus revolt from Antonius, and doe yeld to Cæsar.

of reproch : so assembling all the Senate, he red it before them all. Whereuppon divers were marvelously offended, and thought it a straunge matter that he being alive, should be punished for that he had appoynted by his will to be done after his death. Cæsar chiefly tooke hold of this that he ordeyned touching his buriall : for he willed that his bodie, though he dyed at Rome, should be brought in funerall pompe through the middest of the market place, and that it should be sent into Alexandria unto Cleopatra.

· · · · · · · · · · ·

Nowe, after Cæsar had made sufficient preparation, he proclaymed open warre against Cleopatra, and made the people to abolishe the power and Empire of Antonius, bicause he had before given it uppe unto a woman. And Cæsar sayde furthermore, that Antonius was not Maister of him selfe, but that Cleopatra had brought him beside him selfe, by her charmes and amorous poysons : and that they that should make warre with them should be Mardian the Euenuke, Photinus, and Iras, a woman of Cleopatraes bedchamber, that friseled her heare, and dressed her head, and Charmion, the which were those that ruled all the affaires of Antonius Empire. *Antonius Empire taken from him.*

· · · · · · · · · · ·

The Admirall galley of Cleopatra, was called Antoniade, in the which there chaunced a marvelous ill signe. Swallowes had bred under the poope of her shippe, and there came others after them that drave away the first, and plucked downe their neasts. Now when all things were ready, and that they drew neare to fight : it was found that Antonius had no lesse then five hundred good ships of warre, among the which there were many gallies that had eight and ten bancks of owers, the which were sumptuously furnished, not so meete for fight, as for triumphe : a hundred thowsand footemen, and twelve thowsand horsemen, and had with him to ayde him these kinges and subjects following : Bocchus, king of Lybia, Tarcondemus king of high Cilicia, Archelaus king of Cappadocia, Philadelphus king of Paphlagonia, Mithridates king of Comagena, and Adallas king of Thracia. All the which were there every man in person. The residue that were absent sent their armies, as Polemon king of Pont, Manchus king of Arabia, Herodes king of Iury : and furthermore, Amyntas king of Lycaonia, and of the Galatians : and besides all these, he had all the ayde the king of Medes sent unto him. Now for Cæsar, he had two hundred and fifty shippes of warre, foure score thowsand footemen, and well neare as many horsemen as his enemy Antonius. Antonius for his part, had all under his dominion from Armenia, and the river of Euphrates, unto the sea Ionium and Illyricum. Octavius Cæsar. had also for his part, all that which was in our Hemisphære, or halfe part of the world, from Illyria, unto the Occean sea upon the west : then all from the Occean, unto Mare Siculum : and from Africk, all that which is against Italy, as Gaule, and Spayne. Furthermore, all from the province of Cyrenia, unto Æthiopia, was subject unto *An ill signe, foreshewed by swallowes breding in Cleopatraes shippe. Antonius power against Oct. Cæsar. Antonius had eyght kings, and their power to ayde him. The army and power of Octavius Cæsar against Antonius. Antonius dominions. Octavius Cæsars dominions.*

Antonius too much ruled by Cleopatra.

Antonius. Now Antonius was made so subject to a womans will, that though he was a great deale the stronger by land, yet for Cleopatraes sake, he would needes have this battell tryed by sea : though he sawe before his eyes, that for lacke of water men, his Captaines did presse by force all sortes of men out of Græce that they could take up in the field, as travellers, muletters, reapers, harvest men, and younge boys, and yet could they not sufficiently furnishe his gallies : so that the most part of them were empty, and could scant rowe, bicause they lacked water men enowe. But on the contrary side, Cæsars shippes were not built for pompe, highe, and great, onely for a sight and bravery, but they were light of yarage, armed and furnished with water men as many as they needed, and had them all in readines, in the havens of Tarentum, and Brundusium. So Octavius Cæsar sent unto Antonius, to will him to delay no more time, but to come on with his army into Italy : and that for his owne part he would give him safe harber, to lande without any trouble, and that he would withdraw his armie from the sea, as far as one horse could runne, until he had put his army a shore, and had lodged his men. Antonius on the other side bravely sent him word againe, and chalenged the combate of him man to man, though he were the elder : and that if he refused him so, he would then fight a battell with him in the fields of Pharsalia, as Iulius Cæsar, and Pompey had done before. Now whilest Antonius

Antonius rode at anker at the head of Actius : where the citie of Nicopolis standeth.

rode at anker, lying idely in harber at the head of Actium, in the place where the citie of Nicopolis standeth at this present : Cæsar had quickly passed the sea Ionium, and taken a place called Toryne, before Antonius understoode that he had taken shippe. Then began his men to be affraid, bicause his army by land was left behind. But Cleopatra making light of it : And what daunger, I pray you, said she, if Cæsar

* The grace of this tawnt can not properly be expressed in any other tongue, bicause of the equivocation of this word Toryne, which signifieth a citie of Albania, and also, a ladell to scoome the pot with : as if she ment, Cæsar sat by the fire side, scomming of the pot.

keepe at Toryne? * The next morning by breake of day, his enemies comming with full force of owers in battell against him, Antonius was affraid that if they came to joyne, they would take and cary away his shippes that had no men of warre in them. So he armed all his water men, and set them in order of battell upon the forecastell of their shippes, and then lift up all his rancks of owers towards the element, as well of the one side, as the other, with the prooes against the enemies, at the entry and mouth of the gulfe, which beginneth at the point of Actium, and so kept them in order of battell, as if they had bene armed and furnished with water men and souldiers. Thus Octavius Cæsar beeing finely deceyved by this stratageame, retyred presently, and therewithall Antonius very wisely and sodainely did cut him of from fresh water. For, understanding that the places where Octavius Cæsar landed, had very litle store of water, and yet very bad : he shut them in with stronge ditches and trenches he cast, to keepe them from salying out at their pleasure, and so to goe seeke water further of. Furthermore, he delt very friendly and curteously with Domitius, and against Cleopatraes mynde. For, he being sicke of an agewe when he went and tooke a litle boate to goe to Cæsars campe, Antonius was very sory for it, but yet he sent after him all his

caryage, trayne, and men: and the same Domitius, as though he gave
him to understand that he repented his open treason, he died im-
mediatly after.   There were certain kings also that forsooke him,
and turned on Cæsars side: as Amyntas, and Deiotarus.   Furthermore, his fleete and navy that was unfortunate in all thinges, and
unready for service, compelled him to chaunge his minde, and to hazard
battell by land.   And Canidius, also, who had charge of his army
by land, when time came to follow Antonius determination: he turned
him cleane contrary, and counselled him to send Cleopatra backe
againe, and him selfe to retyre into Macedon, to fight there on the
maine land.   And furthermore told him, that Dicomes king of the
Getes, promised him to ayde him with a great power: and that it
should be no shame nor dishonor to him to let Cæsar have the sea,
(bicause him selfe and his men both had bene well practised and
exercised in battels by sea, in the warre of Sicilia against Sextus
Pompeius) but rather that he should doe against all reason, he having
so great skill and experience of battells by land as he had, if he should
not employ the force and valliantnes of so many lusty armed footemen
as he had ready, but would weaken his army by deviding them into
shippes.   But now, notwithstanding all these good perswasions,
Cleopatra forced him to put all to the hazard of battel by sea: considering with her selfe how she might flie, and provide for her safetie,
not to helpe him to winne the victory, but to flie more easily after the
battel lost.

Domitius for-
saketh An-
tonius, and
goeth unto
Octavius
Cæsar.
Amyntas, and
Deiotarus, do
both revolt
from Anton-
ius, and goe
unto Cæsar.

.   .   .   .

So when Antonius had determined to fight by sea, he set all the
other shippes a fire, but three score shippes of Ægypt, and reserved
onely but the best and greatest gallies, from three bancks, unto tenne
bancks of owers.   Into them he put two and twenty thowsand fighting
men, with two thowsand darters and slingers.   Now, as he was setting
his men in order of battel, there was a Captaine, and a valliant man,
that had served Antonius in many battels and conflicts, and had all
his body hacked and cut: who as Antonius passed by him, cryed out
unto him, and sayd: O noble Emperor, how commeth it to pass that
you trust to these vile brittle shippes? what, doe you mistrust these
woundes of myne, and this sword? let the Ægyptians and Phænicians
fight by sea, and set us on the maine land, where we use to conquer,
or to be slayne on our feete.   Antonius passed by him, and sayd never
a word, but only beckoned to him with his hand and head, as though
he willed him to be of good corage, although in deede he had no great
corage him selfe.   For when the Masters of the gallies and Pilots
would have let their sailes alone, he made them clap them on, saying
to culler the matter withall, that not one of his enemies should scape.
All that day, and the three dayes following, the sea rose high, and was
so boysterous, that the battel was put of.   The fift day the storme
ceased, and the sea calmed againe, and then they rowed with force
of owers in battaile one against the other: Antonius leading the right
wing with Publicola, and Cælius the left, and Marcus Octavius, and

Antonius
regardeth
not the good
counsell of
his souldier.

Battail by sea
at Actium,
betwixt An-
tonius and

Marcus Iusteius the middest.   Octavius Cæsar on thother side, had
placed Agrippa in the left winge of his armye, and had kept the right
winge for him selfe.   For the armies by lande Canidius was generall
of Antonius side, and Taurus of Cæsars side: who kept their men in
battell raye the one before the other, uppon the sea side, without stirring
one agaynst the other.

.   .   .   .

Howbeit the battell was yet of even hand, and the victorie doubtfull,
being indifferent to both: when sodainely they saw the three score
shippes of Cleopatra busie about their yard masts, and hoysing saile

Cleopatra
flyeth.

to flie.   So they fled through the middest of them that were in fight,
for they had bene placed behind the great shippes, and did marvelously
disorder the other shippes.   For the enemies them selves wondred
much to see them saile in that sort, with ful saile towards Peloponnesus.
There Antonius shewed plainely, that he had not onely lost the corage
and hart of an Emperor, but also of a valiant man, and that he was

The soule of
a lover liveth
in another
body.

not his owne man: (proving that true which an old man spake in myrth,
that the soule of a lover lived in another body, and not in his owne)
he was so caried away with the vaine love of this woman, as if he had
bene glued unto her, and that she could not have removed without
moving of him also.   For when he saw Cleopatraes shippe under saile,

Antonius
flyeth after
Cleopatra.

he forgot, forsooke, and betrayed them that fought for him, and
imbarked upon a galley with five bankes of owers, to follow her that
had already begon to overthrow him, and would in the end be his
utter destruction.   When she knew his galley a farre of, she lift up a
signe in the poope of her shippe, and so Antonius comming to it, was
pluckt up where Cleopatra was, howbeit he saw her not at his first
comming, nor she him, but went and sate down alone in the prowe of
his shippe, and said never a word, clapping his head betwene both
his hands . . . and so lived three days alone, without speaking to
any man.   But when he arrived at the head of Tænarus, there Cleopatraes women first brought Antonius and Cleopatra to speake together, and afterwards, to suppe and lye together.   Then beganne
there agayne a great number of Marchaunts shippes to gather about
them, and some of their friends that had escaped from this overthrow:
who brought newes, that his army by sea was overthrowen, but that
they thought the army by land was yet whole.   Then Antonius sent
unto Canidius, to returne with his army into Asia, by Macedon.   Now

Antonius
lycenceth his
friends to
depart, and
giveth them
a shippe
loden with
gold and
silver.

for him self, he determined to crosse over into Africk, and toke one of
his carects or hulks loden with gold and silver, and other rich cariage,
and gave it unto his friends: commaunding them to depart, and to
seeke to save them selves.   They aunswered him weeping, that they
would nether doe it, not yet forsake him.   Then Antonius very curteously and lovingly did comfort them, and prayed them to depart:
and wrote unto Theophilus governor of Corinthe, that he would see
them safe, and helpe to hide them in some secret place, until they
had made their way and peace with Cæsar.   This Theophilus was
the father of Hipparchus, who was had in great estimation about

Antonius. He was the first of all his infranchised bondmen that
revolted from him, and yelded unto Cæsar, and afterwardes went
and dwelt at Corinthe. And thus it stoode with Antonius. Now
for his armie by sea, that fought before the head or foreland of Actium :
they helde out a longe tyme, and nothing troubled them more then
a great boysterous wind that rose full in the prooes of their shippes,
and yet with much a doe, his navy was at length overthrowen, five Antonius
howers within night. There were not slaine above five thowand navy over-
men : but yet there were three hundred shippes taken, as Octavius throwen by
Cæsar writeth him selfe in his *Commentaries*. Many plainely sawe Cæsar.
Antonius flie, and yet could hardly beleeve it, that he that had nyne-
teene legions whole by lande, and twelve thowsand horsemen upon
the sea side, would so have forsaken them, and have fled so cowardly :
as if he had not oftentimes proved both the one and the other fortune,
and that he had not bene throughly acquainted with the divers chaunges
and fortunes of battells. And yet his souldiers still wished for him,
and ever hoped that he would come by some meanes or other unto
them. Furthermore, they shewed them selves so valliant and faithfull
unto him, that after they certainly knewe he was fled, they kept
them selves whole together seven daies. In the ende Canidius, Antonius
Lieuetenant, flying by night, and forsaking his campe : when they
saw them selves thus destitute of their heads and leaders, they yelded
themselves unto the stronger.

.   .   .   .

But now to returne to Antonius againe. Canidius him selfe came
to bring him newes, that he had lost all his armie by land at Actium.
On thother side he was advertised also, that Herodes king of Iurie,
who had also certeine legions and bandes with him, was revolted unto
Cæsar, and all the other kings in like manner : so that, saving those
that were about him, he had none left him. All this notwithstanding
did nothing trouble him, and it seemed that he was contented to forgoe
all his hope, and so to be ridde of all his care and troubles. Thereupon
he left his solitarie house he had built in the sea which he called
Timoneon, and Cleopatra received him into her royall pallace. He
was no sooner comen thither, but he straight set all the city of rioting Antonius riot-
and banketing againe, and him selfe, to liberalitie and giftes. He ing in Alex-
caused the sonne of Iulius Cæsar and Cleopatra, to be enrolled (ac- andria after
cording to the maner of the Romanes) amongst the number of young his great losse
men : and gave Antyllus, his eldest sonne he had by Fulvia, the mans and over-
gowne, the which was a plaine gowne, without gard or imbroderie throw.
of purple. For these things, there was kept great feasting, banketing, *Toga virilis.*
and dauncing in Alexandria many dayes together. In deede they Antillus, the
did breake their first order they had set downe, which they called eldest sonne
Amimetobion, (as much to say, no life comparable) and did set up an by his wife
other which they called Synapothanumenon (signifying the order and Fulvia.
agreement of those that will dye together) the which in exceeding An order
sumptuousnes and cost was not inferior to the first. For their frendes erected by
made them selves to be inrolled in this order of those that would dye Cleopatra,

together, and so made great feastes one to another : for everie man when it came to his turne, feasted their whole companie and fraternitie. Cleopatra in the meane time was verie carefull in gathering all sorts of poysons together to destroy men. Now to make proofe of those poysons which made men dye with least paine, she tried it upon condemned men in prison. For when she saw the poysons that were sodaine and vehement, and brought speedy death with grievous torments : and in contrary maner, that suche as were more milde and gentle, had not that quicke speede and force to make one dye sodainly : she afterwardes went about to prove the stinging of snakes and adders, and made some to be applied unto men in her sight, some in one sorte, and some in an other. So when she had dayly made divers and sundrie proofes, she found none of all them she had proved so fit, as the biting of an Aspicke, the which only causeth a heavines of the head, without swounding or complaining, and bringeth a great desire also to sleepe, with a litle swet in the face, and so by litle and litle taketh away the sences and vitall powers, no living creature perceiving that the pacientes feele any paine. For they are so sorie when any bodie waketh them, and taketh them up : as those that being taken out of a sounde sleepe, are very heavy and desirous to sleepe. This notwithstanding, they sent Ambassadors unto Octavius Cæsar in Asia, Cleopatra requesting the realme of Ægypt for her children, and Antonius praying that he might be suffered to live at Athens like a private man, if Cæsar would not let him remaine in Ægypt. And bicause they had no other men of estimacion about them, for that some were fledde, and those that remained, they did not greatly trust them : they were inforced to sende Euphronius the schoolemaister of their children. For Alexas Laodician, who was brought into Antonius house and favor by meanes of Timagenes, and afterwards was in greater credit with him, then any other Grecian : (for that he had alway bene one of Cleopatraes ministers to win Antonius, and to overthrow all his good determinations to use his wife Octavia well) him Antonius had sent unto Herodes king of Iurie, hoping still to keepe him his frend, that he should not revolt from him. But he remained there, and betrayed Antonius. For where he should have kept Herodes from revolting from him, he perswaded him to turne to Cæsar : and trusting king Herodes, he presumed to come in Cæsars presence. Howbeit Herodes did him no pleasure : for he was presently taken prisoner, and sent in chaines to his owne contrie, and there by Cæsars commaundement put to death. Thus was Alexas in Antonius life time put to death, for betraying of him. Furthermore, Cæsar would not graunt unto Antonius requests : but for Cleopatra, he made her aunswere, that he woulde deny her nothing reasonable, so that she would either put Antonius to death, or drive him out of her contrie. Therewithall he sent Thyreus one of his men unto her, a verie wise and discreete man, who bringing letters of credit from a young Lorde unto a noble Ladie, and that besides greatly liked her beawtie, might easely by his eloquence have persuaded her. He was longer in talke with her then any man else was, and the Queene

Marginal notes:

called Synapothanumenon, revoking the former called Aminetobion.

Cleopatra verie busie in proving the force of poyson.

The property of the biting of an Aspick.

Antonius and Cleopatra send Ambassadors unto Octavius Cæsar.

Alexas treason justly punished.

her selfe also did him great honor: insomuch as he made Antonius gealous of him. Whereupon Antonius caused him to be taken and well favouredly whipped, and so sent him unto Cæsar: and bad him tell him that he made him angrie with him, bicause he shewed him selfe prowde and disdainfull towards him, and now specially when he was easie to be angered, by reason of his present miserie. To be short, if this mislike thee said he, thou hast Hipparchus one of my infranchised bondmen with thee: hang him if thou wilt, or whippe him at thy pleasure, that we may crie quittaunce. From thenceforth, Cleopatra to cleere her selfe of the suspicion he had of her, she made more of him then ever she did. For first of all, where she did solemnise the day of her birth very meanely and sparingly, fit for her present misfortune: she now in contrary maner did keepe it with such solemnitie, that she exceeded all measure of sumptuousnes and magnificence: so that the ghests that were bidden to the feasts, and came poore, went away riche. Nowe things passing thus, Agrippa by divers letters sent one after an other unto Cæsar, prayed him to returne to Rome, bicause the affaires there did of necessity require his person and presence. Thereupon he did deferre the warre till the next yeare following: but when winter was done, he returned againe through Syria by the coast of Africke, to make warres against Antonius, and his other Captaines. When the citie of Pelusium was taken, there ran a rumor in the citie, that Seleucus, by Cleopatraes consent, had surrendered the same. But to cleere her selfe that she did not, Cleopatra brought Seleucus wife and children unto Antonius, to be revenged of them at his pleasure. Furthermore, Cleopatra had long before made many sumptuous tombes and monumentes, as well for excellencie of workmanshippe, as for height and greatnes of building, joyning hard to the temple of Isis. Thither she caused to be brought all the treasure and pretious things she had of the auncient kings her predecessors: as gold, silver, emerods, pearles, ebbanie, ivorie, and sinnamon, and besides all that, a marvelous number of torches, faggots, and flaxe. So Octavius Cæsar being affrayed to loose suche a treasure and masse of riches, and that this woman for spight would set it a fire, and burne it every whit: he alwayes sent some one or other unto her from him, to put her in good comfort, whilest he in the meane time drewe neere the citie with his armie. So Cæsar came, and pitched his campe hard by the city, in the place where they runne and manage their horses. Antonius made a saly upon him, and fought verie valliantly, so that he drave Cæsars horsemen backe, fighting with his men even into their campe. Then he came againe to the pallace, greatly boasting of this victorie, and sweetely kissed Cleopatra, armed as he was, when he came from the fight, recommending one of his men of armes unto her, that had valliantly fought in this skirmish. Cleopatra to reward his manlines, gave him an armor and head peece of cleane gold: howbeit the man at armes when he had received this rich gift, stale away by night, and went to Cæsar. Antonius sent againe to chalenge Cæsar, to fight with him hande to hande. Cæsar aunswered

Pelusium was yeelded up to Octavius Cæsar.

Cleopatraes monuments set up by the temple of Isis.

him, that he had many other wayes to dye then so. Then Antonius
seeing there was no way more honorable for him to dye, then fighting
valliantly : he determined to sette up his rest, both by sea and lande.
So being at supper, (as it is reported) he commaunded his officers
and household servauntes that waited on him at his bord, that they
should fill his cuppes full, and make as muche of him as they could :
for said he, you know not whether you shall doe so much for me to
morrow, or whether you shall serve an other maister : and it may be
you shall see me no more, but a dead bodie. This notwithstanding,
perceiving that his frends and men fell a weeping to heare him say so :
to salve that he had spoken, he added this more unto it, that he would
not leade them to battell, where he thought not rather safely to returne
with victorie, then valliantly to dye with honor. Furthermore, the
selfe same night within litle of midnight, when all the citie was quiet,
full of feare and sorrowe, thinking what would be the issue and ende

Straunge noises heard, and nothing seene.

of this warre : it is said that sodainly they heard a marvelous sweete
harmonie of sundrie sortes of instrumentes of musicke, with the crie
of a multitude of people, as they had bene dauncing, and had song
as they use in Bacchus feastes, with movinges and turninges after the
maner of the Satyres : and it seemed that this daunce went through the
city unto the gate that opened to the enemies, and that all the troupe
that made this noise they heard, went out of the city at that gate.
Now, such as in reason sought the depth of the interpretacion of this
wonder, thought that it was the god unto whom Antonius bare singular
devotion to counterfeate and resemble him, that did forsake them.
The next morning by breake of day, he went to set those few footemen
he had in order upon the hills adjoyning unto the citie : and there
he stoode to behold his gallies which departed from the haven, and
rowed against the gallies of his enemies, and so stoode still looking
what exployte his souldiers in them would do. But when by force of

Antonius navie doe yeeld them selves unto Cæsar.

Antonius overthrowen by Octavius Cæsar.

Cleopatra flieth into her tombe or monument.

rowing they were come neere unto them, they first saluted Cæsars men :
and then Cæsars men resaluted them also, and of two armies made
but one, and then did all together row toward the citie. When
Antonius sawe that his men did forsake him, and yeelded unto Cæsar,
and that his footemen were broken and overthrowen : he then fled
into the citie, crying out that Cleopatra had betrayed him unto them,
with whom he had made warre for her sake. Then she being affraied
of his fury, fled into the tombe which she had caused to be made, and
there locked the dores unto her, and shut all the springes of the lockes
with great boltes, and in the meane time sent unto Antonius to tell
him that she was dead. Antonius beleving it, said unto him selfe :
What doest thou looke for further, Antonius, sith spitefull fortune hath
taken from thee the only joy thou haddest, for whom thou yet reservedst
thy life ? When he had sayd these words, he went into a chamber
and unarmed him selfe, and being naked said thus : O Cleopatra, it
grieveth me not that I have lost thy companie, for I will not be long from
thee : but I am sory that having bene so great a Captaine and Emperour, I am in deede condemned to be judged of lesse corage and

noble minde, then a woman. Now he had a man of his called Eros, whom he loved and trusted much, and whom he had long before caused to sweare unto him, that he should kill him when he did commaunde him: and then he willed him to keepe his promise. His man drawing his sworde, lift it up as though he had ment to have striken his maister: but turning his head at one side, he thrust his sword into himselfe, and fell downe dead at his maisters foote. Then said Antonius, O noble Eros, I thanke thee for this, and it is valliantly done of thee, to shew me what I should doe to my selfe, which thou couldest not doe for me. Therewithall he tooke his sword and thrust it into his bellie, and so fell downe upon a litle bed. The wounde he had killed him not presently, for the blood stinted a litle when he was layed: and when he came somwhat to him selfe againe, he praied them that were about him to dispatch him. But they all fled out of the chamber, and left him crying out and tormenting him selfe: untill at last there came a secretarie unto him called Diomedes, who was commaunded to bring him into the tombe or monument where Cleopatra was. When he heard that she was alive, he verie earnestlie prayed his men to carie his bodie thither, and so he was caried in his mens armes into the entry of the monument. Notwithstanding, Cleopatra would not open the gates, but came to the high windowes, and cast out certaine chaines and ropes, in the which Antonius was trussed: and Cleopatra her owne selfe, with two women only, which she had suffered to come with her into these monumentes, trised Antonius up. They that were present to behold it, said they never saw so pitiefull a sight. For, they plucked up poore Antonius all bloody as he was, and drawing on with pangs of death, who holding up his hands to Cleopatra, raised up him selfe as well as he could. It was a hard thing for these women to do, to lift him up: but Cleopatra stowping downe with her head, putting to all her strength to her uttermost power did lift him up with much a doe, and never let goe her hold, with the helpe of the women beneath that bad her be of good corage, and were as sorie to see her labor so, as she her selfe. So when she had gotten him in after that sorte, and layed him on a bed: she rent her garments upon him, clapping her brest, and scratching her face and stomake. Then she dried up his blood that had berayed his face, and called him her Lord, her husband, and Emperour, forgetting her owne miserie and calamity, for the pitie and compassion she tooke of him. Antonius made her ceasse her lamenting, and called for wine, either bicause he was a thirst, or else for that he thought thereby to hasten his death. When he had dronke, he earnestly prayed her, and perswaded her, that she would seeke to save her life, if she could possible, without reproache and dishonor: and that chiefly she should trust Proculeius above any man else about Cæsar. And as for him selfe, that she should not lament nor sorrowe for the miserable chaunge of his fortune at the end of his dayes: but rather that she should thinke him the more fortunate, for the former triumphes and honors he had received, considering that while he lived he was the noblest and greatest Prince of

Eros Antonius servant, slue him selfe.

Antonius did thrust his sword into him selfe, but died not presently.

Antonius caried unto Cleopatraes tombe.

A lamentable sight to see Antonius and Cleopatra.

the world, and that now he was overcome, not cowardly, but valiantly,
a Romane by an other Romane. As Antonius gave the last gaspe,
Proculeius came that was sent from Cæsar. For after Antonius had
thrust his sworde in him selfe, as they caried him into the tombes and
monuments of Cleopatra, one of his gard called Dercetæus, tooke his
sword with the which he had striken him selfe, and hidde it: then he
secretly stale away, and brought Octavius Cæsar the first newes of his
death, and shewed him his sword that was bloodied. Cæsar hearing
these newes, straight withdrewe him selfe into a secret place of his
tent, and there burst out with teares, lamenting his hard and miserable
fortune, that had bene his frende and brother in law, his equall in the
Empire, and companion with him in sundry great exploytes and battells.
Then he called for all his frendes, and shewed them the letters Antonius
had written to him, and his aunsweres also sent him againe, during
their quarrell and strife: and how fiercely and prowdly the other
answered him, to all just and reasonable matters he wrote unto him.
After this, he sent Proculeius, and commaunded him to doe what he
could possible to get Cleopatra alive, fearing least otherwise all the
treasure would be lost: and furthermore, he thought that if he could
take Cleopatra, and bring her alive to Rome, she would marvelously
beawtifie and sette out his triumphe. But Cleopatra would never
put her selfe into Proculeius handes, although they spake together.
For Proculeius came to the gates that were very thicke and strong, and
surely barred, but yet there were some cranewes through the which
her voyce might be heard, and so they without understoode, that
Cleopatra demaunded the kingdome of Ægypt for her sonnes: and
that Proculeius aunswered her, that she should be of good cheere, and
not be affrayed to referre all unto Cæsar. After he had viewed the
place verie well, he came and reported her aunswere unto Cæsar.
Who immediately sent Gallus to speake once againe with her, and bad
him purposely hold her with talke, whilest Proculeius did set up a
ladder against that high windowe, by the which Antonius was trised
up, and came downe into the monument with two of his men hard
by the gate, where Cleopatra stoode to heare what Gallus sayd unto her.
One of her women which was shut in her monuments with her, saw
Proculeius by chaunce as he came downe, and shreeked out: O, poore
Cleopatra, thou art taken. Then when she sawe Proculeius behind
her as she came from the gate, she thought to have stabbed her selfe
in with a short dagger she ware of purpose by her side. But Proculeius
came sodainly upon her, and taking her by both the hands, said unto
her: Cleopatra, first thou shalt doe thyselfe great wrong, and secondly
unto Cæsar: to deprive him of the occasion and opportunitie, openly
to shew his bountie and mercie, and to geve his enemies cause to
accuse the most curteous and noble Prince that ever was, and to ap-
peache him as though he were a cruell and mercielesse man, that
were not to be trusted. So even as he spake the word, he tooke her
dagger from her, and shooke her clothes for feare of any poyson hidden
about her. Afterwardes Cæsar sent one of his infranchised men called

The death of Antonius.

Octabius Cæsar lamenteth Antonius death.

Proculeius sent by Octavius Cæsar to bring Cleopatra alive.

Cleopatra taken.

Epaphroditus, whom he straightly charged to looke well unto her, and to beware in any case that she made not her selfe away : and for the rest, to use her with all the curtesie possible.

. . . .

Shortly after, Cæsar came him selfe in person to see her, and to comfort her. Cleopatra being layed upon a litle low bed in poore estate, when she sawe Cæsar come in to her chamber, she sodainly rose up, naked in her smocke, and fell downe at his feete marvelously disfigured : both for that she had plucked her heare from her head, as also for that she had martired all her face with her nailes, and besides, her voyce was small and trembling, her eyes sonke into her heade with continuall blubbering : and moreover, they might see the most parte of her stomake torne in sunder. To be short, her bodie was not much better then her minde : yet her good grace and comelynes, and the force of her beawtie was not altogether defaced. But notwithstanding this oughly and pitiefull state of hers, yet she showed her selfe within, by her outward lookes and countenance. When Cæsar had made her lye downe againe, and sate by her beddes side : Cleopatra began to cleere and excuse her selfe for that she had done, laying all to the feare she had of Antonius. Cæsar, in contrarie maner, reproved her in every poynt. Then she sodainly altered her speache, and prayed him to pardon her, as though she were affrayed to dye, and desirous to live. At length, she gave him a breefe and memoriall of all the readie money and treasure she had. But by chaunce there stoode Seleucus by, one of her Treasorers, who to seeme a good servant, came straight to Cæsar to disprove Cleopatra, that she had not set in al, but kept many things back of purpose. Cleopatra was in such a rage with him, that she flew upon him, and tooke him by the heare of the head, and boxed him wellfavouredly. Cæsar fell a laughing, and parted the fray. Alas, said she, O Cæsar : is not this a great shame and reproche, that thou having vouchesaved to take the peines to come unto me, and has done me this honor, poore wretche, and caitife creature, brought into this pitiefull and miserable estate : and that mine owne servaunts should come now to accuse me, though it may be I have reserved some juells and trifles meete for women, but not for me (poore soule) to set out my selfe withall, but meaning to geve some pretie presents and gifts unto Octavia and Livia, that they making meanes and intercession for me to thee, thou mightest yet extend thy favor and mercie upon me? Cæsar was glad to heare her say so, perswading him selfe thereby that she had yet a desire to save her life. So he made her answere, that he did not only geve her that to dispose of at her pleasure, which she had kept backe, but further promised to use her more honorably and bountifully then she would thinke for : and so he tooke his leave of her, supposing he had deceived her, but in deede he was deceived him selfe. There was a young gentleman Cornelius Dolabella, that was one of Cæsars very great familiars, and besides did beare no evil will unto Cleopatra. He sent her word secretly as she had requested him, that Cæsar determined to take his jorney through Suria, and that

Marginal notes:

and to Cæsar came to see Cleopatra.

Cleopatra, a martired creature, through her owne passion and fury.

Seleucus, one of Cleopatraes Treasorers.

Cleopatra bet her treasorer before Octavius Cæsar.

Cleopatraes wordes unto Cæsar.

Cleopatra finely deceiveth Octavius Cæsar, as though she desired to live.

within three dayes he would sende her away before with her children. When this was tolde Cleopatra, she requested Cæsar that it would please him to suffer her to offer the last oblations of the dead, unto the soule of Antonius. This being graunted her, she was caried to the place where his tombe was, and there falling downe on her knees, imbracing the tombe with her women, the teares running downe her

Cleopatraes lamentation over Antonius tombe. cheekes, she began to speake in this sorte : ' O my deare Lord Antonius, ' not long sithence I buried thee here, being a free woman : and now ' I offer unto thee the funerall sprinklinges and oblations, being a ' captive and prisoner, and yet I am forbidden and kept from tearing ' and murdering this captive body of mine with blowes, which they ' carefully gard and keepe, onely to triumphe of thee : looke therefore ' henceforth for no other honors, offeringes, nor sacrifices from me, ' for these are the last which Cleopatra can geve thee, sith nowe they ' carie her away. Whilest we lived together, nothing could sever ' our companies : but now at our death, I feare me they will make us ' chaunge our contries. For as thou being a Romane, hast bene buried ' in Ægypt : even so wretched creature I, an Ægyptian, shall be buried ' in Italie, which shall be all the good that I have received by thy ' contrie. If therefore the gods where thou art now have any power ' and authoritie, sith our gods here have forsaken us : suffer not thy ' true frend and lover to be caried away alive, that in me, they triumphe ' of thee : but receive me with thee, and let me be buried in one selfe ' tombe with thee. For though my griefes and miseries be infinite, ' yet none hath grieved me more, nor that I could lesse beare withall : ' then this small time, which I have bene driven to live alone without ' thee.' Then having ended these dolefull plaints, and crowned the tombe with garlands and sundry nosegayes, and marvelous lovingly imbraced the same : she commaunded they should prepare her bath, and when she had bathed and washed her selfe, she fell to her meate, and was sumptuously served. Nowe whilest she was at dinner, there came a contrieman, and brought her a basket. The souldiers that warded at the gates, asked him straight what he had in his basket. He opened the basket, and tooke out the leaves that covered the figges, and shewed them that they were figges he brought. They all of them marvelled to see so goodly figges. The contrieman laughed to heare them, and bad them take some if they would. They beleved he told them truely, and so bad him carie them in. After Cleopatra had dined, she sent a certaine table written and sealed unto Cæsar, and commaunded them all to go out of the tombes where she was, but the two women, then she shut the dores to her. Cæsar when he received this table, and began to read her lamentation and petition, requesting him that he would let her be buried with Antonius, founde straight what she ment, and thought to have gone thither him selfe : howbeit

The death of Cleopatra. he sent one before in all hast that might be, to see what it was. Her death was very sodaine. For those whom Cæsar sent unto her ran thither in all hast possible, and found the souldiers standing at the gate, mistrusting nothing, nor understanding of her death. But when

they had opened the dores, they founde Cleopatra starke dead, layed
upon a bed of gold, attried and araied in her royall robes, and one of
her two women, which was called Iras, dead at her feete : and her Cleopatraes
other woman called Charmion halfe-dead, and trembling, trimming two waiting
the diademe which Cleopatra ware upon her head.   One of the souldiers with her.
seeing her, angrily sayd unto her : Is that well done Charmion?
Verie well sayd she againe, and meete for a Princes discended from
the race of so many noble kings.   She sayd no more, but fell downe
dead hard by the bed.   Some report that this Aspicke was brought
unto her in the basket with figs, and that she had commaunded them
to hide it under the figge leaves, that when she shoulde thinke to take
out the figges, the Aspicke shoulde bite her before she should see her :
howbeit, that when she would have taken away the leaves for the
figges, she perceived it, and said, Art thou here then?   And so, her Cleopatra
arme being naked, she put it to the Aspicke to be bitten.   Other killed with
say againe, she kept it in a boxe, and that she did pricke and thrust the biting of
it with a spindell of golde, so that the Aspicke being angerd withall, an Aspicke.
lept out with great furie, and bitte her in the arme.   Howbeit fewe
can tell the troth.   For they report also, that she had hidden poyson
in a hollow raser which she caried in the heare of her head : and yet
was there no marke seene of her bodie, or any signe discerned that
she was poysoned, neither also did they finde this serpent in her tombe. The image
But it was reported onely, that there were seene certeine fresh steppes of Cleopatra.
or trackes where it had gone, on the tombe side toward the sea, and caried in
specially by the dores side.   Some say also, that they found two litle triumphe at
pretie bytings in her arme, scant to be discerned : the which it seemeth Rome, with
Cæsar him selfe gave credit unto, bicause in his triumphe he caried an Aspicke
Cleopatraes image, with an Aspicke byting of her arme.   And thus biting of her
goeth the report of her death.   Now Cæsar, though he was marvelous arme.
sorie for the death of Cleopatra, yet he wondred at her noble minde
and corage, and therefore commaunded she should be nobly buried,
and layed by Antonius : and willed also that her two women shoulde
have honorable buriall.